A Look at
BOULDER

To Mother and William
To Gene, my husband
To Sarah and Rachel, my daughters

A Look at BOULDER
FROM SETTLEMENT TO CITY

PHYLLIS SMITH

PRUETT PUBLISHING COMPANY
Boulder, Colorado

©1981 By Phyllis Smith
All rights reserved, including those to reproduce this book,
or parts thereof, in any form, without permission in writing
from the Publisher.

First Edition

3 4 5 6 7 8 9

Printed in the United States of America

Library of Congress Cataloging in Publication Data

Smith, Phyllis, 1928-
   From settlement to city.

   Bibliography: p.
   Includes index.
   1. Boulder (Colo.)—History. I. Title.
F784.B66S64   978.8'63   81-5155
ISBN 0-87108-590-9   AACR2

Acknowledgments

I wish to thank Laurence T. Paddock, editor, Boulder *Daily Camera*, for his patience and unselfishness in allowing me to use photographs from his family's outstanding collection. Further, he took time from his work to help me solve stubborn problems of verification. Sometimes we just chatted about early Boulder, a most enjoyable experience.

Boulder photographer Tom Moen spent many hours duplicating photographs from the Paddock collection. I think that he enjoyed surveying the work of earlier artists. My father, William Cobb, contributed his wisdom and expertise on questions of style. Magda Dulk also criticized the manuscript and read my copy.

As a class, librarians are a wonderful group. Jack Brennan and Sandy Volpe of the University of Colorado's Western Historical Collections were extremely helpful to me, as was Imogene Easton of the City of Boulder's central files. The reference librarians at the Boulder Public Library—Virginia Braddock, Lynn Dyba, Judith Waller, and Lynn Kerler—deserve special thanks for their patience and imagination in handling my numerous requests for information. The members of the Boulder Writers Club gave me inestimable help with their wise criticism and support.

I talked with and enjoyed my conversations with the following people: Edna Harkins, Elizabeth Ricketts, John Charles Smith, Fred Weber, Ernestine Grigsby, A. Gayle Waldrop, Don McInnes, Lyndon Switzer, Bly Ewalt Curtis, J. Perry Bartlett, Thomas Waugh, George Bernzen, Greg Lefferdink, A.A. Wickstrom, Harold Copeland, Leo C. Riethmayer, Martha Weiser, Carl Chapel, Janet Roberts, Walter Slack, Paul Danish, B.J. Miller, Jane Barker, Margaret Coel, Sanford Gladden, Ed Gawf, and Ron Donahue.

I did not talk with E.C. Pickett when she was alive because I was afraid of her, but I enjoyed her messages to the public. Finally, the echoes in our old house on Mapleton Hill made me curious to learn more about past events in Boulder.

Joseph B. Sturtevant takes a photograph of himself in the Boulder sunlight. *Boulder Historical Society*.

Contents

Chapter One 5
The wanderers: the Indians, James Purcell, Zebulon Pike, Stephen Long, the mountain men and their forts, John Charles Frémont, a tragedy at Green Rocks

Chapter Two 11
The first party, their route to Fort St. Vrain, decision to turn west to the Boulder valley, "color" is found in Boulder Creek, the excitement at Gold Run, other gold discoveries nearby, meetings with Chief Left Hand and the Arapaho, the last antelope hunt, letters back home, placer operations, the "rocker," the sluice, the "go-backers"

Chapter Three 17
Land pre-emption, formation of the Boulder City Town Company, government at Gold Hill, discovery of gold-bearing lodes, early descriptions by Sniktau and Reverend Adriance, the first business ventures, a Christmas dance, trouble with the Utes, establishment of stamp mills, the boom at Gold Hill, fire devastates Gold Hill, settlers scatter throughout the county

Chapter Four 25
Early attempts at agriculture and coal mining, the first school, early newspapers, establishment of county government, first steps toward a university, the building of wagon roads, gold at Ward, tragic events at Sand Creek, business developments, the public square, early churches, the first reading room

Chapter Five 47
Silver at Caribou, arrival of the Cornish, a sidewalk of silver at Central City, the "gentlemen" from The Hague, the mill at Nederland, fire and disease at Caribou, death of Caribou, identification of tellurium, re-birth of Gold Hill, new settlements along the tellurium belt

Chapter Six 67
Local government for Boulder, growth of political parties, problems with water and muddy streets, early law enforcement and jails, the lynching of William Tull, Mary Solander's trial, ladies of the evening, the fear of fire, founding of the hose companies

Chapter Seven 81

Boulder life in the 1880s, new schools and "a sort of a" high school, opening of the University, the "flag salute" controversy, Grandma Dartt and the Adventists, Martha Maxwell and her museum

Chapter Eight 105

The first railroads, development of coal as an industry, mine accidents, troubles between labor and management, Josephine Roche, strikes and Mother Jones, underground fires, a dream called Copper Rock, the flood of 1894, a Chautauqua for Boulder, Eben Fine and the glacier

Chapter Nine 127

Railroads for the mountains, the Switzerland Trail, discovery of tungsten, the boom at Nederland, Boulder's oil field, a spa at Eldorado Springs, the 1907 explosion, a semi-centennial celebration, the first park lands, the Olmsted report, developments in business and industry, red sunflowers

Chapter Ten 155

Temperance and prohibition, the murder of Officer Cobb, politics leading to adoption of the Charter, Flora McHarg and the Charter Convention, the Hare system of voting, Charter fight of 1923, Charter fight of 1925, a professional fire department, changes in the police department, buses for Boulder, Boulder's Ku Klux Klan

Chapter Eleven 171

Women's work, a library for Boulder, Spanish influenza, tuberculosis in Boulder, a school for sick children, blacks in Boulder, promise of the Silver Wing Aircraft Corporation, the quiet thirties and the Depression, C.C.C. and W.P.A., Mrs. Hennig and the taxi-cab wars, a first zoning ordinance, the Courthouse burns, Pay Dirt Pow Wow, a new high school, "Minnie and Jake," the first kindergarten

Chapter Twelve 185

A. Gayle Waldrop helps to "wake up" Boulder, the Elks and "tainted money," end of the Hare system, another failure for liquor-by-the-drink, signs of change for an uneasy Boulder, a ski tow at Chautauqua, the Flatirons has a "CU," beer licenses, the Public Service franchise fight, building of the turnpike, big business comes to Boulder, the ambitions of Allen J. Lefferdink, garbage, trash, and back-yard burning, Bly Curtis and the dump, Boulder Creek is polluted, rise and fall of the ward system

Chapter Thirteen   193
"Christmas in the schools" controversy, re-organization of the school district, twenty years of water acquisition, the wisdom of E.C. Pickett, the first sales tax, a Blue Line, an exception to the Blue Line, "Spokes of the Wheel," Boulder goes "wet," a second sales tax and greenbelt for Boulder, the fluoridation fight, Tedesco and the firemen

Chapter Fourteen   201
"Hippies" in Boulder, the Park Allen youth hostel, anti-war demonstrations, riots on the Hill, barricade of the turnpike, return of the buses, a series of bombings, homosexual civil rights and a recall election, Clela Rorex and marriage licenses, "downtown disease," revival of downtown with The Mall, Boulder flirts with shopping centers

Chapter Fifteen   213
PLAN-Boulder, Historic Boulder, P.U.R.E., E.C. Pickett on planning and planners, rise of the neighborhood movement, Comprehensive Plans for Boulder, Pow Wow looks for a new home, the many newcomers, change and alienation, diversity

End Notes   223

Bibliography   233

Appendix
Members, Nebraska City party	239
Members, Boulder City Town Company	240
Members, Boulder Charter Convention	241
Boulder's Educational Institutions	242
Population of Boulder County Communities	243
Boulder County's Newspapers	244
Origin of Boulder County Place Names	247

Index   253

Maps
Early Forts in Eastern Colorado	**8**
Settlements and Camps in Boulder County	**vi-vii**
Wagon Roads in Boulder County	**34-35**

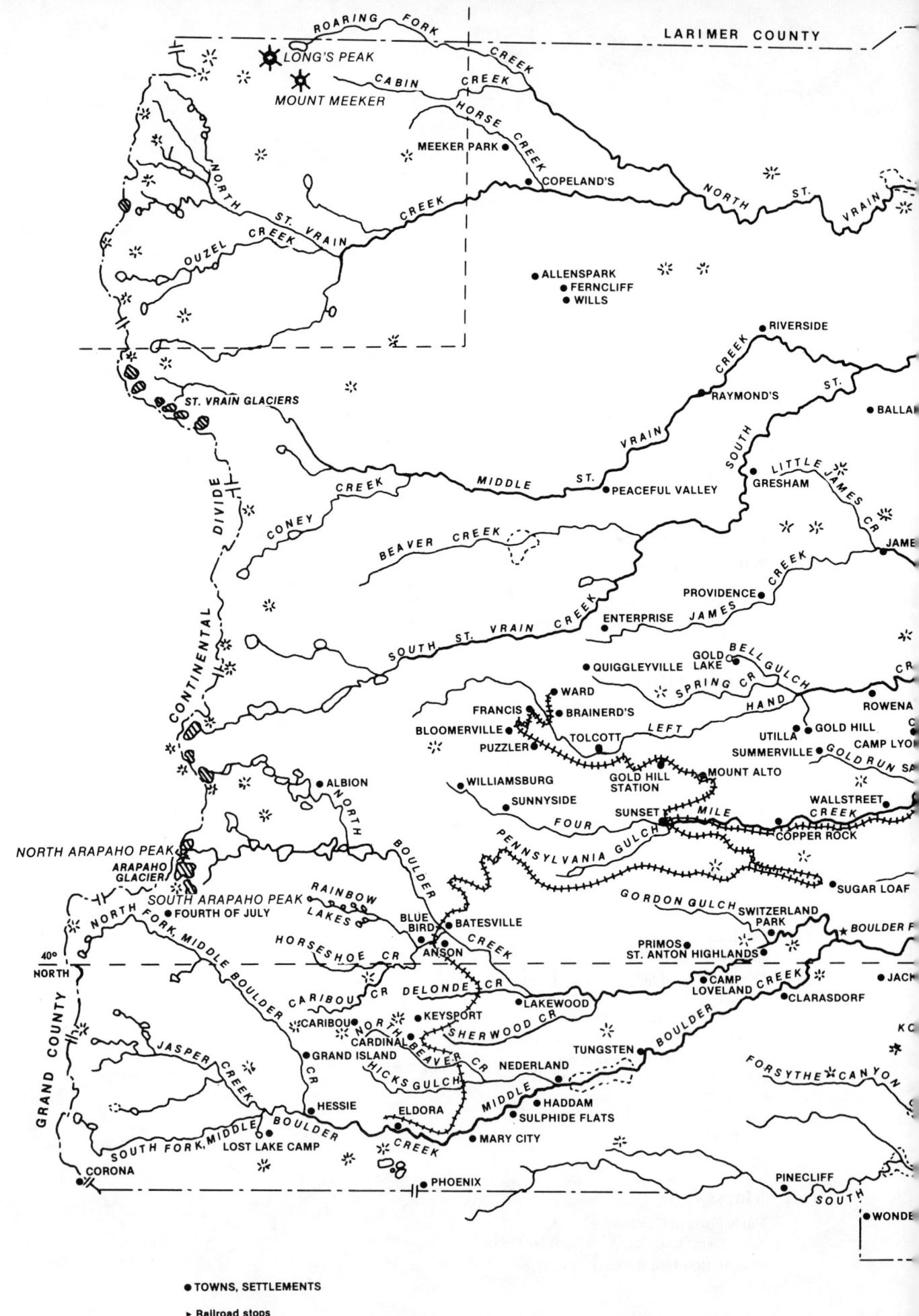

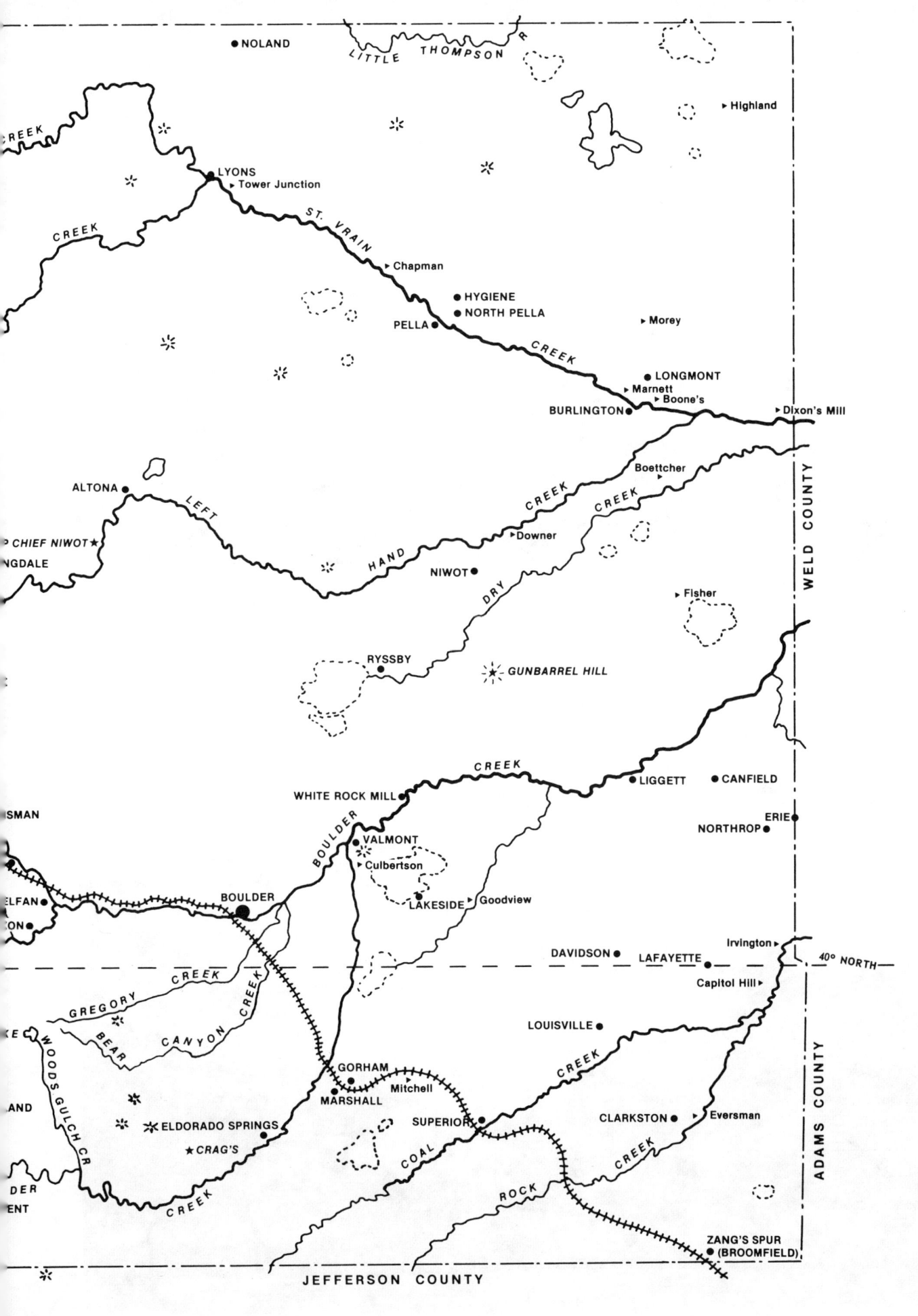

Red Rocks. *Tom Moen photo*

Boulder's children celebrate Arbor Day, May, 1887, as they parade down Pearl Street at Twelfth (Broadway). *J.B. Sturtevant photo, A.A. Paddock Collection.*

Introduction

Sometimes I see early Boulder out of the corner of my eye. For a moment, when the sun first shines on the Red Rocks, I see Andrew Douty's flour mill below, rather than the condominiums that now line Farmers Ditch. When I am on the busy Mall and hear the faint bell from Mapleton School calling the children to their classes, as it has since 1889, I fancy I hear voices of earlier Boulder children as they march down Pearl Street to celebrate Arbor Day. I look up at the facades of the older buildings that line the Mall to read the names and dates of earlier merchants, and I imagine I can hear the stage from Ward, rushing out of the canyon and pulling to a stop in front of Fonda's Drug Store at 1218 Pearl Street. After a rain, the smell of horses is still strong in some of the stables and carriage houses in the older neighborhoods. In the spring, when I hear the ditch runners on Farmers Ditch calling to one another as they prepare the waterway for another summer's flow of water, I deliberately confuse myself for a moment and wonder if they have been calling to one another, in the same manner, since 1862.

This book is an attempt to record some of the history that has shaped the Boulder area. While it does not pretend to be an exhaustive study of Boulder County, some information regarding the settlements surrounding the city of Boulder, both in the mountains and on the plains, is necessary if Boulder's development is to be understood. Boulder did not grow in a vacuum but was dependent upon the fortunes of the mining camps above, as well as on those of the farms and coal mines below. When they flourished, Boulder took hold. When they lost ground, Boulder suffered.

Colorado Territory, one of the last areas of the United States to be settled by white migration, was the western extension of both Kansas and Nebraska territories. The boundary between these two territories runs through Boulder County, indeed, through the city of Boulder itself. Baseline Road marks that division and is the Fortieth Parallel. Colorado became a territory in 1861 and was admitted to the Union as a state in 1876.

Boulder County is a small rectangle (only a dozen of Colorado's sixty-three counties are smaller) stretching twenty-four miles from north to south and about thirty miles east to west. The reason it is "about" thirty miles east to west is that the irregular spine of the Continental Divide forms the county's western boundary, along which lie the Indian Peaks. (Earlier, these mountains were called the Snowy Range.) Long's Peak, the county's only mountain over 14,000 feet above sea level, marks the northwest corner and is now included in Rocky Mountain National Park, established in 1915.

The county's nine hundred square miles have a varied topography. Two-fifths of its lands to the east are high, flat prairie, with farm lands to the north and coal fields to the south. The remaining three-fifths are foothills and mountains. Because the mountains rise so sharply from a desert plateau, Boulder's peaks and valleys seem unusually close together. Boulder is 5,420 feet above sea level, but, a mere twenty miles to the west, the peaks along the Continental Divide rise to just under 14,000 feet. The mountain hiker will observe this close juxtaposition as he views the valley. Amos Bixby, writing in 1880, noted that this peculiarity "brings the mines and farms close together, face to face. From most of the homesteads...in the county may be seen, when the air is clear, the smoke of the furnaces employed in mining...and from points in nearly every mining camp the valley is thrown into full view, so near that each newly established home...may be observed."[1]

The county's five major canyons, the South Boulder, the Boulder, the St. Vrain, Four Mile, and Left Hand, were formed by the mountains uplifting and water erosion. The geologic reason for this upthrust was the coming together of the Southern

A view into Left Hand Canyon, 1918. *Ed Tangen photo, A.A. Paddock Collection*

Rocky Mountain province and the Colorado Piedmont of the Great Plains province. Until the last of the Upper Cretaceous period, 135 million years ago, all of the Boulder valley, including the Front Range, lay under a series of seas. From time to time, the land upraised and the seas drained off. Later, heavy marshy conditions, which prevailed in the eastern part of the county, led to the formation of coal beds. As the land continued to rise, partly by volcanic action, igneous molten rock poured through fractures in the earth's unstable surface, causing the formation of batholiths, sheets, and dikes. (For example, the buttes at Valmont are intrusive dikes.) The mountains continued to rise, and the pressures within the rock formed deposits that man later found valuable—gold silver, lead, tungsten, and uranium. Fountain sandstone, such as the Red Rocks, Mount Sanitas, and the Flatirons, were formed in the Paleozoic era some five hundred million years ago. The smooth front of the Flatirons is probably due to their position under water. A newer formation, geologically, is the pink sandstone near Lyons (Lyons formation), which has been favored as a local building material for many years. Most of the outcroppings west of the Flatirons to the Continental Divide are of Precambrian age, over one billion years old. The county is a geologist's paradise, with examples of new formations as well as very old ones.

The snows of the Indian Peaks feed Coal Creek, the three forks of Boulder Creek (South, Middle, and North), Left Hand Creek, and the St. Vrain. All of these creeks eventually flow into the South Platte River. Efficient use of this water has always been difficult. Unlike in the East, spring rains of any consequence do not regularly occur to start off crops; therefore, the early settlers built ditches and reservoirs to catch melted snow run-off to irrigate their crops. From time to time, warm weather, combined with storms from the southeast, causes the snow to melt too quickly, and the creeks swell with snow water. Flooding occurs periodically. Because of the many rocks that have washed down the canyon, it is not difficult to imagine how Boulder got its name. Since the existing watershed could never support Boulder's present population, the community is indebted to far-sighted council members of the 1940s who were successful in securing rights to a portion of Big Thompson water to the north.

Boulder is the only city in the United States that owns a glacier, which was purchased from the federal government in 1928. During the Pleistocene, the Arapaho glacier may have been ten to fifteen miles

Arapaho glacier had a lake at its base until the 1920s. *Ed Tangen photo, Boulder Historical Society*

long and one thousand feet deep. Today, it is one-half mile square and two hundred feet deep. A small lake, which lay at its base, disappeared around 1922. Most of the crevasses are gone.

Mineral springs are found at Jamestown and Springdale; the warm waters at Eldorado Springs inspired the building of a famous spa just after the turn of the century.

Winters are relatively mild along the eastern half of the county. When they are harsh, heavy snows and cold do not ordinarily occur until February or March. Even then, a gentle warm "chinook" wind can melt many inches of snow within a short time. Boulder is noted for another type of alpine wind, a cold one that is not so gentle and that develops on the leeward, or sheltered side, of mountain ranges. These winds sometimes arrive after a snowstorm when the air pressure differs on either side of the Continental Divide. When high pressure occurs on the western slope, the air shoots straight up to a height of 70,000 to 80,000 feet, then cools and races downward, waterfall fashion. As it gains speed, the wind shrieks down the canyons with a formidable roar that is not unlike the sound of a heavy bomber. These winds are usually nocturnal and occur during the winter, with January being the peak month.

Boulder's dryness is remarkable enough that new residents sometimes find their furniture cracking as it dries out. Those who wear contact lenses have found adjustments necessary; the town's dermatologists attend to many skin ailments caused by the arid climate. Strep throat is more common here since the dryness produces favorable growing conditions for the bacteria. Both the dryness and high winds account for the intense fear of fire on the part of the early settlers.

The pioneers of the Boulder valley and mountains were ordinary people, Americans from the East and immigrants—farmers, merchants, and laborers. A few titled visitors passed through the area, and Dutch investors in silver left some $3 million in the county. Gamblers and gunmen stood out by wearing waistcoats instead of the area's uniform of overalls and heavy boots. As far as is known, only one horse thief was lynched in Boulder, and he turned out to have been innocent. Cornishmen came to mine silver, Swedes came to farm their homesteads, and Italians arrived to mine for coal on the plains. English, Scots, Irish, French, and German settlers—even a few Chinese from California—panned for gold along the mountain creeks. What was somewhat unusual about the early arrivals to the Boulder valley was that a good number of them were sick. Some were tubercular, others had recurrent fevers, but all came west to find the clean air, clear water, and vigorous life that they hoped would cure them.

A number of settlements in the county, which grew up around farm land, coal fields, or gold and silver mines, developed to the size of small towns, often larger than Boulder, and flourished for a time, supported a variety of businesses, gave sustenance to the town of Boulder itself, and then died, sometimes leaving little trace of their existence. Caribou is gone because of fire, the fortunes of the silver trade, and destructive tourists. Ballarat, Springdale, and Copper Rock were among the many settlements wiped out by the flood of 1894. Gold Hill burned to the ground one year after its establishment; residents rebuilt at another location. Hopes for flourishing communities at Altona, Albion, and Gold Lake were never more than dreams. In general, Boulder County was settled by a people determined to build as permanent a community as the one they had left. They carefully platted their streets, planted trees, built schools and churches, and gave some attention to the formation of government.

Despite their apparent ordinary nature, Boulder's citizens have displayed a feistiness and willingness to fight over almost anything—liquor, the method of saluting the flag, paving of the town's streets, celebration of Christmas in the schools. O.H. Wangelin, editor of the *Boulder County Herald,* in musing over this tendency toward belligerence amongst Boulderites, stated in 1888, "human nature...there is considerable of it in Boulder."[2] However, as Bixby sums up his description of Boulder, "It is the pride of the county that people once resident, who have removed, rarely escape a passion for returning."[3]

Surrounded by members of the charter convention, Flora McHarg and Ida Campbell, stern but feisty, were the first women to sit on council. *Western Historical Collections, University of Colorado at Boulder*

The Nancy Mill still stands out from the mountainside at Wallstreet to beguile the curious. Once prosperous and bustling, the mill was part of the Nancy Gold Mine and Tunnel Company. *A.A. Paddock Collection.*

Chapter One

Before 1858, few Americans knew that green valleys and grassy plains lay just east of the Rocky Mountains, for the land was uncharted, unsettled, and nameless. Most people pictured it as remote, unapproachable, and uninviting. From the Missouri River to the Snowy Range, the terrain was characterized as a "rainless, treeless waste."[1] Its skies were "sunny but unsympathetic and lonely..."[2]

The Indians who roamed the Boulder valley—the Comanche, the Kiowa, the Cheyenne, and the Arapaho, —regarded the land as their special winter hunting ground. Had they known that the white men described their valley as arid and desolate, they would have been pleased, for the antelope and buffalo could continue to graze in the quiet valley, undisturbed by unwanted settlement.

In the eighteenth century, this was Kiowa and Comanche country. They lived with the mountain lion and cinnamon bear and watched the elk come down the mountains to feed during the mild winters. By the late 1700s, the Kiowa and Comanche had wandered farther south as bands of Cheyenne and Arapaho moved into the quiet valley. For a thousand years, the Arapaho* had farmed in the Minnesota-Great Lakes area. Forced west to the Black Hills by the Sioux, who pressured them from the east, the Arapaho moved south to a nomadic life on the plains. The Sioux, in turn, were forced to move west by the early white settlement of northeast United States. The Arapaho enjoyed the mild winters here, found the game plentiful, and revered, even worshipped, the warm waters spilling down the rocks above what is now Eldorado Springs. The periodic scourges of grasshoppers across the valley did not bother them unduly, as they no longer put in crops. After each spring thaw, the Indians moved on to No-Man's Land in the Oklahoma Panhandle for the summer.

The Cheyenne had also farmed in northern Minnesota. They, too, felt the pressure from the east and moved on to the Dakotas, traveling south to the plains with their friends, the Arapaho.

The Ute, related to other Shoshone-speaking Indians to the west, were the traditional enemy of both the Arapaho and the Cheyenne. They lived in the mountains above the Boulder valley and roamed the mountains west to the Salt Lake Basin. The Ute were a short, muscular, warlike people, sometimes called "Black Indians" because of their darker skin color. Occasionally, they descended to the valley to hunt buffalo and to kill a few Cheyenne or Arapaho, but, for the most part, they were a mountain people.

During the seventeenth century, both France and Spain claimed this land, which included all the present states that border the Mississippi River, plus the Dakotas, Montana, Wyoming, and part of Colorado. The French explorer LaSalle roamed the southeast portion of this area in 1632 and called it Louisiana to honor his king, Louis XIV. After France's defeat in the French and Indian War of 1762, Spain again claimed the territory as hers, calling it New Spain. However, in 1800, Napoleon Bonaparte traded a kingdom in Italy for the Spanish claims in North America, and the land became French territory once again, for three years.

Despite the fact that by 1802 this was not yet U.S. territory, a few American adventurers quietly explored the valleys and plains east of the Rockies. James Purcell was one such early wanderer. Born in Kentucky, Purcell, along with two other men, traveled up and down the South Platte River and was subsequently captured in South Park by the Kiowa in 1803. He escaped and continued his explorations. Moving south, Purcell met some Apache Indians, who escorted him to the Spanish military garrison at Santa Fe. The Spanish did not put Purcell in jail, nor was he free to leave, since the Spanish preferred that as little information as possible about Louisiana get back to the States. The Spanish also knew that Purcell had found

---

*The Arapaho called themselves "Inunaina," meaning "our people." The Pawnee called the Arapaho "Harapihu" or "Tirapihu," their words for "trader." The Crow word for Arapaho means "many tattoos on the breast." Since the Arapaho had no "r" in their Algonquin language, some early writers referred to them as "N'appaho."

gold along the Platte River and demanded that he guide them to the spot. This he would not do. When Zebulon Pike came to Santa Fe in 1806, also under duress, he talked with Purcell, who told the explorer that "he had found gold on the head of La Platte..."[3]

Zebulon Montgomery Pike, then a lieutenant in the U.S. Amry, and his party of twenty-three men spent several months wandering along the eastern edge of the Rockies. The land was again called Louisiana and encompassed some 830,000 square miles, newly acquired from France by President Thomas Jefferson in 1803 for $15 million. Pike's orders to explore were not from Jefferson, as were those of Lewis and Clark, but from Major General James Wilkinson, governor of the Louisiana Territory. Pike may have been acting on secret orders to let himself be detained by the Spanish in order that he might spy on their operations in Santa Fe.

General Wilkinson, who, it appears, was also in the pay of the Spanish, may have been engaged in a conspiracy with Aaron Burr to detach the lands to the southwest from the United States and to form a new country with Burr as its head. It is doubtful that Pike knew of these plans, but the purposes of Pike's expedition have remained, throughout history, cloudy and mysterious. In any event, Pike published his *Journals* in 1810 and included, in his appendix, Purcell's remarks about the possibility of gold along the Platte. Apparently, little attention was paid them. Pike also noted that the "vast plains of the Western Hemisphere may become in time celebrated as the sandy desarts (*sic*) of Africa..."[4]

It is to Major Stephen H. Long,* who followed the Platte in the summer of 1820 on a side trip to South Park, that we are indebted for another unflattering portrait of eastern Colorado. He called it "The Great American Desert...totally unfit for cultivation, and,

Major Stephen H. Long saw little worth in Colorado's eastern plains when he crossed them in 1820, describing the area as "The Great American Desert." *Western Historical Collections, University of Colorado at Boulder*

Zebulon Montgomery Pike and his party of twenty-three men wandered north along Colorado's Front Range in 1805 to explore what was then part of the Louisiana Territory. *Western Historical Collections, University of Colorado at Boulder*

of course, uninhabitable by a people depending upon agriculture for their subsistence."[5] He did take note of "buffaloes, wild goats and other wild game"[6] and mentioned that Arapaho and Cheyenne were in the area, as well as some Kiowa and Sioux. Someone in his party of nineteen gave out the story that the Arapaho used gold bullets. Long also concluded that the high plains were arid and uninviting but said that if they were "viewed as a frontier, may prove of infinite importance to the United States, inasmuch as it is calculated to serve as a barrier to prevent too great an

---

*Long's Peak is named after the explorer. Earlier, the French called the peak, together with Meeker Peak, Les Deux Oreilles, or "two ears."

The Boulder valley was home to herds of buffalo, elk, and antelope as were other protected valleys along what is now called the Front Range. Bands of Southern Arapaho and Cheyenne wintered here, below the peaks of the Snowy Range. *Western Historical Collections, University of Colorado at Boulder*

extension of our population forward...."[7] Most Americans, with the exception of a few mountain men, believed him, and the winter hunting grounds of the Arapaho and Cheyenne would remain quiet and undisturbed for another thirty-eight years.

Even so, the Indians uneasily watched the business activities of Charles and William Bent and Ceran St. Vrain in the late 1820s. Bent's Fort (then called William's Fort) was established on the Arkansas River in 1833 to capture the fur trade. Louis Vasquez and Andrew Sublette also hoped to profit by the sale of beaver pelts. (The fur provided the felt for men's hats.) They built Fort Vasquez on the South Platte in 1835, near the present town of Platteville. Sublette, a Creole from St. Louis, seemed well acquainted with the Front Range. He wrote back home that his tuberculosis did not trouble him as long as he stayed here.*

The following year, Lancaster P. Lupton built Fort Lupton (sometimes called Fort Lancaster) farther south on the South Platte. By 1837, Fort Jackson was constructed between Forts Vasquez and Lupton (near the present town of Ione) by mountain men Henry Fraeb and Peter A. Sorby, who established a fur trade there.

Andrew W. Sublette, one of several notable Sublette brothers, was born in Kentucky and lived in St. Charles County, Missouri, until the life of the mountain man and the lure of beaver pelts proved irresistible. He helped found Fort Vasquez on the South Platte in 1835 and probably knew the Boulder area well. *Missouri Historical Society*

*Sublette probably spent some time along St. Vrain Creek and above, for early writer Rufus B. Sage, in his *Rocky Mountain Life*, published in 1846, refers to the St. Vrain as Sublette's Creek. Historian LeRoy Hafen believes that Left Hand Creek was also named for the fur trader Sublette, whom the Indians called Left Hand. A more popular explanation for the naming of Left Hand Creek is, of course, that it commemorated Chief Left Hand of the Arapaho.

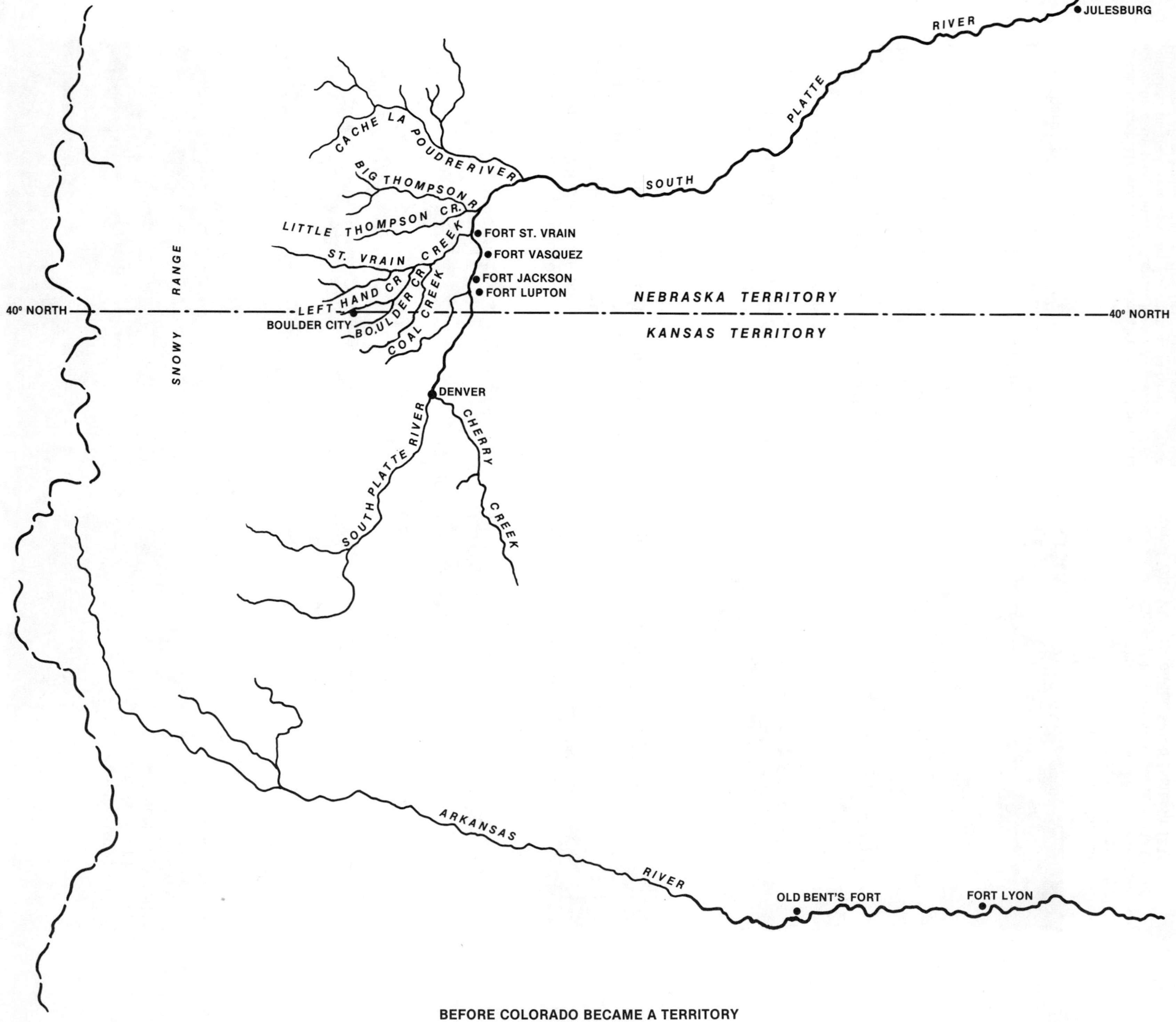

BEFORE COLORADO BECAME A TERRITORY

Map showing rivers, creeks, forts and settlements including:

- Snowy Range
- 40° North
- Arkansas River
- South Platte River
- Cherry Creek
- Coal Creek
- Boulder Creek
- Left Hand Cr.
- St. Vrain Creek
- Little Thompson Creek
- Big Thompson Cr.
- Cache La Poudre River
- South Platte River
- Boulder City
- Denver
- Fort St. Vrain
- Fort Vasquez
- Fort Jackson
- Fort Lupton
- Old Bent's Fort
- Fort Lyon
- Julesburg
- Kansas Territory
- Nebraska Territory

A few months later, feeling the pinch of competition, Ceran St. Vrain built Fort Lookout where the St. Vrain flows into the South Platte. (The fort was later called Fort George, then Fort St. Vrain). Ceran's brother, Marcellin St. Vrain, managed the business there, but the fort was short-lived. By 1840, fur hats had gone out of style, and selling fur pelts was no longer lucrative. The fur trade passed into history almost overnight. Fort Vasquez closed in 1842, and the St. Vrains bought Fort Jackson only to have it closed, but Fort Lupton remained open until 1845.

John Charles Frémont wandered through the area in 1843 looking for an easy route across the Rockies. He visited Marcellin St. Vrain, who was still at the fort, and celebrated the Fourth of July with him. William Gilpin, later to become the first governor of Colorado Territory, was in Frémont's party. He reported that gold probably could be found here, but, again, the news seemed to attract only a few men who lived in the mountains with their Arapaho or Ute wives. By the time Francis Parkman passed by the St. Vrain area in 1846, the fort was in ruins.

Activity of a violent nature may have occurred in the Boulder valley in 1852. The story *Green Rocks*[8] tells of the John Snodgrass family of Kentucky, who was overtaken by Indians en route to Oregon. The Indians killed Mrs. Snodgrass and kidnapped her daughter Josephine (nicknamed Gypsy or Gyp because of her coloring). They took Gyp, as the story goes, toward the mountains, with Mr. Snodgrass and his

These Southern Arapaho men, left to right, Crazy Bull and Friday, pose for their portrait. Modern joggers may enjoy studying the footwear of these gentlemen. *Western Historical Collections, University of Colorado at Boulder.*

John Charles Frémont, in search of a new route across the Rockies, stopped at Fort St. Vrain in the summer of 1843 to visit with its proprietor Marcellin St. Vrain. *Western Historical Collections, University of Colorado at Boulder*

When this young woman sat for her portrait in her Civil War hoop dress, little did she know that, as Mrs. Ebenezer Rowland, she and her family would trek across the country in search of gold. *Rowland Collection*

party in desperate pursuit. They followed the tracks of the Indians to Green Rocks (at the mouth of Sunshine Canyon), where Gyp escaped her captors. As the girl ran out from the cover of the rocks to reach her father, an Indian's arrow killed her. Someone carved the girl's name on one of the rocks, where the word "Gyp" can still be seen today.

Despite this violence, perhaps fictional, the valley remained a peaceful winter home for the elk, the buffalo, and the Arapaho. In July 1858, the discovery of gold elsewhere, along Cherry Creek, would shatter the quiet of the Front Range forever. William Green Russell and his fellow Georgians joyfully told the world of their findings at Cherry Creek. They named the spot Auraria, after the gold diggings that they had worked back home in Georgia. By September, anyone who could read a newspaper knew that exciting times were ahead for an area hitherto regarded as worthless.

Born in the States, these youngsters would spend their childhood in the Boulder valley. Georgina Rowland, at left, would attend the University of Colorado and teach third grade at White Rocks School, Pine Street School, and Mapleton School. *Rowland Collection*

Chapter Two

Thomas A. Aikins moved west in stages, as did so many restless Americans. He farmed in his native Maryland, moved on to Ohio, farmed again in Illinois, then moved to Missouri and farmed there for fourteen years. No doubt he read of Green Russell's gold discovery in the *Missouri Republican*. The descriptions of a near-heaven and easy riches to be found at Cherry Creek must have excited the fifty-year-old farmer, for he quickly formed a small gold-seeking party that included his son James and nephew Samuel, said goodbye to the rest of his family, and struck out for Nebraska City, following the Missouri River north, the first leg on the journey to Cherry Creek.

At Nebraska City, Mayor Alfred A. Brookfield, twenty-eight-year-old grocer and sometime marble salesman, joined Aikins, who was now captain of the party. Brookfield said goodbye to his new wife Emma, telling her that he would write when it was safe for her to come west. Her brother, hotel-keeper Thomas Lorton, decided to come, too. John Rothrock also joined the party at Nebraska City. Born in Pennsylvania, he had worked as a government surveyor, piecing out a living with carpentry work, a skill that would serve the group well a few weeks later. Other names associated with the Aikins party were Daniel Gordon, Theodore Squires, the Wheelock brothers,

Farmer Thomas A. Aikins was captain of the Nebraska City party, one of the first gold seekers in the Boulder valley from the States. *History of Clear Creek and Boulder Valleys*

Alfred A. Brookfield came with the Nebraska City party and was elected first president of the Boulder City Town Company. *History of Clear Creek and Boulder Valleys*

Although John Rothrock was a government surveyor, his carpentry skills were important to the first party because he built the first cabins along Boulder Creek. *Boulder Historical Society*

Captain Abram K. Yount, Charles Clouser, William "Billy" Moore, Henry W. Chiles, and W.H. Dickens.*

This first group was typical of the people who followed them to the mountains and plains of eastern Colorado. They were farmers or small merchants. Most of them dreamed of the riches that they would soon realize from mining gold; most of them knew nothing about how to go about it.

From Nebraska City they followed the Platte, passing through Fort Kearney to Ogallala, then turned their wagons to follow the South Platte to Julesburg. Their goal was to try their luck with others hurrying toward Cherry Creek and Auraria. They planned to move across the Great American Desert, venture into the austere Rockies, get the gold, get rich, and get out. Not all of them, however, planned to return to the States. Some hoped that the new land would provide a permanent living for them and their families. Financial depression back East, resulting in the Panic of 1857, caused their flight. Growing tensions of an approaching civil war added to their restlessness, making the West more attractive. Some wanted to escape the deteriorating living conditions of the industrialized Northeast. Many sought a healthier life. They came because someone in the family had tuberculosis. Undulant fever raged in the river valleys behind them. They hoped it was true, as newspaper accounts proclaimed, that the clear, crystal air and sparkling water of the Rockies would clear consumptive chests and strengthen fragile bodies.

When the Aikins party reached the abandoned Fort St. Vrain on October 16, 1858, the men stopped to reconnoiter. Captain Aikins later reported:

> I mounted the walls...and with my field glass could see that the mountains looked right for gold; could see bands of Indian ponies and bands of deer and antelope grazing close up to the high foot-hills; could see that the valley...was the loveliest of all the valleys in the scope of vision—a landscape exceedingly beautiful, those mountains are so high and steep, the boys said, that it will not be safe to venture up till Spring, on account of snow slides.

> But the following morning was so fair, and the love of adventure and hope of gold so inviting, that we forded the Platte and traveled up, with the bold mountains all before us, till we pitched our tents under the red rock cliff, at the mouth of Boulder Cañon.[1]

No one knows the exact location of the first camp, but the men probably camped where Sunshine Creek flows into Boulder Creek. (In later years, some of the gold-seekers, while speaking to reporters, remembered that they could see the setting sun glow on "Sunset Rock," the most northern ridge of the Flatirons, while the rest of the area was in darkness. This phenomenon can be seen where Sunshine Creek flows into the Boulder, but not on higher ground under Red Rocks, where some have placed the first camp.)

The Aikins party and the men who joined them came prepared for a harsh winter, but they found, to their surprise, that they could work outside in their shirt-sleeves for the early part of the winter. They also came prepared to butcher their oxen, for they felt that if Stephen Long's Great American Desert proved true, the animals would die of starvation. In fact, the oxen thrived on the range, and the men ate deer and antelope meat instead.

John Rothrock, the part-time carpenter from Nebraska City, and others built eleven crude cabins along Boulder Creek. (In fact, the new settlement was called Eleven Cabins for a short time.) They had no nails, they used undressed logs, and they found that animal skins would do for doors. Others in the party scouted Boulder Canyon for a distance, and in November, they found "color" in the creek. However, hiking up the canyon was rough going, so they turned their attention instead to Sunshine Canyon. In mid-January, the weather was still mild, so a party that included James Aikins, Colonel I.S. Bull, Charles Clouser, William Huey, W.W. Jones, and David Wooley continued on up Sunshine Canyon for twelve miles, eventually crossing the ridge between Sunshine Canyon and Four Mile Canyon. On January 16, in a small creek bed, they found gold; before they left, they named the place Gold Run.

*See Appendix for as complete a list of the first party as is known.

About the same time, John Gregory had left Auraria and moved about the Black Hawk area. He found what he was looking for on January 15. Earlier, on January 7, George Jackson, also starting from Auraria, had found gold on Chicago Creek near Idaho Springs. Both men returned to Auraria separately, keeping their discoveries to themselves in hopes that, after the spring thaw, they could extend their finds in peace, without competition.

When members of the Nebraska party went into Auraria for supplies, they reported their Gold Run discovery and learned that B.F. Langley had also found "color" in Deadwood Gulch on South Boulder Creek. How the Ute Indians reacted to the many forays for gold in their mountain territory is not recorded, but surely they were unhappy with the heightened activity.

Down below, on the plains, a band of two hundred Arapaho Indians became acquainted with the Aikins party. The Indians, called "The Ugly Ones," were so named because they wore the facial scars from previous encounters with white man's smallpox. Chief Left Hand (his Arapaho name was Niwot) and his group were camped to the north on St. Vrain Creek; the band visited the Aikins camp from time to time. The Arapaho were the least warlike of the Plains Indians; Left Hand himself was mild of manner, often stating his hopes that Indians and whites could accommodate one another. He knew more of white culture than some Indian leaders, because he had traveled as far east as Iowa to visit white settlements. He was friendly, even though he knew that the Nebraska City party was camped on Indian lands that were guaranteed to the Arapaho nation by the Horse Creek Treaty, signed at Fort Laramie in 1851.

Left Hand told the would-be miners, "Go away, you come to kill our game, to burn our wood, and to destroy our grass."[2] Some of the men offered Left Hand food, giving him such compliments that the Indian was somewhat placated. Not so with Bear Head and Many Whips, who were also camped nearby. Bear Head pointed to a comet (Donati's comet) visible in the sky and asked the white men if they remembered the other year when the stars fell. Yes, the whites replied, that would be November 1832, a time of heavy display of shooting stars. Bear Head stated that that was also the first year white men came onto his lands, and the comet "points back to when the stars fell as thick as the tears of our women shall fall when you come to drive us away."[3] Bear Head gave the men camped under the red rock cliff three days to leave. After a short time, however, he returned and told the white men of his dream. He had been standing on a hill and had seen Boulder Creek swell to a flood. His people had been swallowed in the waters, while the white people had been saved. Thus, Bear Head found a way to back down from a confrontation, but the Arapaho knew that soon they would have to move on.

Left Hand continued to visit the camp. The tall, broad-shouldered, handsome chief was particularly fond of the five-foot-tall Alfred Brookfield. When Left Hand realized that the men were searching for gold, the chief told Brookfield that he knew where to find gold. Left Hand would locate the gold, then Brookfield could return home and leave the Arapaho in peace. For a time, Brookfield was very excited until Left Hand showed him some shiny but worthless mica. Little did this mild-mannered Arapaho chief know that, in less than five years, he would fall by the guns of some of these same men at a place called Sand Creek.

In 1860, the Arapaho held a final antelope hunt near the site of Valmont. Some four hundred Indians on horseback formed a circle around the grazing antelope and chased the animals within the circle, driving them round and round until they tired and fell. They slaughtered five hundred animals.

The following year, a new treaty signed at Fort Lyon (near Bent's Fort on the Arkansas River) cut the Arapaho's hunting grounds by 90 percent. The Indians continued to visit the Boulder area and made friends with a number of the settlers. In fact, some of the settlers were so devoted to Chief Left Hand that

Little Raven, chief of the Southern Arapaho, knew the freedom of his people was doomed after the discovery of gold in Colorado. *Western Historical Collections, University of Colorado at Boulder*

they refused the call to go to Sand Creek with the Third Colorado Regiment.* However, the Arapaho knew that their special hunting place was doomed as the whites continued to pour in.

An examination of letters back to the States illustrates that disagreement existed as to whether or not gold mining was a profitable venture. Alfred Brookfield wrote to a close friend on January 26, 1859:

> We were quite surprised a few days since when we read the glowing account in the Missouri River papers, of what the miners are doing here. I pronounce them a pack of lies, written and reported back by a set of petty one horse town speculators, and are calculated to ruin many a poor devil besides your humble servant.[4]

Elsewhere in the letter, the dour Brookfield adds, if his friend has any confidence in his judgment, he will "immediately abandon the idea of coming out here, without some other discoveries are made than have been thus far. My impression of the mines is that they are a damned humbug. I wish I could write otherwise...."[5]

But another would-be miner wrote, "I want you to come out early in the spring—a fortune is in store for us. There is gold here in considerable quantity, and no mistake. Bring picks and shovels, groceries and provisions, for they are in demand, and sell at high figures."[6] Oliver P. Goodwin was enthusiastic about mining prospects in his February 12 letter, and he could see opportunities other than mining:

> It has the best farming land in the country...One of our citizens has already a saw and grist mill en route from Nebraska City, and another has gone for goods to the states...the population exceeds 280 male, and but one drawback, there is not a single white woman in the country; but we hope when spring comes, with it will come plenty of help-mates for the isolated miners.[7]

Some of the first arrivals to the Boulder valley, Charles Clouser for one, took Indian wives, unwilling, it seems, to wait for warm weather and white ladies from the East.

By the end of February, the mournful Brookfield seemed more cheerful when he wrote to his wife Emma:

> ....our discoveries are creating much excitement at all the settlements and people are coming in every day...The gold which we find is of quite a different quality from any that has been found in other places, and what is called "shot gold"—all that has been found in other places is "scale or float gold."[8]*

Brookfield continued to be conservative and would not advise anyone to come west, but he told Emma that he would come for her "later in the season."[9]

---

*Early settler Robert Hauck, who headed the Wisconsin Gold Mining Company and farmed near Longmont, refused to fight at Sand Creek because of his friendship with Left Hand.

*"Float" refers to pieces of ore that have fallen from a parent vein due to weathering.

Whenever there was a break in the weather, most of the men were in the mountains, moving about the Gold Run area. The first gold was collected by simply panning in the creeks. If a site looked promising, a hand rocker, said to have been invented by the Chinese, was brought in. Then the miner would shovel dirt in one end of the device and "rock" the mud out through holes at the other end. The gold particles, heavier than the mud, caught on riffles built inside. The handrocker was used extensively and most profitably at Gold Run.

By March, Brookfield was (for him) positively ecstatic:

> We have found this gold in nearly every place we have prospected from the mouth of the cañon, for a distance of twenty-five miles in a north-westerly direction, and I know, by actual experiment, that a man can make with a rocker $5 per day...."[10]

Early prospector W.H. Wannemaker taught the inexperienced men to build a sluice, which was tipped so that the water would flush out the dirt, leaving the gold at the bottom. The men at Gold Run realized that the water in the small creek could not support many sluice operations. Before the second summer ended, Thomas Aikins and his men had dug a ditch almost seven miles long from Left Hand Creek to tiny Gold Run. Now it was possible to store the water in boom dams in order to release it down the sluice with such force as to separate out the gold more efficiently. These placer operations could be built by the men very cheaply and ran at quite a profit; $100,000 was realized from little Gold Run alone. Some of this money trickled down the canyon to Boulder City and kept the struggling settlement alive.

Almost immediately upon its founding, the small camp along Boulder Creek lost its population. Would-be miners found gold mining hard work. They despaired of becoming rich. Disgusted, the "go-backers" returned to their homes in the States, telling all that they had "seen the elephant."* Historian Amos Bixby, himself an unsuccessful miner, wrote that these men were here too soon; their ventures were premature. In order to benefit, they had to wait for the proper equipment to be brought in and for the expertise that went along with the equipment. There were others who did not continue with mining, but neither did they go back home. Instead, they came down from the mountains and fanned out across the Boulder valley. They put in the first crops, cut the native grasses for hay, and started cattle-feeding operations. They knew that miners had to eat; someone would sell produce and meat in the mining camps above. They became farmers, barbers, cattle-raisers, butchers, general store proprietors, saloon-keepers, and bankers. They started res-

---

*To see the elephant is "To see the world and gain experience of its sin and glitter, generally at some cost to the investigator."[11]

taurants, boarding houses, and hotels. Bixby wrote that "one good effect of the severe trial has been to eliminate the lazy and the easily discouraged men, and to leave only those of clear grit and of sufficient intelligence to see ultimate success."[12]

Early journalist Amos Bixby despaired of becoming rich from gold mining, became Boulder's postmaster, and wrote a history of the Boulder valley in 1880. *History of Clear Creek and Boulder Valleys*

Have they just arrived? A tent and two low cabins just east of the present Columbia Cemetery. *A.A. Paddock Collection*

A first Boulder home for these settlers, fancier than most, as it has roof shingles and real bricks for the chimney. Note the pole at right to help support the cabin during high winds. *J.B. Sturtevant photo, Western Historical Collections, University of Colorado at Boulder*

Are these folks having a picnic or is it their first stop in the Boulder valley? *A.A. Paddock Collection*

Chapter Three

On February 10, 1859, the mild winter turned harsh for a time, making gold-seeking difficult. Thomas Aikins called a meeting to form what was later named the Boulder City Town Company—an association, not a government. (Some talked of calling the settlement "Boulder Creek.") More than sixty men* signed the company's Articles of Organization, which stated, "whereas we the undersigned, residents of St. Vrain County, Territory of Nebraska, having met the 10th day of Feb., A.D. 1859, for the purpose of organizing a Town Company, and locating and improving a town site on Boulder Creek near the entrance into the mountains...." This document was sent back to the States for the purpose of obtaining a city charter, together with a petition for a post office.

If the foregoing sounds somewhat colonial, perhaps it was. Part of the original town site was a federal land grant of 160 acres, dated August 1865 and awarded to Sarah Emery Weston, a resident of Maine and widow of Joseph Weston, who fought in the Revolutionary War. Widow Weston was in her nineties and could not make the trip west, but by some method she conveyed her grant to Peter Housel, who did come west.* The Pre-emption Law of 1841 stated that a person had prior right to purchase a piece of land if he occupied it and improved it. Such lands were selling for about $1.25 per acre. The Kansas-Nebraska Act of 1853 also referred to pre-emption of "the public lands to which the Indian title had been at the time of such settlement extinguished." Historian Percy Fritz called this phrase in the Kansas-Nebraska Act "a pious one" but said that the men who pushed the Indians off of California's gold fields had used the same logic ten years earlier.

One is forced to conclude that the early settlers of the Boulder valley were squatters and that the lands they pre-empted belonged either to the Arapaho nation or to Mrs. Weston. No evidence points to their feeling guilty about such encroachment. Apparently, those back in the States did not feel guilty either, for in 1866 the U.S. Congress validated the settlers' claims to these lands.

During the first meetings of the Boulder City Town Company, two factions developed. The "lowers" wanted to encourage men to come to the valley and settle their families on relatively cheap land. The "uppers" felt that the company should control immigration by setting a high value on the real estate. At one of the early sessions, someone moved that all settlers along Boulder Creek become automatic members of the company, but that motion was withdrawn. Another motion called for alternating lots to be given free to incoming settlers, but that motion failed. At the February 14 meeting, a peacemaker moved to consolidate the opposing factions, but that lost thirteen to twelve. Three days later, at another meeting, one of the men moved to accept the officers of the "lowers" as head of a joint organization, but he was forced to withdraw the motion. On February 25, the "uppers" and "lowers" again tried to get together, but by the end of the evening they gave up and went their separate ways.

In the end, the "uppers" stayed in control of the company, which turned out to be an exclusive real estate organization. The members divided up 1,280 acres along Boulder Creek, stretching east from the mouth of the canyon for two miles, into 4,044 lots. Each lot was 50 feet wide and 140 feet deep. Each shareholder received eighteen lots in a drawing, with a few lots reserved free for those who promised to provide a needed service in town, such as a sawmill. The rest of the lots went on sale at $1,000 each. (Compare this price with that of homestead lands, selling for

---

*See Appendix for a complete list of the original members of the Boulder City Town Company.

*Peter Housel finally got his land in 1869, a parcel of 158.9 acres elsewhere in the valley.

$1.25 per acre.) Needless to say, there were not many takers. The high cost of the lots was only one of several reasons for the slow growth of the settlement.

The company was to meet on the tenth day of each month. Alfred Brookfield was elected president for a six-month term, Thomas Aikins was vice-president, and W.S. Buckwalter was elected secretary. Eleven men wanted to be treasurer, and, after several ballots, T.S. Scholfield finally earned the trust and votes of thirty-six company shareholders. Seven directors were chosen. The company issued stock, transferred stock, and took back lots for resale when owners did not pay their taxes.*

Already Boulder City had "city planners" and "building codes" at work. The company specified that a cabin foundation must be laid in seven days; the cabin walls must measure more than eight and one-half feet to the eaves. Chimneys must be built inside the cabin. Construction must be finished within sixty days; houses must be oriented north and south. Streets were to be eighty feet wide, alleys twenty feet wide. No stores had been built, and any goods that were available were sold from wagons. One letter-writer was optimistic. "This will no doubt be a good trading post...Boulder City is in her infancy... already some 60 to 75 houses are in course of erection. The Stockholders, satisfied that they have real inducements, have set to earnestly preparing as many houses as possible to accommodate traders in the spring."[1]

When the winter storm abated, however, interest in the company's rules and regulations paled; the shareholders, and everyone else, moved back into the mountains near Gold Run. They, and a new wave of gold-seekers, were not satisfied to placer for gold for any great length of time. They sought the original veins from which the gold had tumbled into the creeks.

With the heavy influx of people around Gold Run, it became obvious that some sort of government was needed. The laws of Nebraska Territory seemed very far away. The miners met together on March 7, 1859 (they may have met earlier) and set up a government fashioned after those of California's mining districts. They called themselves Mountain District Number One, Gold Hill, Nebraska, the first of its kind in Colorado and just as legal as the Boulder City Town Company—for Gold Hill was also on Indian land. That they were squatters did not bother the newcomers to Gold Hill any more than it had at Boulder City, for they adopted a constitution, fixed boundaries (the district was four miles square), elected officers, and passed regulations regarding the filing of mining claims. William Blore was elected president; he also served as justice of the peace and as presiding judge. The men also elected a recorder and a constable, bonded for $100, whose first duty was to make certain that liquor was not sold in the area. The men decided that no saloons would open in the Gold Hill district, although "somehow, the 'boys' would occasionally manage to get a canteen filled on the sly."[2]

Boulder followed the lead of Gold Hill and recorded its own mining district on July 30, 1859. By the following year, mining districts were formed in the Sugar Loaf and Ward areas. Each district had its own constitution, officers, constable, and mining claim regulations. They made laws regulating lodes, gulches, water, mill sites, timber, patch diggings, tunnels, ranches, and cabin construction.

The First Mining Districts

District	Date Established
Gold Hill	Probably March 7, 1859
Boulder	July 30, 1859 or before
Ward	September 12, 1860
Sugar Loaf	November 9, 1860
Gold Lake	February 26, 1861 or before
Grand Island	March 16, 1861
Snowy Range	June 17, 1861
Utilla	September 7, 1861 or before
Bald Mountain	June 10, 1864
Central	September 7, 1866

If one resident perjured himself, stole another's goods, or murdered someone, death by hanging could follow. If a man were caught "salting"* a claim, he could be fined anywhere from ten to fifty dollars, receive twenty-five lashes on his bare back in front of everyone, then be banned from the district. Some of the districts tried to pass laws regarding the collection of taxes with the view that the building of roads should start with public funds. Such ventures were usually voted down; the development of the county's wagon roads had to wait for popular subscription.

On April 23, 1860 the *Rocky Mountain News* started publication. In the first issue, the paper reported that Oliver P. Goodwin had located a vein of gold. In May, J.D. Scott also found a lode which he named The Scott. On June 16, David Horsfal, William Blore, and Matthew McCaslin discovered a lode on the hill above Gold Run (Gold Hill), which was to

---

*In the past, records for this period have been difficult to study because Marcus W. Towner, an original company shareholder, left Boulder City in January 1864, taking the company records with him. By extensive correspondence, local historian Sanford Gladden was able to secure these papers, copy them, and distribute them to local libraries.

*"Salting" is placing ore found elsewhere on a new site, with a view to defraud.

become the famous Horsfal mine. By mere sluicing, the lode gave up $10,000 of ore. (However, one man sold his interest in the Horsfal mine for "one wool hat and damned glad to get the hat.") These and other finds had considerable coverage in newspapers back in the states. Cries of "humbug" were heard no more. Soon, tents, lean-tos, cabins, and crude boarding houses covered Gold Hill. Makeshift meat markets, barbershops, and groceries opened. By the time of the spring thaw, some one thousand gold-seekers poured through Boulder City, leaving those $1,000 lots behind on their way to the Gold Hill area. Perhaps if the site had not been crowded so quickly, more thought would

portals; we had the world by the seat of the britches."[3] Boulder City, according to Sniktau, was "only a collection of log huts built by the pioneers of the year before. There were three families there at the time, the heads of which were white as to the male members, copper-colored as to the female, while the children were a blending of two races."[4] Sniktau also mentions that his party brought in the first white female, Mrs. Williams. That worthy lady made an American flag out of red flannel and flour sacks that waved in the town square, "a proper greeting of the Fourth of July."[5]

By June 1859, Samuel M. Breath and William A.

Winter at the mouth of Boulder Canyon. *Western Historical Collections, University of Colorado at Boulder*

have been given to a proper location for the town of Gold Hill. Since no creek flowed nearby, the new residents had to haul their daily water supply up the hill. This poor location was to result in grave consequences later on.

During the early summer of 1859, a writer calling himself Sniktau* visited a virtually deserted Boulder City. His group had found a small amount of gold in the Big Thompson to the north, and "all were wild with excitement; El Dorado had opened her bright

Davidson arrived from the East, apparently undaunted by Boulder City's dismal appearance and prospects. Both men were college-educated, which was not a common background for most of the settlers. Together, they built a double log cabin on what is now the northeast corner of Eleventh and Pearl streets, where they sold groceries and mining equipment. Their partnership must have been a happy one, for through the years they farmed together, financed a coal company, developed the Ni Wot Mining Company at Ward, built a wagon road, and worked on similar projects in Golden City.* (One of the men gave his name to

*Pen name of E.H.N. Patterson, editor of *The Mining Review* at Georgetown, who was described as a "poet of no mean pretentions" by the *Burlington Gazeteer* in 1867.

*The word "City" was added to the names of early camps in hopes they would become cities in fact.

Beasley Ditch, one of the first to be dug in Boulder City.
J.B. Sturtevant photo, Boulder Historical Society

Davidson Mesa.) Messrs. Horace Tarbox and Ed Donnelly also opened a store for general merchandise.

The first successful business in the valley was supplying hay for the miners' horses and mules. The native grasses of the valley were cut, and wagons carried loads of dried hay into the mountains, a load sometimes selling for as much as $400. Marinus G. Smith came to the area that summer with two dollars in his pocket and, among his many projects, started the Marinus Express, a mail delivery and passenger line between Denver, Boulder City, and other points. He charged fifty cents for each letter to be delivered to the States. (Mr. Smith was called "Marine;" Marine Street is named after him.) Smith and William Pell plowed the creek lands at Seventeenth and Arapahoe* streets and put in a vegetable garden, lining it with cherry trees. Needing water for their crops, the men started digging Boulder's first irrigation ditch, which would head off from Boulder Creek at Broadway and run to Smith's land at Seventeenth Street. (Smith eventually acquired 220 acres at that location, part of which he later donated to the University of Colorado.) Andrew Douty had planted wheat on the South Boulder Creek lands and also set to work on the county's first grist mill, carving the grinding buhrs himself from native stone. Later, he was to build a proper flour mill there and on the creek near Boulder City. Henry Clay Norton, in an effort to turn some of the eleven thousand wagons bound for Cherry Creek west to the Boulder valley, built a toll bridge across the South Platte near crumbling Fort St. Vrain.

In July, the Wellman brothers, Luther, Henry, and Sylvanus, arrived in Boulder City from their native Pennsylvania and surveyed agricultural possibilities in the Boulder valley. Since the area was pretty much deserted, except for herds of elk numbering five hundred, the brothers could pick their spot for farming without much competition. They chose land two and one-half miles from the mouth of the canyon, plowed their first field, and planted turnip seed. As the turnips matured, the Wellmans had their first encounter with Rocky Mountain grasshoppers. The insects came in massive clouds, swooped down upon the turnips, and quickly finished them off.

In August 1859, the Reverend Jacob Adriance, a Methodist circuit preacher, visited Boulder City, delivering the town's first sermon to an audience of fifty persons. The minister's description of the "town" differed from the grand plans of the Boulder City Town Company, for he reported "There were 10 or 12 log houses in town, but none of them completed."[6] Evidently, not everyone was in the mountains now, for Adriance estimated that seventy to one hundred people resided in town, most of whom occupied wagons or tents. He also preached at a place that he called Springville, a settlement north of Boulder.

Understandably, all of this activity spurred the building of cabins. By late fall, when the Reverend Adriance returned on his circuit, seventy cabins had been built. None had windows or wooden plank floors, because no sawmill had yet been constructed. A saloon had opened, however, for the preacher led a prayer service on the second floor over the saloon. By this time, his circuit included "Twelve Mile," a spot near Gold Run.

Despite this activity, Boulder City was not flourishing. The impoverished community had no capital to support road building; Boulder's new merchants and farmers were frustrated in their attempts to sell goods to the miners up above. There were no sewers; flies were everywhere and so were droppings from horses, mules, chickens, and pigs. The mud along Pearl Street caused considerable irritation.

During the fall of 1859, Bill Barney finished his

---

*Arapaho Glacier and Arapaho Indians are spelled without the final "e." Although Arapaho without an "e" is regarded as correct, Boulder's Arapahoe Street and Arapahoe Shopping Centers use the final "e," a spelling used by the whites.

One of the first settlers from Wisconsin, Andrew J. Macky became one of Boulder's early financiers. *History of Clear Creek and Boulder Valleys*

cabin on the southeast corner of Eleventh and Pearl streets. Since his was the only cabin with a real floor of wooden planks, a Christmas dance was held there with 200 men and 17 women in attendance. A midnight supper consisted of black-tailed deer, rabbit, and fish, a pleasant change from parched corn. Coffee was served from wash boilers. Many dressed in flour sack costumes and borrowed shirts; there were "no vests, claw-hammer coats, kid gloves on gentlemen, no silk dresses, kid slippers, diamond pins, and idiotically combed hair...,"[7] but everyone had a good time. Emma Brookfield was one of the dancers. Alfred had returned from Nebraska City with his wife after having been away from her for more than one year.

At Gold Hill, mining activities were temporarily interrupted in October 1859 when Indians, possibly Utes, descended upon the camp and stole some horses. In the process, they fired upon a miner named Barker, wounding him in the hip. A posse of twenty-nine volunteers tracked the Indians for miles, traveling west through country that they had never seen. They lost the Indians, but they did get their first close view of the immense Snowy Range, which stretched grandly before them to the north and to the south.

Captain Ebenezer Rowland pauses on the way to his mines. *Rowland Collection*

An arastra, early Spanish device to crush gold-laden rock, later powered by steam. *Western Historical Collections, University of Colorado at Boulder*

Now that the gold veins themselves were being mined, the extracted quartz ore had to be pulverized, hence the need for different equipment. At first, the men built a crude arastra, a Spanish device that consisted of a flat, circular stone with a revolving sweep above, to which heavy stones or boulders could be attached. As a man or mule (later, steam) turned the sweep, the stones would crush the quartz and thus expose the gold ore.

In the fall, Thomas J. Graham hauled in by ox train a three-stamp mill weighing 500 pounds from Leavenworth, Kansas. This was the first such mill in Colorado. He set it up in Aikins Gulch near Gold Hill. However, by 1860, mining activity was so intense that the mill could not accommodate the ore. In July, the partners of the Horsfal mine, hearing that a larger mill was on its way to the Gregory mines, decided to journey to Auraria to intercept the owners, Robert

Two men above the sluice at Wood Mountain Gulch are watching a group of Chinese placer mining. *J.B. Sturtevant photo, A.A. Paddock Collection*

and Gary Culver and John Mahoney. The Horsfal men persuaded them to bring the mill to Gold Hill instead; it, too, was replaced with a six-stamp mill within a few months. Although the expensive changes of machinery and constant breakdowns must have been hard on some miners, the owners of the Horsfal mine made $300,000 in the next two years.

Associated with much of this gold was a "troublesome purple ore" which the men kicked out of the way. Little did they know that they were disposing of the rare tellurium, which would be recognized thirteen years later at Gold Hill.

Gold Hill now supported 2,000 residents. The men had sent for their families; a school and a hotel opened, and the new residents made ambitious plans for town expansion. Fourth of July in Gold Hill was a grand affair with toasts and speeches by David Nichols and the Reverend Wiley Bunch, who was "a strange compound of ignorance, natural eloquence, quick wit and Yankee shrewdness, who had found his way...from the wilds of Arkansas."[8] Two boys baked a lovely "fruit" pie, the fruit being crushed quartz. By then, the first baby born in Gold Hill had been baptized Mamie (McCaslin).

But nature intervened cruelly. A forest fire moved up the hill from Left Hand Canyon in October 1860. Its fierce flames "ran along in the pitchy sprigs of the green tree-tops...so rapid was the advance that the inhabitants only saved their lives...by diving into the prospect holes."[9] The fire quickly consumed the settlement. Discouraged by the fire, some of the miners returned East. Their lack of expertise in gold mining was a further frustration, because they could not make a living. Concern about the Civil War caused others to go back. By 1861, the community was virtually deserted. Reverend Adriance did not preach at Gold Hill or Springville any more, "as the miners were nearly all gone."[10]

Most of Gold Hill's residents, however, did not move very far away. Their names are associated with many aspects of Boulder County's development. Charles Clouser and his Indian wife settled down to farming near Gold Hill. John Rothrock returned to surveying and farming. Alfred Brookfield came down to Valmont to farm. He also helped to develop downtown Boulder City, and he ran a hotel in Ward for a number of years. George Zweck acquired cattle from the East and moved them up to the mountains to the site of what would become Jamestown. John Pickel started a general store in Middle Boulder (now called Nederland) and was to help finance a mine called Caribou in a few years. Charles Dabney, William Pell, Peter Housel, and others came down to Boulder City with a number of business ventures in mind involving irrigation, farming, ranching, and real estate. Anthony Arnett came down to breed his Morgan horses with a wild California strain (he was also a town trustee in Boulder's first governing body), and Thomas J.

A view of the Continental Divide from Gold Hill. Note mining operations in foreground. *Charles Snow photo, Western Historical Collections, University of Colorado at Boulder*

Graham became the first commissioner of Boulder County in November 1861.

In October 1859, Thomas Aikins took part in a movement to establish a territorial government, and for a short time residents of the Boulder valley lived in an unofficial Jackson County under the jurisdiction of an unofficial Jefferson Territory. Never on firm ground, the movement died, and Aikins turned again to farming. In the fall of 1861, Gold Hill resident Charles F. Holley went to Golden City as Boulder's representative to the first Colorado Territorial Legislature. Another Gold Hill resident, a presiding elder in the Methodist-Episcopal church, John Chivington, was to become a colonel and lead the charge against Indians camped at Sand Creek.

Slowly, Gold Hill was rebuilt, this time on lower ground and nearer a water supply. But the camp remained small and quiet until the mid-1870s, when the "troublesome purple ore" was identified.

Chapter Four

By the spring of 1860, Boulder City could no longer boast of seventy cabins. As disappointed miners returned to their previous occupation of farming, they needed a place to live. They moved some of the town's cabins out onto the plains, staked their fields, and plowed for their first crops. The Wellman brothers, undaunted by their earlier experience with the grasshoppers, went back to farming and planted potatoes and wheat. So did Andrew Douty on the South Boulder. Perry White planted his fields along the St. Vrain with wheat brought in from Salt Lake City. When Charles Harrinton passed through the valley a little later, he noted that Boulder "was not a handsome city,"[1] but he did describe the wheat fields and their rich appearance. (He also took note of destruction to the creek beds from placer mining.)

The grasshoppers came again and again. The Reverend Nathan Thompson later described them:

Sitting in my study one morning, suddenly the light through the window became smoky. There was a striking against the panes much like small sticks or bits of gravel blown by the wind...Looking toward the sun we could see them flying, filling the space and darkening its light...At night, they settled upon the earth and whatever of grass or crops...were ruined if not wholly devoured.[2]

Another grasshopper story has a visitor asking directions to a farm near Hygiene; he was told to follow the onion smell, as the grasshoppers had topped all the onion plants.

These first ventures in agriculture were confined to land near the creeks, as the farmers soon realized that the Colorado plains did not receive the beneficial spring rains that started off crops back in the States. They could see that the melted spring runoff from the mountains had to be captured by some sort of ditch system to irrigate the arid lands that explorer Stephen

What Boulder looked like to an early artist who evidently felt that the Flatirons were not important enough to include. *Boulder Historical Society*

Early Boulder scene looking southwest from corner of Broadway and Spruce streets. *A.A. Paddock Collection*

Early Boulder scene from a point near site of Highland School. At extreme left, Squires-Tourtellot house, built in 1865. Tower of Congregational Church, constructed in 1866, can be seen near the horizon. *A.A. Paddock Collection*

Long had written off as useless desert forty years before. Following the lead of Marinus Smith and William Pell, the men started digging ditches throughout the valley to catch melted snow water.* By 1862, Farmers Ditch was dug; seven miles long, it had the capacity to irrigate 1,500 acres. Along the edges of the ditch, asparagus plants were set, some of which survive today as Farmers Ditch winds through North Boulder neighborhoods on its way to farms northeast of town. Some years later, Granville Berkley dug what is now called Beasley Ditch, a twelve-mile channel. Two more ditches nearby, the Chambers Canal at Valmont and the Davidson Canal off Coal Creek, were also twelve miles in length. Marinus Smith and Joseph Wolff experimented with the growing of a wide variety of fruits, feeling that the slopes along the foothills might be right for such production. Soon patches of strawberries, raspberries, and blackberries began to bear, as did groves of young apple trees and acres of grapevines. The new fruit growers seriously discussed the possibility that the foothills might one day support vineyards suitable for making fine table wines. "No soil or climate appears better adapted to grape culture, and it is foreseen that the rich slopes of the numerous foothills and the thousand little valleys that divide them are natural vineyard lands."[3] The big problem with fruit cultivation, in addition to the grasshopper plagues, was that of winterkill, due to

*For an interesting description of early ditch digging, read Dorothy Gardiner's novel *Snow Water*.

Joseph Wolff wrote abolitionist tracts before settling in Boulder. Here he raised fruit, a more peaceful pursuit. *A.A. Paddock Collection*

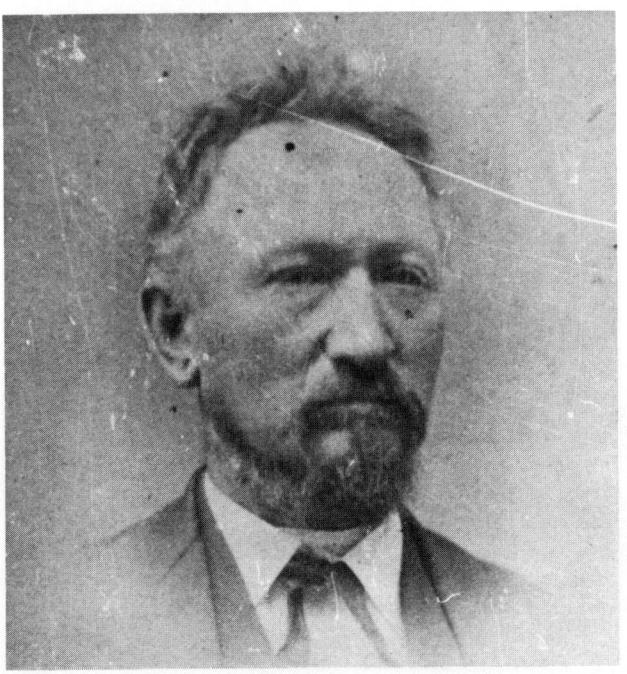

Early resident Granville Berkley is remembered for his florid speeches as well as for digging some of the first irrigation ditches. *History of Clear Creek and Boulder Valleys*

Boulder valley's dry winters. But the miners purchased the wheat, fruit, and vegetables. New storekeeper Jonathan Tourtellot bought, with great ceremony, for fifty cents, the county's first peach, grown by Joseph Rhoades.

Soon cattle, horses, and later, Merino sheep, grazed on the native grasses of the plains where the antelope and buffalo had wintered before. In 1869, some 1,500 people visited the county's first fair and heard a rousing speech by Granville Berkley,* who predicted that the Boulder valley would soon support "railways, telegraphs, academies, manufactories, and other appliances of civilization."[4] He also exhorted the ladies to "cultivate flowers and small fruits to make homes attractive to their male relatives, and thus win them from the ways of temptation."[5]

Longmont started as a colony of 30,000 acres. A group of Chicagoans, eager to come west to good farm land, formed the Chicago-Colorado Colony in 1871 with the Reverend Robert Collyer as president. Memberships were sold to those prospective settlers who promised not to serve liquor in the new land. Although the Longmont group patterned its colony after the earlier one at Greeley, Longmont's economy took hold more easily, perhaps because the colony

*One of Mr. Berkley's thirteen children was named Cloudless Morning, "Cloud" for short, as he was born on a sunny day after a spell of cloudy weather.

soon became the center of the growing sugar beet industry. By 1900, there were 967 farms in Boulder County, 90 percent of them dependent upon irrigation water.

At the same time that families settled on the plains to farm on what looked like fertile land, William Kitchen found coal outcroppings six miles south of Boulder on a site later to be called Marshall. He called his find the Washington lode, but his customers preferred to call the mine Kitchen's Bank. The coal was transported to the Denver market by a team and wagon, a most unprofitable method. Farmers and coal miners alike were frustrated by the absence of good roads and hoped for the speedy arrival of the railroad to the county. Coal production, too, was erratic; during the slack periods, miners tended their fields and vegetable gardens.

Most settlers did not purchase their heating and cooking coal from Kitchen's Bank, however, for they could help themselves to loose chunks of coal wherever they found a surface outcropping. (These outcroppings were part of a geologic formation (lower Laramie) which had thrust up in earlier ages as the mountains and foothills pushed up in the same manner. The veins of coal, some fourteen feet wide, were laid down some 100 millions years ago (Cretaceous era) when the Boulder valley was covered by a series of inland seas and swamps. As the humus and debris built up from the swampy environment, a coal bed formed. From every fourteen feet of swampy debris, one foot of coal could develop.)

Shortly after the discovery of coal, Joseph M. Marshall was on the scene to build the area's first blast furnace that would manufacture pig iron from the red hematite ores associated with the coal fields. William Lee, Mylo Lee, and Augustine Langford also capitalized on this enterprise. By April 1866, Marshall had acquired Kitchen's Bank; two years later, he added to his property with a land grant from President Andrew Johnson. On these 1,480 acres lay the Marshall coal mine and the Black Diamond mine, soon to become prolific producers. The ensuing settlement took Marshall's name, and, at one point, its 800 residents supported three saloons as well as a school for 70 children.

In 1873, when the Colorado Central Railroad completed a branch line across Coal Creek to the coal mines, Marshall amazed everyone by ordering a twelve-ton steam engine from England. When it arrived, Marshall invited all to celebrate its delivery and view the monster. In no time at all, residents complained of the smoke and pollution caused by busy trains hauling tons of coal to market. The Langford* interests at Marshall grew considerably, and, indeed, the settlement was renamed Langford for a time. The name did not stick because most were used to calling the town Marshall or by its nickname, Foxtown, after the nearby Fox mine.

*One of the Langford principals, Nathaniel P. Langford was one of three men who explored the Yellowstone geyser area in 1870 and pressed the federal government to set aside land for the nation's first national park.

A mild winter day near the coal mines at Marshall. *A.A. Paddock Collection*

The teacher is not much older than her students in a school between Marshall and Eldorado Springs. Note the boy's makeshift bat. *A.A. Paddock Collection*

By 1874, Isaac Canfield and his brothers had opened the Rob Roy mine (later called the Jackson) near Tabor Station on the Boulder Valley Railroad line, northeast of Marshall. Canfield filed a town plat, naming it after himself; soon the settlement supported 398 people. They constructed twenty buildings, which included a store, post office, a blacksmith shop, and a school. Canfield, more a traveling speculator than a settled miner, left the area for a time. While he was gone, he learned about locating oil wells, a skill that he was to use twenty-five years later in the Boulder valley.

The Northern Coal Field, which lay in both Boulder and Weld counties, would in the future spur the development of other towns such as Louisville, Lafayette, Superior, and Erie. When the British gentlewoman Isabella Bird journeyed on horseback through the area in 1873, she took note of a "discovery of a coal seam,"[6] but, upon viewing Boulder City itself, she wrote it off as a "hideous collection of frame houses on the burning plain,"[7] with overblown pretentions to a trading center.

As more families moved across the rocky areas from what is now Gunbarrel and north to the site of Hygiene, they became aware of a strong odor of oil; in fact, at some points in the stony terrain they could see oil seepage on the land surface. However, an oil well would not be drilled there until the 1890s.

Boulder City had no school when Abner Roe Brown passed through in June 1860. He was on his way to build a quartz mill at Gold Hill, but he told the townspeople that he was a teacher and that if gold mining did not suit him, he would return to teach. The quartz mill failed, and in two weeks Brown was back. He rented one-half of a log cabin for ten dollars a month. (The Street family lived in the other half.) Calling it Pioneer School, Brown accepted his first pupils for a monthly tuition of $1.50. The classroom measured twelve by thirty feet; in no time, forty students lined the walls. Due to lack of space, he closed the private school in August and joined the residents in building a public school. Marinus Smith donated the land at Fifteenth and Walnut (southwest corner), and Dave Nichols cut logs in the mountains and brought them down (after having a fist fight with a less public-spirited man who said that the logs were his). These logs were sawed into planks at Tarbox and Donnelly's new sawmill, which had opened for

A familiar picture to Boulder citizens, the first building in Colorado built as a schoolhouse, Walnut and Fourteenth streets, southwest corner (across the street from the U.S. Post Office). The two boys in front are R.E. Arnett and Mack Smith. The girls play separately, as was the custom. *A.A. Paddock Collection*

business at the mouth of the canyon. Since Mr. Partridge had just completed his shingle mill, the roof of the school had real shingles. Someone carted in bricks from Denver for the chimney. When a Ralston man heard of this community project, he donated the lime for wall plaster. There being no window glass in town, Boulder parents removed the picture glass from their family photographs and gave it to the school so that it might have windows.

Winter was approaching, and Brown, realizing that the school needed a stove, built one from waste material that he found near Boulder Creek. He also built crude desks and seats. Brown was not paid for this work, but he took his meals and slept at the homes of the residents. To show their appreciation for his work, Boulder ladies held a "gold dust" dancing party, fifty cents a couple, which raised forty-two dollars. With part of the money, Brown was able to buy a suit of clothes so that he would not have to teach in his overalls.

In October 1860, pupils filed into Boulder's second school, the first building constructed as a school in Colorado Territory. Even with donated labor and materials, the building cost $1,200 to erect. The remaining Arapaho Indians took a great interest in the building, because near the front door stood a water barrel with a drinking cup which they enjoyed using to splash one another. Those pupils not attentive to their lessons could watch the antelope browsing near the building. When school was not in session, the townspeople used the building for meetings; the Methodists held regular church services there.

In almost all of the mining camps, construction of a school building had high priority. The building was also used for church services, court trials, and dancing parties. Many of the mountain schools had to be braced on their eastern walls with long, sturdy poles as a safety measure against the seasonal high winds. Some mountain schools were open only during the summer months, because the children found it difficult to walk through the high snowdrifts. By 1863, a school district was formed in Boulder, but the school board found it difficult to collect the necessary taxes with the fathers of pupils away mining in the mountains.

For a number of years, camps and settlements in the county grew faster than did Boulder City. The community at Valmont, surrounded by agricultural lands, grew larger and held greater prospects than Boulder in the 1860s. Valmont supported a school, two drugstores, five general stores, three saloons, and later a cheese factory and a newspaper. The newspaper, the *Valmont Bulletin,* started publication on New Year's Day 1866. Fifteen months later, Boulder merchants convinced the editor, some say with liquor, to move his press to Boulder City. He started publication again in April 1867, calling the paper the *Boulder Valley News.* Two years later, the paper changed hands and was renamed the *Boulder County Pioneer.* After a few months, the management and name changed yet again to the *Boulder County News.**
From the beginning, the paper took advertising,

---

*See Appendix for a chart showing the growth of the area's newspapers.

Some serious, some clowning, students at Sunshine School. Note pole brace for the high winds. *J.B. Sturtevant photo, A.A. Paddock Collection*

School children and their teacher in front of Altona School near the mouth of Left Hand Canyon. *A.A. Paddock Collection*

much of it simple and straightforward. As the town's mercantile base grew, so did the ads with flamboyant and sensational claims for the products advertised. Recent developments in mining occupied much of the newspaper's space, but attention was paid to school programs, sickness, death, scandal, and the travel plans of the residents.

When Colorado became a territory in 1861, Boulder County immediately selected representatives to the territorial legislature and chose three commissioners and other county officials. The frame house of A.J. Macky at Fourteenth and Pearl streets (northeast corner) doubled as a county office as well as a courtroom. The new county could collect taxes, issue permits for toll road construction and irrigation ditch companies, and initiate bond issues for railroads. By 1862, thirteen public roads were being planned. The following year, a local militia formed and was on call to subdue Indians, should the occasion arise. But the county did not offer two important services—fire protection and a system of water rights. This made the townspeople very unhappy.

In 1864, the defunct Boulder City Town Company turned over its remaining unsold lots to the county with the understanding that any profits would go toward construction of a county courthouse. By the late 1860s, however, Boulder citizens were growing increasingly angry with county government. Republican newsmen charged that the Democrats ran the county for the sole benefit of the Democrats. Some charged land swindles and other improprieties. As the *Pioneer* reported, "people were eager to cast this town out of the county."[8] In 1869, the Boulder Anti-Clique Party formed (they were Republicans) and at the next election swept most of the Democrats out of county office. Gloated the *Pioneer,* "The 'Ring' is burst, sure; glory hallelujah!"[9] That issue was the *Pioneer*'s last. Evidently, the Democratic opposition was still strong enough to make sure that the sheriff took possession of the newspaper plant because of outstanding debts.

Very early, a number of Boulder citizens dreamed of a university in their town. When Charles Holley of Gold Hill decided that he would like to represent the area at the territorial legislature, Robert Culver and others told Holley that they would support him if he would attempt to get territorial approval for Boulder as the university site. Holley said he would, the men supported him, and he was successful. For a time, Fred Squires' pasture (Mapleton Hill) was mentioned as a possible site for the new university, but it was generally agreed that stock-raising might interfere with higher education. Not until 1876, Colorado's year of statehood, did the University of Colorado become a reality.

The county was desperate for roads. Historian Bixby, writing in 1880, said, "Few in after years, realize how much of a drain upon the earnings of pioneers is the indispensable expenditure for roads, in a rough, roadless mountain region, where, at first,

A corduroy road, made of logs laid side by side, on the way to Eldora, 1897. *J.B. Sturtevant photo, A.A. Paddock Collection*

it was difficult to cut a foot-path or a pack-trail."[10] At this time, no one seriously thought that a road could be constructed up Boulder Canyon. "The settlers found Boulder Cañon so difficult of access that a man could not make his way up it by food...With them, it was a disputed question whether or not a wagon road could ever be constructed through it..."[11]

The canyon of South Boulder Creek was impregnable, and St. Vrain Canyon was considered too far north. The remaining possibilities were Left Hand Canyon, Sunshine Canyon, Gregory Canyon, and Bear Canyon, four miles south of Boulder City.

Henry Clay Norton, the man who built the toll bridge across the South Platte, was also involved in an attempt to build a road to the mines through Gregory Canyon. Miner Gregory himself had tried earlier. Part of his "road" was "corduroy," built of logs placed close together across the wagon way. It led to the Ute Trail above and from there to his mines at Black Hawk. Gregory's road was not really passable. Norton's venture failed because he could not raise enough money.

Late in 1859, the St. Vrain, Altona, Gold Hill, and Gregory Road Company was formed to build a road up Left Hand Canyon to Altona and above. The company hoped that use of the road would cause Altona to become a business center, but the road failed, and Altona never flourished.

In the early 1860s, the federal government financed the building of a military road up Sunshine Canyon. The road, called the Gordon-McHenry after its two chief engineers, was to cross Arapaho Pass eventually. It ran to the top of Sunshine Hill and turned down Ritchie Gulch to Four Mile Creek. Near Orodell, the road turned to the right and went up Sugar Loaf Hill to Gordon Gulch, then to North Boulder Creek. From there it wandered west, where it was abandoned on the flats north of Caribou.*

Henry Norton, whom Bixby describes as having "a passion for road building," and George Williamson, who owned mines in the Sugar Loaf area, joined forces to build a wagon road up Bear Canyon. They felt that this would be the easiest route to Black Hawk and thence to Central City. A cloudburst washed out their efforts. Later, sawmill owners G.D. Harmon and Onsville C. Coffin built the road again; another cloudburst washed it out. Much later, in 1868, Peter Housel and Ed Donnelly tried their hand with Bear Canyon road building and formed the Bear Canyon and Black Hawk Road Company. With $12,000 in capital they rebuilt the road. The next year, they, too, saw their efforts washed out. Harmon, Coffin, and Eli Metcalf tried in 1873 with another $12,000. This time nature cooperated for a time, but eventually another cloudburst demolished the roadway. In 1885,

*Former Caribou resident, J.C. Smith, remembers picnicking near the road with his mother just before the turn of the century. She told him that President Buchanan ordered the army to build the road, which was to cross Arapaho Pass into Middle Park so that the soldiers could surprise and attack Mormon parties on their way to Deseret.

Freighter Bob McDonald carries goods over difficult roads to Eldora. Note packages in wagon with Eldora address. *J.B. Sturtevant photo, A.A. Paddock Collection*

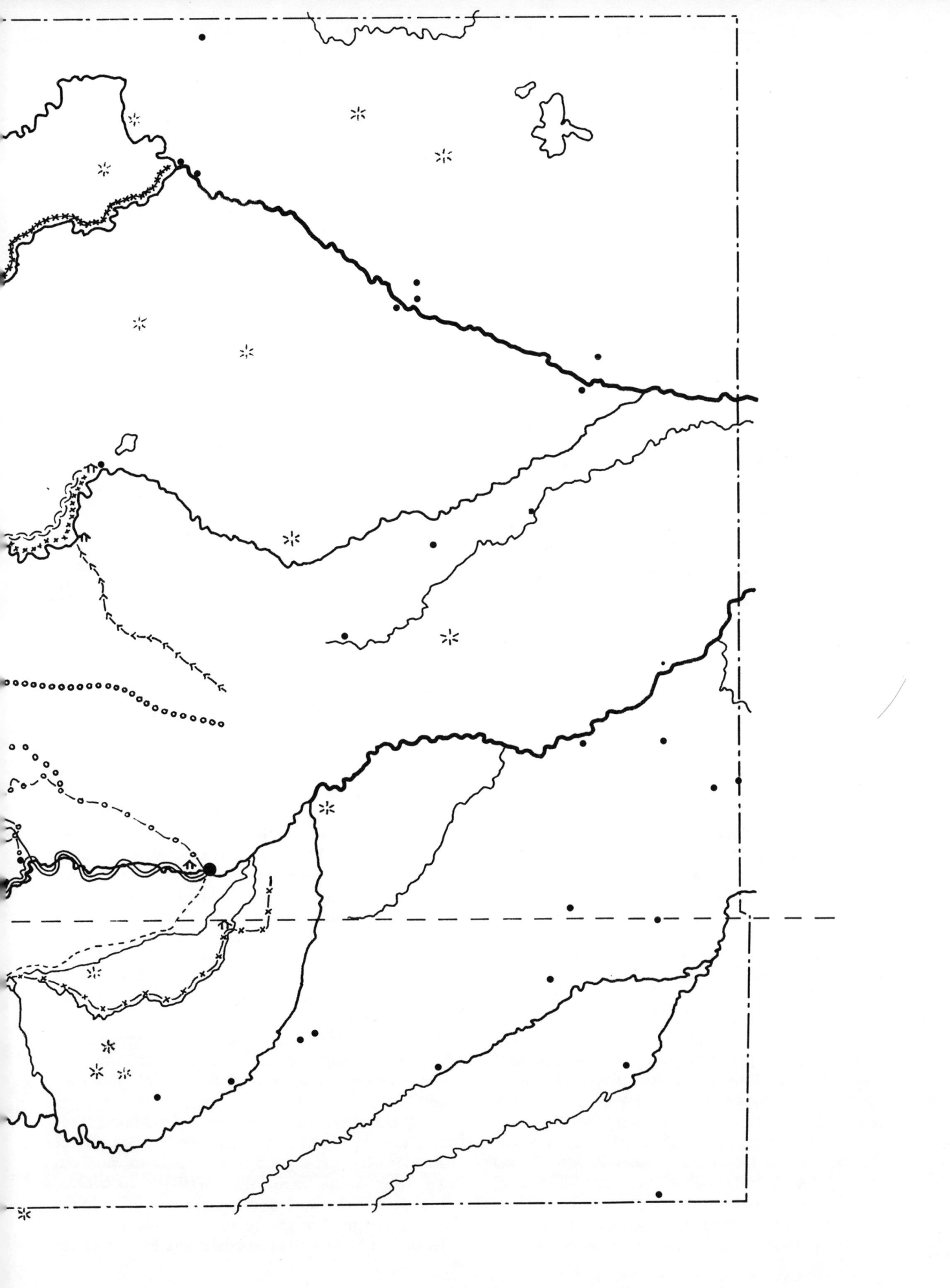

A light snow does not stop a freighter with a heavy load on his way to Ward. *J.B. Sturtevant photo, A.A. Paddock Collection*

the Bear Canyon and French Gulch Wagon Road Company tried road building, but its efforts were washed out, too. (As recently as 1969, Table Mesa Drive, the natural waterway for Bear Canyon was under water because of cloudburst activity.)

In the late 1860s and early 1870s, more men attempted a road through Gregory Canyon. At first, they built a road from up above that descended part way down the canyon, where loaded wagons were dropped by block-and-tackle to a lower level. In 1873, a group started building from Boulder up to Kossler's Lake. This crude road was used until the Flagstaff Road was completed in 1906.

Since James P. Maxwell and Clinton M. Tyler were able to capitalize the Boulder Valley and Central City Wagon Road Company for $50,000, they received a county building permit on March 11, 1864 to attempt a road through Boulder Canyon. They contributed $10,000 of their own money; the Wellman brothers subscribed, for they needed the road to sell their produce to the miners above. Boulder's fledgling merchants, Charles Dabney, Anthoney Arnett, Daniel Pound, Jonathan Tourtellot, and Fred Squires, all helped to raise money.

Actual road construction began one year later. It took three months and $9,000 to get as far as Four Mile Creek, the site of Orodell, three miles up the canyon. Construction continued for another year; Maxwell and Tyler chose a route up Magnolia Hill, over to South Boulder Creek, and to the Enterprise Road, which led to Black Hawk. (The Enterprise Road had been built earlier by Tyler's father-in-law, Nelson K. Smith.) Later on, they constructed a branch road to Ward at an additional cost of $13,000. Two toll gates were established on the road, one at the mouth of Boulder Canyon and another at the foot of Magnolia Hill at Eagle Rock. For many years, C.D. Norton collected a toll of one dollar for each wagon and team (twenty-five cents extra for each additional animal) and seventy-five cents for a carriage. No toll was charged if a group was going to a funeral or to a church. The price for loose stock was ten cents a head. Mrs. Norton had a tame magpie that performed for each traveler, calling out, "Pay your toll, pay your toll!"

When silver was discovered at Caribou in 1869, it became imperative to the economic well-being of Boulder City that a good road be built to carry out the riches of the mountains. Wells Fargo became interested in Caribou and planned a route through the mountains. For this reason, Maxwell and Tyler decided to build a road to Nederland by way of the

Should this family be going to church or to a funeral, they will pay no toll at this station, which was built at the mouth of Boulder Canyon. *Ives photo, 1909, A.A. Paddock Collection*

Calvert's Stage Station, called Eureka House, near Boulder Falls. Toll was collected here as well as at the mouth of Boulder Canyon. *J.B. Sturtevant photo, A.A. Paddock Collection*

Narrows, the present canyon route. The road builders solved tricky construction problems by avoiding cliffs and bridging Boulder Creek whenever the mountain formations seemed impassable. By the time they reached Nederland in 1871, they had built thirty-three bridges.

Wells Fargo never fulfilled its promise to run freight lines into Boulder County, but other commercial lines used the canyon road, which now had a branch to Caribou. Near the Narrows, a way station called American House gave stage drivers the opportunity to change horses and rest after a meal of ham and eggs. Now tally-hos carried parties into the mountains for picnics and sightseeing. The klondike, or storm buggy, an enclosed vehicle, was much favored by doctors and mail carriers. From this time onward, the problems of road building in the mountains seem to have been solved, for many roads crisscrossed the area between mining towns and temporary camps, some deteriorating later from disuse and some disappearing altogether from washouts.[12]

A wagon road established earlier in 1861 to Ward helped that community grow. Calvin W. Ward founded the town seven miles west of Gold Hill and 9,300 feet above sea level. He had found a gold-bearing lode and named it Miser's Dream. A year later, Cyrus Deardorf prospected nearby; he also discovered a lode, the Columbian, a real money-maker that eventually grossed $5 million. The famous H.A.W. Tabor of Leadville nosed around the area too, and in 1865, Davidson and Breath, the first dry goods salesmen in Boulder City, bought the Ni Wot mine. Little towns and camps sprang up near Ward wherever a prospector thought that gold was a possibility. Miners held such hopes for success at Gold Lake that a town plat was filed in 1861. The camp at Sunnyside was another such dream, and much later, so were Sunset and Copper Rock.

Ward in 1895 before its disastrous fire of 1900. The townsite is at 9,450 feet, on the route of the Switzerland Trail. *A.A. Paddock Collection*

A group poses for J.B. Sturtevant in front of Hartley's Store at Ward, 1899. Surveying the snow are Joe Hartley, Dr. Jacob Campbell, and John Hartley. *A.A. Paddock Collection*

After the fire of January 23, 1900, a few Ward townspeople view the wreckage. *J.B. Sturtevant photo, A.A. Paddock Collection*

The miners seldom fought with the Indians. By the summer of 1864, however, news regarding the activities of the Indians spread alarm in some quarters. Perhaps Indians in Colorado took advantage of the Civil War, since most of the military troops were engaged elsewhere. Wagon trains were attacked, and Indians did attempt to stop express wagons along the Smoky Hill route. Incidents of Indian marauders, true or exaggerated, were reported in such a way that some residents became fearful. The *Rocky Mountain News,* well-known for its anti-Indian articles (Editor Byers was not tolerant of black people either), reported on July 20, 1864, "There is a good deal of anxiety among the public to know what steps are being taken to quell the Indian disturbances down the Platte... To quiet sensitive nerves we will just say that efficient steps have been and are being taken; that the plans are working well; that Mr. Lo* will soon find it quite hot down among the sand hills."[13]

Territorial Governor Evans called for "100-day volunteers" and commissioned Dave Nichols of

*At that time, some referred to Indians as "Mr. Lo."

On September 28, 1864, just before the Sand Creek Massacre, these Indians met with Territorial Governor Evans and John M. Chivington at Camp Weld. Seated, left to right: Neva (Chief Left Hand's brother), Southern Arapaho; Black Kettle, Bull Bear, and White Antelope (brother of Black Kettle), all Southern Cheyenne. Standing, left to right: Bosse, Notanee, and Heap of Buffalo, all Southern Arapaho. *Western Historical Collections, University of Colorado at Boulder*

Boulder as a captain. Marinus Smith was named captain of the guard; both Alfred Brookfield and Fred Squires served as lieutenants. Territorial officials threatened Boulder with martial law until it could raise its quota of soldiers; those who "volunteered" mustered into Company D of the territory's Third Regiment. Captain Nichols trained his company at Fort Chambers, a hastily built adobe fort on George Chambers' farm near Valmont. Although some citizens had to be threatened to sign up, friends of Chief Left Hand refused outright to go.

After fall engagements at Beaver Creek and Buffalo Springs, Captain Nichols marched with his men for forty miles in late November, sometimes in two feet of snow, toward Sand Creek, where Indian families camped in accordance with treaties. Some nine hundred men, which included Boulder's "100-day volunteers" and other Coloradoans, formed the First and Third regiments led by John M. Chivington, late of Gold Hill. Earlier, the church elder had been offered a chaplainship, but Chivington wanted to fight as he had earlier at Glorieta Pass. Colonel Chivington told his men, "Off with your coats...you can fight better without them. Take no prisoners. Remember the slaughtered women and children."[14]

The shooting started at daylight on November 29 and, according to George Bent, who was camped with the Indians, did not stop until five o'clock in the afternoon. Chief Black Kettle, thinking there was some mistake, raised his American flag, but the bullets kept coming; he put down his flag and commenced his death song, "Nothing lives long, except the earth

DAVID H. NICHOLS,
BOULDER.
PIONEER 1860. CAPT. D. 3RD COLO. CAVALRY. MEM
4-5-9 GEN. ASSEMBLY. COMMISSIONER C. S. P.
FOR 14 YEARS. LIEUT. GOV. 1893-1895.

David Nichols, who helped found Boulder's first school and the University of Colorado, is also remembered as a captain with the "Bloodless Third" at Sand Creek, 1864. *Representative Men of Colorado*

and the mountains."¹⁵ Little Bear reported later that "bullets were hitting the lodges like a hail storm."¹⁶ Indian women set to work digging holes in which to hide. George Bent was wounded in the hip. Later, he wrote letters describing the scalping of Indian women and children. Dave Nichols fought with his men until the snow blinded him. Two Boulder men died at Sand Creek—Robert McFarland and Henry Foster. Chief Left Hand, the gentle Arapaho who met Boulder's first white settlers under the red cliffs, was one of those killed by the guns of the "Bloodless Third."¹⁷

Life in Boulder returned to normal, even though a number of investigators studied the Sand Creek "affair," as it was called. Although Boulder City was still very small, with a population of less than 350,* by 1866 the town had an air of stability, as if it meant to endure. Its fortunes still paralleled those of the mining interests above. When times were hard, merchants Squires and Tourtellot carried families on credit. The two men had married identical twins, Maria and

*In 1860, there were 238 men and 86 women. In 1870, the population was about the same.

Early Boulder scene, probably 1872, from Lovers (Sunset Hill). Left center is town square (note flagpole). Southwest corner of the square shows Colorado House (site of Majestic Savings, Thirteenth and Pearl Streets. *A.A. Paddock Collection*

Squires-Tourtellot home, 1019 Spruce Street, oldest house in Boulder. Note identical twins, Maria Tourtellot and Miranda Squires, on the veranda. Building is now owned by the Boulder Historical Society. *A.A. Paddock Collection*

Miranda, who worked alongside their husbands. In the front half of the double cabin (Davidson and Breath's original building at Eleventh and Pearl streets), the men sold groceries, mining equipment, and real estate. At the back of the cabin, Maria Tourtellot and Miranda Squires managed a combination restaurant-hotel; for a time, both families lived in the back of the store also. They started out with no furniture—just two boards. They made their original beds and stools from undressed logs. From willows growing along the creek, the ladies made brooms and swept the cabin's dirt floor at least once a day, avoiding the puddles from the cabin's leaky roof. Even though the women worked hard, they found time during their day to watch antelope browsing near the door.

In 1866, Andrew Douty and his son Sylvester moved up from the South Boulder (their mill there had been flooded out twice) and built a three-story flour mill along Farmers Ditch under the Red Rocks. After a number of improvements, the Red Rocks mill had a clientele from as far away as Denver and Colorado Springs.

By the end of the 1860s, seventy-seven buildings had been constructed in town. Residents had completed sawmills, more flour mills, a brickyard, several blacksmith shops, and general stores. Newly constructed stables and liveries kept busy. Each merchant constructed his own wooden sidewalk in front of his business, apparently without noticing the height of his neighbor's sidewalk. Since each walk was of a different

Mouth of Boulder Canyon looking north toward Red Rocks. In foreground is Yount Mill, built in 1878, on site of earlier Red Rock Mill. Yount flour was advertised as "Legal Tender." *J.B. Sturtevant photo, Boulder Public Library from A.A. Paddock Collection*

Boulder businessmen moved around from time to time. This Streamer's Drug Store location is site for future National State Bank, built in 1900. *A.A. Paddock Collection*

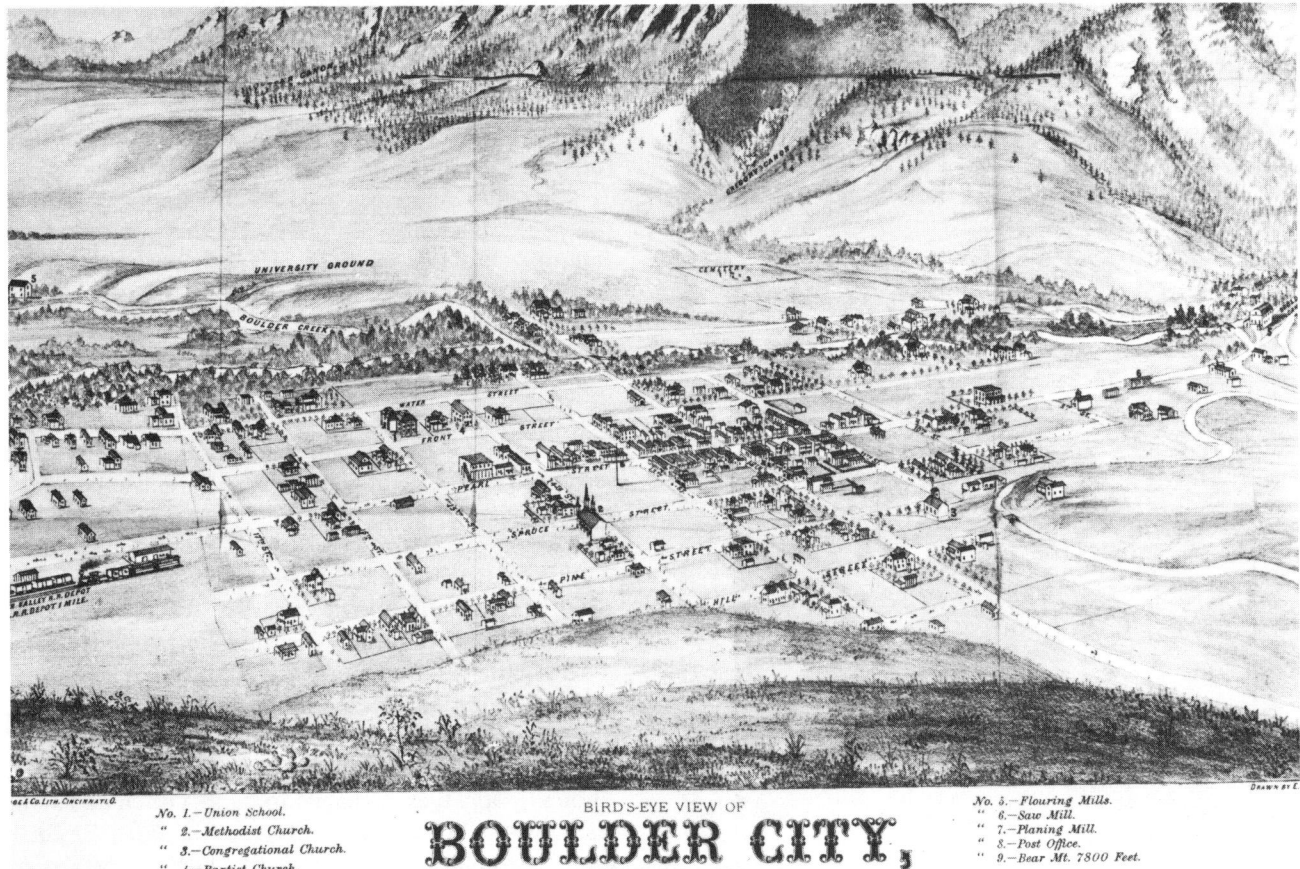

Boulder City in 1874. Hill Street is now Mapleton Avenue, Front Street is now Walnut Street, and Water Street is now Canyon Boulevard. *Boulder Historical Society*

Boulder to the northwest from Fourteenth and Walnut streets, 1876, taken from roof of Central School. Walnut Street runs parallel to white fence. Church spire is Methodist-Episcopal Church at Fourteenth and Spruce streets. Note privies and wash on the lines. *Alexander Martin photo, A.A. Paddock Collection*

A store that seemed to sell everything was Fonda's Drug Store, 1218 Pearl Street, south side. Owner George Fonda, leaning against the door in his shirt sleeves, started in the business in his teens. *A.A. Paddock Collection*

height, the pedestrian would bob up and down as he walked down Pearl Street. Women tore their dresses on the nails that came up from the planks; real injury from the nails was not uncommon. Boys, and even adults, fished through the cracks of the sidewalks, looking for coins and other dropped valuables.

Boulder had improved its town square (site of the present county courthouse) with a fence and a flagpole, but the space was kept fairly open, for it served as a baseball diamond. Boulder City and Sunshine were arch-rivals; residents often gathered at the town's first park to root for their teams.

Circuit ministries were still common, but the preachers concentrated their efforts in the mining camps, often walking from one to another after each sermon. Alfred and Emma Brookfield helped to launch a Presbyterian church at Valmont in 1867. The Congregationalists also met in Valmont in 1864 until their first Boulder church was completed two years later. (They built on the site of Carnegie Library.) Nathan Thompson, their first minister, spoke later of the difficulty of excavation due to the baked clay soil. In 1869, eight families, immigrants from Småland, Sweden, established a settlement on 1,000 acres northeast of town, calling it Ryssby after their home parish. Though poor, they managed to build a ditch and some reservoirs. Shortly afterward, seven more Swedish families joined them. The Methodists stopped using the schoolhouse for services when their church at Fourteenth and Spruce streets was completed in 1870-71. Ten Boulder residents formed a Presbyterian group in 1872, and six Baptists met together that same year. The Methodist-Episcopalians formed a

The original Presbyterian Church at Valmont, built in 1866. Handsome additions were added to the first building but the structure burned in 1978. *J.B. Sturtevant photo, A.A. Paddock Collection*

society the following year, and by 1876 the Catholics had an active parish in Boulder.

In 1872, several Boulder businessmen could see that more settlers were needed if Boulder was to prosper; they formed an immigration society that advertised for newcomers in the eastern papers. They must have had some success, because from 1870 to 1878 seventeen land additions were made an official part of Boulder City.

Some Boulderites believed that the town's young men spent too much time in the saloons. They discussed the possibility of opening reading rooms to counteract the bad influence of saloon life. The first reading room opened in the offices of the *Boulder County Pioneer,* in the 1300 block of Pearl Street, and was used until the paper folded. As an inducement to young bachelors, genteel young ladies were allowed to visit the reading room from time to time. While looking over the young ladies, the men studied a growing collection of books, newspapers, and magazines. The second reading room opened in the offices of the *Boulder County News,* whose editor campaigned for a proper library with a librarian. The reading room was a private venture and was supported by yearly subscription tickets, three dollars for men and dollar for a lady. It was open every evening and on Sunday afternoons. Fortnightly, a ladies' literary society, started by University of Colorado Professor Mary Rippon in 1884, marshalled its forces to fight for a library. However, it was not until the turn of the century that other Boulderites saw the need for a public library.

No room left on the Jain's stage to Ward. Note that only two men have not grown a mustache. *Kauffman photo, A.A. Paddock Collection*

The silver town of Caribou at its height, probably 1873-74. Large building in right foreground is three-story Sherman House. Note trees at edge of town; the site is barren now. *A.A. Paddock Collection*

Chapter Five

During the fall of 1869, silver was discovered on a steep hill twenty-two miles up from Boulder, four miles up from Nederland, and 10,500 feet above sea level. A town grew there and flourished for a time, despite deep snows and nine-month winters, fierce winds, electrical storms, forest fires, epidemics, a nitroglycerin explosion, and even an earthquake. Through the years, heavy snows, the winds, fire, and acquisitive tourists have picked the bones of this once-thriving community clean. There is little left to see. Even the cemetery is pretty much gone. However, the more imaginative visitor to the desolate Caribou site today fancies that he hears voices of the painted girls standing in front of their shacks on Idaho Street, or the music of the Caribou Silver Cornet Band marching down Sherman Street, or the laughter spilling out of the Shoo-Fly dance hall on Potosi Street, or the Cornish brogue of the miners.

Despite the town's unusual setting, which faced the Snowy Range and the Continental Divide four miles to the west, the story of Caribou is representative of many mining communities in the Rocky Mountains. Surely, many people who streamed into such camps had the philosophy of "get rich and get out," but mixed with their desires for quick riches was a yearning to create a stable, lasting community. They wanted

A crowd gathers in front of Pete Werley's saloon in Caribou. *J.B. Sturtevant photo, A.A. Paddock Collection*

neat, well-built houses arranged along quiet, orderly streets. Caribou's sturdy, unpainted houses, built to last, were testimony to this need for permanence. But this was not to be. What we know of Caribou is both romantic and tragic and, as is the case with better romances, its story is short.

The people built a public school; some parents sent their children to a private school for a time. They listened to circuit ministers and for a few years worshipped with resident ministries. They subscribed to the *Caribou Post,* an excellent newspaper, and supported a wide variety of businesses. They even constructed a waterworks, which was considered quite sophisticated for its time. They made jokes about the weather but boasted that the vigorous life of Caribou would cure the consumptive.

Several stories survive regarding the discovery of Caribou silver. The most fanciful concerns Samuel Conger and the Arapaho Indians. According to the story, Conger often lived with the Arapaho, saw their "crude" silver trinkets, and tried to discover the source of the silver from one Moaning Dove, a chief's daughter. "Where is Treasure Mountain?" he asked Moaning Dove. (Treasure Mountain was said to be the Arapaho name for Caribou Hill.) She did not tell him, and he was not successful. Nor does the story hold up too well!

It is more likely that the wandering Conger saw outcroppings of blossom rock* as early as 1860 while he was tracking an elk. Or perhaps he acquired ore samples from someone else and did not realize their significance at that time. One other story goes that Conger, while visiting a town (perhaps Laramie, Wyoming), saw some ore fall out of a broken box, heard it identified as Comstock silver from Nevada, and remembered that he had seen similar rock while elk hunting.

In any event, Conger appeared at the dinner table of the Samuel Mishlers of Black Hawk before August 1869 and showed his ore samples to Mishler's father-in-law George Lytle and neighbors William Martin and Hugh McCammon. The only one of these men knowledgeable about mining was forty-four-year-old George Lytle, who had spent some time in British Columbia at the Cariboo gold diggings. Lytle described the appearance of the Canadian outcroppings, and Conger said that the description resembled the area where he had tracked the elk. The men agreed that the site was worth investigating, and they formed an informal partnership. Lytle and Martin were to go in search of the vein; Mishler and McCammon agreed

*Blossom rock is the term that miners use for the external, weathered, flowerlike rock, reddish to bluish in the case of silver, which indicates that precious metal may lie beneath its surface.

Caribou School. *J.B. Sturtevant photo, A.A. Paddock Collection*

to outfit them. Conger was a partner, for he had located the samples.

Since August had already turned blustery, the two men quickly built a shelter hut below Caribou Hill. Alice Weber writes that her grandfather Lytle "knew that somewhere on that hill was a wonderful silver mine."[1] He found the blossom rock "as big as a cook stove" and shouted to Martin, "Eureka. Eureka. Billy, come up here. I've found it. I've found it!"[2] Maybe Conger found the lode himself earlier as he claimed, and maybe Lytle found it. (The heirs of William Martin believe that Martin found it.) George Lytle is responsible, however, for the name "Caribou," meaning a small arctic reindeer.

When the men returned to Black Hawk, they brought samples with them to be assayed at Professor Nathaniel Hill's new smelting works, and Hill confirmed the high potential of the lode. "At this time," Alice Weber goes on to say, "they decided most firmly for very good reasons of their own that they did not want Conger in a company with them...."[3] (Was it because the men were Masons and Samuel Conger was not?) They proposed to Conger that he relinquish his one-fifth interest in the Caribou lode for full interest in another lode, the Poorman. (Lytle said later that he named the Poorman, "since I am a poor man, that will be the name of my claim.")[4] Conger agreed to the arrangement; he had also discovered another lode higher up on Caribou Hill that he named the Conger. Thus, when Caribou Company was formed with Sam Mishler, William Martin, Hugh McCammon, George Lytle, and grocer John H. Pickel as principals, they started operations on what turned out to be the richest silver mine in Colorado.

Before the onset of full winter, the men had built a cabin, packed in supplies on their backs, and hacked a way through the woods to the Black Hawk Road, four miles away. (Black Hawk itself was twenty miles away.)

By the time spring arrived in June 1870, news of the silver at Caribou had spread throughout the world. The boom was on. Newly arrived miners and speculators lived under the trees. (The Caribou site was heavily timbered then.) Grocers from Central City and Boulder, the first businessmen on the spot, used tents to display their groceries until proper buildings could be constructed. Boulderite Pete J. Werley and his partner Frank Sears opened the first billiards and pool parlor ("three good tables"). Major E.M. Beard built the first saloon and boarding house on Idaho Street. For some meals, tables had to be reset three and four times to accommodate the diners. Soon mining equipment stores were busy, and a meat market opened. (Butchers had to store their meat on poles twenty feet high to escape Caribou's low-flying blowflies.)*

By August 1870, perhaps 460 people were in residence, and more than thirty-five mines were in operation. In September, the partners in the Caribou Company sold the western half of the Caribou lode to Abel D. Breed, a notorious promoter from Cincinnati.

By the summer of 1871, businesses included several hotels and boarding houses, two billiards parlors, four saloons, a dry goods store, a millinery, two blacksmiths, a livery, and a photographic studio. A jeweler, a bootmaker, and a barbershop were also open for business. The Fonda brothers (later of Boulder) opened a drug store that seemed to sell everything. Obviously, a town of Caribou's size could not support this many businesses, and by the following year many merchants had departed.

Sixty substantial buildings had been built. (Travel writer T.H. Tice[5] estimated 250 buildings, but that figure seems high.) Wood from the trees nearby was used with not a thought that their removal would increase the severity of the winds. Caribou's buildings had to be well made to withstand the heavy snows and high winds. ("Caribou is the place where the winds were born.") Even so, most of the structures had to be buttressed on their eastern walls with long, thick poles to support the buildings against the almost constant winds. The Sherman House, a handsome three-story hotel built in 1874, was protected with heavy iron rods that were bolted to the roof of the building and dropped down the western side of the hotel, where the rods were buried deep into the ground.

Early miners loved to tell stories of the violence of the wind and the length of the winters. When asked about Caribou winters, one man is supposed to have said that he did not know how long winter lasted, because he had only been there three years. Another described the glory of the Caribou summer, adding that both days and nights were quite pleasant.

Often, after a storm, a one-story building would be completely covered by a twenty-five-foot snowdrift. Many residents deliberately built a second story on their homes so that in the winter they could enter their buildings by crossing the drifts to their bedroom windows. Snow was everywhere. It even piled up inside the houses at night, silently flowing through cracks and keyholes. The drifts were changeable; supposedly, a hemp rope was secured at the town's center and stretched to the Caribou mine shaft house so that miners could find their way home during a storm. Some unfortunates let go of the rope and were lost in the snow.

*Former Caribou resident John Charles Smith remembers those poles. Smith's grandfather, Alexander Campbell Bennett, immigrated to the Caribou area from Scotland because he feared he had tuberculosis. He became Caribou's constable and was one of the signers of the town charter.

The Caribou Silver Cornet Band, a highly sought-after group of musicians, most of whom had the Cornish last name of Moyle. *A.A. Paddock Collection*

Caribou's city fathers laid out their streets with care, using a square grid running over the hilly terrain. After several changes, the residents named their streets Potosi, Spanish for "city of silver," Main, Idaho, Jones, Brewery, Sherman, and Quigley.

Below the town of Caribou, on the flats near Coon Creek, were the remains of the corduroy road that engineers Gordon and McHenry built and abandoned in the early 1860s. The road may have been used in the summer of 1870 to bring in much-needed heavy mining equipment by oxen train. Mine owners particularly were frustrated that silver could usually only be transported out of Caribou in the summer. The Boulder men who were building, in difficult and expensive stages, the wagon road up Boulder Canyon were more than anxious to get as close to Caribou as they could. As merchants, they wanted to pull Caribou's business away from Central City. After the road was completed in the summer of 1871, regular stage travel was possible on a branch line to Caribou if one had $3.50, the price of a Boulder-Caribou ticket. In winter, the traveler went up by sleigh from Nederland to Caribou, the mail being delivered in the same manner.

Thereafter, several roads, largely financed by Caribou mine owners and Boulder businessmen, came into Caribou. The mountain community dreamed of a railroad through the Caribou flats, but it never came to pass.

In May 1871, Central City newsmen Collier and Hall hired Amos Bixby to edit the *Caribou Post*. This most readable four-page paper featured national and international news, humorous one-liners so fashionable in newspapers of the day, poetry, and serial stories, as well as news of the potential of each mine. Bixby also tried his hand at mining but was never successful at it, concluding, philosophically, that those who came too early to the mining areas had neither the money nor the knowledge to operate successful mines. As is so often the case, said Bixby, the men who made the first finds did not realize the grand profits that other more experienced men gained who came after them. Bixby despaired and moved to Boulder;* the *Caribou Post* ceased publication in August 1872.

Because of the winds and the threat of fire, the citizens designed and built a waterworks in 1878; it included a covered reservoir, several mains, and a

---

*After a stint on Boulder's newspapers, Bixby became the postmaster and started writing the Boulder valley section of *History of Clear Creek and Boulder Valleys*.

number of fireplugs. It worked for a time and saved the downtown from fire in 1879, but residents did not maintain it, and the waterworks rusted out. Its lack of maintenance is one of the factors that led to the town's eventual death.

Miners from Cornwall, noted for their expertise with metal ores, came in great numbers to Caribou. Called "Cousin Jacks" (their ladies were "Cousin Jennies"), their hardworking ways and distinctive brogue gave Caribou a special character. Cornishmen, at home in cold, damp climate, sometimes worked for a percentage of the silver ore itself, as well as for wages. Although they were not apt to join a miners' union, they would strike when they thought it necessary.

Cousin Jacks were a highly superstitious people, says Duane A. Smith in his *Silver Saga, the Story of Caribou, Colorado.* "Little withered, dried-up creatures called 'knackers' or 'Tommy Knockers' lived in and roamed about the mines." A Cornishman always left part of his lunch for the creatures and would not whistle in the mines for fear they would bedevil him. He would repeat this prayer:

> *From ghoulies and ghosties*
> *And long-leggedy beasties*
> *And from things that go*
> *Bump in the night*
> *The good Lord Deliver us.*

Rats down in the mines were a lucky sign. A large gathering of birds up above was unlucky; Cousin Jacks would not work if they saw, for instance, a flock of mountain jays. Moreover, if a woman stepped inside a mine, disaster would certainly ensue.

Sailors also lived in Caribou. Until hemp ropes were replaced by metal ones in the mines, rope-splicing specialists were needed, and sailors were imported. They did not appear to work too hard, and some miners resented them, but the sailors' skills were obviously needed for mine safety.

Chinese miners worked only briefly in the Caribou area. According to Patrick K. Ourada,[6] in 1874 the owners of the Caribou mine imported 160 Chinese from the California diggings, hoping for cheaper labor underground and in the mill at Nederland. As elsewhere in Colorado, resident miners did not take kindly to this idea and threatened the "Celestials" (as the Chinese were called), who left Nederland quickly. Evidently, the few Chinese laundrymen were not considered a threat to the Cornish ladies who took in washing.

A few doctors, teachers, and other professionals lived in Caribou, practicing their profession, to be sure, but their main interest was in their mining claims. Some had several callings; for example, the teacher was also the town barber.

Despite the cruel, long winters and the high winds, the people of Caribou loved a good time. They sang and danced a lot, even though there were not many women for partners. There were baseball games, parties, and weddings. Some homes had pianos and even organs. An inside roller-skating rink provided entertainment. Families and friends picnicked in the spring, bringing

Four ladies on an outing pose atop Goat Hill above Caribou. *J.B. Sturtevant photo, A.A. Paddock Collection*

Most of the cemetery at Caribou is gone now. Many Caribou children who died of scarlet fever or diphtheria lie there. *A.A. Paddock Collection*

back wild raspberries and huckleberries. They sledded, skied, and tobogganed in the winter.

Caribou had both a string band and a brass band, the Caribou Silver Cornet Band, which came out in full uniform for most celebrations. Of the thirteen brass players, six of them, including the director, had the last name of Moyle. They were so good that they were sought after in Boulder and other towns for special entertainment. (Brass bands were popular not only for the music they provided but also because the miners were able to blow mining dust out of their lungs.)

Church was a central part of Caribou life. The Cornish were strong Methodists; as soon as their church was completed, a minister was called in. Most Caribou men participated in the many fraternal organizations so popular in that day—Masons, Odd Fellows, and the like.

Even though saloons flourished (the Cornish were noted for their capacity for beer), and even though prostitutes lived in town, the activities in such places as the Shoo-Fly dance hall were not as wild as those of other mining camps. An old miner once told artist and writer Muriel Sibell Wolle that in 1881 "Caribou got pious, and ran the loose women out of camp."[7] The ladies moved to Cardinal two miles below and resumed business with the same customers. Cardinal, at its height, supported 1,500 residents; some of the buildings were built from lumber charred from the area's many forest fires. Someone said that the town was "conceived in sin and dedicated to the principle that all men were fair game." By comparison to other camps, Caribou was a quiet, stable town and, as Bixby says, "comparatively free from the startling crimes that stain the early annals of so many mining camps."[8]

The people of Caribou had to be special. Their cemetery markers showed, in part, what they suffered. Scarlet fever and diphtheria would sometimes take all of the children in a family in one week's time. A poem on the gravestone of a Cornish lady, Mary Webster, who died in 1879, illustrates the mood of Caribou:

Remember friends as you pass by
As you are now so once was I.
As I am now so you must be
Prepare for death and follow me.

Caribou was built next to what is now called a "magnetic dike." Because of the ground's strong magnetic properties, Caribou residents had more than their share of electrical storms. The children did not like to use their classroom slates during a storm. As they wrote their lessons on the blackboard, the static electricity would jump out at them, giving them a nasty shock. J.C. Smith tells a wonderful tale of Caribou men who, if they walked through town wearing rubber boots, "would get so weak they found it hard to continue...." A number of observers noted that they had seen the tail hair of the horses standing straight up.

By September 1871, the original partners of Caribou Company found ownership of the mine a burden; they sold the other half of the Caribou to A.D. Breed for $75,000. William Martin stayed on as superintendent for a time. Breed managed to pull $1,000 a day from the mine for a year or so. He built a silver concentrating mill at Nederland that employed eighteen men; thereafter, Caribou's silver was transported down to the new mill.

When President Ulysses S. Grant visited Central City in 1872, he stepped down from his carriage to walk on a solid silver brick pathway from the street to Teller House—an imaginative promotional scheme of Abel Breed. The press took note that the silver was from Caribou; that news spread to Europe, or at least to The Nederlands, for after much promotion Breed was able to sell the Caribou mine and the mill to "gentlemen from The Hague" for $3 million.

Dutch operation of the business was doomed from the start. During the change of ownership, Abel Breed did a little "house-cleaning," working "feverishly to remove the rich ore reserves, so that there would be no bothersome clutter of that sort left in the underground workings, and the new owners would have a nice cleaned mine in which to start operations."[9] In any event, since the Caribou mine did not prosper due to mismanagement, the mine eventually became subject to a sheriff's sale. Senator Jerome B. Chaffee and David Moffat bought the property in 1876.

Even though the Caribou mine had its troubles, its silver made news when it was exhibited at the Philadelphia Exposition that year. The mine changed hands again in 1879. This time, R.G. Dun (of Dun and Bradstreet) bought the property, but now silver itself was in trouble. Not only was the price of silver plummeting, but Dun could not get the water pumped out of the mining shaft. The mine opened and closed; it was for sale, and not for sale. By 1888, Dun regarded the whole property as a "white elephant."

The declining fortune of the silver trade was not the only cause of Caribou's death. There had been destructive fires in earlier years; a very serious one occurred in 1873. The next year, a nitroglycerin explosion rocked the town. Even so, residents started to rebuild as they had after each calamity. The fire of 1879 was of holocaust proportions. Forest fires burned in the region that summer, but apparently no one tried to put them out. On September 14, a Sunday morning, the townspeople arose to a red-glowing sky west of town, and the famous Caribou winds grew

What was left of Caribou in 1943. Little trace of the silver camp remains today. *A.A. Paddock Collection*

stronger and stronger. When the fire crowned a few remaining trees near town, many of the residents left their beds and started running downhill as fast as they could, not stopping until they reached Nederland. The flames swept into Caribou, demolishing sixty or more buildings and reducing the eastern half of the town to ashes. Caribou's new water system saved the center of town, but the fire moved down the valley. Cords of wood already stacked for the approaching winter went up in heavy smoke. The same year, scarlet fever and diphtheria plagued the town.

For several years after, Caribou continued to be an active settlement. Its business life remained relatively stable, but a slow decline began with the fire of 1879. By the mid-1880s, the Methodist Church no longer had a resident minister. Many of the Cornish miners moved on, some on their way to Leadville, others to the Black Hills diggings in South Dakota. Some moved to nearby Williamsburg (later called Switchville), hoping that the silver finds there would equal those of Caribou. Others moved down to Boulder.

Winters in the mid-1880s were especially hard. In August 1885, snow from the previous year was still on the ground. Scarlet fever and diphtheria struck again and continued to decimate the population, especially the children. But with each new hardship there continued a strong optimism about Caribou's future. The *Boulder County Herald* said of Caribou, "times ain't quite as lively as they might be, but we think before long we will see a change."[10] However, it was not long before the columns on Caribou activities were dropped permanently from the county's newspapers. As times got harder and harder, the people clung together and helped one another with food and clothing. After the town's doctor died, mining superintendent William Todd learned how to set bones, pull teeth, and treat gunshot wounds.

In 1890, Caribou was twenty years old and "had begun to show her age."[11] The Sherman House was "pretty well beat up,"[12] and the town's rats grew more numerous, their shining eyes scaring the children at night. An earthquake in 1903 shook up the residents but did little damage. Although parts of the town of Caribou had survived earlier fires, the fire of 1905 finished off, in just three hours, the remaining major buildings and "ended the prolonged agony of abandonment."[13] The waterworks had rusted out and was of no help. A defective flue in one of the few stores left seems to have dealt the final blow to Caribou. Residents tried to stop the fire before it reached Sherman House (now called Billy Donald's) by setting off dynamite that could be heard in Old Cardinal below, but the old hotel was consumed by flames.

Even so, some families hung on in the fire-blackened community. As the mine shafts filled with water, the snows and the winds and destructive visitors continued the work of erasing what was Caribou.

Someone said that "Caribou taxes built the Boulder County Court House." Surely, the working of the Caribou mines was responsible for the first real growth that Boulder ever had, as its economy was stimulated by the silver flow from the mountain camp above. By 1910, $20 million had been realized from Caribou silver, half of that from the Caribou mine itself, the property Sam Conger had traded so quickly for another. "Caribou, like the reindeer it was named after, pawed its food—silver—from beneath the frozen snow. The life blood of its silver veins pinched out, and the town stumbled to a stop, and died."[14]

Before the excitement of the silver discoveries at Caribou had died down, the fire-battered settlement at Gold Hill experienced new life. Professor Nathaniel Hill's new smelting works could accommodate the processing of lower-grade ore, which meant that tunneling for gold could be profitable. Those who worked the mines rebuilt the town on lower ground between Gold Run and Aikins Gulch, closer to a water supply. In 1872, prospectors Christian Holk and Joseph Steppler found a vein of metal near Gold Hill that was to cause the camp to "boom" again, inspire the establishment of many new mining communities, and bring more money into Boulder City. Tracing the source of their "float" discovery, the prospectors dug through twelve feet of soil, uncovering what looked like a rich vein of ore. Because they had no money for their own assay, they took samples to Denver, where Territorial Geologist J.F.L. Schirmer and expert J. Alden Smith studied them. After Schirmer finished his test, he felt that he knew what the metal was, but he sent samples to an expert in Philadelphia for confirmation.

The "troublesome purple ore," kicked out of the way by earlier miners, was positively identified as a telluride of gold and silver,* a rare find for the United States. This vein was to become the Red Cloud mine. J. Alden Smith examined the vein, then moved about the mountainous area to determine the direction of what he though must run a telluride belt. Several miles to the east (site of Sunshine), D.C. Patterson began to work the Little Miami mine in 1873, and a year later George Jackson and Hiram Fullen found a telluride vein, site of the American mine, which was to be far richer than the find at Gold Hill. Jackson and Fullen made $17,500 from the American and, fearing that the mine was about to

---

*Telluride is a binary compound of tellurium. Tellurium (Te) is an element occurring naturally with gold and other metals. Sylvanite is a telluride of gold and silver. Calaverite is a telluride of gold with some silver (so named because it was found in Calaveras County, California). Tellurides are also found in the Transylvania district of present Rumania and at the mines of Kalgoorlie, Western Australia.

A rebuilt Gold Hill in 1888.
A.A. Paddock Collection

Great rivals of the Boulder baseball team, the Sunshine Nine pose for the camera at Jamestown on the Fourth of July, 1897. Left to right: Johnnie Jones, Sam Emery, Frank R. Gunn, Bill Emery, Frank Hook, Ed Clark, Lander Smith, Steve Lewis, and Ed Spinney. Note the mismatched socks. *A.A. Paddock Collection.*

play out, sold it to Hiram Hitchcock for another $17,500. Hitchcock, who was going broke because his New York hotel, the Fifth Avenue, was not doing well, gambled and won, for he made $196,000 on his telluride operations. (The mine, supervised by J. Alden Smith, eventually gave up $1,500,000 worth of ore; samples from the American were exhibited at the Philadelphia Exposition in 1876.)

Almost overnight, the town of Sunshine* ("rich as the mines of Sunshine") sprang up; soon its population was greater than that of Boulder. By 1876, some 1,500 people were living there. The *Sunshine Courier* began publication on May 1, 1875, telling its readers that it was the only paper in Colorado "that keeps its columns Free From Politics and aims to be an Organ of the People striking fearlessly at all times in defense of Right, Truth, and Justice. We will be found always reading with our coat off and sleeves rolled up to vindicate and battle for the most sacred Interests of the People."

*Sunshine was named after the first baby born in camp, Susan Sunshine Turner, daughter of the Peter Turners.

Camp Salina, on Gold Run, was also the result of the telluride "boom" when O.P. Hamilton found a vein there in 1873. The Kansans who settled there worked the Melvina and Black Swan mines. Salina, like Sunshine, lost its "boom" population several years later. (In 1878, the *Courier*'s owner, William G. Shedd, moved to Boulder, bringing the paper with him, and it combined with the *Boulder County News* to form the *News-Courier*.) North of Salina, on Gold Run, the town of Summerville was surrounded by mines—the Black Cloud, the Victoria, the Cash, the U.S. Bank, the Bailey, the Tunnell, and the Hoosier Ledge. Camp Lyon and Camp Tellurium, settlements nearby, supported populations of three hundred or more for a time, with a hotel, four boarding houses, two general stores, a shoe shop, and a blacksmith shop.

By the time Obed Crisman founded a town in his name in 1875, two tellurium mines were already in operation, the Yellow Pine and the Logan (named after General John A. Logan). The Logan's gold was considered so pure that the ore was delivered, under guard, directly to the Denver Mint. One of Crisman's

A busy McAllister lumber mill at Clarasdorf along the Middle Boulder. *J.B. Sturtevant photo, A.A. Paddock Collection*

A family enjoys some fishing at Clarasdorf, 1899. *J.B. Sturtevant photo, A.A. Paddock Collection*

Residents of Crisman, gold mining camp on Four Mile Creek, pose for the camera of J.B. Sturtevant. *A.A. Paddock Collection*

The Pacific Express Company and the Crisman bridge. *J.B. Sturtevant photo, A.A. Paddock Collection*

The mining town of Rowena (sometimes called Rockville), north of Gold Hill on Left Hand Creek, 1909. The Gray Eagle Mill is on the right. *A.A. Paddock Collection*

Tunnel of the Lost Dutchman mine near Rowena. *A.A. Paddock Collection*

Magnolia, sometime after 1875. Magnolia whiskey was popular among the gold miners, one theory as to the origin of the town's name. *J.B. Sturtevant photo, A.A. Paddock Collection*

Hoover and Barber's Mountain House resort, two miles northwest of Magnolia. *J.B. Sturtevant photo, A.A. Paddock Collection*

A sleepy afternoon in Sunset, gold boom town in the 1890s. *A.A. Paddock Collection*

Sunset, where the Switzerland Trail narrow gauge railroad branched, with one line running to Eldora and the other to Ward. *J.B. Sturtevant photo, A.A. Paddock Collection*

Everyone is dressed for the Baptist Sunday School Picnic in Sunset, late 1880s. *L.P. Bass photo, A.A. Paddock Collection*

Sometimes called "Colorado canaries," a mule trail outside the Nellie mine. *Byers and St. Claire photo, A.A. Paddock Collection*

A quiet day at Jamestown, 1884. *A.A. Paddock Collection*

Patrons of the Budweiser Palace have their picture taken. Note the mixture of tents and buildings for business use. *A.A. Paddock Collection*

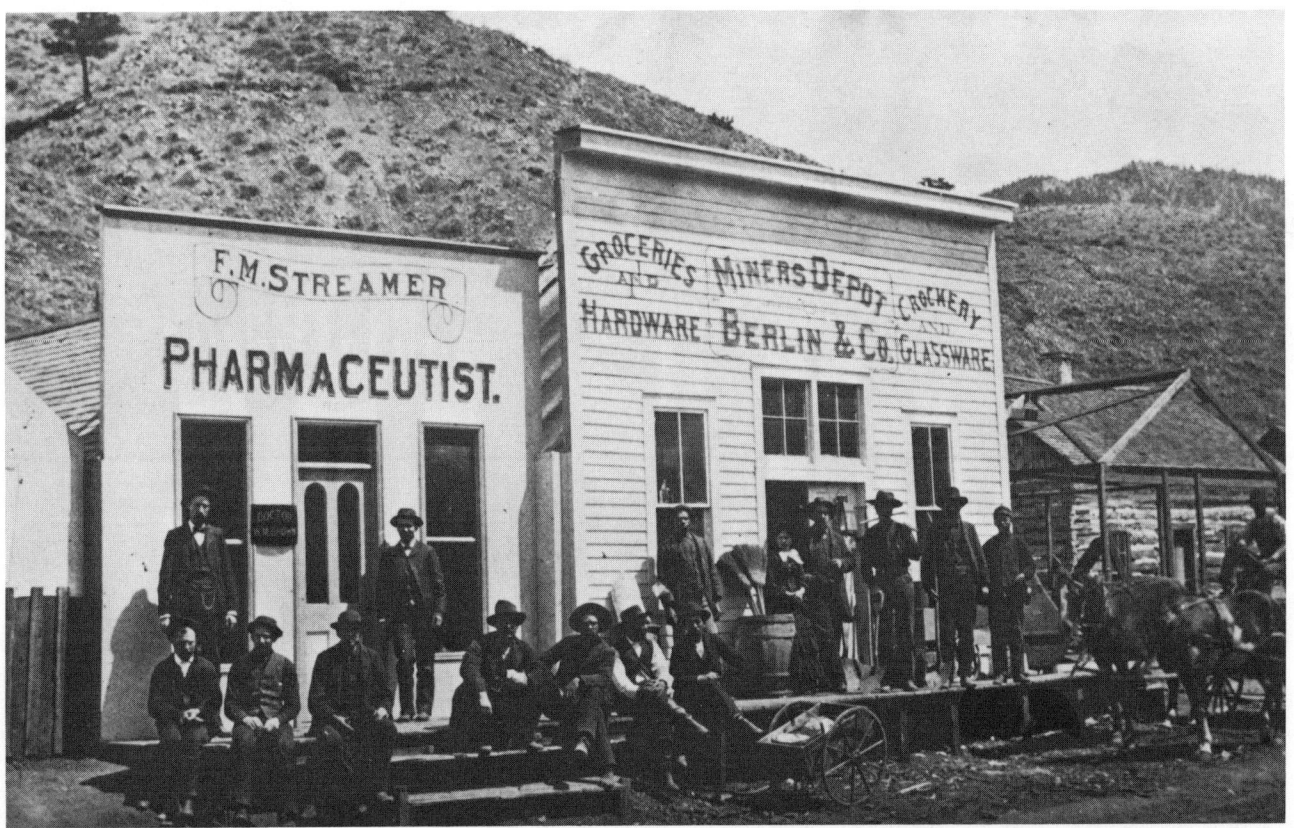
Jamestown folks taking in the sun in 1884. There are black and oriental faces in this shot; note the unusual occupation of F.M. Streamer. *A.A. Paddock Collection*

Springdale's mineral springs drew tourists to its resorts and spas; most of the community was destroyed in the flood of 1894. *L.P. Bass photo, A.A. Paddock Collection*

Springdale's Seltzer House advertised its mineral water as healthful and pure. *Ely and Hildredth photo, A.A. Paddock Collection*

Two hundred settlers, working gold and silver mines, called this lonely place home in the 1880s. Camp Albion, built at 11,000 feet, was five miles northeast of Caribou, close to the Continental Divide. *Meile photo, A.A. Paddock Collection*

As Eldora boomed in 1898, some lived in tents. Merchants might start out business life from tents also. *J.B. Sturtevant photo, A.A. Paddock Collection*

A winter day at the gold mining camp of Eldora. Note a cabin under construction in background. *J.B. Sturtevant photo, A.A. Paddock Collection*

settlers, French aristocrat François Pierre Ardourel, feeling that fine wines were integral to the life of a mining gentleman, built extensive wine cellars at the camp. Hiram Fullen continued his prospecting and in June 1875 found outcroppings of tellurium at the southern edge of the mineral belt at Magnolia. A year later, three hundred people had moved to Magnolia to work in mines with such names as Keystone, Mountain Lion, and Little Maud and Lady Franklin. (Magnolia was the name of a whiskey popular with the miners, or could it be a southern settler's nostalgia for the flowers back home?)

Jamestown also experienced a new life. In 1864, galena (a lead ore) was mined there (the settlement was called Elysian Park then). When Jamestown's early miners met to form their mining district, it is said that they started each proceeding with a rendition of "Sweet Betsey From Pike."

The mid-1870s brought with it a number of telluride strikes throughout the area. Four miles north of Jamestown, the little camp of Ballarat* grew because of the prospects at the Smuggler mine and mill. Southwest of Jamestown, Camp Providence (sometimes called John Jay Camp) was established by J.J. Van Deren, who felt that he received divine guidance with his tellurium discoveries. Nearby was Camp Enterprise, which was a unique settlement in that the population was almost totally Swedish. There was Gresham, and Glendale, and Springdale, whose hot springs drew tourists and sick people to the town's Seltzer House and Peabody's Hot Springs. Those who drank the waters at Springdale were told that it was "effervescent and agreeable...a specific for Rheumatism, Kidney Troubles, Dyspepsia, General Debility, Indigestion...Sure cure for Headaches either Nervous or Bilious, and especially for derangements caused by excessive use of Tobacco or Alcoholic Stimulants." (Years later, Edgar Smith was to sell lemonade in Springdale that he advertised as made from waters of the "Fountain of Youth," a potion "fit for the Gods.")

All of these camps and settlements were a boon to Boulder. Most were larger than the community on Boulder Creek, and their residents had every intention to remain there. But fire, the fortunes of the metals market, and flood caused the people to move on. Most of these camps and settlements passed into history.

---

*Ballarat (or Balarat) was perhaps named after the Ballarat mining center in Victoria, Australia. For the derivation of other Boulder County names, *see* Appendix.

Chapter Six

Boulder was beginning to simmer in the 1870s. By now, a number of local men had amassed considerable money and real estate. They realized the need for local government and hoped to run the town as they saw fit. Political parties grew, some of them based upon local issues; mass meetings were common as Boulder's political climate heated up. One angry citizen wrote to the *News,* saying the town needed local government to solve the dog problem, for there was "not another small town in the world that can support as many, useless, cussed dogs as Boulder. Oh for a municipal government so that we can have a poisonous, killing, exterminating dog law."[1]

For whatever reason, on November 4, 1871, the original town site, plus three additional parcels of land, were incorporated by the county. The commissioners appointed five men to serve as town trustees until the April elections: Anthony Arnett, innkeeper; James P. Maxwell, engineer and road builder; Marinus G. Smith, farmer; Alpheus Wright, lawyer; and Fred A. Squires, merchant. The men elected Squires president of the Board of Trustees, a post similar to that of mayor.

For the next few days, the "founding fathers" spent many hours writing ordinances and appointing civil servants. W.C. Wynkoop, sometime newspaperman, assumed the duties of city clerk; Oscar Allen became constable. Evidently, they paid attention to the angry dog-hater, for the trustees ordered that dogs be tagged and licensed. Citizens paid little attention to these instructions, however, because dogs continued to be a nuisance. Although the high-desert soil did not look promising, the trustees developed an ambitious tree planting program. Recognizing that liquor licenses were a good source of revenue, the trustees charged each saloon $100 to operate.

By the time of the first elections in April 1872, the voters had become suspicious of the businessmen-trustees. They joined the Young American Party (in reality, Republicans) and other newly formed political groups. When the votes were in, the Young Americans won all five seats over four other tickets, Jarvis Gilbert became president, and the "founding fathers" were

JAMES P. MAXWELL,
BOULDER.
MEMBER COLORADO LEGISLATURE 1872-1874.
STATE SENATE 1877-1881. PRES. PRO TEM SENATE 1879.
STATE ENGINEER 1889-1892.

James P. Maxwell from Baraboo, Wisconsin, engaged in varied business ventures, including a wagon road through Boulder Canyon. He is pictured in one of his fraternal costumes. *Representative Men of Colorado*

swept out of office. In addition to the Democratic and Republican parties, the Prohibition Party was a political force, as well as the High License Party, which stood for raising the cost of a liquor license. There were the Non-Partisans and the Citizens Party; both were Republican groups in disguise, for the Republicans found out early in Boulder politics that they were far more successful at the polls if they did not call themselves Republicans.

"Sweet and womanly" was how Amos Bixby described an 1875 speaker on women's suffrage, middle-aged Mrs. Campbell, even though she stated to her audience that depriving women of the right to vote was "assigning them to the same category as idiots, thieves, murderers, and untaxed Indians."[2] Boulder women started early to fight for the right to vote and waged several unsuccessful attempts. (They would not gain the franchise until 1893.)* In 1877, members of the new Greenback Party, which called for a paper dollar as full legal tender, announced that they wished to concern themselves with the plight of the working man. Greenbackers often allied themselves with the Populist Party, but even so, they seldom won at the polls. The Citizens Reform League became active in 1897 and was the precursor to the Better Boulder Party so popular after the turn of the century. As elsewhere in the country, the Socialists made a strong showing in the elections of 1903.

When Boulder City incorporated in 1878, this time under the new State of Colorado, "City" was dropped from the town's name. The only other change was that the voters directly elected a mayor as well as four trustees. That fall, Greenbacker Jacob Ellison was elected for the short term, until the April elections, by a majority of four votes (208 to 204). By 1882, Boulder qualified as a "city of the second class," because its population had risen to slightly more than 3,000. In April of that year, the Board of Trustees passed an ordinance that gave the growing town an alderman-ward system of government (which endured until the passage of the present city manager-council form in 1918). Under this system, the voters elected a mayor and treasurer for one-year terms and four aldermen for two-year terms. W.H. Allison, a cashier at the First National Bank, became the first elected mayor.

The Citizens Party (Republicans) took over all seats on the council; that left a lone Democrat in office—Marshal J.C. Coulehan. Flushed with victory, the new council set about to "revise" all the ordinances that the "founding fathers" had passed ten years before. They forced Marshal Coulehan out of office, replacing him with B.F. Bounds. Mayor Allison was so disgusted with these and other tactics that he resigned and the *Boulder County Herald,* a Democratic newspaper, commented, "We cannot find it in our heart to blame him for his course in laying down an office the possession of which brought with it no satisfaction, but only harrassing, worry, criticism, fault finding and consequent vexation."[3] This was not the end of it, because the following year B.F. Bounds was arrested and fined $100 for assault on the editor of the *Herald.*

Ten years later, each of the four wards was divided and eight aldermen were elected, with the mayor serving a two-year term. As the Populists gained support in the 1890s, many "regulars" from both Democratic and Republican ranks moved into the Populist camp. By allying themselves with the Democrats, they controlled county offices for a time, but they never could beat the Republicans for municipal office. With their "nonpartisan" mantle, the Republicans managed to squeak through by the slimmest margin of votes.

The strength of the Citizens Reform League was growing in the late 1890s; their goal was to close down "all commercialized vice." Campaigning was vigorous, but even so, newspaperman Crockett Ricketts won over the reform ticket. In 1903, in an apparent burst of democracy and with the influence of the Socialists, the voters elected municipal officers that were usually appointed—the city clerk, the city attorney, the engineer, the marshal, a police magistrate, and a supervisor of streets. This "democratic government" was evidently not too successful, for it lasted only until the next election.

Boulder found it difficult to decide in the 1870s whether water belonged to the people or to private enterprise. A committee of three—Fred Squires, Alfred Brookfield, and Ephraim Pound—studied the problem and reported back to the trustees that water belonged to all the people. In 1874, they proposed an $18,000 bond issue to build a reservoir at the mouth of Boulder Canyon, near Douty's mill. The bonds passed, the reservoir was built, and a ditch was dug from Boulder Creek (at Hanging Rock) to the new reservoir. The water was brought down to Pearl Street by means of a small cast-iron main. The next year, Ephraim Pound, who had been county sheriff as well as proprietor of Colorado House, was appointed Boulder's first water commissioner. He canvassed the townspeople to "find out whom (*sic*) will take water and what they are willing to give per annum or per quarter for the use of the water."[4] Up to this point, householders got their water from the creek or from the irrigation ditches. Another $12,000 bond issue passed which allowed the laying of pipes to the cross streets, but the project was a patchwork and a constant source of trouble. A contractor promised "to make tight all joints, connections, and hydrants

---

*Wyoming (as a territory) was first in the Union to grant women the right to vote in 1869; Colorado (as a state) was second in 1893.

now leaking or that may be found to be so leaking within twenty days."[5]

Those who did not have wells drank the creek water that was polluted with tailings from the mines above. The *Herald* recommended that the water be taken out at a higher point in the canyon to avoid mining debris. In 1878, another $30,000 was spent to patch up the water system, but the town's water became more and more clouded with mine tailings. By 1882, the city owned eight shares of Farmers Ditch, but that water was used primarily to flush out the gutters and clean the streets. In fact, the water was allowed to run down the streets for no discernible reason, where it formed "nauseating puddles."[6] In 1884, the *Herald* described the water as "murkier than ever." A professor recommended that households filter their drinking water and treat it with alum and soda, which would "settle ninety per cent of the dirt in twenty minutes."[7] Shortly thereafter, the city stopped the water flow altogether when dead horses were found in the creek.

At some point, small ditches were built on either side of Pearl Street. Lined with cobblestones, they measured two feet wide and eight inches deep. Not only was the water used to settle the dust in summer, but barefoot boys found them a convenient place to wash their feet. The water was also used to put out fires, but if a burning cabin was too far from the ditches, the townspeople watched it burn to the ground, for Boulder was just beginning to develop a firefighting capacity.

Amid great controversy and debate, a $150,000 bond issue passed in 1890 designed to clear up Boulder's water problems for good. A new reservoir was built at the base of Sunshine Canyon to avoid Boulder Creek's mine tailings. One merchant was so thrilled with the prospect of clean water that he offered on sale "the greatest bargains in Pure Toilet Soap ever known."[8] Plans for the new reservoir were somewhat deficient, however, because no one thought to line it with cement. The *Camera* referred to the reservoir as the "mud and microbes"[9] project. Finally the reservoir was lined, but the city asked for an additional $50,000, even though it had not spent all of the $150,000 in what the *Camera* termed "a gaudy show of economy."[10] With the funds now at hand, the city concentrated on improving the water supply lines. This must have helped, for in 1896, *Camera* editor Lucius C. Paddock printed an Iowa visitor's description of Boulder water:

> The city water supply comes from an open reservoir two or three hundred feet higher than the town, which is supplied through pipes reaching several hundred feet still higher several miles 'up the mountains.' It is snow water and the cleanest, coolest, purest, and softest water we have ever seen.[11]

The new commissioner of streets, Dr. George Chase, announced that every able-bodied Boulder man must work two days a year to help maintain the streets or pay a fee of four dollars. Street repair was frustrating because the grades were steep and the clay turned to mud or dust, depending upon the weather. Twelfth Street (Broadway) was graded in 1872. A number of bridges were constructed across Boulder Creek as new homes were built to the south. Pearl Street continued to have a torn-up appearance, because the heavy ore wagons used that route to reach camps in the mountains. When the streets were muddy, the ladies wore black stockings in hopes that the splattered mud would not show. A deeply mired stage coach or carriage was not an uncommon sight. The mud was memorialized in a poem sent to the newspaper:

> *Oh the mud, the miserable mud*
> *Into its depths you go with a thud*
> *That causes the sticky, nasty clay*
> *To slide up your boots in a horrible way!*
> *Sticky, nasty, filthy stuff!*
> *Why, the devil! It's enough*
> *To cause oaths to come from pious saints.*
> *Everything here is damned with the taints*
> *Of the nasty, adhering real estate,*
> *That's loafing around your town at date.*[12]

In later years, crushed rock was added to the mud, and this helped to stabilize the streets somewhat. By 1874, a man had been hired to sprinkle the streets to keep the dust down in summer.

Dr. Chase, also the city's first health officer, complained to the trustees about the "running at large of cattle and poultry."[13] In 1875, it was decreed that no cattle, sheep, or swine should be kept in town, "if offensive."[14] No privy or private sewer (there were no public ones) should be "nauseous, foul, offensive, or injurious to public health."[15] Since Dr. Chase was hired to control epidemics, he tried to get public money for a sewer system. The people twice voted down sewer bonds until 1895, when the first town sewer was constructed. From time to time, Dr. Chase ordered an extensive Boulder cleanup.* Sometimes conditions in town became so appalling that newspapers called for an end to unsanitary conditions. "Waste paper from the size of a circus tent down are constantly drifting about in the gentle zephyrs. Old boots, trunk covers, boxes, green watermelons, decayed fruits, etc., are scattered in all directions. Stagnant water and mud are too common. If this cannot be remedied, we suggest that the swine be turned loose to eat up decaying matters."[16]

Before 1871, Boulder City had no real law enforcement. Law and order consisted of the mining

---

*Our present yearly "cleanup" has its roots in this early practice.

Unpaved Pearl Street after a rain, 1903. One block away, a streetcar. *J.B. Sturtevant photo, A.A. Paddock Collection*

district's "club rules." The rule-breaker might well have his head shaved on the right side (if he wore whiskers and a mustache, they would be shaved off on the left side) and then be expelled from town. In 1860, under authority of the short-lived Jefferson Territory, Captain Aikin's son Lafayette was appointed "town marshal" for the princely sum of seventy-two dollars a year; how he fared is not known.

When Boulder County was established in 1861, sheriffs supervised the town's streets. A "citizens'" court was organized with a justice of the peace presiding. According to historian Amos Bixby, sometimes the proceedings of these courts were great fun and a source of entertainment. The qualifications of some of these justices is questionable, too, for in 1861 Judge Parker left the bench quite suddenly when it was discovered that he was the leader of a gang that stole forty horses and mules. Marinus Smith and Horace Tarbox chased the criminals all the way to the Missouri River; when the two men returned, they reported that the judge and his friends had "joined the army."

Oscar Allen survived the "clean sweep" election of 1872 and was approved ninety-nine to nine. The constable's job was one of piecework with no salary; for each arrest he made, he received two dollars. (William Westlake was the first arrest of record, but the nature of his crime is lost to history.) For each dog that Allen disposed of, he received one dollar. He was also the town's first fire warden for an additional twenty-five dollars a month.

Allen was to "suppress riots, disturbances, and breaches of the peace."[17] He was to arrest those who appeared nude in public or "in a dress not belonging to his or her sex," or in "lewd or indecent dress."[18] What this came down to was that Allen arrested rock throwers, drunks who raced their horses up and down Pearl Street, gun shooters, and those who used profanity. Swearing in public could cost a man anywhere from $5 to $100.

Constable Allen and the four men who followed him in office were also to keep an eye on the bawdy houses, the saloons, the gambling rooms and billiards parlors, all of which were doing a brisk business. Boulder was not unlike other frontier towns with a transient miner population that required such services. From time to time, the press called for the shutting down of these establishments, but such a move had no strong support from the public until the turn of the century.

As one might expect with numerous saloons, drunks were also a common sight. The constable was supposed to arrest them and put them in jail, but this was sometimes difficult, for at times there was no jail. In 1874, the city asked the county for the use of the jail facilities at Fourteenth and Spruce streets. Evidently the county said no, for city prisoners were housed for a time in the basement of the Boulder

Business is lively in Hoover's pool hall, Arnett Hotel, north side of 1000 block of Pearl Street. Note tobacco juice on the floor. In the late 1970s, the handsome Arnett, under extensive renovation, collapsed under the weight of a heavy snowstorm. *Boulder Historical Society*

A cleaner hall, waiting for business. *A.A. Paddock Collection*

Hose Company (one of the firefighting services) at Twelfth and Front streets (site of the Public Service Company building at Broadway and Walnut streets). When visitors to the basement jail complained of "bad air, foul odors, and close quarters,"[19] the city rented "calaboose" space from Anthony Arnett.

In 1881, the city asked the county for jail space, and this time the county acquiesced with cells in the county building at Fourteenth and Spruce streets. In 1888, the county sold the land and asked the city to leave. For a time, city officials were stubborn, kept the key to the jail, and would not get out. By 1890, the city fathers had reserved $600 for the construction of a jail but instead bought an old county building at 1018 Pearl Street, which was known as "the pit." An unusual number of fires occurred at this stone facility; the most interesting one started when someone tied firecrackers to a dog's tail and encouraged the animal to run through "city hall." Fire finally demolished "the pit" in 1924, and the jail was moved yet again to the county courthouse.[20]

There was no jail in 1867 when William Tull was arrested for stealing horses; he was put into the deputy sheriff's room over Dabney's blacksmith shop. Tull was a twenty-six-year-old hired hand who worked on a farm east of town. He decided to visit his Cheyenne Indian wife who was camped north of Boulder toward Fort Collins. He took two horses with him, but since someone questioned whether he had title to these animals, the sheriff arrested Tull and brought him back to the deputy's room, saying ominously, "This will not cost the county anything."[21] A mob found it easy to get the prisoner; they took Tull to a grove of willow trees along Boulder Creek. Although they intended to hang him, they ineffectually roped Tull to a low branch of a willow, and, in fact, he strangled to death. The mob discovered too late that Tull had full title to the horses. After the lynching, newspapers would report every once in a while the sighting of William Tull's ghost, who appeared to be pleading with passersby to remove a piece of rope from around his neck.

Another Boulder scandal led to the jailing of the first woman at the penitentiary at Canon City in 1873. Mrs. (Dr.) Solander was arrested after the death of Mrs. Fredericka Baunn of Left Hand, who "died on Tuesday last under suspicious circumstances."[22] Although the papers did not give the gory details during Dr. Solander's trial (they did later and sold out their editions), the prosecution alleged that Mary Solander

This brick building, sometimes known as "The Pit," located on the south side of 1000 block of Pearl Street, housed city offices and the court until 1921. The jail was housed there until 1924, when the building burned down. *A.A. Paddock Collection*

had performed an abortion on Mrs. Baunn. The doctor pleaded innocent. There seemed to be a division of opinion in the community as to Dr. Solander's guilt, although the jury did find her guilty. She had come to Boulder in 1870, set up her practice, and seemed well received. (Her credentials to practice medicine could not be evaluated, because the territory did not require attendance at a medical school until 1874.) David Nichols and Alpheus Wright came to her defense. Her husband Daniel, a carpenter and a member of the school board, divorced her, however, when she was released from the penitentiary after serving a few months of her sentence. She was given a full pardon by Territorial Governor McCook. When she returned to Boulder, she placed an ad in the paper to thank citizens for their kindness and support, but a doctor's life in Boulder was not for Mary Solander. She gave up her practice and left town.

Boulder residents evidently enjoyed reading about crime in their papers, as the reporting was most uninhibited. Even though two armed men fought it out in Fred Squires' store around Christmas of 1871, newspaper editors generally agreed that court business had been dull. A few years later, the *News-Courier* reported "the criminal record of the town is almost at zero, and it is hoped it will continue so."[23]

A prize fight, possibly Boulder's first, occurred in August 1873 near Boulder Creek on the site of the present Boulder Public Library. Tim Brown fought one Scotty; no gloves were used. Constable Gilbert watched all nineteen rounds, then proceeded to arrest those in the audience, for watching a prize fight was against the law; besides, it was Sunday.

A red-light district developed along the north side of Boulder Creek on Water Street (Canyon Boulevard) stretching from the present Boulder Public Library site to the municipal building. Although Boulder's prostitutes tended to cluster within the "district," "soiled doves" were in business in other parts of town as well. Prostitution and gambling were declared illegal in 1873, but the houses did not close down for long, if at all.* The business was a lucrative one. Some of the houses stood on land belonging to prominent Boulder citizens who profited substantially. The *News* complained that a keno game was "running at full blast every evening"[24] and reported that the "denizens of the house of questionable fame near the old hose house"[25] had asked the law to remove drunks from their establishment.

In 1878, the law was reversed; gambling and prostitution were excluded from the list of illegal businesses. And so it went, on and off, but the "brides of the multitude" did not give up their trade. Madame Susie Brown continued to operate her "boarding

*They were not welcome in Sugar Loaf, nor were gamblers. Ward outlawed gambling also.

These "doves" may be "soiled" but their grins for the camera are infectious. *John Schoolland Collection*

house" at 1045 Water Street, even though her place was burned out seven times. After she built two sturdy brick houses at Eighteenth and Spruce streets, she moved her growing business there. Molly Gordon, a black "lady of the evening," called her place at 1034 Water Street the "Hell-hole." In the January 31, 1878 issue of the *Colorado Banner*, Gordon's place was called the "Temple of Venus." (Miss Gordon and a white man visited the local justice of the peace, stating their intention to marry, but were denied a marriage license. It was against the law for blacks and whites to marry one another.) Other women put up signs "Men Taken In and Done For." No proper lady in town would consider a white poodle for a pet, because the "doves" often walked down Pearl Street with their poodles. Marietta Kingsley, however, had two small pug dogs which she carried, one on each arm.

Although the houses were listed in the U.S. Census as "boarders, fancy," they were not talked about in polite society unless they came to the attention of the press when a fire or a death occurred. Frankie McDonald's overdose of morphine and subsequent death was reported. Lottie Diamond's demise called for this statement in the *Boulder County Herald:* "A lady long known in this community as one fallen from the path of virtue died of mountain fever...Although her life has been checkered with sin the tender chords of human sympathy are yet aroused when we consider

The interior of Gilbert's Drug Store. Note the magnificent soda fountain and revolving fan. *A.A. Paddock Collection*

the circumstances under which she died. Fallen to the depths of infamy and without a friend by her side, she breathed her last...."[26] Yet, on another occasion the same paper complained, "The friends of morality should train their batteries on the houses of ill fame in this city. There is no need for them here and they have a very damaging and deteriorating effect upon the young. The inmates should at least be compelled to leave the city and not be allowed to flaunt their avocation in the face of everyone on the street, nor be permitted to advertise their business publicly everywhere."[27] However, the citizens continued to watch "the young bloods of the town, or some of the sportier of the miners, riding on Pearl Street in swanky buggies with 'Painted Ladies.'"[28]

By the late 1870s, increased activity in the mines was bringing in more criminal problems, so the town trustees hired the first official marshal, William DeBord. Marshal DeBord added a night watchman and instituted a work program for his prisoners. When J.C. Coulehan became marshal in 1883, he added one more to his staff. Coulehan was paid seventy dollars a month, the evening officer sixty dollars, and the night watchman thirty-four dollars. The men also wore uniforms for the first time. The miners would "whoop it up" on Saturday nights, but the night watch stopped all boisterous activity exactly at midnight, the beginning of the Sabbath. Even so, the *Herald* continued to complain, "Too many small boys are allowed in the saloons. Is there not an ordinance against this?"[29]

Despite Boulder citizens' great fear of fire, the town made no provision for fighting one until 1871. The combination of wooden structures, Boulder's high winds, and the lack of an adequate water system were evidence enough for their fear. The newly appointed board of trustees began to tackle the problem and appointed themselves fire wardens, in addition to the services of Constable Allen. The trustees passed an ordinance which provided that anyone who did not obey their commands during a fire was fined five dollars. They inspected buildings for faulty fireplaces, stoves, chimneys, and the like. They required the proper burial of ashes and prohibited the use of candles and kerosene lamps near hay. No mining explosives were to be stored in town.

A fire at Spruce and Twelfth (Broadway) on a

Interior of early Pearl Street barbershop, complete with spittoons. *A.A. Paddock Collection*

The statue and fountain in front of the railroad depot at Fourteenth and Water streets, now moved to Thirtieth and Mapleton. *J.B. Sturtevant photo, A.A. Paddock Collection*

Waiting for the train. Note one lady is carrying copy of *Cosmopolitan*. A.A. Paddock Collection

windy September 18, 1874 caused such alarm that construction of a waterworks was begun. "The danger to which the town is exposed is vividly illustrated by an accident during the gale," the *News* reported.

> About the time the walls of Allen's block toppled before the blast, a chimney burning occurred in the Parker house...The flying sparks ignited a parcel of gunnysacks in the yard of George Tourtellot...and extinguished just in time to save a haystack nearby. In another minute, the hay would have been in flames, and before that driving wind a burning town would have terrified the inhabitants....[30]

Now the fear of fire was so strong that the trustees ruled that no more wooden buildings could be constructed on Pearl Street or Front (Walnut) Street between Tenth and Eighteenth streets. They also gave orders to "ascertain the probable cost of getting hooks and ladders sufficient for a fire company."[31] Such a vehicle was bought in Denver for $400, and in February 1875, eleven men signed on as charter members of the Boulder Hook and Ladder Company. The following month, the group swelled to fifty men; it changed its name to the Phoenix Hook and Ladder Company, and uniforms were designed. Local tailor Mr. Hernandez made the company's shirts of red California flannel. Their pants and belts were black, and their hats (made to order in New York) were also black, decorated with a golden wreath.

The original hook and ladder was eventually sold to Louisville, and in 1882, a second vehicle costing $500 was escorted into town, its red and gold paint glittering in the sun, by the Boulder Cornet Band. (This vehicle is on display at the Central Fire Station, Thirteenth and Portland streets.)

Until 1875, citizens fought fires by passing buckets of water from hand to hand. A few merchants had their own firefighting equipment. Although Boulder's water system was barely adequate in 1875, the use of fire hoses was then possible. When Boulder Hose Company No. 1 formed in July of that year, its twenty men went into training, for these sturdy firefighters literally ran to each fire dragging water carts behind them. They wore dark blue shirts and bought a 1,200-pound hose cart, or "jumper," for $1,000. One of their first actions was to meet with the Phoenix group to plan an immense ball to raise money for a fire alarm bell.

The next hose company, Macky Hose No. 2, formed on January 5, 1877, was so named because financier Andrew Macky put up the money for the uniforms. They were of bright blue opera flannel trimmed with gold braid and had a flaring, gold-buttoned cape. The men wore white belts; their cone-shaped white hats were trimmed with gilt, and each officer had his name in gilt letters on his hat. Their hose cart, built in Boulder, was bright carmine with gold and white stripes. When the cart was stored at 1000 Broadway in 1906, a high wind toppled the building, and the fire cart rolled down Pennsylvania Avenue to its destruction.

In addition to the yearly balls and other social events sponsored by the hose companies, A.J. Macky

The martial bearing of the Macky Hose Company, stretched across Pearl Street at Twelfth (Broadway), 1887. This fire fighting unit was sponsored by financier A.J. Macky, who stands in the center of the group in his top hat. *J.B. Sturtevant photo, A.A. Paddock Collection*

The Champions of 1896. This hose company includes runner George Fonda, front row, second from left. Their trainer, Bob Davis, is second row, extreme right. *A.A. Paddock Collection*

There's no fire! The Langford Hose Team has its turn down Pearl Street for the day's trophy. *J.B. Sturtevant photo, A.A. Paddock Collection*

entertained his group each year on New Year's Day. The *Herald* reported that "while the delicacies were being enjoyed the Italian band enlivened the occasion with 'music's voluptuous swell.' After dinner the room was cleared and for an hour the fire laddies and their wives, sweethearts, etc., indulged in a pleasant dance."32

In 1878, the East Boulder Hose Company was formed, but the group was never as active as the first two. The Buckingham Hook and Ladder Company had brief mention in newspapers of the 1880s. Highland Hose Company, organized in 1894, served the area around Highland School.

As the hose companies became expert at their jobs, they began to compete with one another to see who could do his job the fastest. Boulder Hose No. 1 won a silver urn and tray in Georgetown during the summer of 1877. Five men ran 400 feet, pulling a 1,175-pound wagon in 34½ seconds. The same group won the Colorado championship in 1886 for running 700 feet in 36½ seconds, dragging the fire wagon behind them. Macky Hose No. 2 won the world's record in Greeley in 1890 in the "dry hose" contest, and Boulder Hose No. 1 achieved the world's record at Cañon City in 1896 for the "wet hose" contest, finishing in 30⅖ seconds.

Although these early volunteer firemen were referred to as "boys" or "laddies," many of them were from the cream of Boulder society. Their exciting tournaments were enjoyed by all, as were their balls and parades. When the fire bell sounded, Boulder's "gallant fire boys" raced to fires (with the town's hero-worshipping young boys running alongside them) where "the flames subsided like magic."33 Since the firemen's elections of officers were far more hotly contested than those for city officials, it appears that Boulderites had a higher regard for the firemen than they had for the town trustees. By 1876, the fire companies elected their chiefs, who served without pay. O.E. Henry was the first such volunteer chief.

One of the town's worst fires started during another wind storm the day after Christmas 1883. Tin roofs blew away, and the bell-and-hose tower on Boulder Fire Station No. 1 (1038 Pearl Street) fell down, the heavy alarm bell crashing through the room of the station itself. The downtown fire demolished a number of small businesses at Broadway and Pearl streets—two saloons, a grocery, a restaurant, a dry goods store, a clothing store, and law offices. Although Boulder winds "helped" the fire along, an arsonist may have started the blaze. In fact, arson was often mentioned as a possible cause for fire. Temperance-minded residents threatened to burn down the Boulder City Brewery from time to time; in fact, a fire did break out there in 1883. Some buildings could not be

Victorian ladies enjoy the spring thaw along Boulder Creek. In the background, across the creek, is the home of Martha and J.A. Maxwell, site of Eben Fine Park. At right is Yount's mill. *A.A. Paddock Collection*

saved, for they were beyond the reach of the hoses. Thus, on June 14, 1878, the White Rock mill burned to the ground, and in March 1899, Sternberg's flour mill ("Lily White Flour") located on the banks of Boulder Creek also burned.

Boulder firemen had to deal with low water pressure, ice in the hydrants, and split hoses damaged by mildew. Further, some citizens criticized the "fire laddies." However, the *Boulder County Herald* stood by the "boys" in 1885, writing with some asperity,

> Too lazy to take hold of the ropes and help, too dainty to get into the mud, too effeminate to act the part of men, these lung testers could walk or run along the sidewalks to see the sights, but they could not exhibit enough manliness to help the boys along. They ought to be ashamed of themselves.[34]

When it became apparent that a building was needed to house fire equipment, the town bought Erik Anderson's building on the northwest corner of Twelfth and Front streets (Broadway and Walnut streets) for $1,800. For a time, all of the fire equipment was housed there, in addition to the water department and the board of trustees; two jail cells were in the basement. When the Macky Company was formed, the town added another building to the complex and built a bell tower (the tower was tall enough to drain the fire hose after each use), which was dedicated with champagne just after Christmas of 1877. Four years later, the trustees bought a little two-story building at 1921 Fourteenth Street (site of the Colorado Building), and the trustees, together with the Macky Hose Company and Phoenix Hook and Ladder, moved in. (The police stayed behind in "the pit" at 1018 Pearl Street.) There were bedrooms for the firefighters, and a sixty-foot bell tower rose above the roof.

By 1882, Chief Coulehan saw to it that the Boulder Hose Company had its own building at 1038 Pearl Street, next to the jail. (This building was to become Fire Station No. 1.) Brussels carpet, installed here and there in the building, added touches of elegance. The company purchased an alarm bell for $166 from proceeds of one of its many balls. Fire hydrants were installed a few at a time; by 1887, there were thirty-six. Ten years later, the Gamewell fire system, consisting of twelve alarm boxes, had been installed, with the alarms scattered throughout a growing town. Because the fire bells could not be heard at any great distance, eventually a fire whistle was mounted on the roof of the Boulder Electric Light Company. By 1899, the ultimate in modernity was reached when Fire Station No. 1 got a telephone, which meant speedier response to fires.

Downtown Boulder from roof of Central School. Congregational Church in near left background. *1880s photo, Edna Harkins Collection*

Chapter Seven

"One of my very early memories was of crying because mother would not let me go down to see a horse thief hanged."[1] Thus, W.H. Burger recalled his early life in Boulder during the 1880s and 1890s in a memoir that he wrote for the Boulder Historical Society. (Professor Burger was born in Caribou, and his mother, who followed successive silver and gold strikes throughout the region, ran boarding houses and hotels in a number of mining camps before settling in Boulder as manager of Boulder House.)

At the first sign of spring, young boys removed their shoes for the season. (Young girls no longer had the freedom to roam that they had enjoyed in the 1860s and 1870s but remained "sheltered" at home.) "The streets were thick with droppings from horses and mules—and millions of flies abounded...."[2] No matter, bare feet went everywhere, even climbing on mountain trails. Young Burger's summer job was to herd the family cows. He went barefoot into the hills with a pinto pony, a dog, and a slingshot to aim at rabbits, gophers, and chipmunks. In spring, boys loved to climb newly planted silver maples downtown to "suck the sweetish sap that oozed out."[3]

They swam in the yellow muddy water of the clay pits south of town. "Clay was a source of joy to a Boulder boy,"[4] wrote Burger. It was "carefully wetted and pounded to the right consistency; then a small wad of it was pressed tightly to the tip of a willow switch and 'flipped.'"[5] Citizens were not happy when mudballs hit their houses. Burger remembers "a crowd of us being chased by Tone Arnett, who had been hit, though a half-block distant, and by Lige Forsythe, who objected to having his freshly painted buggies splattered."[6] Hot tar, oozing from flagstone sidewalks, also made excellent trajectory weapons. Moreover, one could chew the tar and be certain of offending the teacher with a smile of black teeth. At school, Burger was fascinated with Professor Webb, who told his classes stories of military prison life during the Civil War. The teacher maintained a spittoon, which he used frequently and accurately. Outside school, the boys chewed too; the *Herald* complained, "A little eight year old boy of Boulder chews tobacco as he would so much cole slaw."[7]

Meticulous washing, starching, and ironing led to this portrait. *Rowland Collection*

Portrait of another era. Courthouse block on Pearl Street, 1900. National State Bank is in center. Note umbrellas over some of the wagons. *A.A. Paddock Collection*

Is something cooking on the small stove at the tent's entrance? The gentleman at right holds a violin. *A.A. Paddock Collection*

View of Boulder from Sunset Hill looking southwest, 1899. Mount St. Gertrude Academy, left center background. Note gravestones of unfenced Columbia Cemetery, right center. Courthouse, extreme right center. *J.B. Sturtevant photo, A.A. Paddock Collection*

Street fakirs were a common sight downtown. Under flaring glass torches, the peddlers gave entertaining spiels for their patent medicine cures. Some of these salesmen were also ventriloquists. Young boys would also get up early to watch circus tents go up in the vacant lot on Pearl Street between Tenth and Eleventh streets, for the unloading of the animals could not be missed. Two shacks south of town (site of Mount St. Gertrude Academy) excited the imagination of boys, as miners' dynamite was stored there and occasionally exploded, much to their delight.

In winter, bobsledding down Mapleton Hill was very popular. For those who had no bobsled but who were especially hardy, sailing down the hill on a "jumper" was exciting, if not dangerous. A "jumper" was made from the curved stave of a whiskey barrel. A short post was nailed to the stave for steering, and another cross-piece was used for the seat. If properly handled, the jumper could cruise over bushes and rocks. Ice skating was also dangerous because of the warm spells that melted ice; nevertheless, skaters could be seen on Boulder Creek, Farmers Ditch (the water ran in the winter also) or Weisenhorn's Lake near Valmont (adjacent to the present Public Service Company plant). When Captain Clinton Tyler announced in the papers that his lake (on his estate at 2940 Twentieth Street) was safe for skating, Boulder's young people gathered there.

Roller-skating indoors at the rink at Fourteenth and Spruce streets could be indulged in for five cents an evening. The *Boulder Herald* announced the grand opening of the rink in September 1884 and noted that Boulder's youngsters were practicing their skating skills in Allen's block; their noise sounded "like a defeated candidate rumbling."[8] As the Boulder Brass Band played, skaters participated in a Grand March; prizes were given for unique homemade costumes. First prize for ladies was won by Annie Stevens, whose cream-colored skating dress was decorated with black musical notes. George Fonda won the men's first prize; he came as a huge beer bottle. The *Herald* instituted a new column called "At the Rink," which included social notes of Boulder's skating society. The *Herald* also noted that Gold Hill had its own skating rink now; Erie's was under construction. On October 13, 1886, the big news in roller skating was that electric lights had been installed at The Rink. This devotion to roller-skating must have been short-lived, because the newspapers of the 1890s spoke wistfully of the pastime, hoping for renewed interest in the entertainment.

Boulder's first "auditorium" was the old roller-skating rink. Called Rink Auditorium, L.C. Paddock of the *Daily Camera*, in his characteristically florid style, described it in 1892, saying "the amphitheatre at Rome was a woodshed compared to Boulder's opera house with its tasselated floors of native Spruce and its Etruscan dome with its itaglio of nail holes"... with "space intervening between the planks to admit of splendid ventilation." Another popular meeting place was Berlin's (later called Feeney's) on the second floor of the building at Broadway and Pearl (south-

A roller skating rink at Fourteenth and Spruce streets, later called Rink Auditorium, where operas and lectures were given. *A.A. Paddock Collection*

west corner). This hall was booked for lecturers, revivalists, dances, and grand opera. Baseball games were still frequent; almost everyone came out to watch the hose races by the town's volunteer firefighters. Each year, large crowds were attracted to the fairs held at Pine and Twenty-eighth streets.

Boulder's young boys hung around the livery stables during the winter, listening to stories of the hostlers and watching the stage coaches come and go. A favorite spot was the hayloft; one could swing into the hay from a trapeze overhead. The boys could also hear stories from the loft not meant for their ears. Now and then, a hostler would send a boy with a dime and a pail to the saloon "to rush the growler."*9 Five cents was for the bucket of beer, and five cents was for the boy. As the youngsters went about town, they were aware of the consumptives sunning themselves on bright corners. Some seekers of the sun were badly crippled due to accidents in the mines.

Boulder was still considered ugly. Although most homes were built of wood, some with two stories, a few brick houses stood out. A number of log cabins survived. Mapleton Avenue (then called Hill Street) had no permanent buildings as yet; two or three shacks were surrounded by Fred Squires' grazing cows. In 1882, when the city handed over its town square to the county, a handsome courthouse with a bell tower was built on the site. As the town grew, the fire bells were no longer used for an alarm because they could not be heard. The Women's Club of Boulder insisted that one of the old alarm bells be installed in the courthouse tower. (The other bell went to a church in Nederland in 1915.) Boulder's wooden sidewalks never were acceptable, and by 1898 the old plank walkways were so unbearable that the city fathers ordered them to be removed. Flagstone walks had been on Pearl Street since 1886. Some of this flagstone on neighborhood streets survives today. Pearl Street, itself unpaved, continued to be the dividing line between "better" and "poorer" families. East Pearl, beyond Fourteenth Street, was known as Culver's Flats (Robert Culver of Gold Hill owned the land), and the town's poor lived there, being regularly subjected to spring flooding from the runoff down Boulder Creek. The town's few black families lived within a small area near Water (Canyon Boulevard) and Goss Streets, from Nineteenth and Twenty-second streets.

Many trees, most of them silver maples, were planted during the 1890s. James P. Maxwell planted 200 silver maples along Hill Street (Mapleton). Each sapling was protected by a wooden box so that horses would not nibble the trees to death. "Boulder was a mighty dark town in the early 80s after the sun had set."[10] Soon a few kerosene lamps lined Pearl Street.

*"Rush" means "to work." "Growler" is a bucket or pail. To take a growler to a saloon, have it filled with beer, and carry it home.

Some electricity had been used in town since 1886, but proper lighting of the streets came slowly; by the 1890s, a few arc lights had been installed on an experimental basis. Residents complained that with the lights would come bugs. But the *Herald* welcomed street lighting, saying, "when the train comes in from Denver at night, these lights will loom up grandly and impress everybody, strangers especially."[11]

By 1889, in order to get free mail delivery, Boulder went "urban" and numbered its lots and houses for the first time. For some reason, this numbering was not successful, because in 1893, the lots were numbered again (making the tracing of present addresses difficult). City directories now listed a proper address rather than the vague "east on Pine Street." Street signs made of spruce posts sunk into the ground at each corner were common by 1896. Although telephones were available by 1881, few residents had them, for they were considered a luxury; no vital service such as a school, police, or fire department used telephones until the turn of the century. To induce residents to install a telephone, the Colorado Telephone Company advertised with this poem:

"Hello"
Why don't you have a telephone?
You will find it just the thing
With which to call the grocerman
And tell him what to bring.

The caterer and the butcher,
Perhaps you'd like to call.
The whole dinner you can order,
And never leave the hall.

If baby has the measles,
Or you think he's very sick,
Just telephone for Doctor,
He'll get there twice as quick.

One thing you need I'm certain,
To make your home just right.
That's the ever ready telephone,
To use both day and night.[12]

Two railroad lines started to serve Boulder City in 1873 after several earlier attempts had failed due to financial problems. The Colorado Central brought the first train in from Golden in April of that year; by September, the Denver and Boulder Valley Line had instituted service. At first, trains did not come into town, and one sent a carriage to pick up visitors at the train depot, located east of Boulder. Eventually, a rail spur ran along Water Street (sometimes called Railroad Street, now called Canyon Boulevard) to Ninth Street. From the 1870s onward, group after group received a franchise to operate a horse-drawn streetcar line, but twenty years passed before one was in actual operation. When a line was finally established in 1891, it ran for one year only. The horse-drawn double-decker car, open at both ends, ran along tracks laid on Pearl Street between Eighth and Twentieth streets. Many small boys enjoyed the streetcar's first run on September 13, 1891, but they, as well as their parents, neglected to pay the five-cent fare to Mr. Roots, the conductor. This continuing oversight, plus the mess made by the horses, caused the line to fail; one year later, the city ripped out the tracks.

Bicycles were used as early as 1869 in Boulder. The *Boulder County Pioneer* reported that blacksmith Peter Jasper and friends were hard at work building a three-wheeled velocipede, adding that the "bicycle in its first management is said to be worse than a broncho, but we don't believe it."[13] News must have been sparse that spring, for the *Pioneer* continued with regular bulletins on the progress with the velocipede. As soon as the "builders" would mount the device, it would weave around in circles and then collapse. By May, however, the *Pioneer* reported success. The men had "tamed the animal until it has become quite docile and tractable."[14]

By the 1890s, Boulder was a bicycle town. When the Boulder Wheel Club was organized, the group indicated that special clothing was to be worn while cycling: a gray suit, black stockings, and a gray cap. When the club was "on parade," the bicycle was to be decorated with crimson ribbons woven through the spokes. On Sunday, April 23, 1893, eighteen members of the Boulder Wheel Club started for Louisville on their first long outing with the idea of circling around through Lafayette, Erie, Canfield, then to Longmont, where they would board the train back to Boulder. One member missed the train and cycled back to Boulder alone.

Most of the men in Boulder wore overalls and heavy boots. Beards and mustaches were still fashionable, although the clean-shaven look would be more common by the turn of the century. The merchants wore suits with celluloid collars, and a stiff hat marked them as "upper class." However, because of the mud, their trousers were stuffed into heavy boots. A man who wore a frock coat was most apt to be a gambler. All wore long johns in winter; some men wore floor-length sleeping gowns at night. Others retired with their heavy clothing on to keep warm. Someone in the family had to get up in the middle of the night to see that the fire was still going.

Women wore bustles, rather large ones. Hoop skirts, so popular during the Civil War, were on their way out. Plainer garments were more practical in a town of muddy streets. Even so, the skirts were long and trailed in the mud or picked up tar from the new flagstone walks. High-button shoes, which were put

Two cyclists pose in front of the Boulder Railway at the Texado Park stop (Chautauqua), 1899. *J.B. Sturtevant photo, A.A. Paddock Collection*

A special occasion. *Rowland Collection*

A very mature-looking seventh grade on an outing in the mountains. *J.B. Sturtevant photo, A.A. Paddock Collection*

on and removed with a buttonhook, were the rule. Proper ladies did not "paint" their faces; however, a piece of red flannel, hidden away, would produce the desired effect when brushed across the lips and cheeks.

Boulder residents, as well as those in the mining camps above, did a lot of dancing, particularly in the winter. Dancing parties often lasted until dawn. The Virginia reel, the barn dance, the polka, and the quadrille were popular, and at the university, students were learning the two-step.

The little school that Abner Brown helped build and in which he taught was no longer big enough for the town's girls and boys. Anthony Arnett bought the building for a rental and moved it away (it burned down shortly thereafter, but a model of it can be seen in the Boulder Historical Society Museum) to make room for a brick-and-stone Central School, an elegant two-story building that cost $15,000. It was surrounded by a white picket fence and had room for 113 students. Still, within a few years an annex was required. Now the school

Yesterday's RTD? P.F. Little's Rapid Transit mail wagon bound for Salina, Gold Hill, and Ward. *A.A. Paddock Collection*

A Sunday excursion by tallyho, "The Columbine," up Boulder Canyon. S.R. Wheeler wearing duster, H.M. Wheeler on top, T.L. Clark, wife, and Alfred Wheeler sitting in back. *A.A. Paddock Collection*

Jay Church turning his stage around to carry members of a band to an engagement, 1890. *A.A. Paddock Collection*

A light snow covers University Hill as seen from Red Rocks. Extreme right near horizon, Chautauqua Auditorium. Mount St. Gertrude Academy is center. *A.A. Paddock Collection*

consisted of seven rooms. Grades one through twelve, a total of 720 students, were taught in the building. When the University of Colorado opened its doors in 1877, Central's top grades moved into Old Main to form a college preparatory department. Although fires broke out in Central School from time to time, the place was built to last, and it did last for 100 years.*

*Razed in the early 1970s to make way for a parking lot, this incident sparked the formation of the Historic Boulder group.

As the town grew, Pine Street School was built in 1882 to accommodate Central's overflow student population. Pine Street students corresponded with a favorite poet, John Greenleaf Whittier, and after this exchange of letters, petitioned the school board to change the school's name to Whittier in 1903. The town's advanced students were using the preparatory school on the campus to such an extent that citizens around the state were becoming very critical. Boulder was using the university for its high school, and there were hard feelings about it. Moreover, the university

Boulder's first school was replaced by Central School on the same site in 1872. Note the young trees planted in front of the building. For a time, the building housed all twelve grades. *W.H. Jackson photo, A.A. Paddock Collection*

"Upward and Onward—Always Busy" graced the walls of this Pine Street School room (now Whittier). In the background, his white cuffs showing, is Principal William V. Casey, soon to become Superintendent of Schools. *A.A. Paddock Collection*

William V. Casey, Boulder's Superintendent of Schools for forty years, 1894-1934. *Western Historical Collections, University of Colorado at Boulder*

wanted to get out of the high school business, because it took considerable energy by the faculty members who wanted to concentrate on developing a college curriculum. Thus, when Mapleton School was built in Fred Squires' pasture in 1888, a "sort of a high school"[15] with a combined ninth and tenth grade was housed there for a time, in addition to the elementary grades and an office for the superintendent. Students spilled out of the space almost immediately; some had to sit on apple crates in the aisles. (The following year, the school board passed a resolution authorizing a high school.) By 1892, overflow classes were held downtown and in the basement of First Congregational Church. Even the additional construction of Highland School in 1891 did not ease the situation for any great length of time. Those who were studying high school subjects to prepare for college moved over to the third floor of Highland. Because of an 1893 agreement with the University of Colorado (the university would pay some of the expenses), the city would operate the State Preparatory School. Students could choose one of three courses of study—the classical (Latin and Greek), the scientific, or the Latin-scientific. Highland School was essentially an elementary school, however, and too great an age range was housed in one building. It became imperative that State Preparatory School have its own building. Construction started in 1895 on the southwest corner of Seventeenth and Pearl streets. When Jefferson School was completed in

Schools were so crowded in 1888 that Miss Jessie Gates taught her class in one of the rooms of the old *Camera* building. Note the magnificent hats. *Fecher photo, A.A. Paddock Collection*

Taking a break on the construction site of Mapleton School, 1888. The stone is from the Lyons quarry. *A.A. Paddock Collection*

Mapleton School as it looked in 1907. The fountain in front of the school is in place, built by the children and their principal, Miss Lovelace. *Edna Harkins Collection*

Susan Mary Lovelace, principal at Mapleton School in the 1890s, first principal of North Side Intermediate School (Casey Junior High School), is remembered for her bright red hair, flowing green veils, and strict discipline of children. *Boulder Public Library from the A.A. Paddock Collection*

1899 at the same location, it, too, had elementary grades in most of its six rooms for a time, but the school was converted to a house a growing State Preparatory School that educated high school youngsters until 1936. The first headmaster, Dr. Henry White Callahan, instituted, among other traditions, the custom of head boy and head girl.*

*See Appendix for a list of educational institutions and their construction dates.

A private school was built in 1892. Sister Mary Lumina and other Sisters of Charity were responsible for the construction of Mount St. Gertrude Academy, replacing the dynamite shacks. The sisters advertised the school as a perfect place for "young children and girls who desire health as well as a primary education."

Before 1889, public school teachers were paid on an A, B, or C basis. "A" was "excellent" at seventy dollars per month, "B" was "needs improvement"

When Mapleton School opened its doors in 1889, these youngsters comprised the first fifth grade. Teacher Miss Johnson is at the back of the group. *Elizabeth Ricketts Collection*

1895 scene from Mapleton School, looking southeast. Note snow in Farmers Ditch, courthouse in background, Congregational Church to the left. *J.B. Sturtevant photo, A.A. Paddock Collection*

Boulder from Lovers (Sunset) Hill with first Sacred Heart of Jesus Church in foreground; Mapleton School and Klingler home on nearby hill are on south side of Mapleton Avenue. *J.B. Sturtevant photo, A.A. Paddock Collection*

The children of Highland School in 1906. A careful look at early school photos will show that Boulder had a small black population. *Elizabeth Ricketts Collection*

Three cadets at State Preparatory School, around 1904. Left to right: Frank Moorhead (soon to be city attorney), Arthur Roose, and Art Streich. *A.A. Paddock Collection*

at sixty-five dollars, and "C" was "quality unknown" at fifty dollars. One year's experience was required, and married women, unless they were widowed, were not allowed to teach. The principal also taught classes and was paid one hundred dollars a month. Primary students paid monthly fees of $1.00, and secondary students paid $1.50 each month. Corporal punishment was the rule; special discipline cases were referred to the board of education. Most schools had segregated playgrounds, one for the boys and one for the girls. By 1884, classrooms were graded, that is, children were separated by grade level—a radical innovation for that day.

Great attention was given to the celebration of holidays, particularly May Day, when elaborate parades and programs took place. After kings and queens were crowned, the children performed intricate dances in front of their parents. (Before the 1900s, the school board questioned the propriety of "folk dances.") The school janitor raised the flag for Washington's Birthday, Lincoln's Birthday, Decoration Day, and the Fourth of July—days that we still celebrate. But in that time, school children also celebrated Longfellow's Birthday, Arbor Day (third Friday in April), School Board Election, Discovery of America Day (October 12), William Jennings Bryan's Birthday (November 3), and Whittier's Birthday (December 17). By the turn of the century, Dewey Day (May 1) and Flag Day (June 14) were added to the list.

First graders learned to print and write script at the same time that they learned to read. They also were expected to conquer punctuation and capital letters as well as memorize Eugene Field's "Little Boy Blue," Tennyson's "What Does Little Birdie Say?," "God Bless Our Native Land," and numerous Bible stories. Bulletins to teachers warned that they were to "allow no writing with the left hand unless physical deformity makes it impossible to write with the right hand."[16]

Each student brought a slate and rag from home. (Some used a sponge to erase their sums, but that was considered "sissy.") By the third grade, the student knew his Roman numerals and studied the mysteries of the adjective and adverb, as well as geography and hygiene. He had memorized Longfellow's "The Children's Hour," Shakespeare's "Hark, Hark, the Lark," and could recite the Twenty-third Psalm. By fifth grade, the student was expected to memorize Tennyson's "Charge of the Light Brigade," Whittier's "Barbara Frietchie," and "Columbia, Gem of the Ocean." By eighth grade, he read *Rip Van Winkle* and studied U.S. history and something called hygenic physiology. He knew by heart Kipling's "Recessional," Whitman's "O Captain, My Captain," Julia Ward Howe's "Battle Hymn of the Republic," the Gettysburg Address, the Preamble to the Constitution, and Webster's "Reply to Hayne." He was ready to start Latin and Greek, advanced mathematics, physics, botany, literature, and prepare himself for college entrance.

Although Boulder City had been approved as the site for a university in October 1861 by the territorial legislature, it was sixteen years before the doors of Old Main officially opened to receive forty-four preparatory students in the fall of 1877. Boulder had some competition for the site. In 1864, nearby Burlington (a town later absorbed by growing Longmont) petitioned the legislature for a university. By 1870, twenty acres had been contributed for a site at Boulder, and, in an effort to get the legislature to put up some money, more lands were acquired south of town. Finally, in 1874, Colorado Territory appropriated $15,000 for a university with the provision that Boulder, too, raise $15,000. Marinus Smith,* David Nichols,

---
*The varied activities and energies of "Marine" Smith, a Mexican War veteran, certainly belied the Reverend Nathan Thompson's description of him as "seldom known to work" and "constitutionally tired."[17]

Was the tallest girl in school "Queen of the May?" May Day at Highland School. *Elizabeth Ricketts Collection*

Dancing around the May pole at Highland School. Note the giant hair bows. *Elizabeth Ricketts Collection*

Costumes for these holiday dances were made at home.
Edna Harkins Collection

Making a spring garden was part of the curriculum.
Edna Harkins Collection

and Andrew Macky led the drive and convinced 104 Boulder families to contribute to the matching fund.

By September 1875, the cornerstone for Old Main was laid on a windy mesa south of town. It was to be a gala occasion with 2,000 invited guests, but snow came early that year. By December, with three stories completed, work on the building's bell tower began. In February, however, high winds destroyed the bell tower; a new design called for a lower tower on Old Main. With another $15,000 territorial appropriation, Old Main got a furnace, gas fixtures, outbuildings, fences, a sewer, and a 2,929-foot water line up the mesa. (Boulder decided that the university's water would be supplied free of charge.)

When Colorado achieved statehood in 1876, the university became a land-grant institution, receiving seventy-two more sections of land. A heavy roof of slate was added to Old Main, but incoming first President Joseph A. Sewall of Illinois State University feared for the safety of the building and ordered the roof to be replaced with lighter cedar shingles. When Sewall and his family arrived in July 1877, his daughter Jane described her first view of Old Main: "It loomed before us gaunt and alone in the pitiless clear light.

Young trees circle Old Main, the first university building, constructed in 1875. *1889 photo, J.B. Sturtevant photo, A.A. Paddock Collection*

No tree nor shrub nor any human habitation was in sight. Vast expanses of rock and sagebrush were its only surrounding."[18]

Opening day, September 5, 1877, was noisy and memorable. Boulder's three fire companies, in full dress uniform, marched in front of the distinguished guests, which included the governor of the new state and newly appointed regents, "bearded, high silk hatted and solemn as Egyptian mortuary figures."[19] Gilman's Brass Band played "Onward Christian Soldiers," and someone pealed the bell, which lay on Old Main's front steps, not yet installed in the tower. Justin Dow, professor of Latin and Greek, the only faculty member besides President Sewall, was on hand. Many visitors toured Old Main. The building served as living quarters for the Sewall family, for the janitor and his wife Selma, who occupied the basement. It also had classrooms for the students and, eventually, a university library—a $2,000 gift from banker Charles Buckingham. (When a chemistry laboratory was added, it was placed on the third floor so that the fumes from experiments could be carried away by the winds.) The visitors studied every room, including the indoor bathroom. They "stared with awe at the vast shining tin tub, at the marble washbowl and throne...all magnificently encased in polished wood."[20]

When Mary Rippon was considering an offer to teach here (she became the university's third faculty member and the first woman in the United States to teach at a state university), a minister visited her in Detroit and warned her that Old Main was built so poorly that it would "fall down and kill all within." However, Miss Rippon decided to come west when she heard about Buckingham's gift for a library and when she read about Colorado's wild flowers in *Atlantic Monthly*. When she arrived, Sewall met her at the station, saying, "How does it look to you?" Her reply was "Glorious!" President Sewall relaxed but told her, "My wife had told me you would not stay two days in this lonely place."[21] Miss Rippon stayed fifty-seven years as professor of French and German.

Mrs. Sewall, trying to soften the harsh desolation that surrounded Old Main, ordered fifty wagonloads of topsoil for grass and flowers. With the next wind, the topsoil was blown off the mesa, so she ordered another fifty wagonloads of soil. By 1881, she had managed to grow two acres of lawn and had planted

Mary Rippon, third faculty member at the university, first woman to teach at a state university in the United States, is remembered for her work to found a public library for Boulder. *Boulder Public Library from the A.A. Paddock Collection*

being threatened with expulsion from school if they did not do so. The controversial salute went: "We give our Head! and our Hearts! to God and Our Country! —One Country! One Language! One Flag!"

The manual required that, as the flag was presented to the students, they were to "seize" their seats and rise "as one" at a signal. They were to extend their right arm, "bent so as to touch the forehead lightly with the tip of the fingers of the right hand. The motion should be quick, but graceful, the elbow being kept down...." Boulder's Adventists, many of whom came from Puritan New England families, had no trouble with this part of the salute. But it was the "Sixth Signal" that they felt was in violation of their religious privacy. "The head is thrown slightly back, the face turned upwards, the countenance expresses deep reverence, the right arm is outstretched high in the air, the fingers of the right hand being held close together, the expression that of looking and pointing upwards. As the motion is accomplished, all will exclaim slowly and in reverential tones, "to God...."

Class of 1886: Clarence Pease, Vic Norton, Fred Chase, Ed Wolcott, and Judson Rowland. *J.B. Sturtevant photo, Rowland Collection*

trees and flowers. The university's development was modest but was beginning to attract attention. Crofutt's *Grip-Sack Guide to Colorado* for 1881 described the fledgling university as "particularly favorable to the exercise of the intellectual facilities." In 1882, six young men were graduated from the university with a ceremony appropriate to the first class. "Rocky Mountain Joe" Sturtevant painted a mural on one wall of the chapel in Old Main in their honor. By 1900, the faculty had grown to 80 and the student body to 433, and the preparatory school consisted of 356 students.

Members of the Seventh Day Adventist Church made educational news in 1897 when trouble erupted between them and the board of education. The board had just published a school manual called "The American Patriotic Salute." Adventists were patriotic, too, said Dr. E.D. Clark, but parts of the manual were "inconsistent with their beliefs." Adventists children at Mapleton School were being forced to use the name of God in their salute to the flag and were

In explaining the Adventist stand against the school board, the *Daily Camera* reported that "Seventh Day Adventists are uncompromisingly opposed to any and every union of church and state."[22] The *Camera*, sympathetic to the Adventist point of view, pointed out to its readers that Colorado state law prohibited "religious tests" in the classroom. The Adventists

Hale Science building has been added. The trees are taller. *J.B. Sturtevant photo, Boulder Historical Society*

Ella Tyler Whiteley, first woman to graduate from the university. *Boulder Public Library*

The men's dormitory at the new university (building is gone). *A.A. Paddock Collection*

One of the earliest fraternities on campus. Men who can be identified are: front row, left, Vic Norton; third from left Fred Chase, fourth from left, Gustave Beauregard Blake. *Rowland Collection*

Without a smile, four young fraternity men pose in front of a painted backdrop: Nat Chedsey, Ben Holstein, young Tyler, Frank Boyd. Note their feet. *A.A. Paddock Collection*

RICHARD HENRY WHITELEY,

BOULDER.

ATTORNEY AT LAW. EX-STATE SENATOR.

Richard H. Whiteley, Jr., university regent, expert in mining law, and state senator, built "The Poplars" at 1709 Pine Street in 1891. *Representative Men of Colorado*

Andrew J. Macky made a lot of money in Boulder and was a generous contributor to the university. *Western Historical Collections, University of Colorado at Boulder.*

Early drama group at the University of Colorado, 1900. *J.B. Sturtevant photo, Boulder Historical Society*

University Hill from the top of Old Main on campus. Columbia Cemetery is in background. *A.A. Paddock Collection*

were persistent and threatened to sue the school board. Finally, one year later, the board voted to eliminate the word "God" from the flag salute. For the next half century, Boulder students saluted the American flag in this way until the presidency of Dwight Eisenhower, who put the word "God" back in the salute to the flag.

There had been at least one Adventist in town since 1871, when Amy Dartt followed her daughters to Boulder and settled here.* Known as "Grandma" Dartt, a fearless missionary, she trudged in and out of Boulder's saloons, handing out religious tracts about her church. Grandma Dartt also walked from mining camp to settlement, handing out her literature to the miners. As others of her faith settled here, they established the Seventh Day Adventist Church in 1879. By 1895, the Adventists had acquired ninety acres of land on the hill above Fourth and Mapleton and built a sanitarium there, modeled after the Kellogg sanitarium in Michigan, a facility that treated tubercular. The main building was five stories high and was surrounded by a powerhouse, a bakery, a laundry, a dairy barn, and, later, a dormitory for the nurses. For a number of years, a little lake graced the front of the sanitarium, but some free spirits decided to go swimming there. The conservative elders of the church frowned upon such activity and drained the lake; now this area serves as a parking lot for Boulder Memorial Hospital.

A unique display of stuffed animals, housed in what was called the Rocky Mountain Museum, was started by one of Grandma Dartt's daughters, Martha Maxwell. The museum opened in 1874 with a brass band and hoopla in the A.J. Macky building (site of the National State Bank addition) on Pearl Street. Reporter Helen Hunt Jackson gave readers of the *New York Independent* her first impressions:

> I went to the museum expecting to be much amused by a grotesque exhibition of stiff and ungainly corpses...I stopped short on the threshold in utter amazement...there is found stuffed owls, eagles, bison, deer and many other species all executed with artistry and reality.[23]

---

*Her daughter Mary married Nathan Thompson, minister of the First Congregational Church. Her daughter Elizabeth married Hal Sayre, another Boulder pioneer. Her daughter Martha married J.A. Maxwell, a businessman and road builder.

Martha and James A. Maxwell were among the first parties to come down from Baraboo, Wisconsin, to settle in the Boulder area. She was twenty-two and he was forty-two. Mrs. Maxwell had always been interested in animals and plants, had roamed her native Pennsylvania countryside with her grandmother, and had learned to sew expertly when she was four years old. As a girl of ten, when she saw a rattlesnake coiled near her little sister, she ran to the house, got a gun, steadied it on a rock, and shot the rattler. Her stepfather, Josiah Dartt, was so impressed with her quick actions that he taught her how to shoot, an unlikely avocation for a young girl in those days. J.A. and Martha Maxwell had a daughter, Mabel, whom they left temporarily in Wisconsin with Grandma Dartt, and moved to Colorado, following Maxwell's son James P. Maxwell, one of his six grown children. Mrs. Maxwell discovered that a squatter on their newly acquired lands near Boulder was a German taxidermist; she asked him to teach her how to stuff animals. At first he was willing, but when he realized she might be competition for him, he refused to instruct her. The Maxwells evicted him, but not before Mrs. Maxwell took some of his materials to study. When she had learned enough of the art of taxidermy, she prepared some 1,200 animals (shooting even the larger species herself), but the family finances were such in 1870 that she was forced to sell the entire collection to Shaw's Botanical Gardens in St. Louis. With the money, the Maxwells bought a modest cottage on Boulder Creek (site of Eben Fine Park). While Maxwell interested himself in the cultivation of fruit trees,

Diminuitive Martha Maxwell taught herself the art of taxidermy and revolutionized museum display methods. Her specimens were housed in Boulder's Rocky Mountain Museum for a time. *A.A. Paddock Collection*

Early scene at the Sanitarium (now Boulder Memorial Hospital), built in 1895. The little lake in front of the tubercular facility was drained when a number of free spirits decided to swim there. *A.A. Paddock Collection*

Mrs. Maxwell started a new collection. She began to exhibit at county fairs and even journeyed to California for her animals. No mountain was too high, no area too remote to stop Martha Maxwell from collecting a new specimen.*

Even though she was referred to as the "Colorado huntress" (she aimed with her left eye), Mrs. Maxwell was a shy, feminine woman, four feet, eleven inches tall, and barely weighing 100 pounds. In 1876, the Boulder taxidermist took her collection to the Philadelphia Exposition; her lifelike exhibits, ranging from hummingbirds to grizzly bears, caused a sensation. "Did she kill them buf'lo?" "Did she poison 'em?" "Does she live in that cave?" "Is she an Indian?" "If she's married, why ain't it called Mr. Maxwell's collection?"[24] The petite matron stood quietly in the middle of her exhibit, gun at her side, with a modest sign in front inscribed, "Woman's Work."

Because she arranged her animals in a natural setting, *Harper's Magazine* for November 1876 called Mrs. Maxwell's taxidermy fresh and natural. The magazine predicted that her work would influence the way in which museums would display animals for the public. And so it has. Throughout her life, Mrs. Maxwell was a vegetarian. When she was asked why, then, she shot animals, she replied, "There isn't a day that you don't tacitly consent to have some creature killed that you may eat... I leave it to you. Which is the more cruel? To kill to eat or to kill to immortalize."[25]

---

*Mrs. Maxwell's sister, Mary Dartt (Thompson) wrote a charming account, *On the Plains and Among the Peaks, or How Mrs. Maxwell Made Her Natural History Collection*, published in 1879.

Chapter Eight

*The hard working miner his dangers are great,
So many while mining have met their sad fate,
While doing their duty as all miners do,
Shut out from the daylight and darling ones too.*[1]

The profitable mining of coal had to wait for the establishment of railroad lines across the eastern part of Boulder County. When they came, the coal business came alive, too. C.C. Welch of Golden looked over the region and hired Louis Nawatny to prospect for coal. Nawatny found coal 200 feet under settler David Kerr's farm land; Welch bought Kerr out and established the Welch mine. Nawatny also bought up the land nearby. As other coal mines opened, attracting more and more people, Nawatny registered a town plat on October 24, 1878, calling it Louisville after himself. In two years, 500 people had settled there; Nawatny was on hand to greet the newcomers and sell them some real estate. The Welch mine employed 175 men, the Rex #1 employed 48 miners, and the Hecla hired 19 men. Four years later, the Louisville population doubled. Eventually, twelve mines were to operate in the Louisville area. By now, Marshall's mining was most active and included such mines as the Peerless, the Graham, the Red Ash, the Black Diamond, the Fox,* the Peterson, the Cracker Jack, and the Mitchell. There were two mines at Canfield.

John Simpson opened the first coal seam at Lafayette in 1887; five years later, five mines were producing coal. Two hundred homes had been built as well as several rooming houses to accommodate the single miners.

As news of the coal discoveries spread, immigrants from Poland, Italy, Greece, and France joined the Welsh, Scots, and English miners who had been there since the 1860s, all of them accustomed to working underground. Some of the immigrants were used as strike breakers until they understood how they were being used. Their numbers increased until the 1920s, when the coal industry was the largest employer (1,000 men) in Boulder County. One to two million tons of coal had been pulled from the Northern Coal Field, a relatively small field.

As the miners tunneled underground, they braced chambers with timbers. They built entries two by two, with these twin entrances occurring every twenty-five to thirty feet. Storage facilities, called "tipples," were built to accommodate the coal when it was brought to the surface. As the tunneling continued, life underground resembled that of a small city. Mules used to pull the coal cars to the top were stabled underground; with the exception of the first and last years of their existence, the animals spent their lives in the dark chambers. Danger from cave-ins was always present, because the mine owners were reluctant to spend money to replace rotting timbers. Boulder's coal contained more moisture than that found in other fields; hence, it could not be stored for long, because it could explode by spontaneous combustion. Again, mine owners did not like to spend money to keep the chambers free from coal dust.

When explosions did occur, and they did, the "black death," or carbon monoxide fumes, could quickly snuff out the life of a miner or a mule. Underground fires were common; miners stored "brattice" cloths (partitions that were hung in the mines in the event of fire) below which would help to seal off a fire so that oxygen from above could not

---
*Although the name of this mine gave Marshall its nickname, "Foxtown," less charitable people called Marshall "Dagotown."

Marshall as it looked in 1875. The town's nickname was "Foxtown," after the nearby Fox coal mine. *Western Historical Collections, University of Colorado at Boulder*

Dressed in their Sunday best, these coal miners obviously enjoy having J.B. Sturtevant take their picture on Point Lookout near Marshall (Langford). *A.A. Paddock Collection*

Three coal miners pause in their work in a tunnel near Marshall. The lines at the top of the photo show cracks to the original glass negative. *A.A. Paddock Collection*

fan the flames. When railroad cars were used underground, brake failure was also a threat to life. Runaway railroad cars were a nightmare for the miners.

In addition to the noise of chugging locomotives above the ground, residents listened for the sounds of the mine whistles. Each mine had its distinctive whistle. A change in shifts was announced by whistle. If there was to be work next day, that news was announced by whistle. And if an accident occurred, that was also told by seven short blasts on the whistle. The women knew all the whistles and thus knew which mine entrance to run to. Often the whistle was not even necessary, for many of the explosions were felt above ground. In 1936, eight men were killed by an explosion in the Monarch #2 mine at Louisville. Ten men were just coming off the graveyard shift at six in the morning when the blast occurred. Twenty minutes later, there would have been 100 men in the Monarch. Three men "ran like rabbits" up the ladders and got out, but miner Joe Jaramillo, thinking he had left a $900 money belt below, went back to get it and did not return. (The money was found safe in the bank.)

Considering the almost constant dangers to the miners and the apparent callousness of most of the owners, it is a small wonder that miners made a daily stop for pails of beer on the way home. The women drank, too, although not openly. Children were sent to the back door of saloons to replenish an empty pail for a lady drinker.

Coal could be found at 50 feet, but some of the tunnels went as deep as 500 feet into the ground, for the better quality coal was deeper. Most of Marshall, Lafayette, and Louisville lie over honeycombs of empty coal chambers. Louisville is built over the Acme mine; only the northwest corner of the town is built on solid ground. The Simpson mine lies under Lafayette; Superior is built over the Industrial mine. Along Colorado Highway 36 are spots where subsidence (the uneven settling of the earth caused by the underground collapse of empty coal chambers) causes the need for frequent repairs. Houses settle and tip miles from the mine entrance, for hundreds of miles of black chambers run beneath the ground in eastern Boulder County.

Although a young man of fourteen was considered ready for the mines, some boys of nine or ten were already experienced underground. Miners had to buy their own equipment and were responsible for its repair. They paid for their own blasting powder, and if an accident occurred, they paid the doctor. At first, the miners were paid in script for each ton mined (rental of a company house had already been taken out of their pay). With the script, they bought groceries at the company store. Should the miner in later life suffer from black lung disease, no benefits came from either the mine owner or the government.

Problems between management and the miners occurred all over the country at this time, and Boulder County was no exception. Most of the owners would not bargain with the unions. At Erie, the miners struck for better conditions in 1871, but strike-breakers quickly moved in and ended the strike. In November 1903, the miners at Louisville went on strike. The workers were treated to a visit from Mother Jones, a seventy-four-year-old labor organizer for the United Mine Workers* who spoke with a bawdy tongue and "fervid eloquence."[2] Compared to other coal fields, however, the Northern Coal Field was easily organized. A contract between management and the United Mine Workers was signed in July 1908 which provided for a closed shop, a controversial eight-hour day, and some improvements in mine safety. Even so, the miners in the Louisville-Lafayette area struck again in 1910. The strike lasted for five years. Emotions on both sides, labor and management, were heightened by the massacre at Ludlow, Colorado.* In April 1914, Louisville residents were subjected to searchlights and machine-gun fire from guards at the Hecla mine. Out-of-work miners would from time to time shoot out the searchlights. Strike-breakers fired upon the miners at the Columbine mine (near Frederick in Weld County) in 1927, killing several people and wounding twenty or more.

When John Roche, owner of the Rocky Mountain Fuel Company, died in 1927, he willed his business to his daughter Josephine. She was most interested in social work and had been Denver's first policewoman. The new mine owner bought out the other shareholders in the business, and the following year, Miss Roche signed a contract, containing very liberal terms, with United Mine Workers, who used the contract to good advantage by distributing signs at competing coal firms reading "Buy from Josephine." The other coal companies retaliated by lowering their coal prices to force Miss Roche out, but the miners at Rocky Mountain Fuel loaned the lady the equivalent of three months' wages so that she could keep the company afloat. The workers' faith in Miss Roche was rewarded. The Rocky Mountain Fuel Company flourished and became the highest coal producer in the state.

Boulder County residents are still reminded today of the once-active coal industry by an unusual phenomenon. Coal burns just as efficiently underground as it does in a stove, and in 1870 a fire started in the #1 mine (near the junction of Colorado Highways 170 and 93). It burned for years, fanned by the occasional breaths of oxygen that it received from cracks in the unstable ground above. Another fire, which started in the 1930s at the Peerless mine near Marshall

---

*Later, Mother Jones despaired at the "stodginess" of the United Mine Workers and joined the Socialist Industrial Workers of the World, becoming a "Wobblie."

*The Ludlow camp was between Trinidad and Walsenburg. In April 1914, the National Guard was brought in to the coal fields to quell labor troubles. The guardsmen killed a number of people, including women and children.

Smoke and steam rising from underground fires in a mine near Marshall. *Western Historical Collections, University of Colorado at Boulder*

(junction of Marshall and Cherryvale roads), is still burning today. Even now, during snowy or rainy weather, smoke and steam from this fire can be seen rising through fissures in the ground. As recently as 1974, the fire from the Peerless broke through the ground, and for a time flames shot three and four feet above the ground. The fire has moved at least 100 feet up a nearby hill, turning coal into coke with temperatures as high as 2,000 degrees underground.

By 1938, the coal industry was suffering because of the emphasis upon the use of other fuels. Boulder County coal miners were offered the opportunity to go to "retraining" school for education in other fields.

Even though Boulder had experienced the excitement of several gold booms, a silver strike, and a telluride discovery, its citizens had not lost their innocence, but rather continued with a hearty lack of sophistication to enjoy the excitement that would result from further "finds" in gold, tungsten, oil, and uranium. In the spring of 1891, the big news was at Copper Rock, a camp twelve miles west of Boulder in Four Mile Canyon, halfway between Wallstreet and Sunset. For the next two years, the fledgling *Camera* reported the "good news" from Copper Rock and the Orphan Boy mine with exciting daily bulletins, despite the apparent and obvious lack of interest by the other newspapers of the day. "...The camp is growing steadily and that, too, in the face of sneers and back bitings from ignorant croakers, who live on the principle that nothing good can exist in Boulder County."[3] Each day the paper reported the building of another shack, the raising of a few more tents, the visit of important experts in from Denver to survey the possibilities of gold, or a new tunnel for the Orphan Boy. According to the *Camera*, the only thing that was holding Copper Rock back was the weather: "Success is just around the corner. Drat the weather."[4] The paper also bemoaned the lack of a railroad depot, the lack of a stamp mill, and the lack of sufficient capital. No matter, "lively times are coming"[5] and "Copper Rock will be the great gold camp of the state in a very few months."[6]

A town plat for Copper Rock was filed with two streets, Main and Willets. A grocery tent-store opened,

"The Jungle," west of Eleventh and Water (Canyon) streets, an area targeted for early slum clearance. Lady at extreme right of group is Em "Bugtown" Birge, "Queen of the Jungle," an early unfortunate character in Boulder. *Boulder Historical Society*

Copper Rock, located just beyond Wallstreet, held great promise of riches from gold mining in 1891, but became just a memory in short order and was wiped out by the flood of 1894. *A.A. Paddock Collection*

as well as a tent-saloon. Even Superintendent of Schools Robert Casey, who was never completely cured from "prospecting disease," left his students and poked around the area. Robert Coulehan sold his Boulder hotel and moved to Copper Rock. The *Camera*, hurt that other papers did not take up the lure of Copper Rock and stung by jibes in the Denver press, continued to predict that, when the weather cleared, "By May 15, there will be 1,000 people in Copper Rock. See if this is not true."[7] Some skeptical readers canceled their subscriptions. Even so, some 1,500 people did come to Copper Rock for a short while to support a restaurant, hotel, general store, saloon, grocery, butcher, blacksmith, lumber yard, and real estate office, which sold twenty-five foot lots for fifty dollars each. The big problem with Copper Rock, the skeptics maintained, was that no one had shipped any gold to the market. Do not worry, defended the *Camera*, we have been informed that the first shipment will be made "next week and that a railroad depot" is about to open.

In December 1893, the *Gold Nugget*, a Denver mining publication, summed up the experience:

> Many people will recall the excitement over the wonderful gold discoveries at Copper Rock some eighteen months ago. Nothing like it had ever been seen in the State. For a few days even the glories of Creede and the growing wonder of Cripple Creek were obscured. Excitement ran high. Even the most experienced and conservative lost their heads. The great shop windows of the city flashed samples of the new-found treasure upon the passing throng. The air was full of it. Men talked about, ate and drank it, and then went to bed and dreamed it.
>
> Masses of beautiful quartz big as your hat, big as a tub, stood in the windows, spattered with gold, filled with gold, interlaced, festooned and spangled with gold—gold enough in a single place to make a collar for my lady's poodle or a girdle for the waist. To the new find men rushed in hundreds; clerks laid down their pens, and professional men their dignity—everybody went, and—alas for human hopes—everybody returned. If there was more of the beautiful stuff, no one found it. The boom died, was buried and forgotten.

A few miners continued to work the Orphan Boy. From time to time, the *Camera* would report that prospects at Copper Rock were still good, but the price of gold was not steady. An unusual weather pattern late in May 1894 caused this settlement to be erased completely except for the coppery, green stain on the cliff above it.

If certain weather conditions occur in the right sequence, and they do from time to time, the Rocky Mountain creeks may swell, sending such a torrent down their courses that destruction is sure to follow. The winter of 1894 was a long, cold, snowy one. The mountains held a heavy snow pack. By the end of May, eastern humid winds brought warm spring rain that melted the snow pack far too rapidly. It rained for sixty hours. The *Denver Republican* summed up the situation afterward: "Waterspout after waterspout seemed to break on the hillsides and added to the fearfully swollen streams."

Flooding began in the early morning darkness of May 31. One by one, mountain roads, bridges, rooming houses, even mines, broke apart. The narrow gauge railroad to Sunset washed out. Four Mile Creek was in flood also; its waters rushed into Boulder Creek. Jim Creek, Left Hand Creek, and the St. Vrain boiled over. For five days, Boulder was cut off from the world; neither news nor mail came from the outside. Editor Fred Lockwood of the *Camera* dramatically headlined his first story, "Flood in Boulder—The Windows of Heaven Opened and Boulder was Submerged—Many Lives are in Danger—And Thousands of Dollars Worth of Property Completely Destroyed —Boulder Creek on a Rampage."

First reports spoke of six buildings gone at Camp Crisman, eight down at Sunset, and extensive damage at Jamestown and Ballarat. Jamestown's church floated downstream with its bell ringing, and the two-year-old boom town of Copper Rock was wiped out. Parts of Sugar Loaf and Salina were gone. The lower section of Lyons was wiped out, and the Estes Park toll road was no more. At Glendale, on Left Hand Creek, "The entire creek bed, from one side of the canyon to the other, was one seething mass of black water, bowlders [sic] and crushed buildings. Nearly every tree has been torn out by the roots and the road bed is entirely destroyed."[8]

In Boulder itself, the first to go was the long Fourth Street railroad bridge; its tracks were twisted into a semicircle. Then, one by one, the bridges at Sixth Street, Ninth Street, Twelfth Street (now Broadway), and Seventeenth Street collapsed, piling up along the way. The swiftly moving debris, including large "bowlders" from the canyon, added to the danger. Those who lived along the creek remember the terrifying noise of rushing water filled with trees and the remains of houses, bridges, and railroad tracks.*

For several days there was no way to cross Boulder Creek; South Boulder was separated from North Boulder. Photographer "Rocky Mountain Joe" Sturtevant got caught on the wrong side of the stream from his camera, but Marshal Bass was out taking pictures of the flood scene. As the *Camera* stated, "From the Boulder Hotel to the University Hill was one vast lake with here and there a small patch of an island."[9]

---

*Miss Elizabeth Ricketts, at ninety-nine years, still remembered the noise of the flood as its waters rushed by her Arapahoe Street home.

What Ninth Street looked like on June 1, 1894. The number of umbrellas suggest it is still raining. *L.P. Bass photo, A.A. Paddock Collection*

View of Ninth Street looking west, 1894. Note, at center, the narrow gauge engine mired in the receding floodwaters. *Meile and Sturtevant photo, A.A. Paddock Collection*

Sheets of heavy rain hit the roof of the depot at Fourteenth and Railroad streets. *L.P. Bass photo, A.A. Paddock Collection*

Black residents at Twenty-third and Water streets assess the flood damage to their neighborhood, May 31, 1894. *Biles Studio Photo, A.A. Paddock Collection*

Blacksmith Jacob Faus' house has finished its journey down the floodway. *Meile and Sturtevant photo, Boulder Historical Society*

A brave young woman uses a makeshift pulley to cross Boulder Creek because the Sixth Street bridge is no more. House in background still stands at Sixth and Arapahoe streets. *J.B. Sturtevant photo, A.A. Paddock Collection*

What the flood left at Twentieth and Goss streets. *Meile and Sturtevant photo, A.A. Paddock Collection*

After another flood, a Springdale store tilts precariously after a cloudburst in 1913. *Wiswall photo, A.A. Paddock Collection*

Jamestown residents view road damage from the same cloudburst. *Wiswall photo, A.A. Paddock Collection*

Newspapers, in the journalistic style of the day, ran such one-liners as "Good Baptist weather," or "The more rain, the fewer strawberries," or "Was the Populist Party responsible for the flood?" "Poor Dan McAllister! His best girl lives on the other side." The northern half of the town experienced a temporary beer famine until the brewery, by means of ropes, hoisted kegs of beer across the creek. The ropeways were perilous as the creek bed kept changing.

Dr. Jay put on his hip boots and went fishing on Water Street; he caught a seven-inch trout. A certain Madame Kingsley, a pug dog on each arm, was carried to safety in the vicinity of the red-light district, with "misery depicted on her countenance."[10] To the east, Culver's Flats was completely under water. Nearby, engine #155 from the narrow gauge railroad was sunk in the mud and debris. A bawling cow, tethered by the stream, could not escape the rising waters. Several "humanitarians" shot at the tether rope with their rifles but evidently hit the cow, for the animal went down. Towards noon of May 31, blacksmith Jacob Faus and his family scrambled out of their creekside home and joined a crowd to watch their residence sail rather grandly downstream. The neighbors of Mr. Mallinckrodt helped him move his factory equipment to higher ground; Mr. Mallinckrodt manufactured antinicotine pipes.

In the first excitement, the rumor spread that the reservoir was damaged. George Whitney is said to have rushed through the streets crying, "Get to the hills, the reservoir is busted." Mayor James Cowie was worried about it, too, for he spent that first day hiking up the canyon to assess the damage. Some seventy-five Boulder citizens camped on Lovers' Hill (now Sunset Hill) until they were assured by the mayor that the reservoir was intact.

On the morning of June 1, the rains stopped and the sun shone for the first time in days. Townspeople came out to assess the damage. "There will have to be some changes in the Assessor's office," Editor Lockwood wrote thoughtfully. "Some citizens of Boulder who owned real estate, now find they have none. Farmers in the valleys, whose land has been added to, should not, however, be assessed to this gift of an all wise, but inscrutable Providence."[11] Moreover, the soil that was dumped on the plains was of very poor quality. Farmers had to bring in new topsoil before their farms produced to their previous standard. Some worried that the destruction to Beasley Ditch would make it no longer possible to irrigate farms in that area.

Most miners were out of work for a time, because some of the mine shafts had filled with water from the extensive rains. They put their dynamite to good use, however, by exploding it to free dangerous debris caught along the creek. The explosions sounded like an early Fourth of July.

The most outstanding outcome of the flood of 1894 is that apparently no one died because of it. For a while it was feared that Milkman Tunnel was drowned, because someone had seen his empty milk wagon overturned. But he was found alive in the vicinity. Joe Monroe, a fireman on the narrow gauge railroad, fell in Boulder Creek while trying to save his chickens, but he rose from the swirling floodwaters, undamaged. He had managed to climb onto a submerged log and came out safely, minus his hat and the chickens. Others fell into either Left Hand Creek or Boulder Creek, but they were rescued or they rescued themselves. In the area of Eagle Rock, Mr. and Mrs. John Merryman and their two children were buried temporarily by a mud slide. All were saved. Mrs. Merryman was found waist-deep in mud, holding one of her children aloft. Others were presumed dead, but everyone was eventually accounted for.

No crimes were reported with the exception of the arrest of "Bug Town" Birge and R.M. Randall, who were caught ransacking someone's trunk. There had been a concert just before the flood, and its principals, Signor Sobrino and soprano Madame Sobrino—forced to stay in Boulder until the waters receded—gave an additional benefit concert for flood relief; it raised $33.25. The Sisters of Charity, who ran the girls' school at Mount St. Gertrude, provided a program at Feeney's Hall to benefit the needy. Sternberg's flour company gave away some fifty sacks of flour to those who were certified as "needy" with a note from Mayor Cowie.

Commencement was postponed, and the new graduates of the university had to wait a few days to receive their diplomas. A news item, lost in the reports of flood developments but which came to light later, was that Mrs. Jeanette B. Durham, a faculty wife, had received the first law degree ever granted a woman in Colorado.

By June 4, 1894, life was returning to normal in Boulder. The first mail in five days arrived, as well as news from the outside. Boulderites discovered that flooding was extensive up and down the Front Range. Colorado's coal strike had not been settled. Boulder also learned that, during its flood ordeal, Alferd Packer, celebrated eater of Democrats, had been denied a pardon and continued to serve his forty-year prison term. All available men started to work on the roads; the miners started to pump the water out of shafts. Newspaper articles were entitled, "And now to rebuild." A committee of eleven was chosen to coordinate clean up and rebuilding activities. "One touch of Nature makes the world kin," reminded Fred Lockwood, who wrote, "Cheer up those despondent ones, remembering that their calamity is ours and all who are not stricken will comfort those who are."[12]

In the 1890s, Boulderites, as did Americans all

across the land, thirsted for new ideas, new ways of doing things, and new forms of entertainment. Whenever there was an opportunity, homesteaders and city dwellers joined together to listen to lectures, evangelists, politicians, musicians, or magicians. Citizens from another state would provide this forum for Boulder. In 1897, a group of Texas professors had visited Boulder to determine if the town was an appropriate spot for their proposed Chautauqua,* a retreat from the Texas heat and dust. After conferring with Boulder's Mayor Crocket Ricketts, they decided it was. The council proposed a $20,000 bond issue that would buy land for the summer retreat, provide water and electricity, and construct the first two buildings. The bonds passed overwhelmingly, because Boulder wanted a Chautauqua just as much as did the Texans. Thus, the city of Boulder bought its first park land (then called Texado Park) of about seventy-five acres of Batchelder's orchard, and the Texans had a place for "retirement without loneliness," or what a 1903 brochure proclaimed, "not a casino" but "quiet without ennui."

*Derivation of the word "chautauqua" is varied. Some say it is an Indian word meaning "foggy place." Others say it means "place where a child was washed away," or "place of easy death." Still others claim it means "place where the fish were taken out." Most scholars, however, use the Algonquin Indian meaning, "bag tied in the middle," which is the shape of Lake Chautauqua in New York.

Chautauqua from the mountains, 1898. *J.B. Sturtevant photo, A.A. Paddock Collection*

Chautauqua, the first year, 1898. Auditorium is at center and dining hall is middle left. *J.B. Sturtevant photo, A.A. Paddock Collection*

Flags fly over the new Chautauqua auditorium (called a tabernacle then) which was built in less than two months. *J.B. Sturtevant photo, A.A. Paddock Collection*

An attentive audience in Chautauqua's auditorium. *J.B. Sturtevant photo, A.A. Paddock Collection*

A Chautauqua afternoon of music. *Boulder Historical Society*

The Rischar orchestra from Chicago was a standard summer attraction for a number of years at Chautauqua. *A.A. Paddock Collection*

Official Chatauqua photographer Joseph Bevier Sturtevant had a way with a camera and with the ladies. *A.A. Paddock Collection*

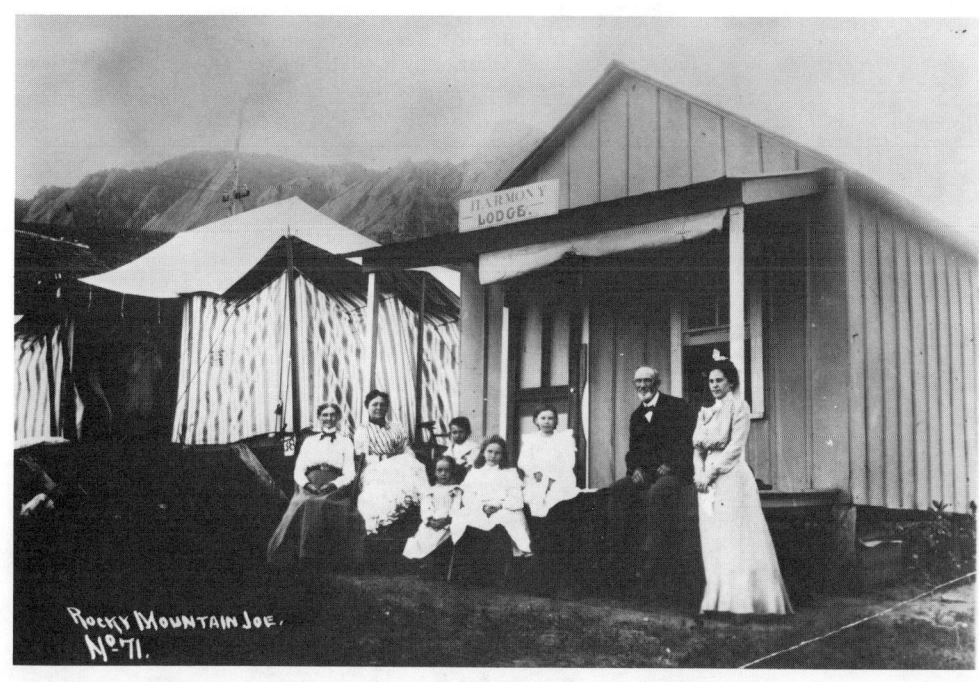

A Chautauqua family sits for a portrait by J.B. Sturtevant, "Rocky Mountain Joe." *A.A. Paddock Collection*

Boulder's first electric streetcar stops at the Chautauqua gate, 1899. *J.B. Sturtevant photo, A.A. Paddock Collection*

Boulder school teachers on a mountain hike around the turn of the century. Note Miss Georgina Rowland's hiking costume, the skirts pinned back and the pantaloons showing. *Rowland Collection*

A Boulder school teacher cools her feet near Red Rocks. *Edna Harkins Collection*

This Chautauqua climbing group pauses in Bluebell Canyon. *Ed Tangen photo, Edna Harkins Collection*

A steep climb to the Royal Arch was a yearly goal for some Chautauquans. *Edna Harkins Collection*

Construction of the Chautauqua's first buildings, a tabernacle (the present auditorium) and a dining hall, began on May 12, 1898. Two months and $10,000 later, painters gave the last finishing touches to the eight-sided building on the morning of the Fourth of July—the official opening of Boulder Chautauqua.* (The dining hall had been completed one month earlier.) With flags raised, Colorado Governor Alva B. Adams walked across the platform to dedicate the building and welcome several thousand visitors. M.A. Spoontz of Fort Worth spoke, then Senator Richard H. Whiteley for the university, followed by Mayor Ricketts, who introduced the keynoter, the Honorable Henry Watterson of Kentucky. (Watterson was one of a group of circuit orators, well-known to audiences of that day but now forgotten, who could speak on a variety of subjects.) A contralto sang, and the Kansas City Symphony performed, after which Maro the Magician amused both children and adults. The crowds cheered at the announcement that the Spanish fleet had been destroyed at Santiago. They watched fireworks that evening.

That first summer, Joseph Bevier Sturtevant, "Rocky Mountain Joe," was named Chautauqua's official photographer. (Two years later, on the site of the present Community House, he built a studio which he called the Photo Gallery.) Sturtevant thrilled Chautauqua youngsters with his campfire stories of Indians and mountain exploits. He acted as guide and driver for groups of ladies who wished a short expedition by tally-ho into the mountains.

Despite the crowds and the excitement of the first summer, there were problems. Transportation, or the lack of it, was one. Visitors either hiked across the prairie to Texado Park from the downtown train depot, or they hired a hack and walked in from the entrance on Baseline Road. Carriages (except those of important personages) were not allowed on the grounds.

Ever since the failure of the horse-drawn streetcar, Boulder's city fathers had been contemplating an electric streetcar line; the coming of Chautauqua inspired the council to build Boulder's first line from downtown to the Chautauqua gate. It took two months to build and was in full operation by the beginning of the 1899 season. Visitors "sped" up to Chautauqua at fifteen miles per hour, having paid a five-cent fare. (By 1903, a line was operating along Maxwell Street to the sanitarium, Boulder Memorial Hospital. Later, the line was extended along Fifth Street to Fifth Avenue, and another line went east on Pearl Street which ended at Twenty-third and Pine streets.)

*Once there were 8,000 Chautauquas thriving across the country. Now two remain, the original Chautauqua in New York State and the one in Boulder. Perhaps it is because there were permanent buildings constructed on the two sites, while others were tent Chautauquas.

That first year, everyone lived in a tent. Some did not favor the primitive tent accommodations even though their healthful virtues were extolled. A simple twelve-by-fourteen-foot tent could be rented for the entire season for eleven dollars. Many of the tents were luxuriously appointed with several rooms of fine furniture and oriental rugs. By the next summer, however, a desire for comfort led to the construction of some fifty permanent cottages. By 1909, the last of the tents were replaced by cottages, and most had hot running water. Trees were planted and gardens planned. The visitors grumbled about the food, though. A meal cost thirty-five cents at the dining hall the first season. By the following summer, the price had gone up, but the food had also improved. By 1900, the Texas-Colorado Organization was in trouble, for the Chautauqua had lost money in two out of three years of operation. The group dissolved, and a new eleven-member organization, the Colorado Chautauqua Association, formed, which still guides the affairs of Chautauqua today. Their first job was to give a more sensible financial foundation to Chautauqua.

Chautauqua's program was divided into four categories: platform, lyceum, academy, and institute. Platform included such keynote speakers as William Jennings Bryan, lecturers such as Charles Evans Hughes, evangelists such as Billy Sunday, and social reformers such as Jane Addams. Chautauquans heard speeches on Jewish theology as well as the Russo-Japanese "struggle." They listened to music of all kinds: symphonic, band, and choir. Singers, pianists, harpists, organists, banjo players, and flautists performed each summer. John Phillip Sousa was on the platform in 1904; the Deep River Plantation Singers entertained Chautauquans in 1935. Visitors saw operas and magic shows as well as "lantern shows," which employed a stereopticon and photo-slides of faraway places or unusual animals. During the 1920s, the "bird man," Charlie Bowman Hutchins, entertained Boulder's children by drawing pictures of birds, whistling their songs as he drew. Some lucky child would get the artist's drawings after the performance. One Boulder resident summed it up by saying, "One can't talk about Boulder entertainment without talking about Chautauqua."[13]

Lyceum encompassed moral and ethical questions which were discussed at study groups and round tables. One such discussion was entitled "The Harp of the Senses; or the Secret of Character Building." At this time, club women were expected to discuss gardening or sewing techniques. At Boulder Chautauqua, however, the Women's Council discussed "Why Should Women Study Law," the graduated income tax, the benefits of kindergarten, should the government support a hot-lunch program, or such environmental questions as should ladies use feathers to decorate their hats, thus reducing the numbers of bird species.

Academy was for the serious student; courses were offered in literature and the sciences and mathematics, as well as in French, German, Greek, Latin, Anglo-Saxon, and even Esperanto. The final category, Institute, featured a program of oil painting, water colors, pastry making, voice culture, lace making, china painting, or military tactics. The children enjoyed spelling bees and nature study. Special programs were arranged for teenagers. One could choose from parties, picnics, coffees, teenage dances, missionary teas, folk dances, and fishing trips. (One Chautauqua picnic was for young ladies, all of whom came dressed as George Washington.) Rock-drilling contests by the miners had their start at Chautauqua before they were incorporated into Boulder's yearly Pay-Dirt Pow Wow (1934). There were baby shows, food booths, luncheon pavilions, fish hatchery exhibits, photo contests, children's races, sideshows, and gypsy camps.

From the very first year, physical exercise and health were emphasized at Chautauqua. Colorado's children were described in Chautauqua bulletins as "full chested, strong limbed and bronze." To dispel any concern on the part of prospective visitors who might know that tuberculars were moving in large numbers to the Boulder area, the bulletins stated, "It is amply proved that the tubercule bacilli and spores do not live long in this place." Indeed, many tuberculars were on the hikes and excursions offered at Chautauqua. In 1898, the Chautauqua Climbers Club was organized. (The name changed to the Rocky Mountain Climbing Club in 1908.) Groups of hikers left the grounds for short but steep climbs to the Royal Arch or for day-long expeditions, complete with steak-frys, farther into the mountains. Many summer visitors, out of physical shape, came hoping for immediate and intensive hiking, but they were required to proceed through proficiency hikes so that by the end of the summer, as climber Ernest Greenman said, "those fat, old schoolmarms" were "ready for Long's Peak."[14]

One of Chautauqua's regular climbers, druggist Eben Fine, could find no one to hike with him on July 14, 1900. He left Silver Lake at 6:00 in the morning and started for South Arapaho Peak. He decided to cross a giant snow field, and when he reached the middle of the field, the climber began to realize that he was "on a living glacier."[15] "If the glacial character of that snowfield had ever been suspected, certainly no word had ever appeared in print...."*[16] Fine was so excited that he nearly fell into one of the glacier's crevasses, but he made it home safely and said, years later, that the discovery was a splendid way to bring in the new century.

*Caribou teacher J.W. Barnard took a hike in that direction in 1892 but did not return. In 1905, John Williams found a skull near the glacier which he identified, in some way, as Barnard's. Another version of the discovery of the glacier gives credit to H.M. Wheeler of the U.S. Forest Service and D.M. Andrews, a nurseryman, who hiked across it in August 1897 but were forced back to Camp Albion because of an early blizzard.

Boulder Cañon

Chapter Nine

The building of railroad lines into the mountains, although difficult, made the transporting of supplies to the mountain camps and the carrying out of ores a more efficient alternative to the dangerous freighting with a team and wagon. By 1883, the Union Pacific Railroad had built fourteen miles of narrow gauge* track to Four Mile, Salina, Wallstreet, and Sunset. Twelve miles of this line washed out with the flood of 1894, but four years later, not only was the line rebuilt but 12.8 miles were added, with tracks laid to Ward. Although the narrow gauge roads were built with an eye to transporting greater amounts of metal ores, tourist excursions provided another source of revenue for the railroad companies.

Chautauquans loved to travel into the mountains for a day, resting at the Mount Alto pavilion for lunch, enjoying the dance hall, and stopping along the way for wild flower picking and snowball fights. By 1904, another branch was completed by the Colorado and Northwestern Railroad to Eldora, thus completing "The Switzerland Trail," a famous tourist attraction the short while it lasted. Boulderites took advantage of the trains, too. A truly exciting day could be spent by three couples and a railroad handcar. The men would take turns pumping the open car; up the mountain they would go to Eldora, Wallstreet or Sunset—perfect spots for an elegant picnic luncheon. The ride down was quite a bit faster as they coasted down the slopes.

In 1907, the railroad switchmen went on strike. Because they were not working, a boxcar half-filled with dynamite was left standing near the freight depot (present site of the Chamber of Commerce). It was against the law to store dynamite in town. A man named Reeves set a fire under the freight depot, and the flames spread to the boxcar. The ensuing explosion blew out many Boulder windows, destroyed a number of buildings, and killed three people. The blast was so fierce that it lit up the mountains. Some thought that Halley's comet had returned three years early to hit Boulder. Reeves confessed and was sent to prison.

In 1909, the narrow gauge route had such financial troubles that the Colorado and Western folded. The line reorganized under the name of the Denver, Boulder, and Northwestern Railroad, but for ten years its management discussed abandonment of the train along the Switzerland Trail. A cloudburst in July 1919, resulting in a washout of 2,500 feet of track in effect made the decision for the railroad company. The line was never rebuilt, and the Switzerland Trail became a happy memory.*

*The stone from the bridge abutments along the Switzerland Trail was salvaged, and in 1932, when the courthouse burned, the stone was used for the façade of the present courthouse.

At work at the freight depot, Ninth and Water (Canyon) streets. *A.A. Paddock Collection*

*Rails for a narrow gauge bed were placed three feet apart to accommodate the sharp turns of mountain travel. Standard gauge on the plains was four feet, eight inches.

Boulder surveys what was once the freight depot. The August 1907 dynamite explosion occurred in the middle of the night, causing some residents to fear that Halley's comet had returned early to hit downtown Boulder. *Above, Western Historical Collection, University of Colorado at Boulder; below, Ed Tangen photo, A.A. Paddock Collection*

Excursion train rounding a bend in Boulder Canyon. A cloudburst in 1919, with subsequent washouts, ended these pleasure trips. *A.A. Paddock Collection*

The Sixth Annual Wild Flower-Picking Excursion along the Switzerland Trail, near Mount Alto. Narrow gauge train in background. *Black photo, A.A. Paddock Collection*

Chautauquans watch a snowball fight at a stop along the Switzerland Trail in July. *J.B. Sturtevant photo, A.A. Paddock Collection*

This party has climbed to the summit of Arapaho Peak in late August of 1904. *J.B. Sturtevant photo, A.A. Paddock Collection*

An observer considers the work to cut away a snow slide near Ward in 1899 so that the Colorado and Northern Railroad might pass. *J.B. Sturtevant photo, A.A. Paddock Collection*

A June snowstorm produces a monstrous slide near Ward, cutting off the Denver, Boulder and Western Railroad for a time. *A.A. Paddock Collection*

The pavillion at Mount Alto along the Switzerland Trail. Tourists came for a day of picnics and dancing. *J.B. Sturtevant photo, A.A. Paddock Collection*

A train runs into trouble along Boulder Creek in June of 1891. Note the folks sitting on the overturned engine. *A.A. Paddock Collection*

Although Nederland had been settled since the early 1860s, the little mountain town came into its own, at least for a while, with the discovery of tungsten in the area. The value of tungsten as a strengthener of steel* was known as early as 1859, but local miners dismissed the heavy float and deposits as that "damned black iron" or "barren silver" and used it to pave roads.

Before Nathan W. "Bolly" Brown settled there in the late 1860s, Nederland was called Dayton. The balding Brown built a boarding house, named it Mountain House, and renamed the settlement Brownsville (sometimes written Brown's Crossing). John H. Pickel, recently moved up from Gold Hill, started a grocery nearby, and as the settlement grew, he established one of the first telegraph stations in the area. About 1871, Brownsville became Middle Boulder. When Dutchmen bought the Caribou mine above and the concentrating mill in town, the mine management stayed at Nederland House. They rechristened the mill community Nederland (their word for "low lands"—apparently the settlement seemed low compared to Caribou). By 1881, Nederland's population was a healthy 350, but the town lost ground for some time afterward until gold was found at nearby Eldora in the 1890s. When this strike revived the region, such settlements as Hessie, Grand Island, Sulphide Flats, Mary City, and Camp Enterprise sprang up nearby. With more people attracted to the Nederland area, the elegant Antlers Hotel was constructed in 1897.

Just before the turn of the century, Samuel P. Conger and W.H. Wannamaker, two prospectors associated with earlier finds of silver and gold, heard elsewhere that tungsten might have value. They recognized it as the mineral that they had passed over in earlier days and rushed back to the Nederland region to buy up claims. At about the same time, John H. Knight of Ward sent samples of the mineral to the Colorado School of Mines, where experts identified it as "wolframite," a tungsten-bearing ore. When Knight took his ore samples to the Paris

*Tungsten was also used in the manufacture of the electric light bulb.

A snow field on Grassy Mountain is site of April 1901 train wreck on the Colorado and Northern line. *A.A. Paddock Collection*

Universal Exposition in 1900, his exhibit was studied by European financiers, including Bavarian Hugo Krupp. Krupp eventually wrote Knight, placing a monthly order for fifty tons of tungsten. After U.S. steelmakers followed suit with orders for the "damned black iron," at least two Pennsylvania steel firms moved into the area. Firth Steel Company sent principals William G. McKenna and William Loach to Nederland; their families have remained in the area ever since. The two men bought Scrooby Mining Company as well as R.G. Dun's "white elephant," the Caribou silver mill. They called their enterprise the Wolf Tongue Company (wolframite combined with tungsten). The Primos Chemical Company also operated in the area with a mill at Primos, a few miles away. (C.F. Lake, Primos' superintendent, gave his name to another tungsten camp nearby, Lakewood, established in 1908.) Both Conger and Wannamaker sold their claims to the larger firms (Conger also sold his Midget Mill) and went on their way, no doubt to prospect something new.

From 1900 to the start of World War I, Nederland was the primary source of tungsten in the United States. Indeed, for a time, the town was called Tungsten Town.* The price of tungsten rose as the major powers of the world geared up for war. Although Nederland flourished—with three saloons, two theaters, a newspaper (the *Tungsten Light*), busy stage lines, and a real bank—it was not a pretty town. Writer Helen Hunt Jackson called Nederland "that dismal little mining town."[1] Nederland's appearance did not improve with two damaging fires, one in 1900 and another in 1911. By 1919, however, American tungsten was still priced so high that South American and Chinese interests were able to take over the market with cheaper tungsten. As Nederland quieted down, some of its population moved to Boulder.

*Tungsten Town is not to be confused with Tungsten, a mining camp just east of Nederland which was first called Stevens' Camp (after founder Eugene Stevens), then Ferberite.

Nederland as it looked in 1877. Helen Hunt Jackson called it "that dismal little mining town." *A.A. Paddock Collection*

How Nederland looked after the concentrating mill for Caribou silver was built, extreme left. Hetzer Hotel is a little right of center. *A.A. Paddock Collection*

The elegant Antlers Hotel, completed in 1897, had unusually fine accommodations for a little town of two hundred. *J.B. Sturtevant photo, A.A. Paddock Collection*

A parlor ready for guests at the Antlers Hotel. *J.B. Sturtevant photo, A.A. Paddock Collection*

Afternoon tea is served in one of the rooms at the Antlers. *J.B. Sturtevant photo, A.A. Paddock Collection*

The town of Wallstreet has a float in a parade turning to the main street in Nederland, followed by the Nederland Tungsten Band. *Black photo, A.A. Paddock Collection*

Another Nederland band from the 1940s. *A.A. Paddock Collection*

Nina Tanner poses with her father, W.L. Tanner, at the right, and the miners of the Elsie mine, located southeast of Nederland on the road to Pinecliffe, 1916. *A.A. Paddock Collection*

A view of Sugarloaf from the Kikionga mine. *J.B. Sturtevant photo, A.A. Paddock Collection*

Although most of Boulder's residents had recovered from various gold booms, from the rush for silver and tellurium, and from the excitement over tungsten, some never got over "prospecting disease." Hence, the citizens were to lose their heads again—this time over oil. The discovery of oil northeast of Boulder was not a complete surprise. From the time of the first settlement in the area, there had been speculation as to the possibility of oil between Boulder and Longmont. People could see it and smell it. Some drilling for oil occurred in the 1890s. In 1892, a well called "Old Whiterock" was sunk at the top of what is now Gunbarrel Hill. In 1901, after some study, geologist Ferdinand V. Hayden announced to Boulder's 7,500 citizens that the county "lies over a veritable sea of oil."[2] Another geologist, B.A. Langridge, further excited the population with his prediction that "the time is not far distant when the eastern edge of the mountains to the Wyoming line will present a forest of oil derricks."[3] The following year, a Chautauqua bulletin modestly stated, "the Boulder oil field gives promise of outranking in every way any previously discovered field in the world."[4]

Interest in oil wells heightened with the explorations of speculator Isaac Canfield in the spring of 1901. Canfield managed the Boulder Oil Company, backed by investors from Denver and Colorado Springs. Canfield had come to Boulder County in 1875 when he and his brothers mined coal (Rob Roy mine) near a railroad stop called Tabor Station, eleven miles east of Boulder. Tabor Station became the town of Canfield, even though Mr. Canfield had left the area for more than twenty-five years.

During that time, he developed oil fields in Ohio and Pennsylvania. He returned to Colorado to bring in the first oil at the Florence field near Cañon City. Perhaps he remembered the talk about the possibility of oil near Boulder. He returned to the area an experienced oil speculator, but he also brought with him a divining "bobbler," a sprout from a witch hazel bush.

Neil McKenzie's 480 farming acres* (near Niwot along the present Independence Road) looked promising to Canfield. He secured a lease and started drilling early in August 1901. After boring down 1,700 feet, he hit oil sand, but before he could bring in oil, a bailing bucket was accidentally dropped into the well. Since no one could get it out, oil exploration ceased

---

*McKenzie, a free-silver Populist who spent years in Caribou, managed his interests in the silver mines, then retired to Boulder to raise trotting horses, for he was very fond of sulky racing.

Resting before a new gas and oil well around 1902. *J.B. Sturtevant photo, A.A. Paddock Collection*

139

The Great Oil Basin, a sea of derricks east of Boulder, 1902. It was predicted they would stretch to the Wyoming border. *J.B. Sturtevant photo, A.A. Paddock Collection*

The first oil to be shipped from Boulder's oil fields, 1902. Note misspelling of "McKenzie." *J.B. Sturtevant photo, A.A. Paddock Collection*

A well-hatted group study the board and the tape in an early stock market.
Boulder Public Library

Neil McKenzie owned silver mines at Caribou, later moved to Boulder to operate a flour mill, still later bought farm land near Niwot where Isaac Canfield successfully drilled for oil in 1902. *Representative Men of Colorado*

at that spot. Later that month, Canfield sunk a drill close by, but the hole turned out to be dry. By January 1902, Canfield had a crew working on the nearby William Arnold property, where on January 2, Canfield brought in gas at 1,500 feet; oil flowed up at 2,720 feet. The crowds of people who had been watching his crew were not disappointed. Canfield, not unmindful of public relations, piped a gas line to the top of the rig and set a match to it. At night, the flames could be seen for miles.

Canfield also had a crew drilling again on the McKenzie land; a week after his Arnold find, he brought in the McKenzie #2 at 2,540 feet. This well was such a good producer—70 to 100 barrels per day—that a railroad spur was built to transport the oil to the Denver market. Now the new rush was on for sure.

Every few days, the Boulder *Daily Camera* would report the establishment of a new oil company, the selling of more leases, or the visit to the area of a noted "oil expert." Companies from the Florence field at Cañon City opened branch offices here. Boulder now had its own oil stock exchange, and a specialized newspaper, *Oil News*, started publication. Both geologists Hayden and Langridge were enthusiastically drilling their own wells, and the Rockefellers were expected momentarily.

The population was about to double, some predicted. Perhaps that influenced the school board to buy more land for two more schools, Washington and Lincoln. An important issue of the day was whether or not drilling should be allowed on Sundays. Evidently greed won out, for rigs continued to operate on the Lord's day.

By now, the dimensions of the Boulder oil field had taken shape. It appeared to be six miles long and two miles wide, stretching northeast of Boulder. Sometimes the region was called the Parallel Dome or the Haystack Field, because rigs operated close to Haystack Mountain.

The oil seeped from the porous layers, or fractures (Pierre shale) which had developed about 100 million years before. Boulder's oil was of high quality and was heavy with paraffin, but it was hard to find. Since drilling through the shale layers was relatively easy, conventional boring equipment was used. Rotary drills did not work too well, for the mud generated by the circular motion would seal off the oil.

By March 1902, ninety-two oil companies operated in the area of the present Longmont Diagonal. By April, the number had increased to 117. But the original speculator Isaac Canfield had departed. Since he and his business associates had illegally moved some money to the Boulder operation, the government was looking into the matter. Canfield defaulted on the McKenzie lease and left the area two days after he had brought in the well. Perhaps Canfield would have moved on anyway, for he seemed to enjoy the speculative part of oil development, always moving on to something new. Perhaps he was smart enough to know that Boulder's oil boom was to be a short one.

Even so, the development continued. In 1903, 44,000 barrels of Boulder County oil were shipped out, some on their way to Denver. By 1905, a refinery had been built by the Boulder Oil and Refining Company; another plant was constructed in 1907. A pipeline to Denver was under discussion. By now, 100 rigs had been built. In 1908, a real "gusher" came in, producing some 250 barrels a day, but the well, like the others, slowed down after a time. The reason that many of these oil wells declined in productivity is that the oil was quickly depleted from the Pierre fractures. For a few wells, as was the case with the McKenzie #2, seepage was constant, and although the number of barrels per day was no longer spectacular, the supply of oil was steady. (The McKenzie #2 still produces today.) The peak year for Boulder's oil production was 1909. The "real" wells produced 85,709 barrels of oil. Plenty of "paper" wells and "paper" organizations were selling bogus stock. Some of the wells were encouraged to produce more heavily by "well shooting." Quarts of nitroglycerin (dynamite was also used) were dropped into the bores. This technique produced favorable results for a few wells, totally ruined a few, and did nothing for most. Even so, "well shooting" caused the establishment of another industry for Boulder County—a nitroglycerin factory.

Gas was associated with most of the oil wells in this region. Early on, no one really appreciated the merits of the gas, which was regarded as a nuisance. Some of the rigging crews capped off the supply, finding it inconvenient to deal with. In 1910, gas was sold from the Buffalo well, two miles south of the McKenzie #2. Most of the gas rights were bought by the Federal Gas Company in 1924. In 1923, twelve oil wells operated in the county, but the newspapers no longer spoke of an oil boom; nor were the Rockerfellers still expected. Altogether, 183 holes were drilled in Boulder County; 102 of them were dry. Despite the many companies in the area, only eighty-one wells were functioning. Of those, seventy-six produced oil and five produced gas.

Throughout the Southwest, thermal areas were being developed as spas. Eldorado Springs, with its warm waters and proximity to new railroad lines, was destined to become a fashionable resort. Since the 1860s, settlers had farmed and raised cattle there. Andrew Douty built the region's first gristmill on the South Boulder.* Early resident Caroline Barber planted walnut trees, some of which still bear. The Kneale family, immigrants from the Isle of Man, operated several sawmills in the area.

The canyon property changed hands several times before the resort was built. First, George Taylor bought 480 acres from the Union Pacific Railroad in 1904 to benefit a spiritualist group who held seances and religious dances near the warm waters. At one point, Taylor had differences with the railroad men, which he expressed by dynamiting one of their tunnels.

W.A. Garner and L.C. Stockton then bought the land; by 1905, Frank Fowler bought into the project and became president of the business—the Moffat Lakes Resort Company. Shortly thereafter, the name Eldorado Springs, Spanish meaning "gilded," was used in advertisements which described the brilliant blue "radium waters" as mineral-free and health-producing. Fowler built a swimming pool that first year. Eventually he built three, one with a forty-foot diving tower. Fowler constructed the New Eldorado Hotel in 1908, a fancy building of forty to fifty rooms decorated in the "mission" style.

During the resort's "grand" period, guests could dine on fresh trout, dance to the waltzes of Strauss, hike to Harmon Falls, take a burro or horse trip, and swim in one of the pools. Pool filters had not yet been invented, so one pool was always being cleaned while the others were in use. At one point, a double-decker building held a roller-skating rink below and a dance hall above. Fowler also built, in 1906, the "crazy

---

*The 1894 flood destroyed the mill, but Douty rebuilt it. Shortly thereafter, he constructed another flour mill downstream, close to Loveland.

stairs," a series of 1,350 steep stairs that started from the base of the canyon and zigzagged up to Castle Rock (now called "The Bastille" by climbers). The stairs led to a picnic area near an old railroad bed, site of an abortive attempt to build a narrow gauge railroad. The line was intended to compete with the 1,500-foot-higher Moffat Road, which went on to Leadville. Construction difficulties and lack of financing caused the project never to be completed. On June 23, 1908 the electric Denver and Interurban train, established by the Colorado and Southern line, made its first run from Denver to downtown Boulder on what the railroad called the "kite route"—their ads describing the journey as "along the foothills and into the mountains." A spur line from the Interurban ran to the entrance of Eldorado Springs; eight daily trains brought guests to the resort area. The train was not without its dangers. One month after its establishment, an engineer "fried" to death while adjusting the lines on top of the car. J.B. Sturtevant, the famous Chautauqua photographer, died in an accident on the Interurban in 1910.

The resort at Eldorado Springs at its height after the turn of the century. All three of the swimming pools can be seen in this photo. *Boulder Public Library from the Eldorado Springs Historical Society*

A quiet 1870 scene at Eldorado Springs, long before the resort development. *Boulder Public Library from the Eldorado Springs Historical Society*

Well-dressed customers provide a holiday atmosphere at the entrance to the Eldorado Springs resort, 1908. *A.A. Paddock Collection*

Victorian visitors line one of the pools at Eldorado Springs. *Boulder Public Library from the Eldorado Springs Historical Society*

The famed Ivy Baldwin in the middle of one of his Sunday afternoon walks along a high wire, stretching from Castle Rock to the Eldorado Springs canyon wall, 1908. *A.A. Paddock Collection*

The "crazy stairs" to Castle Rock (now called the Bastille), a series of 1,350 steep stairs built in 1906 by Frank Fowler, resort owner. Hard to maintain, the steps were closed after World War II. *J.B. Sturtevant photo, A.A. Paddock Collection*

These lovelies grace an Eldorado Springs tour bus which was run by the Denver and Interurban. *A.A. Paddock Collection*

Crag's, a resort above Eldorado Springs, could be reached by a tramway which operated by means of pulleys; a water tank at the top provided ballast for the cars.
Boulder Public Library from the Eldorado Springs Historical Society

Guests used the many picnic spots and trails and rented small cabins. (Young Dwight and Mamie Eisenhower honeymooned in one of the cabins.) Visitors looked forward to Sunday afternoons, when a slight but wiry little man, Ivy Baldwin, completed his high-wire walks. A three-eighths-inch cable was strung from the top of Castle Rock to the canyon wall on the other side of South Boulder Creek, a distance of about 600 feet; its height averaged 582 feet. (Resident Helen Kneale remembers watching Baldwin from up above near the old railroad bed.) Baldwin used a balancing rod with weights on either end, rubbed rosin on his shoes, and always looked straight ahead as he walked the wire. He had grown up with circuses and not only balanced himself in high places (Cliff House rocks in San Francisco, for one) but also worked with balloons. He was the featured balloonist at Elitch's in 1890.* Ivy Baldwin made eighty-nine high-wire trips from 1907 to 1948, the last when he was eighty-two years old.

Through the years, many celebrities were attracted to the resort. The young musician Glenn Miller would leave his studies at the University of Colorado to play with the resort band. Band leader Paul Whiteman played there. Guests included actress Mary Pickford and her actor-husband Douglas Fairbanks, Sr. (a native of Jamestown), writer Damon Runyon, fighter Jack Dempsey, and gossip columnist Walter Winchell. From 1926 to 1938 the resort was owned, at least in part, by Frederick Bonfils, owner of the *Denver Post;* Horace Bennett managed it for him. In 1938, the resort returned to the Fowler's family management.

Flood and fire have changed the character of the resort. In the late 1920s, high winds and fire destroyed one of the pools, sixteen cabins, and a dance hall. The Interurban stopped its operations in 1926, which slowed the flow of tourists to the spa. Flooding occurred in 1938, destroying another dance hall (at one time there were four). In 1940, Fowler's New Eldorado Hotel burned down, possibly due to the work of an arsonist.

Above Eldorado Springs, Crag's, another resort hotel operating before 1907, was built near tunnel No. 10 on the Moffat Road, near Rattlesnake Gulch. Crag's could be visited either by train, by a difficult road, or by a two-car tramway. The tramway operated with pulleys at the top and bottom; its covered cars held ten rows of benches, seating four across. As the tramcars passed each other at the halfway mark, a water tank at the top of the tramway served to counterbalance the weight of the cars. When Crag's burned down in 1912, the tramway was discontinued.

Around the time of World War II, Jack Fowler took out the dangerous "crazy stairs," for they were hard to maintain. Ivy Baldwin's high wire remained in place for many years. Once, a low-flying airplane hit one of the underwires. In the early 1970s, Fowler ordered the removal of the wires when a few enterprising college students tried to imitate Ivy Baldwin. The thermal waters are not as warm as they once were, possibly due to faulty engineering in piping water to the remaining pool. Today, some of the water is bottled and sold to residents in the Boulder area. Castle Rock and other craggy areas are favored by technical climbers from all over the world. (A local climbing group, the Marmots, started climbing there in the 1950s.) In 1978, the Eldorado Springs Canyon became a state park.

---

*Gene Fowler, Frank Fowler's brother and noted author (*Good Night, Sweet Prince*), writes of Baldwin's exploits in *Solo in Tom Toms.*

A Boulder streetcar after the turn of the century. *Hardy photo, A.A. Paddock Collection*

Boulder Railway has a wreck near Chautauqua, Fourth of July, 1902. *J.B. Sturtevant photo, A.A. Paddock Collection*

Following the "kite route," the Denver and Interurban stops for passengers. The railroad's motto: "Along the foothills and into the mountains." *A.A. Paddock Collection*

Emma Brookfield, now called "Auntie," was one of the dancers at the first Christmas dance in 1859. At the semi-centennial celebration, Emma reigned as queen. *Jones Studio photo, 1912, Western Historical Collections, University of Colorado at Boulder*

For several days during the fall of 1909, Boulder citizens celebrated fifty years of settlement. They held a parade, complete with floats. Queen of the celebration was Emma Brookfield, the lady who had danced at Bill Barney's fifty years before. Now called "Auntie," Mrs. Brookfield rode in style down Pearl Street in an open victoria. The town welcomed a group of Ute Indians who left a reservation near Ignacio for the Boulder festivities. Johnny Carmack, veteran stagecoach driver and early-day freighter, participated in a mock stagecoach robbery made more "real" by the presence of the Indians, led by their "chief," Buckskin Charley. The Utes joined the townspeople to watch a football game, the hose companies gave one of their last demonstrations, and some watched a movie entitled "Custer's Last Stand." In the evening, most residents paid a dollar to attend a pioneer banquet.

The early 1900s could be characterized as Boulder's "golden age" of park acquisition. Until 1898, the year that Chautauqua was established, Boulder had but one park—and the city fathers gave it away. The town square (site of the present Boulder County Courthouse) was laid out by the Boulder City Town Company in 1860 and became a social gathering place. The town pump was there as well as a diamond for baseball games. At some point, musicians played from a bandstand on the site. After the Boulder City Town Company dissolved, title to the land passed to Boulder County. Trees were planted and a chain fence with wooden posts was placed around the square. By 1881, however, the area showed signs of serious neglect. A few citizens wrote angry letters to the papers decrying its condition. When the board of trustees proposed to subdivide the square and sell it, lot by lot, Boulder became aroused. Several made offers for the land; Lewis Cheney said that he would pay $10,000 for the property. The *Herald* guessed that the land was worth $30,000. Outraged, Dr. Charles Ambrook wrote to the paper: "Sell? Close up the streets, why don't you, so as to get rooms overhead to rent!"[5]

In response to the threat of subdivision, the Boulder City Improvement Society was formed with businessman Charles Dabney as its first president. After the private group had collected $1,000, members began to clean up and beautify the area. Since questions arose as to the validity of the original title, C.E. Akins brought in a wagon and camped there for a time, claiming that the square was his by pre-emption. Evidently, the title problem was solved, for in 1882 Boulder gave the town square to the county for perpetual use as long as it was used for a courthouse, which was built that year.

When Boulder citizens voted to buy the Batchelder tract for Chautauqua use, precedent was set for the acquisition of both city and mountain parks. The city bought the eastern slope of Flagstaff Mountain—some eighty acres—from the United States. On July 5, 1898, the day after Chautauqua opened, Boulder petitioned the federal government for another 1,800 acres stretching from Flagstaff Mountain west to Four Mile Creek and from Sunshine Canyon south to South Boulder Creek. Congress approved the gift in 1899. Some talked of making a private park atop Flagstaff Mountain which would be called Huggins Park. Boulder

Autos line diagonally in front of the newly-opened Hotel Boulderado. Note the open porches on Thirteenth Street. *Black photo, Boulder Public Library from the A.A. Paddock Collection*

A winter snow melts quickly in front of the old courthouse at Fourteenth and Pearl streets. *A.A. Paddock Collection*

continued to acquire lands in the area, either by gift or by purchase. Some were federal property, and some were state-owned lands. The privately owned Red Rocks and the Flatirons were bought because gravel-mining operations threatened the region.

In 1903, the Boulder City Improvement Association became active again under president Junius Henderson. Texado Park (Chautauqua's grounds) was bare; the group hired landscape architect W.W. Parce to plant greenery there. The Women's Club of Boulder raised $400 for the planting of trees. By 1907, a parks board became an official city department and slowly acquired Boulder Creek lands from the Colorado and Southern Railway. It was the board's intention to have a park along Boulder Creek stretching from the mouth of Boulder Canyon to the eastern edge of town. The city acquired one parcel of Central Park land in 1906, bought more lots in 1915, leased parcels from the railroad in 1921, and by 1933 completed the land purchase for Central Park. (Before that time, the land was commonly referred to as Railroad Park because most of the land was railroad-owned.)

There followed a spate of park naming; the top of Flagstaff Mountain was now called American Park. The land surrounding the reservoir in Sunshine Canyon and the Red Rocks was called Washington Park. In later years, even the sewage plant, now lying underneath part of Scott Carpenter Park, received a name—Valverdan Park.

Dr. and Mrs. William J. Baird gave 160 acres of their holdings in Gregory Canyon for park land in 1908. In 1911, Hannah Barker gave a small parcel of her land at Fifteenth and Spruce for a city hall or public building. (In 1929, part of this land was used as a day nursery.) Mrs. Barker's Nederland holdings would eventually be sold for Barker Dam. The C.G. Buckingham banking family donated their mining claims to the city in 1914. This donation included Boulder Falls and was given with the understanding that any tungsten found there would be extracted first. The Buckinghams, continuing their interest in parks for Boulder, gave thirty acres of Eldora land for a campground and in 1929 gave sixty acres of Left Hand Canyon land to Boulder. In the mid-1920s, Theodore Lashley sold five acres of his land to the city; the area was located next to the present Community Hospital. He then donated the purchase price of $3,000 so that the city could improve the land. William Beach gave twenty-two lots to Boulder in the late 1930s for the present Beach Park on University Hill.

Boulder would have developed quite differently if council had continued with its plans to create a War Memorial Park just south of Boulder Creek and east of Broadway. In 1919, Boulder voters approved by a very narrow margin of votes a $100,000 bond issue for a central recreation center. The site was to include a swimming pool, bandstand, playground, tennis courts, walks, drives, and even an auto camp. Those who supported these ambitious plans felt a patriotic duty to provide such a center in honor of those men who fought in World War I. (Boulder County had sent 773 men to fight; 51 died.) But in

1923 the soldiers were home, and times were getting hard. Public sentiment turned against the project, and the center was put to another vote and was defeated.

Boulder was also acquiring watershed lands near Nederland. A reservoir was built at Chautauqua in 1902, another in 1922. In 1906, James P. Maxwell sold his Silver Lake lands to Boulder for $46,000; 2,300 acres nearby were added in 1919. Ever since Eben Fine celebrated the turn of the century by climbing Arapaho Glacier, purchase of the ice field, called the "perpetual icebox," had been on the minds of some Boulder residents. In 1919, Boulder asked the U.S. Congress for permission to buy the glacier, saying that a proposed toll road threatened the area. However, Rocky Mountain National Park officials wanted to expand their park boundaries to include the glacier, so a strong lobby against the Boulder purchase was waged by the U.S. Parks Department. Boulder offered to pay $1.25 an acre for 3,695 acres surrounding the glacier, but the parks people thought that the price was too low. After years of delay, Boulder paid $4,618 to the United States and officially received title to the glacier and surrounding lands on August 7, 1929. By 1932, Boulder owned sixty-two acres of city park land and 6,300 acres in the mountains. In 1935, Green Lake was purchased, and in 1941, Glacier Lake was added to the city's watershed lands. In the mid-1930s, park land was reserved in both North and South Boulder for future use. North Boulder Park was improved in 1936.

Ten thousand people lived in Boulder when the Boulder City Improvement Association hired Frederick Law Olmsted, Jr. in 1908 to study the physical appearance of Boulder. Both Olmsted and his father were Harvard-trained in a new field—landscape architecture. The senior Olmsted was responsible for many park developments across the country, notably, New York's Central Park.

Olmsted was to answer the question, "What physical improvements within the reach of the city will help to make it increasingly convenient, agreeable and generally satisfactory as a place in which to live and work?" His answer was the report, "The Improvement of Boulder, Colorado," a beautifully written document published in 1910. (Many of the problems raised for immediate solution have not yet been solved; some have not even been addressed.) He stated his prejudices in the most agreeable prose. Boulder should never arrange itself for the benefit of the tourist, warned Olmsted. Tourists are of a class "who hastily pass through a place which attracts them, leaving a few nickels behind...taking not the slightest interest in the welfare of the community and often conducting themselves so as to interfere seriously with the comfort and welfare...of the permanent residents."[6] Olmsted was suspicious of suburban developers as a group, observing that they were not running "charitable enterprises;"[7] moreover, he said, they usually were from out of town. Dirty industry only denigrates a community, Olmsted advised; keep it out of Boulder.

Introducing his remarks about park lands and other beautification efforts, Olmsted remarked, "As with the food we eat and the air we breathe, so the sights habitually before our eyes play an immense part of determining whether we feel cheerful, efficient and fit for life, or the contrary."[8] He was concerned with the "mental and nervous condition of the people."[9] "Our object in all cases is to achieve Order."[10] Quoting an earlier planner, Olmsted continued, "We aim at Order and hope for Beauty."[11]

Olmsted saw Boulder as a city of homes. Everything that the municipality does, underlined Olmsted, should be to insure the stability of Boulder's residential neighborhoods. In other towns less fortunate, he said, people save their money to get out. Boulder should be a city of high quality homes surrounded by irrigated small farms and gardens. He hoped that Boulder's city officials would realize that a sign of civilized society was the effectiveness of "police" powers to insure good land use. (The planner recommended the city manager form of government.)

Olmsted felt that a clear distinction should be made between thoroughfare and residential streets. This would serve to raise real estate values, he predicted, for "there is a coziness and quiet attractiveness about a street of moderate length and width through which no heavy traffic has inducement to flow,"[12] and "the more certain a man can feel that the character of a given street is pretty well fixed, the more he is willing to pay for the privilege of having a lot on the kind of street he wants."[13]

The Harvard planner recommended the undergrounding of all wires, warning that delay would ruin the appearance of the town. Street lights have been built too high, Olmsted observed. As the trees grow, they will cover the street lights. Why not have them lower in the first place, said Olmsted. And further, he recommended, why should not Boulder's lamp posts be unique in design, distinct from any other city. The use of silver maples and cottonwoods was overdone; they are brittle and short-lived, Olmsted felt. He also discoursed at length at what he regarded as tree butchery, or the improper pruning of trees which turned them into "miserable cripples."

Olmsted studied the floodway at length and recommended that the safest and "the cheapest way of handling the flood problem of Boulder Creek"[14] was to have it committed to park land throughout the city. He saw the floodway as a series of playing fields, benches, and walkways. Delay, Olmsted warned, would result in a "costly piece of engineering construction serving no purpose other than the prevention of floods, whereas if the matter is taken in hand now the city will spend less money on the hydraulic improvement and get a beautiful parkway to boot."[15]

Boulder residents did not like industry. Planner Olmsted's view of Boulder as a nonindustrial community where careful attention would be given to the placement of necessary business expressed in the opinion of most residents who, from the first settlement of the town, felt that industry would damage Boulder. As early as 1871, the *Herald* chided the townspeople about their reluctance to attract industry, saying "We have laid idle, half asleep as it were, so long that we are letting many chances slip while other towns in our territory are taking advantage of the sloth and indolence manifested by us and are reaping a rich reward."[16] But L.C. Paddock reminded his Boulder *Daily Camera* readers in 1902 that the town "never enjoyed a boom and consequently has never been compelled to pay the penalty for one of those sporadic, feverish manifestations of ill-advised activity and speculation."[17]

The industries that were essential to Boulder's early development were here, to be sure. The sawmills, lumberyards, blacksmith shops, liveries, foundries, and brickyards were busy. In 1876, Abram K. Yount, a member of the first gold-seeking party, and his wife Ella took over the Red Rocks Mill, changing its name to the Colorado State Mill. Their flour was advertised as "Legal Tender." After the death of Mr. Yount, who died tragically under the wheels of a train moving out of the Boulder station, Mrs. Yount took over management of the mill until 1883 and did very well. Successive businessmen operated the flour mill after that, but the building burned down in 1900, was rebuilt, and burned again in 1905.

The DeKalb Sternberg family built their first flour mill at Twenty-sixth and Boulder Creek, but it, too, burned down. Their new mill, the Boulder Milling and Elevator Company at Eleventh and Walnut streets, sold premium "Lily-white" flour, advertised as more digestible than other flours because Jay Sternberg had invented the "Centennial Separator," which took the gravel out of the wheat.

Where wheat is grown, there may be a brewery; Boulder supported one until the time of prohibition. Frank Weisenhorn founded the Boulder City Brewing Company at Lincoln and Arapahoe streets. He built a handsome facility with rooming houses for his employees and surrounded it with beautiful landscaping and public beer gardens. Weisenhorn dug caves into the hillside to store kegs of beer. When the brewery was sold, its name changed to Crystal Springs Brewing and Ice Company; a side business was the sale of ice from a pond that the owners had dug near the site of the Boulder Public Library. The word "beer" did not receive a prominent place in Crystal Springs ads; rather, it was described as an "appetizer at meals and for strengthening the human system."[18] Even though Boulder became a "dry" community in 1907, 3.2 beer was allowed to be manufactured here because the beverage was not considered to be intoxicating.

James Develine and his son Edward established Boulder's first foundry in 1877 at Ninth and Pearl streets, calling it Boulder Foundry and Machine Shops. They manufactured steam engines and milling equipment. J.D. Long established his flower and vegetable seed business in 1905; three years later, he published his first catalog and offered flower bulbs for sale. (The Long family still operates Long's Gardens at 3240 Broadway.) Another Boulder family became interested in seeds. Professor and Mrs. Cockerell, both noted biologists, saw to their amazement, while breakfasting by a window one 1910 morning at their home at Eleventh and Aurora, a red sunflower. They took its seeds, bred several generations, and eventually sold the seeds to an English firm. While the Cockerells were involved in improving the strain of red sunflowers, there were constant visitors to the Aurora site to see the unusual flowers. The Deavenport Poultry Company was started in 1915 with one hen. The facility was located at 1900 Bluebell; Mr. Deavenport delivered his eggs to his customers on his bicycle.

Certain types of businesses disappeared because of changes in society. The many liveries in downtown Boulder closed down, and the names Telephone Stable and Tally-ho Stable became lost in history. Blacksmiths became less numerous, and the number of assaying offices downtown declined. Before the mining industry slowed down, Fred Mitchell had an assaying furnace at 1120 Pearl Street that could accommodate sixty samples of ore at one time. There continued to be calls for factories, but the townspeople continued to drag their feet. L.C. Paddock of the *Camera* tried to change public opinion, saying, "Boulder must have factories and the only way to get them is to seize them when in sight. Sugar catches more flies than vinegar and bilious traitors to their own city should be weeded out...."[19]

Boulder had so few industries just before World War I that when one said "the plant," everyone knew that it meant Western Cutlery and Manufacturing Company. H.N. Platts established the family business in 1913 at Broadway and Marine streets. By 1920, twenty employees manufactured the cutlery, which included pocketknives, hunting knives, and kitchen knives. During World War II, since Western Cutlery's main customer was the federal government, the company concentrated on the manufacture of various "survival" knives. (The business is now located in Longmont.)[20]

Mining prospects were not totally dead in the mountains. In 1918, Richard G. Place, mining engineer for the Golden Age Mining and Milling Company, Jamestown, analyzed some unfamiliar samples, but his tests were inconclusive. After several unsuccessful tries, Place decided to use the Madame Curie test, which showed that he was testing pitchblende, a uranium ore. Although little uranium mining is being done today, there is still much speculation concerning the amount of uranium that could be found in Boulder County, particularly in the Indian Peaks area.

A few men join the WCTU ladies, Women's Christian Temperance Union, for a July 1915 group portrait at Chautauqua. *Nelson photo, Western Historical Collections, University of Colorado at Boulder*

Chapter Ten

And now resolve we will not take,
Nor give, nor buy, nor sell, nor make,
Through all the years of mortal life,
Those drinks which cause pain, woe and strife
Rum, Brandy, Whiskey, Cordials fine,
Gin, Cider, Porter, Ale, and Wine.

—Old Temperance Vow

When the United States went "dry" in 1920, the state of Colorado had already been dry for four years; Boulder had been dry for thirteen. Some say that Colorado went dry early because it gave women the right to vote in 1893. (However, consider "wet" Wyoming [except for the time that the Volstead Act was in force], the first in the Union to give women the right to vote in 1869.) Even though Boulder City was considered a "wide-open" frontier town in the 1870s, never more than thirty saloons were open at one time, not counting the liquor served in houses of prostitution. Since miners passing through Boulder to the mines above demanded liquor, some of Boulder's new businessmen were not averse to taking the miners' money. Several of the mining camps, however, were dry by choice.

As the town was settled and agricultural people made their homes in the valley, saloon life and liquor were less in demand. Moreover, from the first year of settlement, strong pressure was exerted against the sale of liquor. In 1869, 100 women gave $93.50 to a local newspaper when the editor refused advertising from liquor merchants. Before 1871, the county taxed the saloons. That year, however, the city decided that it should benefit from "liquid sources" and licensed saloons at $100 a year to sell "spiritous, vinous, fermented and intoxicating liquors."[1] (Saloon keepers were also required to post a $300 bond and to obey all city ordinances.) In 1873, the city collected more revenue from saloons and billiards parlors ($2,425.95) than it did from property taxes ($1,800).

By the late 1870s, two groups of voters, very much polarized, had developed. On one side, the Good Templars (formed in 1876), the Prohibition Alliance (formed in 1879), the Anti-Saloon League, a "Blue Ribbon" committee, and the Independent Champions of the Red Cross allied themselves to back dry candidates for public office. The presence of a university was a strong part of their argument. On the other side were the High Licensers, businessmen, and most of the town's trustees, who preferred what they called a more realistic approach. They wanted the miners' trade and could see the benefit to the town from imposing high license fees on the saloons.

A first victory for temperance, though small, was the vote to close saloons at midnight and to force saloon keepers to refrain from hiring "lewd women." With each local election, temperance as an issue grew in strength and appeal. Laws were sporadically adopted to close saloons on Sundays and to compel businessmen not to sell to minors, but such ordinances were difficult to enforce. The town trustees were not that enthusiastic about curtailing the financial benefits that they saw coming from open saloons. As the license fees went up, and they did every year or so, the number of drinking establishments decreased. In 1883, twenty-eight saloons paid yearly license fees of $240 each; by 1888, six or seven saloons paid $1,000 for a license, a victory claimed by the temperance movement. W.H. Allison was mayor in 1883 when temperance forces prevailed and saloons were again closed on Sundays. When Allison quit, in disgust with politics in general, dry Alpheus Wright, a lawyer, became mayor. Even so, the saloons opened again due to public demand.

In 1889, when Marshal "Shep" Madera took office amid cries that saloon life was out of control, he restored order, but the fight between the High Licensers and the Prohibitionists went on. In 1895, one dry alderman tried to raise the license to $1,500 a year, but he could not get a second to his motion. In 1896, the Jim Conway Saloon (northwest corner of Broadway and Pearl streets) had to close because of an ordinance that prohibited saloons to operate on a corner lot. Local brewer Frank Weisenhorn served as alderman in the 1880s and 1890s. His firm, Boulder City Brewery, marketed, among other brews, Zang's Pilsener Bottled Beer, a popular drink at that time. In general, the wets prevailed, but each election was more closely contested.

The Women's Christian Temperance Union (WCTU) held its state convention in Boulder in August 1881 under the leadership of Mrs. Adrianna Hungerford. When the Union discovered that one of its members owned real estate rented to a saloon keeper, the WCTU gave the "offender" one month to evict the saloon. Evidently, no eviction occurred, and the group "allowed" the member and her daughter to resign.

Around 1900, formation of the Better Boulder Party served to coalesce temperance and prohibitionist groups. In addition to being antiliquor, they were antigraft, against the use of chlorine in the city's drinking water, for strong Sabbath laws, and, incongruously, for municipal ownership of utilities. Newspaper editor Lucius C. Paddock was enraged with what he felt was a lack of logic on the part of the prohibitionists. They were willing, he said, to set up a reading room to "lure" the young men away from the saloons, but they were unwilling to see that high saloon licenses would provide the necessary revenue, $37,000, to establish a proper library. He said of the Better Boulder Party, "They don't grasp an idea. The idea grasps them, takes possession of them and drives out of their minds all other ideas."[2] Paddock said further, "A touch of the old Pilgrim spirit is a good thing in any community, that is to say a little of it, just enough to give flavor like...a few drops of vanilla in a barrel of ice cream...but let the spirit dominate and the result is as deadly as the torrid winds that sweep the Sahara, withering all things with its fiery touch."[3]

At one point, an ordinance was proposed to require all saloons to have a large front window (no back rooms, please) so that one could see who was inside, but it did not pass. Each saloon had its own flavor, of course. Henry's, on the north side of Pearl Street between Twelfth and Thirteenth, appealed to the "elite" trade. Charley Johnson's, located on the southeast corner of Eleventh and Pearl streets, and Fred Burger's on the north side of Pearl Street between Eleventh and Twelfth, appealed to the moderate drinker. However, Garbarino's ("two schooners for a nickel") at Eleventh and Pearl and the Board of Trade Saloon, Twelfth and Pearl, were considered so disreputable that temperance groups forced their closing.

In 1907, after years of steadily building their political base, and after two WCTU conventions in Boulder, the Better Boulder Party won most of the seats on council. Prohibitionist and former Gold Hill shopkeeper Isaac T. Earl became mayor and closed down the drinking establishments. Boulder's era of saloon life passed into history. An ordinance was adopted that no liquor would be sold in Boulder or within one mile of the city limits, with the following exceptions: sacramental wines required in church services (taxed at one dollar a year), and the liquor kept in stock at a few pharmacies for doctors' prescriptions. At first the pharmacy was taxed five dollars a year, but that fee rose. Since the pharmacist paid dearly for a license to dispense liquor by prescription, it must have been worth it. Some doctors in town were not concerned with the local laws and wrote prescriptions for liquor to trusted customers. Druggist Eben Fine, himself a teetotaler, tried to stop this practice by buying a liquor license himself, then refusing to sell alcohol.

In 1909, the Prohibitionists lost the local elections by four votes to a businessmen's ticket that had "had enough of the Better Boulder Party."[4] L.C. Paddock of the *Camera* crowed, "the municipal nightmare is over and a reign of sanity in public office here has come again."[5] But the saloons did not open again. As revivalist Billy Sunday was a Chautauqua speaker that year, he must have inspired temperance groups, for two years later, seven dry alderman were back in office. Under the direction of dry Mayor E.D. Webb, council passed an ordinance prohibiting billboards to advertise liquor. At a 1913 city council meeting, W.L. Armstrong suggested that the Crystal Springs Brewery be burned down. Mayor Webb replied that he felt *all* breweries in Colorado should be burned to the ground. (Indeed, the Crystal Springs Brewery did burn to the ground in 1921.) When the charter passed in 1918, the temperance group was strong enough to get the following provision included: "No license shall ever be granted for the manufacture or sale of intoxicating liquors within the city limits of the City

The boys are home! Armistice Day parade crossing Broadway at Pearl Street. The First National Bank (replaced by the Broadway Building) is in background. *Western Historical Collections, University of Colorado at Boulder*

Boulder looks over a World War I tank, part of the Armistice Day parade. Note "Pike's Peak or Bust" lettered on the tank. *Charles Snow photo, Western Historical Collections, University of Colorado at Boulder*

of Boulder, or within its territorial jurisdiction."

As elsewhere, liquor was smuggled in. Some came in from Wyoming. Until 1916, California grape growers delivered their wines to Denver, where Boulderites could quietly pick them up. Boulder ladies, who took the Interurban train to Denver for a day of shopping, found that large handbags were very convenient to hide their alcoholic purchases. A fruit dealer in St. Louis found it profitable to disguise his cider (6 to 7 percent alcohol) with layers of olive oil and salad dressing on the top of his packing cases. After national prohibition in 1920, liquor came in from Mexico or Canada. By this time, the sugar beet industry was established in northern Colorado. One sugar beet liquor recipe for "Sugar Moon" suggested:

120 pounds sugar beets
50 gallons spring water
1½ pounds yeast

This concoction was to be set aside to ferment for ten days at eighty degrees, then boiled. The steam from this recipe produced a passable liquor.

Although bootleggers operated in the mountains during the time of the Volstead Act, liquor making was not as prevalent in Colorado as in other parts of the country. The majority of the stills were in the Pueblo area, although Louisville had a still disguised as a coal mine. Members of the Ku Klux Klan devoted themselves to knocking over still operations throughout the state. In 1923, Sheriff Blum celebrated his first day in office by raiding two bootlegging operations. At about the same time, Chief of Police Claud F. Head and members of the sheriff's office staged a raid at the establishment of Mrs. Ethel Bellairs, where they found a big "booze stock."[6] Thus began a Boulder mystery that was never solved. Chief Head did not use any of his own officers in the raid; he knew that one of his men had a personal relationship with Mrs. Bellairs, and he feared that the officer would alert her in advance. Rumor had it (did the Ku Klux Klan start it?) that a city truck was used to haul sugar beets to a still. After Head's raid, five police officers and the sheriff met with the city manager and asked him to fire Chief Head. The city manager instead fired the officers for insubordination. Elmer Cobb was one of the officers. The other four were reinstated but Cobb was given notice. On November 19, 1923, Officer Cobb was found dead at Ninth and Canyon, shot in the head. Many groups, including the Klan, offered rewards for information relating to Officer Cobb's death, but only a derelict came forward with confusing information. Evidently, it did not confuse the grand jury, for on January 30, 1924, Chief Head himself was indicted for the murder of Officer Cobb. Although Head was tried, he was acquitted; the affair was never resolved to anyone's satisfaction.

Boulder's finest sit on the running board of their first police car. Second from right is Officer Elmer Cobb who, in a year or two, will be found murdered downtown. Extreme right: Chief Bass, who will also die in the police car. *photo, Boulder Police Department*

Boulder's municipal building at 1921 Fourteenth Street, site of the Colorado Building. *A.A. Paddock Collection*

On May Day of 1928, Sheriff Blum, acting on a tip, traveled with a posse to Spring Gulch, two and one-half miles east of Ward. He found yeast tailings in the creek nearby, entered a cabin, and moved a burning wood stove. Behind the stove, the men opened a trap door that led to a still which produced $1,500 worth of liquor a day for its owners. These ingenious liquor makers brought their product out of the foothills by sled in the winter and thus managed to make around $450,000 each season by selling mash to Boulderites.

Through the years, fourteen elections were held to repeal Boulder's dry law. A successful fifteenth attempt in 1967 allowed Boulderites to drink legally in public.

By 1915, a veritable bureaucracy had developed in city government with the addition of a building inspector, an assistant city clerk, a supervisor of sewers, a dairy inspector, professional firemen and policemen, a paid scavenger (a volunteer job since 1866), and a salaried dog catcher. It was also in 1915 that terms for aldermen were staggered—four were elected for four years, and four for two years.

Since 1909, the notion of a city manager form of government had been discussed, both locally and nationally. Frederick Olmsted recommended it for Boulder. In 1910, a petition was delivered to council to authorize an election to see how the voters felt about home rule and the city manager form of government. Home rule lost 1,804 to 1,129, which expressed the general feeling that a convention to write a charter would be too expensive. By 1913, the businessmen were again in charge of city government with a candidate they felt would be a perfect mayor. W.L. Armstrong was retired, wealthy, and conservative and had the energy to be a full-time mayor. The following year, the idea of a business manager form of government was again put to a vote and was defeated 832 to 676. By this time, however, those devoted to the city manager scheme knew that if they kept working at it, Boulder would eventually support it. And they were right.

Early in 1917, Boulderites elected Mayor F.J. Klingler, who opposed the conservative incumbent Armstrong. Klingler wanted home rule, while Armstrong stood for the status quo; Klingler won 1,450 to 1,327. Although the new mayor wanted Boulder to have a charter, he was regarded as rigid in temperament. One alderman described him as "either a tyrant, a lunatic, or striving for political favor."[7] Another alderman is reported to have said to Klingler's face: "cooperation is impossible—might as well try to cooperate with a porcupine as with you."[8]

In a series of three special elections beginning in the late spring of 1917 and ending in December of that year, Boulder had its home rule convention, drafted a charter, and approved it. Among the men who made up the charter convention were two ladies—temperance-minded Ida Campbell, a widow active in civic affairs, and the diminutive, aristocratic Flora McHarg. Mrs. McHarg was graduated in 1901 from the University of Colorado's first three-year law class, having passed the bar a year earlier,* reversing the usual procedure. Although she did not practice law actively, she used her knowledge to help write and revise the charter and design the voting system. She served on Boulder's first parks board (1905-1917), then on the new parks and planning board until 1920, when she was elected to a term on council. She helped to start a day nursery, establish Community Hospital, started the visiting nurse program in Boulder, encouraged the building of the university's first dormitory for women, served on the board of Blue Bird Cottage (for professional women), helped establish the first juvenile court system in Colorado, acted as legal

*The Colorado Supreme Court held a session to decide whether or not Mrs. McHarg would be allowed to use Esquire after her name. It decided that she could do so if she used only the abbreviated form, "Esq."

These Boulder citizens pause in their work of writing a city charter: back row, left to right: O.E. Heinrich, city manager, Bob Nafe, assistant secretary, Charles Fawcett, William V. Casey, superintendent of schools, H.P. Gamble, Ed Fair, and E.S. Evans. Third row, left to right: Wesley Foster, S.A. Greenwood, Dr. W.P. Harlow, Joe Bergheim and W. Flint Smith. Second row, left to right: H.O. Andrew, H.B. Millard, Ida Campbell, F.C. Moys, and Louis Herman. First row, left to right: Charles O. Sundquist, Flora S. McHarg, Clair V. Mann, secretary, J.E. Ingram, vice president, and Ira M. DeLong, president of the charter convention. *Western Historical Collections, University of Colorado at Boulder*

Boulder's first city council meet in elegant chambers. The woman is Ida Campbell, who helped draft the charter, adopted in 1917. To the right of Mrs. Campbell is F.C. Moys, Boulder's first mayor under the charter. *Western Historical Collections, University of Colorado at Boulder*

adviser to women's groups, and worked in the Presbyterian Church, the Red Cross, Fortnightly, the AAUW, and the DAR. (During the last years of her public service, she accomplished her work from a wheelchair.)

From a list of twenty contenders, nine council members were elected in 1917 for six-year terms. The winners selected hardwareman F.C. Moys as the first mayor under the new charter, and lawyer Frank L. Moorhead was chosen acting city manager. Of the nine, one woman, Ida Campbell, was elected, and, due to her presence, the first order of business before council was "should smoking in chambers be allowed?" Mrs. Campbell was described as "faithful, sensible, and businesslike. She doesn't run wild with fads—nor did she talk bonnets when the subject was bridges."9

Boulder was the second city in the nation to adopt the Hare system of voting for local candidates (Ashtabula, Ohio, was the first) and Flora McHarg was largely responsible for its acceptance. Boulder used the complicated system until 1947. The Hare system was an attempt to give fair representation to minority points of view at the local level, but the system itself figured in a number of vicious political fights in the 1920s. The voter, instead of merely voting for the candidates of his choice, ranked them in order of his preference. Before the votes were counted, a formula was established whereby the number of ballots was divided by the number of offices to be filled. In order to win, a candidate must have received more votes than the formula's quotient. In the first round of counting, a candidate who received more than enough votes under the formula was declared a winner. The counting began again. Candidates receiving the lowest number of first-choice votes were declared losers, and their ballots were reassigned to the second-choice candidates. This process continued over and over again, sometimes eight or nine times, until enough candidates received the right number of votes according to the formula.* Although the strengths and weaknesses of the Hare system were the subject of much political fighting, the system lasted in Boulder longer than in any municipality in the country.

City government was divided into five departments: Public Service, Public Health, Public Welfare, Finance and Records, and Public Safety. (The last department was headed by the city manager.) Two appointive commissions were created: the Library Commission

---

*Former council member J. Perry Bartlett once said that Christian Recht, a mathematics teacher at Boulder High School, was one of the few who fully understood the system.

161

Eleven employees make up the city administration in 1918. Second from left is Marshal Lawrence P. Bass (now Chief Bass); fifth from right is Fire Chief Emil A. Johnson; third from right is the first city manager, O.E. Heinrich. *Western Historical Collections, University of Colorado at Boulder*

and the Planning and Parks Commission. Boulder's first city manager was a police chief recruited from California with a reputation for solving serious crimes. O.E. Heinrich was a sort of American Inspector Poirot, and, as he took office in February 1918, he stated simply, "I shall do nothing precipitate."[10] Heinrich was chosen from a field of candidates as a man "with the engineering ingenuity of General Goethals, the business acumen of William McAdoo, and the diplomatic wisdom of Woodrow Wilson."[11] He lasted one year. As he resigned, under threat of being discharged, Heinrich stated, "One's country may inspire one to die for it, but a municipality is scarcely worth the supreme sacrifice."[12] He returned to the life of Inspector Poirot and won national acclaim for crime deduction. F.C. Moys, while musing on the difficulties of the city manager's job, said in 1922, "If Christ himself were city manager of Boulder, there would be some people who would want to recall him."[13]

In 1922, after a short period of municipal peace, the first of two wild, disorganized, and vicious political fights broke out in Boulder. Former Mayor F.J. Klingler, a previous supporter of the charter, now led the "reform" movement, whose numbers felt that the city manager had too much power. Further, it was believed that council was abusing its power by overuse of the charter's emergency clause; citizens complained that council could effect changes before objections could be raised. Just four years after the charter was in place, members of the first Boulder City Council faced the threat of recall, although nothing came of it. The main issue was the city's ambitious program to pave Boulder's streets. Pearl Street had been paved, finally, during World War I. By 1923, only ten miles of Boulder streets had been paved. However, a group of ladies from Mapleton Hill demanded that the city discontinue its street paving program. They feared that "maniacs" in city hall were attempting to pave the whole city of Boulder. In addition, some charged the use of inferior materials and graft. At one point, a court injunction was obtained to stop further paving of streets in the Mapleton neighborhood. This anti-paving climate continued to such an extent that, by 1932, only fifteen miles of local streets had been paved. The Hare system of voting was also under fire; its critics maintained that voters lost their franchise because of a confusing ballot. In a special election the following year, the charter was supported by the people with the largest vote in Boulder history to that point—2,730 to 1,340. Klingler's group retired from battle, but only briefly.

The charter fight of 1925 made the fight of 1923 look like minor squabbling. It was dirty. The same issues were raised, but new ones were added. Some accused the city manager of poisoning the populace

Fire horses are moving briskly along the 900 block of Pearl Street with T.C. Black, Jr. at the reins. *A.A. Paddock Collection*

by putting chlorine in the city's drinking water. A grand jury investigated the charge and found "nothing wrong."[14] Lack of law enforcement was charged. The allegation that a city truck was used to transport a load of sugar beets to a still was brought up again. The circumstances surrounding Officer Cobb's murder were whispered, then shouted; someone in the city administration had done him in. Supporters of the charter shouted back that their opposition was really led by the Ku Klux Klan. The Ministerial Association issued an appeal for peace, urging "all well-disposed citizens to refrain from personalities, the spreading of rumors, the casting of reflections upon the reputations of men and women of tried integrity by suggestion or innuendo, and to try to promote good-will and a fair discussion of the real issues that we may keep unbroken the fellowship that has characterized Boulder."[15] Again, the charter survived. Council members, under threat of recall, survived also by a vote of 1,709 to 1,284.

In 1933, Boulder suffered a milder outbreak of hostilities, this time centered on the Hare system itself. Because the voters could not "X" their ballots, some regarded the elections as unfair. The method of counting was arduous and confusing. Since the last names of candidates were always alphabetized, it was charged, with some truth, that no one ever won a seat on council whose last name began with a letter from the last half of the alphabet. The charter survived again, and by the 1940s, four candidates, whose last names began with letters in the second half of the alphabet, finally won seats on council.

Boulder's fire department became professional in fits and starts. In 1898, Chief Robert May was the first department head to receive a salary—sixty dollars a month. His three firemen were paid as well. From the beginning, rules of behavior for professional firefighters were strict. No overt politicking was allowed, nor could a fireman appear in a saloon in his uniform. He had to be careful to abstain from "violent, abusive, or immoderate language. Immorality, indecency, or profanity will not be tolerated, nor will any controversy upon religious or political topics."[16]

When George Fonda became chief in 1906, for the fourth time, his was an "outside" appointment, since he did not rise from the ranks as a professional. He gave his salary to his wife for "pin money" on the condition that she would locate each fire by telephone while he cranked up his sixty-horsepower auto out in the stable. It had not been too many years earlier that Fonda's fire horses were stabled there; when the fire alarm bell pealed, the horses automatically moved down a ramp in the stable in order to be harnessed to the fire wagon. Druggist Fonda had a lifelong love affair with the fire department. As a young man, he took honors as the town's fastest runner on the hose

163

team. He was often praised for his public spirit in working to expand the fire department, but his desire to be in the thick of the fray was not for the good of the city alone, he said, for racing to fires was "just bully good fun."[17]

In 1908, Chief Fonda told council that five firemen and one fire station were not enough. (Fire Station No. 1 was at 1038 Pearl Street.) "Boulder is no longer a village,"[18] he said, recommending two more stations and three more paid firemen. Station No. 2 was built at 1020 Aurora and was sometimes called the University or Mt. St. Gertrude Station. (Presently it is used as a pottery lab by the Recreation Department.) Station No. 3 was built on the sanitarium's property (Boulder Memorial Hospital) facing Fourth Street, near Maxwell. The Mapleton Station was added because neither men nor horses could pull fire equipment up Mapleton Hill. However, the station was used for ten years only; it closed in 1918 and was converted to a dormitory for the hospital's nurses. (Later, a grocery used the old fire station until it was razed to make way for the present Dakota Ridge Medical Building.)

Another "outside" chief, W.W. McAllister, raced to each fire on his motorcycle. During his administration, the city's first fire truck was brought in 1913. It was a six-cylinder, ninety-horsepower Seagrave (cost: $5,000) with the facility to carry hoses, chemicals, and ladders. The machine was touted as having enough power to climb any hill in town. Chief McAllister reported to council that the "auto had made all of the hills around the city and, with one or two exceptions, has done so on the high gear. The low gear has not been used."[19] A siren for the vehicle was added later. By 1915, the city added a chemical truck to its firefighting capacity—a converted Ford with a white chassis, trimmed with gold and silver (University of Colorado colors), left-handed steering, and electric lights and starter. These two purchases marked the end of fire horses and running hose men. The last of the city's beloved hose companies, Boulder Hose No. 1, celebrated its disbanding by giving $500 to a fund for injured firemen. The city almost sold the hose cart to Lafayette, but popular sentiment forced the city to keep it.

Until the tenure of Chief Emil A. Johnson,

Boulder's firemen are proud of their conversion to motor vehicles. In front of the Mount St. Gertrude Fire Station No. 2, they display a 1915 White at left, a 1914 Ford in the middle, and a 1913 Seagrave at right.
A.A. Paddock Collection

firefighters worked a twenty-four hour shift. Johnson worked for the platoon system in 1921, so that while some firemen worked, others rested. Chief Johnson, who enjoyed a long career with the fire department (he was chief from 1916 to 1956), not only kept careful records of alarms, fires, and loss of property, but he expanded his department to include inspectors, fire prevention educators, parade supervisors, and guards. (He also took care of the town's flags and Christmas decorations.) By 1944, the force consisted of thirteen professional firemen. The following year, council authorized $10,000 for a more modern fire truck.

In 1901, Boulder's police department not only installed a telephone but also ordered a supply of Nelson's Humane Police Clubs, made of hard rubber. Lawrence P. Bass, a noted photographer and sometime miner and expert rock driller, was in and out of law enforcement* for some years. He produced the department's first rules and regulations for police officers:

*Bass was city police officer from 1894 to 1900 and from 1903 to 1905. He was marshal from 1900 to 1901 and from 1909 to 1917 and was the first chief of police under the charter from 1918 to 1920.

Marshal Lawrence P. Bass, active in police work from the 1890s to 1920, was also known for his rock-drilling ability and his photographic skill. *A.A. Paddock Collection*

officers were not to drink, nor could they visit a saloon unless on police business. For the first time, police officers would wear the same uniform. The department acquired a motorcycle, a sign of progress of which the police were very proud.

By 1916, the number of automobiles in town had grown so that the department was obliged to post speed limit signs. At the time of the charter, Marshal Bass, a twenty-eight-year veteran in law enforcement, became Chief Bass, although most continued to call him "Marshal." Linda M. Lee assumed the duties of police magistrate and justice of the peace. In March 1920, Chief Bass proudly displayed the town's first police car. One week later, as he sped to a fire, the new police car collided with a fire truck. Chief Bass, as well as the son of City Manager W.D. Salter, were killed. During the 1920s, three police divisions were created: traffic; investigation and juvenile; and radio, records, and patrol. Six to eight police officers patrolled all of Boulder on a twenty-four hour basis.

During the 1930s, Boulder boys, as elsewhere, joined the Junior Police; some played in the Junior Police Band. By 1939, Boulder's only patrol car was installed with a one-way shortwave radio, a sign of progress but difficult to use, because the police radio band was shared with Denver, Longmont, and Brighton (and continued to be shared until well into the 1950s). By 1944, Boulder had two police cars with two-way radio service as well as a motorcycle and a force of seventeen men. In 1957, a third fatality* occurred in Boulder's police department. Patrolman Raymond McMasters was shot and run over by criminals Vernon and Revilo Sides, who were wanted in connection with a robbery in Lyons; both men were convicted.

After the "light plant"* acquired Boulder's modest streetcar system in 1901, the franchise continued with the understanding that the streetcars would probably operate at a loss but that residents' power bills could be raised instead. When streetcar fare was raised to ten cents in 1902, the dwindling number of patrons was reduced even more. The following year, buses were discussed as an alternative to the streetcar; however, buses did not come to Boulder until 1931. The bus line operated in the black once in its history. When gas rationing was imposed during World War II, Boulder's buses made a profit. With the establishment of the Regional Transportation District in 1972, Public Service Company was finally able to divest itself of the burden of running Boulder's public transportation system.

During the 1920s, Boulder did not escape

*In addition to Marshal Bass' death in an automobile accident, Officer Cobb was murdered by unknown parties in 1923.

*Officially called the Boulder Electric Light Company, then the Northern Colorado Power Company

In the 1920s, Boulder's police department consisted of four officers, two motorcycles, and one car. *photo, Boulder Police Department*

Posing in front of the new courthouse fountain, members of the Boulder Junior Police Band look soberly at the camera. *photo, Boulder Police Department*

Boulder's first bus system, June 1931. *Charles Snow photo, Western Historical Collections, University of Colorado at Boulder*

America's passion, however temporary, for the Ku Klux Klan and its tenets of hate; indeed, Denver, Colorado Springs, Boulder, Pueblo, and Grand Junction were the western stronghold for Klan activities.

> *I would rather be a Klansman
> in a robe of snowy white,
> Than to be a Catholic Priest
> in a robe as black as night;
> For a Klansman is AMERICAN
> and AMERICA is his home,
> But a priest owes his allegiance
> to a Dago Pope in Rome.* [20]

This poetic invective was published in Boulder in 1925 by the *Rocky Mountain American*, organ of Colorado's Ku Klux Klan. On December 11, 1922, a different sort of parade came down Pearl Street—a nighttime parade with no children, no bands, no horses, just three hundred white-hooded figures riding in sixty-three autos (the license plates covered so that their owners could not be traced). A single float was decorated with signs that read "100 percent American," "Join the Invisible Empire," and "Watch Us Grow in Boulder."

The Klan movement in Colorado started as the Denver Doers Club, directed by John Galen Locke, a doctor who was denied membership in the Denver County Medical Society. By 1921, the Klan came out into the open to form Klavern No. 1 in Denver. In Boulder, the *Rocky Mountain American* warned, "Insane, feebleminded and diseased undesirable aliens are being freely admitted to this country."[21] The Klan's declared purposes were to gain control of the state, keep "non-Americans" out, get rid of those already here, remove the state civil service, and sponsor a bill making it illegal to use wine as a sacrament. (This last was aimed at the Catholic Church.) Not only was the Klan against Catholics, but blacks, Jews, orientals, and most foreign-born. Klansmen believed that the rise in the number of female smokers was due to Jewish influence in the movies. Further, Jews were out to do the small businessman in, as they were behind the growing chain business movement in the United States.

The Klan did gain control of the state by infiltrating the Republican Party. They took over its

On a summer evening in 1922, a Denver newsman took the first photo of a Colorado Klan ceremony to initiate 150 Boulder citizens into Klavern No. 3. The reporter stated that five hundred cars circled the area, their headlights lighting a canyon north of Boulder, while some 2,500 Colorado Klansmen watched the proceedings, then enjoyed a barbeque. *Denver Public Library*

convention in 1924, replacing Republican candidates with Klan candidates. (Just before the election, specially marked ballots were sent throughout the state, including Boulder, to Klan members so that they would know how to vote.) When Klansman Clarence Morley was elected governor, he took daily orders from Grand Dragon Locke. In 1925, both houses of the state legislature were controlled by Klansmen. Colorado national senators were Klan-supported as was the mayor of Denver. Longmont was controlled by the Klan for a time. A number of these officeholders stated publicly that they were not Klan-supported, but they said otherwise at Klan meetings. The Klan published lists of newspapers that it did not like (i.e., those that criticized the Klan) and "advised" Klan businessmen not to advertise in them.

Grand Dragon Locke never recovered from the insult of being denied membership in a medical society; hence, he was delighted when Governor Morley appointed him to the State Board of Medical Examiners. Dr. Locke also tried to gain control of the National Guard, but Adjutant General Paul Newlon fought back and kept the group free of Klan control.

On a July 1922 evening, a Denver Klan group met with about two hundred prospective Boulder Klansmen and, in a remote area five miles north of town, initiated them into Klavern No. 3. (Klavern No. 2 was in Colorado Springs.) They taught the new members the secret handshake, passwords, passages from the Klansmen's manual, and other Klan ritual. The new recruits paid a $10.00 initiation fee and $6.50 for a white sheet and hood. That the membership was growing could be determined by taking "inventory of excessive numbers of sheets and pillow cases"[22] on Monday morning's wash line.*

A local department store newly established in downtown Boulder knew its customers when it advertised "Spring values in our White Goods Department." Wizard Sheets were ninety-eights cents, and Wizard Cases were twenty-five cents. The Paris Dry Cleaning

*James H. Davis,[23] scholar of the period, estimates three hundred to five hundred Boulderites in the Klan. On the other hand, historian Robert G. Athearn feels that one thousand Boulder citizens joined Klavern No. 3. The Colorado Historical Society has in its archives a membership list of 25,000 names, purported to be Klansmen, which it acquired from Lee Casey, a *Rocky Mountain News* reporter.

Parlor advertised its services for "Klothes Karefully Kleaned." The *Daily Camera* was not highly regarded by the Klan when the newspaper referred to the group as the Komic Kapers Klub.

James H. Davis, in his work on the Klan, tells the story of a Boulder widow who, when she visited the new grave of her dead husband, found members of the Klan burning a cross to commemorate the passing of a fellow Klan member. Until then, she never dreamed that her husband was a member and later wrote to the paper that she would "have trouble facing the world"[24] knowing that her husband might have been a Klansman. Klansmen often appeared at graves of nonmembers, however, to give the impression of wide membership. Crosses burned on Catholic lawns in Louisville and Lafayette. A giant fifty-foot cross burned on Flagstaff Mountain in May 1924. Hooded Klansmen appeared silently and suddenly, as was their style, at meetings of Boulder's Salvation Army with gifts of money. Members of the local Christian Church applauded heavily if not nervously after eight hooded figures invaded their meeting.

George Norlin, president of the University of Colorado, had his troubles with the Klan. Klansman W. Rice Means, candidate for the U.S. Senate, asked if he could participate in the kickoff for the Colorado-Utah football game. The university replied, "Mr. Means can kick-off anywhere he wants, except in Boulder."[25] Norlin was also told by Klansman Clarence Morley to rid the faculty of Catholics and Jews or suffer financial consequences. Norlin refused to do so; little money came to the university from the legislature that year.

Recovering from the shock of takeover, Colorado Republicans began to regroup and, together with the Democrats, kept Klan-sponsored bills in committee in an effort to thwart the Klan. Governor Morley's position was weakened by the legislature that fought his proposals. By the end of 1926, many of the Klan-supported officeholders were on their way out. The Invisible Empire collapsed with the removal of Dr. Locke as the Grand Dragon. He had neglected to pay his income taxes since 1913; further, it appeared that he had appropriated some of the Klan's treasury for his personal use. Dr. Locke then formed a local Minute Men of America. The Boulder Klavern joined this group, but it did not survive, nor did the *Rocky Mountain American.* Editor William Francis' last editorial on July 23, 1925 stated, "Boulder Klavern No. 3 officially died at the stroke of midnight...."

A climbing party rests on Arapaho glacier on August 30, 1921. *Western Historical Collections, University of Colorado at Boulder*

A Boulder school teacher looks over the Arapaho glacier. *Edna Harkins Collection*

No men are present at this mountain outing. Young school teachers bare their legs in a shocking manner. *Edna Harkins Collection*

A hiker studies a crevasse on the glacier. *Charles Snow photo, Western Historical Collection, University of Colorado at Boulder*

Having spent the night on Flagstaff Mountain wrapped in blankets, this group watches the sun come up over the Boulder valley. *Ed Tangen photo, Edna Harkins Collection*

Chapter Eleven

Boulder's traditional feisty nature may be due in part to the great number of highly educated women with the will and the time to devote to civic life. By the turn of the century, women had organized in a variety of ways. Not only did they take an active role in political life, they were the backbone of the Better Boulder Party. They also formed groups and clubs to discuss such "unwomanly" subjects as politics, history, and literature. The women's group, Fortnightly, was organized in 1884 by language professor Mary Rippon and Mrs. Robert Culver. Eager to use her time wisely, Mrs. Culver read books while washing dishes and studied newspapers while churning the family butter. The Recluse Club, precursor of Hypatia, was composed of six female teachers of history who started meeting in 1890 to discuss matters of mutual interest. Other groups in which women could get together and stretch their minds were the Classics Club, Forget-Me-Not, the Current Events Club, the Mothers' Club, and the Domestic Science Club. Activities at Chautauqua provided excellent opportunities for women eager to expand their horizons.

A University of Colorado president's wife, Jennie Hilton Baker, is credited with the formation of the Women's Club of Boulder in 1901. With 180 charter members, the club vigorously pressed for a day care nursery and visiting nurse program, for a maternity ward at University Hospital (the present Wardenburg Student Health Center), for a cafeteria at State Preparatory School, for public restrooms at the courthouse, and for improvements in Boulder's sanitary conditions. Not only did the ladies loan money to women wishing to go to college, but they bought items that they thought were needed, such as a $300 organ for Macky Auditorium. Jennie Baker also formed the Women's League on the university campus in 1896, a group for those women who did not join a sorority.

Throughout Boulder's history, there have been more than a few women who owned or managed businesses or who worked in traditionally "male" jobs. Ella Yount took charge of the family's flour milling business when her husband died. In the 1870s, Clara Peterman was a local barber; Hattie Church learned to set type at the *Boulder News and*

One cannot doubt the popularity of the artist Gibson after viewing this Pi Phi sorority portrait taken before the turn of the century. *Rowland Collection*

Graduation Day, 1920, Central School. Some of these youngsters will go on to State Preparatory School. *Ed Tangen photo, A.A. Paddock Collection*

Courier. In 1887, nine Boulder matrons, wives of local businessmen, incorporated the Boulder Creamery Company and sold stock for ten dollars a share. Gertrude W. Eaves, daughter of pioneer Alpheus Wright, became a local minister. Boulder was served by several lady physicians, two female morticians, a photographer, and a manager of a popular cafeteria— Helen Marshall. Marie Cowie was the local postmaster for a time. Two women, Suzie Parkhurst and Margaret Read, were noted local architects. Ward's Hazel Schmoll was a reknowned botanist, and Willamette Porter Cockerell earned a reputation as a naturalist; Martha Maxwell was one of the country's early taxidermists. Martha M. Russell ran the University Hospital; Felicia Grace Hall was university registrar. Susan Mary Lovelace became principal at Mapleton School in the 1890s and served as the first principal at North Side Intermediate School until 1936. (The school's name was changed to Casey Junior High School in 1944.) Kate Harbeck's money founded the Boulder Humane Society; Jean Wirt Sherwood's fortune helped to found Blue Bird Cottage, a retreat for professional women, in 1910.

Just after World War I, Florence Molloy and Mabel MacLeay brought their families to Boulder from Syracuse, New York, in a Pierce-Arrow touring car, and both families moved into the Squires-Tourtellot house. The two women started a taxi service which they operated from offices in the Hotel Boulderado. Business was brisk (female travelers often preferred to ride with the lady drivers), and soon the ladies added Packard touring cars to form a "fleet." In later years, when someone asked Mrs. Molloy, who was an imposing six feet tall, if either she or Mrs. MacLeay ever had trouble with "fresh" male customers, she replied sadly, "No, and it's been a terrible disappointment." Eventually, the ladies bought a dude ranch near Gold Hill and raised cattle and quarter horses. (The ranch is now called Trojan Ranch.)

Establishment of a real library was largely the work of Boulder's women. In 1895, various ladies' groups met to form a library board, with Mary Rippon as its first president. (An earlier all-male library association had little success in raising money for a library.) They incorporated, issued a share of stock at ten dollars each, and decided upon a yearly budget of $600 for books and supplies. They went door-to-door to raise money and sponsored suppers, concerts, and lectures to help fund the reading room. Soon, a private library, stocked with some two hundred books, opened in the Boulder Theatre building on Fourteenth Street. Mrs. Clara H. Savory was hired as librarian. Although she had no professional background, she held the job for twenty years, devoting herself to expanding the reading room with a proper library. In 1898, the reading room moved to the Willard building at Broadway and Spruce streets. Since its financial condition continued to be critical, the ladies sought

One of the Boulder's first taxi drivers, Florence Molloy used her Pierce Arrow to transport patients during the World War I flu epidemic. Later, with Mabel MacLeay, she raised quarter horses on land that is now known as the Trojan Ranch. *Boulder Public Library*

help from new sources. Council gave the reading room a fifty-dollar-per-month stipend and bought from a local union a five-hundred-volume library that added to the modest selection. When a patron complained to council that he had to pay to read in the reading room, council decided that it was time to make the reading room accessible to all Boulder citizens. With promises of regular support in 1901, council agreed that the private reading room was now the Boulder Public Library.

After the city had received a $15,000 grant from the Carnegie Foundation in 1906 (industrialist Andrew Carnegie helped to build more than 2,800 libraries in this country and abroad), land was purchased at 1125 Pine Street for $2,750. (This was the site of the Congregationalist's first church.) When the Carnegie Library opened, it offered to the reader some 3,000 books, 28 magazines, 7 weekly and 7 daily newspapers, although it took another year to establish a card catalog using the Dewey decimal system. By 1915, Mrs. Savory was earning an extravagant eight dollars per month, with her living quarters provided. She was on duty from 8 a.m. to 10 p.m. every day of the week. Before she resigned to make way for Boulder's first professional librarian, Claude Settlemire, Mrs. Savory had started a children's collection and instituted the children's story hour. The Carnegie Library served Boulder residents until the present building at 1000 Canyon Boulevard was completed in 1961. (The old building now houses historical documents and photographs.)

Both Mrs. Molloy and Mrs. MacLeay used their Pierce-Arrow to carry influenza victims to medical attention just after World War I. In 1918, Boulder suffered, as did people all over the world, from an epidemic called "Spanish flu." The high mobility of military personnel throughout the world must have helped spread the disease. Nederland was particularly hard hit; out of a total population of 600, 150 were struck down with influenza, resulting in 41 deaths. After Dr. Miles, public health officer, announced 588 cases of flu in Boulder, he ordered a general quarantine on October 7, 1918. Schools were closed and fumigated. All public gathering places were either closed or used on a limited basis. "Stores shall be kept well ventilated, customers shall be served as rapidly as possible, and urged to depart promptly."[1] If one went to the grocery, druggist, or barber, business had to be conducted quickly. Dr. Miles required new health regulations, including the rule "that soda fountain glasses and dishes had to be cleansed in hot water and washing soda or that there be used sanitary paper receptacles."[2] There were no dances or beefsteak frys in the mountains, court trials were suspended, and street meetings of all kinds were banned. Longmont was also hit with the Spanish flu. An Episcopalian minister there was arrested for persisting in holding church services. The quarantine must have helped, for the bans were lifted early in November. The *Camera* noted that a "restlessness in the younger set has been noticeable. Indications are that the city will plunge into an orgy of theater going, parties, and meetings next week."[3]

Another disease, tuberculosis, sometimes called "phthisis," had always been a part of Boulder's life. From the beginning of the town's settlement, consumptives chose to move here as elsewhere in the Southwest, hoping that the pure air, arid climate, and a vigorous life would make them healthy again. Some of the university's distinguished professors were healed tuberculars. The Seventh Day Adventists built the sanitarium in 1895 with Boulder's climate in mind; moreover, they felt that a location farther west would be unwise, believing that Pacific currents brought unhealthy humid winds to inland areas. British traveler Isabella Bird maintained that nine out of ten persons whom she encountered in her Colorado travels were consumptive, an exaggeration perhaps.* But the presence of tuberculars was noted by almost all early observers.

Tuberculars were feared. Chautauqua bulletins made a point of reassuring prospective summer visitors that they would not contract the disease. Advertisements for jobs and rooms might state "Tuberculars need not apply." In Denver, a law was passed to forbid spitting on the streets, except in the gutters, because most people assumed that the soles of shoes would transmit the disease from spit on the sidewalks. Former teacher Edna Harkins remembers that some of the arriving tuberculars were lifted off the train on stretchers, they were so weak from the disease. Dr. Ruth Flowers recalls that when she and her sister came down from Cripple Creek, they had to "thread [their] way through the invalids"[4] on some streets. A few of the early homes had solariums—unheated sleeping porches with rows of windows—built on the north side of the house to accommodate ailing relatives in the hope that sleeping in cold, pure air would clear their lungs.

The "cold-air" philosophy prompted Edna Harkins, herself a tubercular, to establish an open-air school in 1916 on the grounds of Mapleton School. Not only were tubercular children in attendance, but also those recovering from long bouts with scarlet fever, diphtheria, measles, or whooping cough. Some wore back braces, and some were supported by leg braces. All required special educational programs so that they might catch up with their studies. Miss Harkins taught regular second grade at Mapleton School, but she also taught the convalescent children for two hours a day in the little wooden building, the windows flung wide open even on the coldest winter day. Called the "House of Happiness," this special school lasted for twenty years, although its clientele changed when it became the first Boulder classroom for mentally disturbed children and slow learners.

Mount St. Gertrude Academy had tubercular children in mind when the Sisters of Charity opened the school in 1892. Mesa Vista Sanitarium, 1910 Alpine Street, was renovated in 1952 for the specific care of tubercular patients. Navajo Indian children, a group particularly prone to consumption, were treated there.

From the very first years of Boulder's settlement, a few black people lived in the area. They came as runaway slaves or as freed men. Some mined for gold and silver, some were freighters and stage coach drivers, and some worked in small businesses in Boulder itself.* Those who lived in the mining camps experienced less prejudice than they had back East.

*Billy M. Jones, in his *Health Seekers in the Southwest, 1817-1900*, (Norman; University of Oklahoma Press, 1967), estimates that one-fourth to one-third of all those who migrated to the Southwest were sick people looking for a healthy life. He mentions a town in Texas where 95 percent of the settlers had at least one tuberculosis sufferer in the family.

*The presence of black children in school photographs during this early period attests to this.

Youngsters recovering from tuberculosis, scarlet fever, or diphtheria, were taught by Edna Harkins, herself a tubercular, in the House of Happiness, a small open air school on the Mapleton School grounds. The school opened around the time of World War I and operated for twenty years. *Edna Harkins Collection*

Junius Lewis, a runaway slave, came to the Denver area in 1882 and worked at menial jobs for a time, but he eventually bought into the Golden Chest Mining, Milling and Tunnel Company in 1896. Most of his fellow stockholders were black families living in Denver or Central City, some of whom had achieved a degree of wealth and were members of what was called the Blue Vein Society, a group open to those who were mulatto, for "black was not beautiful in those days."[5] By 1907, Lewis was living near Sunset as sole operator of the mine, although he answered to 122 stockholders. On weekends, Lewis would walk from Sunset to Boulder to visit the McVey family. (John W. McVey operated a billiards parlor on Pearl Street.) Miner Lewis suffered from severe asthma but found life in the Boulder mountains most agreeable. Although quiet and well-spoken, Lewis spent a great deal of his time, over a twenty-year period, in legal battles over ownership of the Golden Chest mine. His principal adversary was Delia McMenamin, a gun-toting and somewhat irrational lady who felt that she and her partners were the rightful owners of the mine. At one point, she arrived at the Golden Chest with salt and a frying pan, the traditional way to prove squatters' rights to a mine. Miss McMenamin's "attentions"[6] were so constant (Lewis' attorney, H.O. Andrew, referred to the lady as Lewis' "best girl"[7]) that Lewis had difficulty expanding his interests (he controlled gold and tungsten deposits) or selling his mines.

As Boulder became less of a mining supply center and more of a settled community, the number of black families decreased. Black women could get jobs as cooks or maids in fraternity houses, in hotels, or in private homes, but black men had to travel elsewhere for jobs as porters or menials in industry. As more and more Southern families moved into Boulder (many came because someone in the family had tuberculosis), Boulder's black population found prejudice increasing. Even so, a few black families stayed.

George Reeves worked at Papa's Shoeshine Parlor at Pearl and Twelfth streets (Broadway). The Reeves settled in Boulder in 1903 (there were perhaps a dozen blacks in town then), and the Reeves' daughter, Alice Cleora, remembers that "restaurants and hotels wouldn't serve colored then. And if you tried to go in, they'd meet you at the door and say, 'you'll have to go somewhere else.'"[8] Burgess Drug Store at Seventeenth and Pearl streets would serve black customers at the soda fountain. By the time Ruth Cave Bradford (Flowers) and her sister came to Boulder from Cripple Creek in 1917, few social opportunities were available for the seventy-five blacks who lived in Boulder. Dr. Flowers remembers that her childhood in Cripple Creek was relatively free of such prejudice; it became difficult for her to "adjust" to segregated life in Boulder. Blacks lived on either Goss or Water streets

Although Ruth Cave Flowers was denied a high school diploma from State Preparatory School because of her race, she went on to earn a doctorate in Romance languages and a law degree. *Boulder Public Library*

(Canyon Boulevard) between Nineteenth and Twenty-second streets. When Ruth Flowers attended State Preparatory School, she was aware of the frustrations of the few black male students because they were not allowed to participate in sports activities at the high school. Black students could attend classes at the University of Colorado (Ruth Flowers did and went on to earn a doctorate in Romance Languages at Catholic University of America and a law degree as well), but they were not allowed to live near campus, nor could they participate in recreational activities on the campus.

Under these circumstances, one can understand why the two black churches in Boulder, Second Baptist Church at Nineteenth and Water streets and the African Methodist Church at Eighteenth and Pearl streets, became centers for black social life. Ice cream socials were important to the black citizen who could not buy an ice cream cone downtown.

O.T. Jackson, founder of the all-black farming community called Dearfield, located twenty-five miles southwest of Greeley in Weld County, was able to earn a little money in Boulder to support his "society." After some reflection, Jackson had decided that blacks should live separately from white society; he dreamed of an all-black colony in Colorado. A caterer by trade, Jackson had come to Colorado in 1887. In addition to catering at the University of Colorado and serving a stint as manager of the Stillman Hotel (Arnett Hotel*) at 1200 Pearl Street, he was a messenger for several Colorado governors (until Klan-supported Governor Morley took office), and he farmed east of Boulder. Jackson even operated an ice cream parlor in town for a time. In May 1910, he acquired the first parcel of land that was to become Dearfield; by 1914, he had amassed enough farm land to support some seven hundred black people, at least for a short time. Dearfield had a prosperous appearance, and its future looked good. But the hard times of the Depression affected Dearfield's economy as well. Most of the settlers left to look for other opportunities. By 1930, one lone woman lived in Dearfield, waiting, she said, for the others to come back.

By the late 1920s, Boulder had lost its characteristic bustle as well as some of its population. (In 1900, 6,625 lived in Boulder; in 1920, the number had risen to 13,118, but these numbers included the university students, for the university grew slowly and steadily even though the town itself declined in population.) By the time the Depression took hold, Boulder seemed a sleepy university town surrounded by a farming community. The only industry of note was Western Cutlery. There was a brief flurry of excitement in 1928 when the Silver Wing Aircraft Corporation opened its factory in the old Superior Metals building at Twenty-eighth and Pine streets. Edward "Jack" Euler thrilled a crowd of seven hundred Boulderites as he flew the company's first plane overhead. He and partner A.J. "Toots" Hogue Jr. planned to roll a Silver Wing airplane off the assembly line every six weeks. Boulder's setting would provide the perfect spot to study high-altitude stress on aircraft, they said. The men also planned to open a flying school. Certainly, the Depression crushed the hopes of the two entrepreneurs. They could not acquire enough land, nor could they get the proper financing; further, Boulder public opinion was against the Euler and Hogue operation, for people feared that the business might encourage a "lunch bucket brigade." Boulder continued to discourage blue-collar industrial workers from either living or working in the community.

The Depression, of course, affected everyone, including the city government of Boulder. No one had enough money to do anything unusual. There had not been an annexation to Boulder since 1908, nor would there be one until 1941. No one suspected that Boulder would soon have to search for additional water. Council discussed the dangers of flooding from Boulder Creek but saw no reason to do anything about it. The irrigation ditches were considered a threat to the lives of Boulder children, but council found no inexpensive remedy. Boulder's families were struggling to make ends meet; few social services were available because it was assumed that "everyone would take care of their own."[9] Council meetings were short. Occasionally, they met for more than one hour. Seldom were other citizens present.

"The only thing that stirred us up was Mrs. Hennig,"[10] recalled Don McInnes, who served on council from 1929 to 1934. Lillie E. Hennig owned and operated the City Taxi and Sightseeing Company. Her competition and the constant object of her wrath was the Independent Taxi Company, operated by Alphonse Ardourel. (Mrs. Molloy and Mrs. MacLeay had left the taxi business by this time.) Lillie Hennig appeared regularly at council meetings to complain, at considerable length, about a variety of subjects. Her main concern, however, was the town's other taxi driver, who, she maintained, used unfair business tactics against her. What was usually meant by this charge was that Mr. Ardourel, Mrs. Hennig claimed, might "solicit" a prospective customer's business before his turn. (Taxicabs were to line up in back of the depot* at Fourteenth and Front streets [Walnut Street]). Furthermore, Mrs. Hennig reported, Mr. Ardourel would "push ahead"[11] of her in other ways. He would say "Good morning" before she could get to the customer. (Several extensive court sessions were devoted to whether or not Mr. Ardourel's "Good mornings" were, indeed, the solicitation of trade.)

City Manager McClintock, irritated by Mrs. Hennig's constant attentions and "public bickering,"[12] suspended her cab license for the last few days of 1934, an act to which the lady paid not the slightest attention. Late in January 1935, Mrs. Hennig was fined twenty-five dollars for ignoring the suspension. In September 1936, "after several months of comparative quiet on the taxi-cab battle front,"[13] Lillie's husband, Louis F. Hennig, was in jail with a broken finger. Hennig had insulted a black woman who had entered his cab, and the police had been alerted.

---

*A snowstorm in the 1970s demolished the handsome Arnett Hotel, which was in the middle of renovation.

*The depot was moved by the Boulder Jaycees to Twenty-eighth and Mapleton when its existence was threatened by the city, who felt that Fourteenth Street should be a through street to Canyon Boulevard.

A December evening in front of the old courthouse.
A.A. Paddock Collection

A view of Boulder from Green Mountain, showing Gregory Canyon approach.
A.A. Paddock Collection

Some of these men are construction workers, others are members of the Chamber of Commerce, seeing that the building of the Flagstaff Road gets off to a good start. *A.A. Paddock Collection*

Photographer Ed Tangen views Boulder from above. *A.A. Paddock Collection*

Hennig said later that the police called his wife a "liar" and that he was defending her honor. Hennig was accused of cursing the police, and the verbal fight over "the old trouble on Front Street"[14] turned into a physical one. Officer John Worthing, Captain A.F. Masters, and Chief Rolla C. Prather tried to subdue Mr. Hennig, who appeared to be reaching for Chief Prather's gun. According to the chief, he accidentally broke Mr. Hennig's finger while trying to control Mr. Hennig's flaying arms. According to Mr. Hennig, his finger was broken when Chief Prather attempted to beat Hennig over the head with a gun. The following year, as might be expected, Louis Hennig filed suit for $15,150 in damages against Chief Prather; the city, in turn, filed "malicious assault" charges against Mr. Hennig.

Most of the Hennigs' legal battles were tried again and again, some of them ending up in the Colorado Supreme Court. Lillie Hennig was back visiting council in 1938, the meetings that she attended "contrasting with the usual placid sessions."[15] She wanted separate licenses for taxicabs and sightseeing vehicles. She accused the city of allowing other sightseeing vehicles to operate without licenses. Finally, in 1939, Mr. Hennig won part of his suit against the chief of police, now retired, and was to receive $400. An argument then ensued among some in the community as to who should pay the $400. Should the city back up its employees in such matters (the *Camera* thought so), or perhaps the city had no legal responsibilities in this matter. In any event, the police force passed the hat, and members of the public contributed the difference. Louis Hennig finally got his $400 in 1940; the taxicab wars did not make news again.

Most of Boulder's streets were as yet unpaved by the late 1920s and were still sprinkled with water in the summer to keep the dust from flying. T.H. Fitzpatrick, supervisor of streets, with the help of council member Don McInnes, worked for additional street paving despite continued resistance from residents of Mapleton Hill. Even so, the men were able to pave Mapleton Avenue with cement in 1928.

There was little resistance, however, to Boulder's first zoning ordinance, which was passed in January of the same year—the first of its kind in the western United States. Planning consultant S.B. DeBoers was asked to draft such an ordinance in 1926 after reports of "promiscuous erection of places of business in what has been the residence district of the Hill"[16] (University Hill). DeBoer divided the town into seven zoning districts: three were residential, two commercial, one business, and one industrial. DeBoer recommended that a Board of Zoning Adjustment with five commissioners be established to oversee zoning problems. An ordinance prohibiting advertising signs was also proposed (Boulder citizens had been complaining about

Fire breaks out at the county courthouse on February 9, 1932. The handsome Victorian one was replaced with a "modern" courthouse the following year. *photo, Boulder Fire Department*

the litter of advertising signs since 1902), but it failed, and a similar ordinance failed again in 1937. (Even though a sign ordinance was passed in 1971, illegal advertising signs continue to plague the community.)

Banker Don McInnes remembers an exciting day in February 1932 when he was locking the doors of the First National Bank at 3 p.m. He heard shouts and the sound of running feet. When he joined them outside, he found that the courthouse was on fire; it appeared to have started in the bell tower. When it became obvious that the fine old building could not be saved, citizens stood around to watch it burn. Even the children took a holiday from school and hiked to the top of Lovers Hill (Sunset Hill) to view the fire. Almost immediately, despite the Depression, citizens made plans for a new courthouse. In a display of either thrift or sentiment, the stone from the railroad bridge abutments along the washed-out Switzerland Trail was used to face the new courthouse. Since the county planned a bigger building than before, with less lawn, the bandstand had to come down. No longer was there room for rock drilling contests in front of the courthouse. One resident who had viewed both buildings said, "The old Court House...was more cordial."[17]

In July 1933, the first group of CCC "boys" (Civilian Conservation Corps) moved into town and camped along Boulder Creek at Sixth Street. At first, the young men, most of whom were from Oklahoma, lived in tents; later, five barracks were built on the site. The men were paid thirty dollars a month on the condition that they send twenty-two dollars of that salary back to their families. The number and variety of their accomplishments throughout the United States is well known. In the Boulder area, they opened up fire lanes in the mountain park lands, made horse trails, and improved hiking trails. In addition to other forms of tree care, the men pulled out those trees infected with the Black Hills beetle, much to the outrage of local conservationists who did not feel that the removal of the infected trees, some 67,000 in all, would save other trees.*

Flagstaff Road was virtually rebuilt by the CCC. In later years, one of their commanders reported in a Park Service bulletin, "The road was unsuited to even a moderate amount of traffic. It was too narrow for cars to pass comfortably, all curves were banked the wrong way, surfacing had been washed off by initial errors in construction...." A back road down Flagstaff Mountain, called Chapman Drive, which came out near Blanchard's (now the Red Lion Inn) was built by the CCC boys. They also built the Sunrise Amphitheatre on Flagstaff Mountain, a lodge on Green Mountain, and a rock garden for the Chautauqua grounds.

In 1936, the WPA (Works Progress Administration) was also active in Boulder with the opening of a day car nursery in the basement of Whittier School. Their accomplishments, too, were varied and included the building of the Mary Rippon Outdoor Theatre, the golf course at the Flatirons Country Club, and Beach Park. They replaced some of the seats in Chautauqua Auditorium, did some construction work on Nederland School, and built a town hall for Jamestown. Out-of-work graduate students read old newspapers and developed what is known as the "WPA file," a subject-area file still heavily used by researchers at the University of Colorado.

Local climbing clubs, the Rocky Mountain Climbers Club, and the Colorado Mountain Club also contributed their services in the Depression for trail-building in the mountains. Hiker Ernest Greenman is responsible for the planting of apple trees in Gregory Canyon. The Boulder Lions Club also has a distinguished record in the improvement of city parks. They built the Panoramic Park Shelter on Flagstaff Mountain in 1918, the Bluebell Canyon Shelter in 1923, another Flagstaff shelter in 1933, one for North Boulder Park in 1954, and another shelter for Martin Park in 1962. The Lions were also responsible for the Central Park band shell, which was completed in 1938.

In 1934, times were hard in Boulder, and it seemed as if the Depresssion had taken the spirit out of the people. When the Junior Chamber of Commerce, the Senior Chamber, and the Boulder County Metal Mining Association met together, all agreed that something should be done to "stir up" life, to provide a time for laughter and lightness, to bring people together. Pow Wow (called Pay-Dirt Pow Wow at first) opened August 1, 1934, the anniversary of Colorado's entrance into the Union, with the hope that the miners would come down from the mountains and the farmers would come in from the plains to enjoy a variety of activities. Pow Wow started with a strenuous forty-mile bicycle race from Boulder to Longmont and back. At a bathing beauty contest, the judges gave first prize to Mary Molloy, daughter of Florence Molloy, who had operated the touring service just after World War I.

During Pow Wow's first year, the Hard Rock Drilling Championship of the World was established. Miners came down from Nederland, Leadville, Jamestown, and Climax to compete. The miner who could drive a steel drill the farthest into granite rock in a ten-minute period was the champion. In the city of boulders, rocks suitable for drilling could not be found, and rocks had to be brought down from

---

*In 1924, fire destroyed two hundred acres of Flagstaff Mountain timber. All of Boulder worked together to replant the heavily damaged area, including the Boy and Girl Scouts and the Campfire Girls, who collected pennies for new trees. Eben Fine directed the effort, and citizens came out in force to plant the new trees.

For forty years, 1916-1956, Chester Johnson sold popcorn and peanuts from his wagon at Thirteenth and Pearl streets. *A.A. Paddock Collection*

The first Pow Wow parade, 1934. The Oddfellows float is followed by the Rebeccas in white gowns. Note Valentine Hardware sign, Broadway and Pearl streets. *photo, Lyndon Switzer*

Organizer of Pow Wow parades Lyndon Switzer, left, and Oscar Gilbert show how it's done. Note Arnett Hotel, 1000 block of Pearl Street, in background. *photo, Lyndon Switzer*

Mr. and Mrs. Leonard Wittemyer add a special note to an early Pow Wow parade. *photo, Mrs. Leonard Wittemyer*

Jamestown for the event. (Some of these drilling rocks still lie in Chautauqua's park grounds.) These rock drilling contests were held on a baseball field—the green space between the Boulder Public Library and the municipal building. These contests were part of Pow Wow for only a few years, but other events attracted Boulderites, who participated in hay-pitching contests, hog-calling competitions (separate contests for men and women), softball games, greased-pole climbing, and egg-rolling. The ladies competed in rolling-pin-throwing and slipper-throwing contests as well as needle-threading relays. Boys could participate in pie-eating contests or dive for apples. Children competed in sack races, three-legged races, or footraces; all looked forward to the yearly Pow Wow parade down Pearl Street. The first Pow Wow parade featured Colorado Governor Ed Johnson, who was followed by great number of hay wagons, tally-hos, stage coaches, fire wagons, and even a few hearses. There were 286 horses, a scattering of Arapaho Indians and U.S. marshals, a few ladies riding sidesaddle, and a float containing a replica of Colorado's first schoolhouse in which Abner Brown had taught many years before. Another float featured some of Boulder's pretty girls, who threw snowballs at the parade spectators. The day was a success. It did lift Boulder's spirits, and for a short time everyone forgot the miseries of the Depression.[18] It was not until the 1940s that Pow Wow began to take on its rodeo flavor.

Despite the need for a new high school (the old State Preparatory was now considered unsafe), a 1934 bond issue for a new high school building was defeated. Boulderites had just built a new courthouse. Furthermore, the proposed location for the school bothered some voters, because the site was in the flood plain. (Some parents were already angry with the school administration because of the new grading system just introduced—"S" for satisfactory and "U" for unsatisfactory).

Teachers had received no salary increases during these years and plans for beginning a retirement system had to be shelved. Book fees were established during this period, because the school board no longer had adequate funds for the purchase of books. (Book fees are still charged at all levels in the Boulder Valley School District.) The school board was also exploring the possibility of federal grants and loans that would help in the building of a new school. The following year, however, enough voters had changed their minds to pass a second school bond issue, and the old State Preparatory School, as well as its name, passed into history. Boulder High School was built on the controversial floodway site for a sum that was to exceed one-half million dollars.

Denver sculptor Marvin Martin was commissioned by the Board of Education to design an appropriate panel for the entry to the new school. His work, a bas-relief called "Strength and Wisdom," caused another of Boulder's periodic fights. The school board had approved the artwork on paper, but when the members viewed the finished product, they were appalled by the "modern" work, described as "squat, exaggerated, massive,"[19] and ordered its removal. That started it. The Art Department at the University of Colorado called the board's action censorship of art. One resident likened the sculpture to "wads of chewing gum,"[20] while a favorable critic pronounced it "powerful and effective."[21] The only problem, the writer went on to say, was that the building was wrong for the sculptures. Someone suggested that the sculp-

The once-controversial bas reliefs which adorn Boulder High School, nicknamed "Minnie and Jake." *Tom Moen photo*

tures, known as "Minnie and Jake," be covered and placed beside the track field. As runners would line up for track meets, the statues would be uncovered and frighten the young athletes into faster sprints. At a special meeting of the school board in the spring of 1937, everyone had a chance to have his say. The sculptures were eventually regarded as "harmless," and they remained in place when the school was dedicated in November 1937. Thereafter, it became customary for freshmen to bow to Minnie and Jake when entering the front door.

During the 1930s, Boulder supported a kindergarten, although kindergartens were generally regarded as a frivolous waste of money. Miss Faye Curtin had directed a private kindergarten in her home at 811 Mapleton since 1922. Boulder children loved Miss Curtin's; some met their future husbands and wives there. Families were close, the population was homogeneous, and "the children had a sense of belonging, and this feeling was strongly expressed in school life."[22] When the school board decided in 1938 to allow kindergarten on a tentative and experimental basis, Miss Curtin moved her brightly painted small tables and chairs across the street to Mapleton School and continued to teach kindergarten there until her retirement in 1959.

The playing fields behind Mapleton School. Many of the trees are gone and so is the drinking fountain built by the children. The cobblestone benches remain. *Boulder Historical Society*

Chapter Twelve

Boulder was still a sleepy, quiet little town when Professor of Journalism A. Gayle Waldrop decided to run for council in 1945, but the community showed signs of waking up from the Depression and returning to its former feistiness. Waldrop himself was a little feisty and may have helped Boulder regain its fighting spirit. Since most councils were made up of businessmen, a professor's candidacy was considered unusual, even suspect. He was one of the few winning candidates whose last name occurred in the second half of the alphabet; also, he was the first council candidate to advertise his qualifications. His ads cost him thirty-five dollars. As Waldrop was elected under the Hare system, some observers believed that the professor could not have been elected otherwise, and Waldrop himself is inclined to agree with this view.

For most of his tenure on council, Waldrop's motions did not receive a second. Whenever he brought up subjects for discussion, they often "precipitated a brisk exchange among councilmen."[1] His colleagues did not like it when Waldrop questioned the use of city cars for out-of-town pleasure trips; even so, the practice was banned, and Waldrop asked that "City of Boulder" be painted on the town's five cars. When incoming City Manager Robert E. Baumberger first addressed council, he asked for an "off-the-record

Boulder in the 1950s. *A.A. Paddock Collection*

round table discussion by the Council." Baumberger immediately received a blast from Waldrop, who objected to all closed meetings of governmental bodies. Council still used the "emergency clause" of the charter and passed even zoning changes on first reading, finding it troublesome and wasteful to wait the prescribed period of time for a second reading. When Waldrop asked that the charter be examined to clean out "dead wood," City Attorney Frank Moorhead replied that he could see no reason to do so. Waldrop complained to council that the Elks Club had slot machines in its headquarters and claimed that council should do something about it. Because his view was most unpopular, no action was taken on the matter. Some years later, when the Elks offered to pay for the lighting of a playing field for night baseball games, Waldrop complained that the council was "accepting tainted money."[2] Council member A.A. Wickstrom after some thought replied that the real problem was that the Elks money "t'aint enough."[3]

Boulder was again in good fighting form in 1947 when, after many unsuccessful attempts, liquor-by-the-drink was again placed on the ballot. The Hare system of voting was also before the voters for reconsideration. Those opposed to the voting system maintained that it was ineffective, that only one of the voter's selections counted, and that minorities were unduly favored. Waldrop complained of willful misrepresentation of the Hare system. Its defeat, he feared, would turn back the clock twenty-eight years; Boulder would then be susceptible to machine politics such as existed back East. One anti-Hare letter writer felt that the election system was responsible for the "...definite minority in Boulder who do not wish to see dinner pails and overalls on Boulder streets."[4] Another heated letter writer managed to cover his subject thoroughly. First, he said, the Hare system is "UnAmerican"[5] and "UnDemocratic."[6] Hitler and Mussolini rose to power under the Hare system, which was the "slick tool of the minorities,"[7] with Gayle Waldrop as their mouthpiece. Moreover, "the pinks, the reds, the political actionists never sleep even in Boulder."[8] All was "talk-blab and blab-bark, wrangle and fight."[9]

In November, the Hare system was defeated 3,159 to 1,370 and passed into history as a voting curiosity. Liquor-by-the-drink lost for the eleventh time, 3,303 to 1,450. Boulder drinkers would continue to travel to Louisville for their refreshment or be obliged to patronize one of four package stores operating beyond the half-mile limit from the city. (As years passed, the city would grow around these stores, causing the formation of "liquor islands.")

The character of council discussions and the nature of letters to the newspaper during the mid-1940s illustrate that Boulder residents knew that big changes were in store for their town, but the possibilities made them uneasy and uncomfortable. What would these changes bring? Council discussed the possibility of banning backyard burning of trash, much to the dismay of many residents who regarded trash burning as one of the unalienable rights, even if such burning knocked down the neighbors with noxious fumes. Council also discussed the advisability of banning livestock within the city limits, something that Public Health Director Dr. H.L. Morency had wanted for years. He was also worried about the raw or poorly processed milk that was sold within the city. The haphazard collection of "wet garbage" by local farmers who "cooked" it and fed it to their hogs was

Former Superintendent of Schools William Casey returns to Whittier School on his birthday in 1940 to listen to poetry. *Edna Harkins Collection*

not too appealing either. By 1950, smoking was banned in theaters, school auditoriums, buses, and elevators. Plans for a community hospital were being drawn, because the university hospital could no longer serve the growing community. Citizens were getting used to married women teaching in the schools, and the ban was lifted in 1942 when the men went off to war. Up to that time, only single or widowed ladies were allowed to teach in Boulder's schools.

Bikers were licensed for the first time in 1947 and were charged a fifty-cent fee. In 1948, Harris "Tommy" Thompson proposed to council that he operate an 850-foot ski tow on the Chautauqua hills. With council approval, Thompson cleared away the rocks (he needed a bulldozer for the big ones), and the Mesa Ski Slope was born. It ran for only a few seasons, because the chinook winds did not cooperate and melted the snow below the Flatirons. In 1947, a young college man "autographed" the first Flatiron with

"Joe," and thus was easily apprehended and fined fifty dollars. One month later, two more college men climbed the first Flatiron and painted a "C" on its flat surface for all of Boulder to appreciate. Council did not and required the students to remove the "C" until it was decided that the climb was too dangerous; several experienced mountain climbers volunteered for the job. Council proposed a jail sentence for the next Flatirons artist. In the ensuing years, both the third and the first Flatiron have been painted with "Cs" or "CUs." One perhaps more creative citizen came forward to suggest that the "C" remain in place on the Flatiron, that it could be decorated with lights at Christmas and Easter. William Simons wanted council to adopt a city motto of "City of the Flatirons" and an official flower—the hollyhock. John Schoolland presented his plan to install in Central Park a narrow gauge engine and car from the Switzerland Trail. He had found old No. 30 pushing a snowplow on Lizard Head Pass above Telluride. The Colorado and Southern had renumbered it No. 74. The train was dedicated in Central Park on August 6, 1953. A leash law for dogs was discussed, but no ordinance was passed. Interest was renewed for a war memorial park to honor the 4,077 Boulderites who went to war and the 77 who did not return. This time, the favored site was along Boulder Creek and would have carried out the recommendations of Planner Olmsted of thirty-five years earlier, but the project never left the discussion stage. A tax on cigarettes was under consideration from time to time, mainly because council was hesitant to try for an across-the-board sales tax. Some felt, as did Gayle Waldrop, that sales taxes "soak the poor."[10] Twenty years would pass before Boulder would approve its first sales tax.

Downtown angle parking along Pearl Street became a thing of the past when council ordered 340 parking meters in 1946; three years later, 168 more were installed. For $424, council bought fifty-two street signs for the downtown area; concrete signposts were still used in residential neighborhoods. It became obvious during the mid-1940s that Boulder's north-south traffic problems would increase. Citizens were not happy when council looked at Ninth Street as a through-street possibility; the street stopped at Pearl Street and started again at Spruce. Council wanted to buy the intervening property, move the houses, and put the street through, but again, it would be twenty years before the through-street would become a reality. The old irrigation ditches were pleasant reminders of the past to some, but others, fearing for the safety of children, pleaded with council to cover the waterways. When council received an estimate of $600,000 to cover the city's ditches, they looked for other ways to make them safe and ended up doing nothing.

The first pressures for additional housing came from the university, whose officials came to council in 1946 and reported that student housing needs were getting serious; they proposed to winterize the city-owned Chautauqua cottages for year-round living. Some wanted to remove the rent controls that had been in force since the war, but council kept them for the time being. From 1947 onward, local developers attempted to change single-family zoned properties into multiple-family zones, but in most instances they lost. A business rezoning was proposed for the northwest corner of Eighth and Pearl streets to make way for a supermarket, but Mapleton Hill residents objected; the project was abandoned in August 1949. The year before, a revised zoning ordinance had been presented to council; in characteristic fashion, Boulder residents came out in force and "nearly all proposed zoning changes in the city were protested."[11] The ordinance was sent back to the Planning and Parks Commission* for further study and revision and was accepted later that year. Another attempt to rezone for business occurred on University Hill at Thirteenth and College in February 1950. Council granted the rezoning, "over-riding the protests of most of the property owners in the block."[12] Apparently, council was unsure of itself, for it reversed its decision and denied the rezoning, then reversed itself again and approved the business use the following months. The call for a new building code in 1950 alarmed a number of the local builders, for the proposed code included licensing builders for the first time. In an effort toward uniformity, a 1950 ordinance required that all new lots have a fifty-foot frontage.

In 1949, Tulagi was the only establishment on University Hill that had a license to sell 3.2 beer. In February, a ban was proposed on all 3.2 beer sales near campus, despite the popular view that the brew was not regarded as intoxicating. The ban was sought because another spot, the Sunken Gardens, even then called The Sink, wanted a beer license too. The Sink was turned down that year, but it obtained its beer license in 1950. Council decided to limit beer licenses to ten. (This was not counting the three already given to fraternal organizations.)

In 1946, the Public Service Company* cut the cost of gas service to its Boulder customers by 20 percent. A few months later, the company announced a 13 percent cut in electricity rates as well. A cynic would assume, of course, that Public Service was preparing

---

*In 1951, council divided Planning and Parks into two separate commissions.

*At first, Boulder's power needs were served by the Boulder Electric Light and Power Company, known as the "light plant," which began its operations in 1887. By 1906, Northern Colorado Power Company absorbed the "light plant," and by 1914, the name changed again to Western Light and Power Company, which, in turn, was absorbed by the Public Service Company in October 1923.

for the periodic review of its franchise with the city—an election was slated for February 1949. The company offered to pay Boulder $20,000 in taxes rather than the $7,800 it had been paying. Gayle Waldrop was the only member of council who believed that Public Service was taking advantage of Boulder, despite the claim that the utilities firm paid one-sixth of all taxes collected by the city. Waldrop had similar reservations about the business practices of Mountain Bell, but he did not recommend that the town run its own telephone system. He moved that the city hire a consultant to analyze advantages and disadvantages of the franchise and to investigate municipal ownership of utilities. His motion died for lack of a second.

Although Waldrop's position on council was a lonely one, his views on municipal ownership of utilities had a following in Boulder; his supporters wrote letters and attended public meetings. They accused the company of unfairly trying to influence the voters by using its employees to hand out circulars and talk to residents during service calls. Those who supported Public Service pointed out its low rates; Waldrop countered with Longmont's low rates. Boulder's neighbor owned its own power plant. At a crowded council meeting just before the February election, Waldrop asked that the city publish, as required by the charter, financial statements of both the Public Service Company and Mountain Bell. Council member Thomas J. Peyton replied, "there's lots of things in the Charter we don't follow,"[13] and another of Waldrop's motions died for lack of a second. "No one seems interested in getting the facts,"[14] lamented Waldrop. (Shortly thereafter, the *Camera* printed articles on the two companies' financial statements.) When one speaker pleaded for a municipal power plant, Council member Peyton answered, "We're not going to have one."[15] Further insults and charges were exchanged. Edwin Salomon felt that only one side was being heard and scolded council, "I used to attend Council meetings regularly and I gagged at what you gentlemen did here."[16] Despite the Waldrop charge that council was "abdicating our function of regulation,"[17] the Public Service Company won the franchise election in February.

In 1945, the building of a toll road between Boulder and Denver was under serious discussion. It was a project that would do more to change the face of Boulder than any local ordinance and, when finished, it would be called "the magic carpet to Progress."[18] Boulder County Surveyor Fred Fair had first discussed the possibility of a connecting road between Boulder and Denver as early as 1912, but the engineering problems seemed insurmountable at the time, much as a wagon road up Boulder Canyon had been regarded many years before. Engineering Professor Roderick L. Downing spoke of the road's chances in 1928 and for years afterward took his students out in the field to survey various routes for a Denver-Boulder turnpike. Toll roads back East were in trouble because they did not pay for themselves. A Kansas consulting firm conducted a feasibility study and presented to council and to the state a discouraging report. The firm felt that the road would not pay for itself until 1980, if at all. Longmont, naturally, was very much against a turnpike that did not serve its citizens. Even so, the Colorado General Assembly passed an authorizing bill to construct a 17.3 mile road; the bonds were let, and by October 10, 1950 a first section of road had been graded between Denver and Broomfield. On January 19, 1952, the Boulder-Denver Turnpike was completed and open for traffic; toll was ten cents from Denver to Broomfield and twenty-five cents to Boulder. Not only did the turnpike cut down the travel time between Denver and Boulder, but it also made commuting in either direction a real possibility. Business interests began to look over Boulder now that the turnpike was in place. By September 14, 1967, the toll station near Broomfield was able to close down. The turnpike had become the country's first toll road to pay for itself—thirteen years ahead of schedule.

During the construction of the turnpike, a dog, a sort of a shepherd, befriended the men who worked on the highway. When the toll station near Broomfield

For fourteen years after the opening of the Boulder-Denver turnpike a dog named Shep stood at the tollgate near Broomfield inspecting each car as it passed through. When Shep died, he was buried near the Broomfield exit, south of the turnpike. *Tom Moen photo*

was finished, Shep took up residence there, carefully regarding each toll payer as he passed through. Shep was fed and cared for at the toll station for years; money was collected for Shep's occasional trips to the vet. The only time that Shep would not stay on duty was during the heavy traffic to Boulder for Saturday football games. On those occasions, Shep took up an observation post on a hillside, away from the cars. When Shep died, he was buried just east of the Broomfield exit, south of the highway. His grave is marked by a stone of white marble, surrounded by a wrought-iron fence, under a small shady tree—a reminder that at one time all cars stopped there to pay toll.

The first Eastern business to look over Boulder as a possible site was *Esquire Magazine* in 1949. Originally based in Chicago, Esquire was later called Esquire-Coronet; when A.C. Neilsen bought the firm in 1963, the business became Neodata. The company rented office space for one year, decided that Boulder was a suitable site, and bought land on Portland Place the following year. When Esquire applied for rezoning, no one objected very loudly; perhaps Boulder citizens saw this as a "clean" company that would not foster a "lunch bucket brigade." However, Esquire asked council to consider low-cost housing for some of its employees. Council considered it from time to time but did nothing about it.

Besides Western Cutlery, other local businesses were showing new life. Ray Surguine established his book business in 1936, operating from his house until the company could support proper office space. In 1946, a group of young University of Colorado graduates, desirous of remaining in Boulder, founded Arapahoe Chemicals. The company was most successful, although some residents objected to the smells drifting from the chemical plant at Twenty-eighth and Pearl streets. In 1965, the company was bought by Syntex and moved out into Boulder's Industrial Park.

In 1950, the National Bureau of Standards chose Boulder as its main base of operations after looking over twenty-six cities. The choice was made easier when Boulder citizens voted to buy 217 acres of land for the Bureau, which they gave to the United States. When the Bureau began construction of its complex, most people assumed that the buildings would be far removed from the southern boundary of the city; but, in fact, developers began almost immediately to buy up the surrounding lands for housing development. By 1965, the Bureau was a major Boulder employer, contributing some 10 percent to Boulder's income. In 1951, the Atomic Energy Commission decided that Rocky Flats was an ideal spot for its hush-hush project. Some residents experienced considerable apprehension regarding such an installation to the south of the city but accepted it with reluctance. In 1954, Thompson Engineering Companies were established. "Tommy" Thompson, the man who wanted a ski tow for Chautauqua, designed respirators for people with breathing problems; his first customers were polio victims. In 1955, Automation Industries settled in Boulder. Now the face of Boulder was changing rapidly.

The Chamber of Commerce bought an eighteen-acre tract, called it the Boulder Industrial Park, and convinced Ball Brothers Research Corporation to be its first tenant in 1957. The company was known for its canning jars back in Muncie, Indiana, but with its expansion into space-age technologies in Boulder, its payroll grew. Beech Aircraft Corporation also chose Boulder in 1955 and settled its Aerospace Division on 1,500 acres of land to the north of the town.

Walter Orr Roberts had engaged in solar research in Colorado since 1940. Under the auspices of Harvard University, Roberts established the High Altitude Observatory at Climax, Colorado, where he and his wife Janet reared their family. In 1947, the University of Colorado involved itself with the High Altitude Observatory as well as Harvard. When Dr. Roberts accepted the directorship of the National Center for Atmospheric Research in 1960, he recommended that NCAR locate in Boulder and that the observatory become part of it. After the National Science Foundation studied several locations, the group agreed with Roberts that Boulder was an ideal site. The State of Colorado donated some 530 acres of mesa land to the National Center for Atmospheric Research, which began to study its plans for a building designed by architect I.M. Pei. Granville Phillips, manufacturer of vacuum products, moved to Boulder in 1962. International Business Machines came in 1965; the firm had bought 604 acres of alfalfa fields northeast of Boulder eight years earlier.

All of these firms brought people from other parts of the country to settle in Boulder; most hired Boulder residents as well and were the "clean" businesses that Boulder craved.

A native Nebraskan, however, provided Boulder with the "ultimate businessman"—Allen J. Lefferdink. Born in Lincoln, young Lefferdink attended the University of Colorado. He returned to Boulder in 1945 after his military service as a naval officer. The twenty-seven-year-old started Allen Enterprises, then Allen Enterprises Loans; soon there were Colorado Credit Life Insurance Company and the Boulder Acceptance Corporation. Lefferdink was handsome, charming, and persuasive and could "sell anything to anyone."[19] He bought the old city hall property at Fourteenth and Walnut with plans to build Boulder's first skyscraper, the nine-story Colorado Building, on that site. (No height ordinance governed Boulder's buildings at that time.) Lefferdink needed a large building to house his growing number of companies; he even planned a heliport on the roof. The building was completed in 1953; by that time, Lefferdink's holdings were mushrooming. Many Boulderites bought stock in his growing companies and were excited about his plans to renovate the Daniels and Fisher tower in Denver, about his scheme called Magic Mountain, a Disneyland-type project near Golden (site of Heritage Square), and about his luxury motor hotel at the mouth of Boulder Canyon. "Here It Is, Boulder—Your Luxury Motel Hotel"[20] was a *Camera* headline for April 2, 1958. "Tuesday was April Fool's Day but there was no fooling about the start of the new two-million dollar plus Park Allen Hotel...Tuesday may well go down in Boulder's history as one of its most eventful days...."[21] Mayor Leo C. Riethmayer was on hand for the ground-breaking ceremonies as was Governor Dan Thornton. The Park Allen would "sit like a jewel in a beautiful park"[22] on seven to nine acres, would have 150 rooms, a pool and ice rink, dining rooms, a barbershop and beauty shop, stores, a theater, convention facilities, and lighted walkways to a nearby dance pavilion.

Unfortunately for Lefferdink, an Oklahoma insurance department employee began to investigate Lefferdink's business practices, and this put the first crack in the Lefferdink empire of fourteen companies. That investigation led to others, which ended in his indictment on eighteen counts of mail fraud. He was convicted in Denver in 1960 and given an eleven-month jail term on charges of defrauding his own employees. Somehow Lefferdink obtained a new trial; this time he was acquitted. At this point, Lefferdink departed Colorado, leaving behind some 22,000 stockholders who lost an estimated $25 million. The foundation for the Park Allen, which came to be called "The Ruins," lay vacant until 1970, when it figured into another story. The brilliant businessman, called by the *London Times* "the greatest man in the business world,"[23] surfaced next in San Juan, Puerto Rico, and Miami, Florida. From 1967 to 1971 he had business interests in Luxembourg, Belgium, The Netherlands, the Isle of Guernsey, Australia, South Vietnam, Panama, Mexico, the Netherlands Antilles, Bermuda, the Bahamas, and the Grand Cayman Islands. When Lefferdink became a friend to Elliott Roosevelt, he acquired the former president's son's shares in a Miami bank. The man from Nebraska now had an ocean-going yacht, a mansion and limousine in Bermuda, a luxurious apartment in Miami's prestigious Four Ambassadors Hotel, and a membership in the Jockey Club. Too good to last, he lost control of the Miami bank, which was central to his operations. Before he was indicted again for fifteen counts of mail fraud, one count of wire fraud, and one count of conspiracy, he controlled twenty-six companies, four banks, and four mutual funds operations. In 1978, when the sixty-year-old Lefferdink was sentenced to an eight-year term in prison, the Lefferdink empire was down to two companies—Money Machines, Inc., a computerized money-dispensing operation, and Aeromarine Inc., a company selling underwater hardware.

In the early 1950s, conditions at the dump were deteriorating so rapidly that Bly Ewalt Curtis was convinced by friends to run for council so that she could do something about the problem. Although her public campaign consisted of one speech on the radio, she came in second in a field of nine candidates—the third woman to sit on council. As executive director of Sewall Hall (University of Colorado's first dormitory) for thirty years, one of Mrs. Curtis' jobs was to supervise food service for the university's growing coed population. She saw raw milk sold within the city limits, meat delivered in open trucks, and rats running through Boulder gardens near the town's waterways. She was appalled at the lack of sanitary conditions throughout the city.

Sewage and trash problems had always abounded in Boulder. It seemed as if the town did not find sewage and garbage fit subjects for any concentrated effort or thought, even before the turn of the century. There were no sewers then. The small cobblestone ditches that lined some of Boulder's streets were convenient for tossing refuse. From time to time, a town cleanup would occur. In 1881, the town was tidied when the public health officer was able to get an ordinance passed stating "No refuse is allowed to remain in a decaying condition within the city limits,"[24] but this state of cleanliness did not last for long. The *Herald* reported to its readers in 1891, "the ditches on all the streets are clogged with rank vegetation which not only makes the city untidy but breeds disease to a great extent."[25] A $33,000 sewer bond issue was proposed, but the townspeople voted it down. The following year, the *Herald* reported that Boulder was in a "fearful state."[26] But the citizens continued to vote down sewer systems, apparently finding sewage an uninteresting subject. In 1893, sewer bonds were voted down again 149 to 92. In 1895, the city fathers realized that the situation had reached emergency proportions, and, although the people had voted down yet another sewer proposal, they collected some $25,000 to buy land for $2,000 at the eastern city limits (now the site of Scott Carpenter Park)* and establish a dump and sewage settling basin. A single sewer main brought the waste material to the basin, where it rested for a time before being expelled into Boulder Creek. Extensions were added to the sewer main, and by 1920 most of the community was served by sewers. Farmers

---

*This park was first called Valverdan Park. Some observers feel that, while the city wished to honor astronaut Scott Carpenter, his name was proposed to quiet critics and make it difficult for them to fight the park site. Some did not fancy the idea of children playing over a former city dump.[27]

and ranchers below the settling plant complained regularly that Boulder was polluting the creek. The city consulted engineers for advice in 1908, 1909, and in 1921, but nothing was done. A proper sewage disposal plant was built over the settling basin in 1933 for $70,000, and the nearby dump was closed. Now, Boulder citizens, when they felt like it, could dump their refuse at a 106-acre facility north of town on Twenty-sixth Street (at the junction of Twenty-eighth and Broadway). Farmer Earl Juhl, as had his father before him, continued to pick up "wet" garbage in the city, cook it, and feed it to his pigs. Bly Curtis remembers seeing dead pigs and horses in the Twenty-sixth Street dump; no landfill methods were used, and nearby residents complained almost constantly of flying debris and noxious smells. Since the dump was in a flood plain, its materials were moved to other properties during the flood season; needless to say, this state of affairs caused hard feelings among the dump's neighbors.

At Mrs. Curtis' somewhat cantankerous insistence (she was known as Captain Bly in some circles), the 1952 council created a city-county health department. (Mrs. Curtis served on its board for seventeen years.) Now, for the first time, a facility could demand that raw milk not be sold in the city. Alleys were cleaned up, and a rat extermination program was put into effect. At some point during each council* meeting, Mrs. Curtis would turn to her colleagues to say, "And now, gentlemen, what about the dump?"*28 Sometimes they called her Mrs. City Dump. The matter was discussed repeatedly while the dump received more and more complaints about its management. In 1954, a group of taxpayers sued the city, claiming that the dump was now polluting adjacent waterways with chemicals; the flying paper and trash were unbearable. It was not until 1965, after the threat of more lawsuits, that the Twenty-sixth Street dump was closed. (A rifle range is now on the site.) A new facility near the old coal-mining town of Marshall was developed with a view to using proper landfill methods. In fact, the Rich-land Corporation, which had a ten-year contract with the county, built a $200,000 composting plant there. The composting plant was considered so innovative that it received national attention. The plant's machinery, however, kept breaking down mysteriously, and the town's trash haulers could not be depended upon to carry the city's refuse to the Marshall landfill. They often deposited where they pleased, despite threats from the city. The composting operation was not successful, its employees claiming that the lack of cooperation by trash haulers was the cause of its failure.

*Council was temporarily meeting at Central School, because the new municipal building was finally under construction at Broadway and Canyon Boulevard. The municipal building was first proposed in 1946. At first, the building was to include a public library and a museum as well as municipal offices. When the library and the museum were cut out of the plans, Eben Fine suggested that the old Carnegie Library would make a good museum site. The city building was started in August 1951 and dedicated in July 1952. It housed 43 city employees, including 25 police (there were 111 city employees in all). One year later, 81 city employees worked there, including 44 police (now there were 205 city employees in all). In 1962, a $185,000 bond was passed to build an addition to the ten-year-old building.

*It may be of some interest to the modern observer that in 1951 council held its first four-and-one-half-hour-long meeting.

Boulder citizens fought long and hard to keep burning trash in their back yards. *Tom Moen photo*

191

Meanwhile, most Boulderites continued to burn trash in their back yards. The general populace still regarded back-yard trash burning as a God-given right and resented any municipal interference. In the summer of 1954, council seriously considered the banning of back-yard burning with a compulsory pickup of trash and garbage from each Boulder home and business. The very thought of a burning ban enraged some citizens to such an extent that they willingly lent their support to a new organization, the Civic Association for a Better Boulder, started by John Pudlik, owner of a package-liquor store on one of Boulder's "liquor islands," and Esther Crystle Pickett, owner of a real estate loan company. Their mission was to convince Boulder voters that a return to the ward system of government would stop what they believed were the capricious actions of the city council. (Boulder had used the ward system around the turn of the century.) The city had ordered numerous studies by various engineering firms in the early 1950s with no tangible result, as far as Mrs. Pickett and Mr. Pudlik could see. Moreover, council talked of spending tax money to cover the town's ditches to protect the lives of curious children. Mrs. Pickett referred to council as the "Ditch-dominated city government."[29] Petitions for a charter amendment were accepted, and on October 26, 1954, the ward system question was put to a vote. The town would have nine wards, condidates must have lived in Boulder for three years, only taxpayers should vote for council members, and all council members would serve for two years, with no staggering of terms. The ward system won at the polls 2,972 to 2,568. (A proposal to fluoridate Boulder's water failed at the same election, but the voters did approve purchase of the town's first voting machine.) Members of council felt that they were about to be thrown out and were hesitant to tackle any big jobs. The matter moved into the courts. The following October, in 1955, the case was heard by the Colorado Supreme Court, which determined that the election was unconstitutional. Although the voters were asking for a change in the form of government, they were, in effect, recalling the present council members without a recall election. The election, said the court, was circumventive and "nothing more than a device to unseat incumbents."*[30] Much relieved with the ruling, council went back to work.

In 1955, voters approved a $1 million bond issue to build a new sewage plant at 5050 Pearl Street. Even so, in 1962, the state of Colorado declared that Boulder Creek was polluted beyond any sensible standard and gave the city ninety days to come up with a solution. The pollution was "critical to the entire South Platte River Basin,"[31] and the town of Frederick and others nearby threatened suit. No one had expected the city of Boulder to grow so fast. The sewer plant had to be expanded after seven years of operation. Boulder voters, as independent as always, paid little attention to this news, and in March 1965, in a taxpayers' election, voted against a $3 million sewerage bond issue by 110 votes (3,848 to 3,738). They also voted against a ban on back yard trash burning and against a municipal trash collection franchise. (In January 1968, the state gave discretionary powers to each county on back yard burning. Boulder County used that power to prohibit such activity.)

Voters were particularly displeased with the proposed trash collection franchise because they felt that there had not been competitive bidding. The city was dealing with Monarch Haulers; it was reported, however, that some of the sixteen independent trash haulers had to pay $5,000 to Monarch to be part of the "trash package."

Some voters found it difficult to realize that their community was growing this fast; moreover, those that did realize it did not like it. One writer to the *Camera* expressed her views on the pollution of Boulder Creek this way: "Let the outside users pay to correct it."[32] Another writer described council as "ambitious zealots of enlargement."[33] In order to make a second election more attractive, council passed an ordinance dealing with sewer plant investment fees, $300 for a new user inside the city and $450 for a new user outside the city, described as "the cost of buying into a going concern."[34] Builders said that the fee was too high; others said that the fee was too low. With increasing pressure from the state, Boulder held a second sewer bond election in July 1965; this time it passed 3,880 to 2,695, and the ten-year-old plant was expanded.* Boulder finally paid attention to its sewage problems, at least for a little while.

---

*Perhaps the "ward" election did influence the decision to change the terms of office for council. In 1956, the charter was amended so that in 1959 the four top vote-getters would receive four-year terms and the fifth would receive a two-year term.

*Two sewage plants presently serve Boulder. The old one is at 5050 Pearl Street, and the new one is on 75th Street near Jay Road. Sewage is sent through both facilities in a "double treatment" manner. In 1963, the Department of Public Service was divided into two departments—Public Works and Public Utilities.

Chapter Thirteen

The "Christmas-in-the-schools" controversy was a full-blown Boulder fight, actively participated in by various segments of Boulder society. On a number of occasions during the 1950s, parents, religious groups, and civil liberties organizations complained to the superintendent of schools whenever one of the schools put on a pageant at Christmas time with strong Christian themes. They objected to crèche scenes, religious hymns, and other evidence of Christian dogma. Finally, in early December 1960, Superintendent Natt Burbank ordered that Boulder schools "eliminate visual manifestations of sectarian symbols."[1] The letters-to-the-editor column filled up, and public meetings were scheduled. To support his unpopular decision, Burbank quoted portions of the Colorado State Constitution and the U.S. Constitution; the Board of Education backed him up with the statement that "no child shall be exposed to religious beliefs and practices contrary to those of his own religion."[2] Burbank further stated that the decision had been made after numerous meetings held the summer before, that there was to be a "gradual de-emphasization," that music programs were not affected by this ruling, and that religious activities after school were not affected.

As public meetings grew more heated and tense, insults were exchanged at meetings and through the press. Most of what Superintendent Burbank had said by way of explanation was apparently forgotten. Local artists, including Frances Trucksess, were outraged because they felt that the ruling discriminated against the art programs in the schools. The *Camera* described tearful and confused little children who brought home unfinished artwork; in an editorial, the newspaper questioned whether "partial de-emphasis"[3] was possible. By failing to notify the public in October, the *Camera* went on to say, the School Board kindled the fire under the hot water in which it now finds itself."[4] Traditional Christmas decorations on downtown streets, on the courthouse, and on the municipal building all came under fire, as did the Christmas star and the Easter cross on Flagstaff Mountain. On December 7, 1960, speaking before 1,200 irate citizens, Mrs. Florence Grieder, president of the Board of Education, emphasized that Boulder school children were a "captive group"[5] and should not be subjected to religious information. Boulder's Council of Churches agreed with the board and made a public statement of support. Those who criticized Burbank's action said that the decision had been made in secret, that leftists were running the Board of Education. "...Old Khrushchev may have his agents, working in their subversive ways, right here in little old Boulder."[6] The issue was broadened to include fears that "socialist" texts were being used in the schools, that the ideals of UNESCO were taught to young children, and that the Boulder Public Library was a communist "dupe" because it allowed a Great Decisions program to form under its auspices.

Since a number of professors belonged to the local American Civil Liberties Union, some questioned the loyalty of university employees. Were they subversive? Certain businessmen supported Natt Burbank's views. Perhaps their businesses should be boycotted. J. Corder Smith, speaking for Boulder's American Legion group, asked, "What minority group has forced this action?"[7] Christianity is on trial, said some; others blamed the *Camera* for allowing this issue to "boil along."[8]

On the evening of December 11, 1960, a cross was burned on Natt Burbank's front lawn and four youths were arrested, although it was later determined that a larger group of young men and women were involved. The following day, district court ordered the school board to refrain from "any action whatsoever interfering with the customary and traditional religious observance of Christmas."[9] This order was to be in effect until December 26. Christmas was back in the schools; the children could finish their art projects. But the situation was still tense; bomb threats were phoned in to Base Line Elementary School and Longmont High School. At least one attorney for the school board was accused of being a communist.

Of the boys and girls who participated in the cross burning, only one apologized to the superintendent's family; the others told authorities that they believed they had done no wrong. There continued in the *Camera* letters on both sides of the Christmas issue. By December 17, however, people were becoming tired of the arguments. That day, after a three-hour hearing, the district court handed down its decision. It favored the Board of Education and the superintendent of schools who, the court decided, had every right to remove religious symbolism from the school curriculum; further, the court told opponents that they had drawn up their objections improperly. When Christmas of 1961 rolled around, the Board of Education had issued a full report on the subject. Compared to the earlier letters in the newspaper, the report was dull; few bothered to read it.

All this while, a group of Boulder citizens was meeting to consolidate the county's twenty-nine school districts. Their plan called for the union of fourteen school districts and portions of others that lay in the southern half of the county to be called the Boulder Valley Unified School District. The northern half of the county would also form a district from a number of small districts, to be called the St. Vrain Unified School District. The reorganization group must have worked under difficult conditions with citizens fighting about Christmas all around it; nevertheless, it sent its plans to the state for approval and set and election for January 1961.

It was during the Christmas-in-the-schools fight that E.C. Pickett started to use her advertising space regularly in the *Camera* for her messages to the public. Since the space was in the real estate advertising section, many Boulder newspaper readers formed the habit of reading each issue backwards. They checked E.C. Pickett's daily message before moving to the comics and local news. These messages, always framed in black, served to anger or delight Boulderites until Mrs. Pickett stopped writing them in 1973, one year before her death.[10] At first, Mrs. Pickett used quotations from other writers:

> "There's not much difference between an Alabama bigot and a Colorado liberal." Vernon Jordan, Jr., executive director of the National Urban League.
> E.C. PICKETT LOAN

Eventually, she became skilled enough to write her own biting indictments against aspects of Boulder society that displeased her—the University of Colorado, professors (especially law school professors), students, young people in general, communism, UNESCO, city managers, their staff, and members of city council.

> How do you make an "A" on tests and papers prepared for CU's radical profs? Just be very sure that you always spell America with a 'k.'
> E.C. PICKETT LOAN

> Isn't it great to bleed for the poor—And live in a plush mansion featured on the Democratic Women's House Tour?
> E.C. PICKETT LOAN

> We are the victims of an illusion. The heart of the illusion is in the view that the meaning of life is to be found in participation in the political process thru which Utopia is to be achieved.
> E.C. PICKETT LOAN

> CU's Legal Aid and Defender Program has made a massive contribution toward transforming Boulder from a beautiful, safe community to a dirty, crime-ridden city.
> E.C. PICKETT LOAN

> Why do rabid "environmentalists" drive air-conditioned cars that consume 20% more gasoline, thus adding to the pollution they condemn?
> E.C. PICKETT LOAN

> One trouble with the world is that so many people who stand up so vigorously for their own rights fall down miserably on their duties.
> E.C. PICKETT LOAN

> Boulder badly needs anti-monopoly laws. Ultra-liberal profs took full control of CU long ago. Now their "liberal" spouses are doing the same thing on city council.
> E.C. PICKETT LOAN

> Has a university that participates in a fraud by granting degrees to incompetents any more right to respect than a manufacturer of shoddy goods?"
> E.C. PICKETT LOAN

> Now that CU has Black Studies and Mexican-American Studies, how soon can we expect a Nordic Studies course? Or is the University only selectively racist?
> E.C. PICKETT LOAN

One University of Colorado professor retaliated in this manner:

> To E.C. Pickett Loan In Appreciation of All Your Messages of Love Thru The Year:
> A HAPPY NEW YEAR
> Adhoc Committee of University Professors Lester Goldstein chairman.

As Boulder's population shot upward in the early 1950s, few residents apparently realized that Boulder would need more water. Some citizens kept their faucets running all winter long so that their pipes would not freeze. In the 1940s, council discussed the notion that the city should require higher fees for water and sewer service for those locating outside the city limits. The largest out-of-city users at that time were Public Service Company, the Sanitarium (now Boulder Memorial Hospital), and the Colorado and Southern Railroad. Council considered doubling the fees but, fearing such action would be regarded as extreme, they added 50 percent to those outside the city who sought water and sewer hookups. During the Public Service fight, franchise opponents suggested that Boulder get its power, as well as its water, from the Big Thompson River to the north. In October 1949, a Kansas City firm, Black and Veatch, presented a study to council which estimated that $500,000 would be needed to improve the existing water system. The engineers did not recommend that Boulder convert from a flat-rate charge to metered water, but they warned council that meters would be necessary soon.

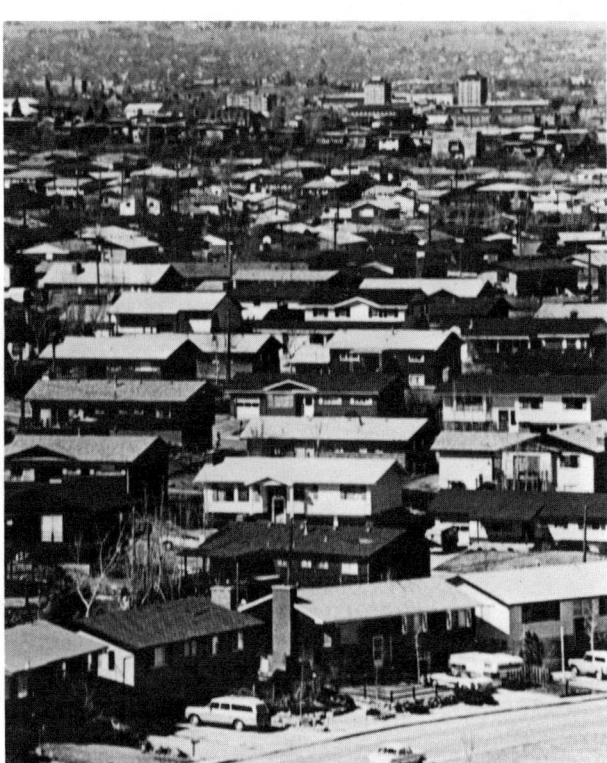

1950 additions to the Boulder landscape. *A.A. Paddock Collection*

Water and its availability were often discussed by council; members could not agree how to estimate the number of people that Boulder would attract in the next few years. (Most of the estimates, it turned out, were too low.) A former chief of the Water Department charged that the facility operated in a wasteful manner; he demanded that the office be investigated. The city attorney did so but reported that he found no evidence of waste. In 1950, council asked for a water survey, because there had not been one since 1925. The possibility of receiving 10,000 acre feet of water from the Big Thompson seemed so attractive that some council members voted to turn down the purchase of other Western Slope water for $1,647,000 in 1951. (At a later

On the way to Arapaho glacier. *A.A. Paddock Collection*

date, they turned down the offer again.) Membership in the Big Thompson District, called officially the Northern Colorado Conservancy District, would increase Boulder's water supplies by 50 percent. When Bert Johnson was hired as city manager in 1950, his top priority was Boulder membership in the Big Thompson District. Communities farther north, in eastern Colorado and in western Nebraska were not thrilled with Boulder's entrance into the race for Big Thompson water and did what they could to discourage the prospect. But "Boulder had the foresight to go after it,"[11] concluded one water attorney, even though the *Camera* was dubious about the project. At about this time, Boulder spent $118,000 for eleven water improvements and passed a $400,000 water bond which, among other things, built Maxwell and Kohler reservoirs.

In December 1952, Council member A.A. Wickstrom, Bert Johnson, and others started meeting regularly with the Northern Colorado Conservancy District. Boulder agreed to pay its share of back taxes to 1937, the year of the district's formation. The city also agreed to build Boulder Reservoir, which took most of the $2 million from a water bond passed in the summer of 1952. The rest of the money went to improve Silver Lake Dam. Boulder also voted to approve membership in the district in a "now or never" election; membership in the district would never again be offered. Boulder's new water supply came from the Western Slope, flowing from the Colorado River into Grand Lake through pipes to Estes Park and down the eastern side of the mountains.

Although a water bond for $1 million was defeated in July 1959, Boulder voters did see the wisdom of establishing a Blue Line. The Blue Line, a first project of the newly formed PLAN-Boulder,* was a boundary line drawn through Boulder's mountain backdrop at a height averaging 5,750 feet. Beyond this line, no water or sewer facilities would be extended. Voters hoped that Boulder's beautiful setting would be secure for all to enjoy. However, one and one-half years later, an exception to the Blue Line was made on the January 1961 ballot. Shall the National Center for Atmospheric Research's proposed building site be an

---

*A group of activist citizens who devoted themselves to attempting to direct Boulder's changes in order that the town's unique qualities might be preserved.

Lakes which lie below Arapaho glacier—Triple Lakes in foreground, Goose Lake, Island Lake in background; Silver Lake is not in photo—and formed the first water supply for Boulder. *Western Historical Collections, University of Colorado at Boulder*

Arapaho glacier in late summer. No longer does a little lake form at its base. *Western Historical Collections, University of Colorado at Boulder*

exception to the Blue Line? Voters agreed to the exception although there was considerable opposition. Why, some argued, should such a scenic spot be used for a building complex? Is it a proper use of our precious water? (Ten years had passed since Boulder residents ran their "precious" water through their pipes all winter long.) Would Table Mountain be covered with houses? Director Walter Orr Roberts assured voters that NCAR would disturb as little of Table Mountain as possible. After another Black and Veatch study in 1961, Boulder citizens voted in April for another $4 million water bond. The bond issue passed handily (3,474 to 1,332), although City Manager E. Robert Turner was accused at one point of restricting water use in order to influence the election. Boulder's original water supply was improved. Fed by the Arapaho Glacier and the snows along the Continental Divide, the water moved through a number of little lakes into Silver Lake, then through a seventeen-mile pipe (the water was chlorinated at Lakewood) to a new water treatment plant called Betasso, thence to four covered reservoirs: Sunshine, Maxwell, Chautauqua, and Kohler. Learning that water meters were now necessary, Boulder residents grumbled only a little; meters were installed for around $700,000. With the 1964 acquisition of the Bijou water rights, which amounted to an additional 1,016 acre feet, Boulder's water prospects were unusually good.

Perhaps a feeling of "water affluence" stimulated a controlled growth plan which was tested in the 1965 elections. The "service area" concept, which was popularly called "Spokes of the Wheel," called for water supplies to be granted to residents outside the city limits along radials in each direction. The hoped for result by such action was to control the nature of growth outside Boulder's boundaries. One "spoke" went straight east along Arapahoe Street and was primarily directed at encouraging the establishment of business and industrial interests to the east of Boulder. Another "spoke" extended northeast along the Diagonal highway, reaching toward the new IBM plant. It was the third "spoke," planned to run seven miles south to the Rudd property, that sparked what turned out to be a strong citizens' revolt.

Florence Sibert started things rolling when she wrote to the *Camera*, "If the Council can, without a vote of the people, arbitrarily decide that Boulder will supply with water we have bought for ourselves any unannexed area Council chooses, as big an area as Council chooses, at any price Council chooses...people have lost control."[12] E.C. Pickett wrote, "This is America or does Council consider itself the master instead of the servant of the people."[13] Although Boulder voters finally approved sewer bonds at the same election, they turned down "Spokes of the Wheel;" the Rudd property to the south remained undeveloped. Boulder passed another water bond in 1967 for $3 million which provided another water treatment plant at the reservoir to process Big Thompson water.

With the November 4, 1969 election, an issue was settled that had been simmering for years. The questions of fluoridating the town's drinking water was a volatile one. In 1903, a Colorado Springs dentist noticed that his patients native to Colorado had a brown mottling on their teeth; those who came from other places did not. Eventually, it was discovered that many Colorado communities had natural fluorides in their drinking water which produced what was called "Colorado brown stain." Those who saw nothing wrong with the additive and considered fluoride essential to the formation of healthy teeth could not understand the "backwardness" of fluoridation opponents and wrote somewhat condescending letters to the *Camera* supporting fluoridation. After all, did not Boulder's water already have some natural fluoride in it? Did we not want to protect our children? Opponents regarded fluoridation as a form of mass medication, that citizens would no longer have freedom of choice if they were forced to drink fluoridated water. Some nervous residents wondered about those who might be allergic to fluorides. Could fluorides cause disease? Cancer? Gum disease? Those against fluoridation suggested the Clifton Plan, a system of distributing free fluoride tablets to those families who wished their children to be so protected. When the fluoridation question appeared again on the November 1969 ballot, after having been soundly defeated three times in recent years, the conflict started all over again. Mayor Knecht said, "Boulder is becoming an island in a fluoridated state."[14] All of Boulder's dentists, save one, supported the effort. Fluoride was an expensive additive, they said, costing eleven cents for each person each year. Pro-fluoride forces called the anti-forces superstitious. Some opponents spoke of fluorides in the same breath with DDT, thalidomide, cyclamates, MSG, and smog. Writer Jane Fitz-Randolph questioned whether fluoride could do all that was claimed for it. Just before the election, Donna G. Jones wrote to the newspaper defending her anti-fluoride position saying, "Conservationists have always been called crackpot."[15] When the Boulder City-County Board of Health took a vote on the question, all were for the fluoridation of water except the lady who established the board—Bly Curtis. She voted against fluoridation for all of the stated reasons, plus one more. She had visited the holding lakes above Boulder's water supply and had seen the cavalier way in which city employees tossed in chlorides without measurement. It made her nervous. Even so, Boulder approved the fluoridation of drinking water.

Even more than the fluoridation issue, the subject of liquor caused voters to take a strongly positive or negative position. Boulder citizens had gone to the polls to defeat liquor-by-the-drink fourteen times since the town went dry in 1907. A few package stores in the county did a brisk business. The town grew around the package stores, which became unannexed "liquor islands." Proprietors of these establishments fought side-by-side with the temperance-minded against an amendment to allow the selling of mixed drinks, for they enjoyed a monopoly of the liquor trade. Of the city's thirteen unannexed "islands," four sold liquor; of the eight "peninsulas," one sold liquor. According to state law, forcible annexation could only take place after a twenty-year wait. When the state of Colorado amended its annexation laws so that a municipality need only wait three years before annexing land islands and peninsulas, passage of a liquor-by-the-drink amendment seemed a real possibility. With each election, the vote came closer and closer. In 1967, the fifteenth attempt to amend the charter with regard to the sale of liquor passed handily 9,701 to 3,965. Perhaps this poem, which appeared in the *Colorado Daily,* amused Boulder voters:

*We never eat cookies
Because they have yeast.
and one little bite
Turns a man to be beast.*

*Oh, can you imagine
a sadder disgrace
Than a man in the gutter
With crumbs on his face.*[16]

One would think that a library bond issue would not be controversial, but Boulder voters made it so. When a $450,000 bond issue was proposed in 1959, the old Carnegie building was bursting at the seams, literally as well as figuratively; some of its walls were unstable. Residents, however, were not sure that Boulder needed a new library. It was true that a new library had been contemplated as part of the new municipal building, but both the library and the museum had been cut for financial reasons. Was not Norlin Library at the university close by? Norlin would serve the city's needs as it had in the past. Moreover, the proposed site was in the flood plain. Would the books be ruined? As usual, some did not want to spend the money. Would citizens come forward who "with good common sense...will help us control these wild and silly spenders?"[17] Despite the opposition, the measure passed. Boulder's new library was dedicated November 11, 1961. A bequest from Nell Buckingham furnished the east reading room. In 1969, library patron George Reynolds made a gift to the city for library use; his bequest, together with federal funds, built a branch library in South Boulder. Two years later, voters approved another bond issue to add a south wing to the main library.

Bond issues for park land and recreation have suffered at the hands of the Boulder voter. E.C. Pickett expressed the views of some:

> Boulder's Parks and Recreation director complains his dept is inadequately funded. Thousands of Boulder taxpayers are also "inadequately funded" & work too hard to play tennis.
> E.C. PICKETT LOAN

In 1957, Boulder turned down a $500,000 recreation bond, although voters did approve money to improve the airport. Council was more specific in its bond requests two years later, saying that the money would build two swimming pools. Even so, the bond failed. In 1961, voters were more kindly; they approved a parks-recreation bond. The following year, at a taxpayers' election, two swimming pools for Boulder were finally approved 2,132 to 2,042. Scott Carpenter Park would get a swimming pool, and the old pool at Spruce Park would get a face-lift. (Swimmers had used an indoor pool at that location since the early 1900s.) In 1969, voters turned their backs again on recreation bonds, but two years later they decided that a north and a south recreational center sounded like a good idea and approved bonds for $1 million.

Boulder voters were not reluctant, however, when it came to greenbelt acquisition. Both liberals and conservatives liked the idea of buying land in the mountains and on the plains that would "belt" the city with undeveloped land. Even E.C. Pickett was silent on the subject. In order to stop the establishment of a luxury hotel atop Enchanted Mesa, voters approved the purchase of 155 acres there at a cost of $105,000. The prospect of more greenbelt helped to lessen the sting of the second sales tax. After having been discussed for twenty years, a 1 percent sales tax proposal went before the voters in November 1963. Perhaps it failed because liquor and cigarettes were not included and because no clear spending program was outlined for the people.

The voters knew, however, that the city planned to make Ninth a through street; this prospect did not appeal to them. Merchants were not happy with the proposal because it exempted food and drugs from taxation, which would complicate their bookkeeping. Although Reuben Zubrow, professor of economics, warned council that a sales tax with food and drugs included was regressive and a burden on the poor, the following year council proposed the sales tax again with food and drugs included. It won, even though the League of Women Voters came out against the measure because of its regressive nature. By this time, a 2 percent state tax was already in place. In November 1967, another 1 percent sales tax measure passed easily, for the voters liked the idea that 60 percent of the collected tax would go for street improvements and 40 percent would be reserved for further purchase of greenbelt lands. In November 1971, voters gave council the power to reserve funds for the purchase of greenbelt.

Eighty-eight years had passed since the angry letter writer had demanded local government for Boulder City in hopes that the dog population would be contained. When a leash law was proposed in 1959, those opposing it saw their free way of life disappearing as a town changed into a city. "We want a place where the kids can roam with their dogs,"[18] wrote one lady to the newspaper. A newcomer disagreed with her picture of the "good life" in Boulder. "You people of Boulder have altogether too much freedom. Your lives are not organized and neither are those of your pets."[19] The leash law passed but was brought up again in two years in a much-weakened form. Dog owners would be required to leash their dogs only in business districts and other selected spots. The measure failed.

In the fall of 1968, City Manager Ted Tedesco announced a consolidation of police and fire services which would bring him nose-to-nose with the Boulder Fire Department. Boulder's charter does not specify separate jurisdictions for police and fire services but places them under a Department of Public Safety. Tedesco was concerned with what he thought was the "excessive free time"[20] of fire department employees. He wanted to trim down the force and train police officers to assume some of the firefighting duties. This type of consolidation was used in some smaller communities in the United States and in quite a number of towns in Canada. Needless to say, the Fire Department was not happy with the turn of events. As they gathered signatures for a petition to amend the charter to prohibit consolidation of police and fire departments, the city manager accused the firemen of spreading a "smokescreen to cover up their plans for self interest and personal gain."[21] In short, he said, they were "fighting over who puts the fire out."[22] Assistant City Manager Robert Westdyke said that the firemen were "feather bedding."[23]

Since the petitions were properly drawn, council had no choice but to set a charter election for February 11, 1969. Thus, the city manager was in the unusual position of fighting against one of his own departments. A month or so before the election was to take place, Mother Nature appeared to take sides in the controversy. An unusually fierce windstorm came up on the evening of January 7, and the firemen answered fifty-six calls. Up and down the Front Range, municipal fire departments and volunteer organizations helped one another as the gales continued to spark fire after fire. (One Cherryvale volunteer was killed.) Although a few Boulder policemen had been designated public safety officers, they had not received their training yet and could not assist the firefighters that evening.

Popular sentiment was for the firemen. When it looked as though the firemen were going to win the election, both sides sat down for a week of conversation. After five months of discord, the city manager announced to the public that consolidation of the police and fire departments was "not now in the picture."[24] Some of the firemen wanted to continue with the election and were not too pleased with the agreement. As Mayor Knecht put it, they "weren't real nuts about it."[25] But the charter election was called off, and the city manager commented on the affairs: "We never intended to consolidate."[26]

Chapter Fourteen

In the late 1960s, Boulder experienced what was called, euphemistically, the "transient problem." Throughout the United States, the sons and daughters of middle-class families were "taking a vacation from society."[1] They were attracted to beautiful places, just as "the lost generation" went to France and Spain after World War I, and just as Jack Kerouac and "the beat generation" went to San Francisco after World War II. Boulder and other spots in the Rocky Mountains were the destinations of 1968's "flower children." They hitchhiked into town carrying a sleeping bag and a few belongings on their backs, or came in colorful but untidy vans. Most were bedraggled and dirty but seemingly free from shackles of the "straight" society of their parents. They congregated in the city's parks, unrolled their sleeping bags wherever they could find a place to rest, and, in general, upset the Boulder populace.

Hitchhiking, sleeping overnight in cars in front of Boulder residences, panhandling, jaywalking and open use of drugs—all these activities enraged many Boulderites who demanded new laws to prohibit such goings-on. Since City Manager Ted Tedesco could not rid Boulder of the transients, he was accused of being "soft on hippies." Central Park was overrun. "I'm from a small town where no one sits on the grass unless they're under 12,"[2] wrote one resident to the *Camera*. A more tolerant writer stated, "the thing is that kids today just don't care to take the Gray Line Tour."[3] As the flower children ran out of money and got sick, welfare agencies were swamped with requests for food stamps and medical care. The People's Clinic, now a respected Boulder institution, was formed to provide doctors and medicine that the young transients could afford.

The visitors caused health problems. Since many of the young people came from urban centers and were apartment dwellers where the "super" did everything, they were either ignorant of basic sanitation or were unwilling to correct the unhealthy conditions that they caused. They polluted the creeks and the parks and camps in the mountains. Nederland complained of hippie squatters on nearby communes and the pollution of forest camps and park land. E.C. Pickett had a comment:

> Hippies already outnumber—and can outvote—the "straights" in Boulder's mountain areas. The freaks and their leftist CU allies will also control the city within 3 years.
> E.C. PICKETT LOAN

Sanitary conditions in Central Park deteriorated to such an extent that Tedesco declared the park "partially closed," calling it a "potential hazard."[4] Public Health Director Charles H. Dowding, Jr. pronounced Central Park a serious health hazard, for the number of hepatitis cases was growing at an alarming rate; he felt that the lack of sanitation was the cause. Boulder residents no longer used the parks, and band concerts were canceled.

A growing number of young runaways, attracted to the Boulder scene, required special attention. St. John's Episcopal Church made headlines when Father James McKeown allowed a certain number of youthful travelers to sleep in the building. Father McKeown wanted to establish a "youth hostel" to accommodate some of the summer transients, so he went to council with an idea. Why not clean up "The Ruins," what was left of Lefferdink's dream of a luxury motor hotel at the mouth of Boulder Canyon, and turn it into a hostel? Council determined that such a hostel would be illegal, for it would be against the city's housing code and a zoning variance would be necessary. Although council denied Father McKeown's request in May 1970, some transients slept there anyway. (Eventually, the Boulder Hall of Justice was built over its foundation.)

For some of these young people who were "taking a vacation from society," the holiday ended; they went back to their families, back to school, or back to the job. Then a quite different group of transients descended upon Boulder. Highly educated, their politics were anarchist and their methods of social action often violent and destructive. These young people were far more dangerous than the first group of visitors, not only because of their revolutionary views, but also because of their increased dependence upon drugs. The police department added more narcotics officers to the force.

Paralleling the hippie disturbances in Boulder were the activities of some students at the University of Colorado. With passage of the Twenty-sixth Amendment to the U.S. Constitution, which guaranteed the right to vote to eighteen- to twenty-year-olds, an organization called BURP, Boulder Union to Register People, claimed to have added 7,000 names to the voting roster. Some of the students were politically aware and, like students everywhere, left their studies to demonstrate against the war in Vietnam. Outraged by each news development in Southeast Asia, they marched in the streets, they sat down in university buildings (in April 1970, they occupied Regent Hall), and they joined with other Boulder citizens in various "public witness" demonstrations to show their anger at the escalation of war in Vietnam. In June 1970, Boulder citizens went to the polls to vote on a Vietnam War referendum which, if passed, would have notified the president and the congress of Boulder's concern with the direction of policies in Southeast Asia. The referendum lost, however, by 289 votes (4,690 to 4,401). Even so, antiwar demonstrations grew in number and intensity on University Hill; some of them got out of hand.

When students, hippies, anarchists, and Boulder residents joined together in May 1971, they participated in three days of violent actions in a "senseless and destructive riot that left stores looted and thousands of dollars worth of windows broken."[5] The police had to use tear gas to subdue the rioters, forty of whom were arrested. Jones Drug Store was vandalized; its owners were forced to install iron grills over the store's windows. Colorado Bookstore gave up glass windows altogether, replacing them with concrete walls. CURB, Citizens United to Restore Boulder, demanded that the laws on marijuana be enforced and that the jails be used to clear the area of "street people." E.C. Pickett suggested:

> The new jail should be located on Unihill near its main source of business—preferably on the CU campus, where defiance of law and order is nurtured.
> E.C. PICKETT LOAN

> Our mayor says he's disappointed" over the Unihill riot. Goodness, gracious, golly, gee! Shouldn't he stop using such strong language over mere looting, assault and arson?
> E.C. PICKETT LOAN

When President Nixon ordered the mining of Haiphong Harbor in North Vietnam in early May 1972, the university students and others joined together to demonstrate in a way that would be remembered by Boulder's commuter population. In the early morning hours of May 8, youthful demonstrators carried barrels, concrete blocks, and stacks of firewood to U.S. Highway 36, barricading the turnpike interchange at Baseline Road. Boulderites who worked in Denver had to find some other way to get there. During the day, the number of demonstrators varied from two hundred to three thousand. For the most part, the demonstration was a peaceful one, with good humor and singing, although a few motorists tried to ram the barricade with their cars, knocking down some of the demonstrators. A few rocks and bottles were thrown, and the police and a family living nearby had an altercation. Shortly after lunch, City Manager Tedesco asked the police to reopen the highway; by 3 p.m., traffic was flowing to and from Denver again. Mrs. Pickett, of course, was inspired to write:

> Peacenik roadblocks didn't inconvenience radical CU profs, who can cancel classes as they please without penalty. It was the hourly-paid working man who was the innocent victim.
> E.C. PICKETT LOAN

A third group of transients arrived in Boulder in the early 1970s, quite different from flower children, college students, or the anarchists, who "passed from the scene...via physical departure or felony conviction."[6] This third group was essentially nonpolitical, was seldom well educated, did not believe in working for a living, and was addicted to a variety of drugs, including alcohol. Some residents lumped all the transients together as hippies, seeing no distinction between the bedraggled free spirit (some are affluent Boulder merchants today) and the hard-core bum. Hippies themselves made the distinction and referred to drug-oriented transients as "red necks." These folks were reminiscent of the gun-toting and knife-carrying motorcycle gangs that had plagued rural California a generation before. One *Camera* reporter, writing in 1970, said that it was a mistake, however romantic, to link hippies with earlier society dropouts, "the lost generation," and "the beat generation," for modern hippies, he said, lacked the creative energies which characterized earlier groups and were "basically inert, interested only in exploring themselves."[7] The *Denver Post* quoted another Boulder resident who said that she could not understand why such people were called transients since she saw "the same people there at 8 a.m. every morning with their beer and their wine."[8] In 1979, there were brief skirmishes between the remaining "street people" and the "Rat Patrol," a high school vigilante group. Despite years of the transient problem, some Boulderites continued their "straight" lives. A policeman reported that at Beach Park he encountered "a mother and her three children playing on the swings...It has been a long time since I have seen that."[9]

Others acted violently during the early 1970s, with far more tragic results. In May 1971, an unexploded pipe bomb was discovered at the door of United Bank. During the occupation of Regent Hall, dynamite sticks were found at the old Security Bank at the edge of the campus. In February 1974, a bomb exploded in Flatirons Elementary School; fortunately, no children were in the building. In the following weeks, the offices of the campus police were bombed, as was the air-conditioning unit of the Hall of Justice Building (just west of the courthouse, facing Thirteenth Street). The Board of Education's auditorium at 6500 Arapahoe Street was firebombed. Theories were expressed and accusations made, but hard evidence was not available; the city was uneasy.

On the evening of April 26, 1974, an explosion rocked Chautauqua Park and was heard by residents throughout most of Boulder. Three young activists,

A number of bombings took place in 1974, this one at Flatirons School. *Boulder Public Library from Town and Country Review*

Reyes Martinez, Una Jaakola, and Neva Romero, were blown to bits in their car, which was parked at the southwest corner of the old Chautauqua Auditorium. Since the windows of the car were closed, the explosion was intense, and debris scattered for some distance. (One of the investigating policemen remembers that an aerosol can of rug cleaner, which was lying in the back seat of the car, was activated. When he opened the back door of the bombed car, white foam poured out.) Three days later, another violent explosion woke up at least part of Boulder. This time, Florencio Granado, Heriberto Teran, and Francisco Dougherty died in a car parked in front of Burger King, next to Pudlik's Liquor on Twenty-eighth Street. A fourth victim, Antonio Alcantar, survived. At the time of the explosion, he was outside the car and claimed that he was merely hitchhiking with the group. He said that he did not know the dead people. Alcantar was close enough to the open car door to be seriously hurt; he lost a leg. Were the cars booby-trapped, as some of Colorado's Mexican-American community claimed? Or were "Los Seis de Boulder," as they came to be called, preparing bombs for more explosions?

In late 1973, council learned the hard way that some governmental business should not be undertaken without a public hearing, at least in Boulder. A teacher had approached Mayor Penfield Tate, asking him to sponsor a protective law regarding the employment rights of homosexuals. On December 18, council, by a vote of five to four, quietly passed an amendment to the Human Rights Ordinance which would ban discrimination in employment with regard to age, marital status, and sexual preference. When the amendment came up for second reading on January 1, 1974, the traditional swearing-in day for a new city council, some residents appeared at the council meeting to denounce the action. The old council tabled the second reading until a public meeting could be scheduled. With that, Boulder geared up for what promised to be a first-class fight; in short, the "community was foaming."[10] Merchant Mary Conner and others formed Concerned Citizens to combat what she saw as the "forces of hedonism and decadence."[11] Housewife Hilma Skinner, who spent a great deal of time outside the home speaking on the subject that a woman's place was in the home, said that she was "sickened,"[12] that the proposed amendment would turn Boulder into a "sexual deviate mecca that will become as vile and corrupt as Sodom and Gomorrah and Pompeii."[13] The public meeting was so crowded that closed-circuit television had to be installed in the halls. Of those who attended, many insisted on publicly declaring their homosexuality by wearing lavender arm bands. After the hearing, council voted, five to four, to place the sexual preference amendment on the ballot.

At this point, some residents initiated the recall of the five council members who voted for the amendment. Three of the five, Ruth Correll, Janet Roberts, and Karen Paget, were saved by a charter provision which stated that newly elected council members may not be recalled for a specified time period. That left Mayor Penfield Tate and Tim Fuller, the man whom the students saw as their representative in government. Fuller did not pick up more support in the community, however, when he described his oppostion as "arrogant"[14] and "politically immature people."[15] Furthermore, his position had weakened earlier in his tenure when the question of his residency became public. When Fuller was elected to council in 1971, a three-year residency requirement for candidates was still in force. It was alleged that Fuller was a resident of San Francisco at the time he claimed residency in Boulder. An independent investigation produced no proof of either residency. In July 1972, the Colorado Supreme Court ruled that such residency requirements were unconstitutional. Although Tim Fuller's residency became a moot question, some voters still brooded over the discrepancy.

The sexual preference election came first. Those in favor of the employment amendment formed an organization called Concerned Citizens for Human Rights, describing the threats to the homosexual as a "sore in the side of the community."[16] A second group, the Boulder Committee for Individual Freedom, worked against passage of the amendment. On May 7, 1974, after a five-month fight, Boulder defeated the amendment two to one (13,107 to 7,438). The *Camera*, in summing up its views, said that the whole affair from the beginning was the result of "poor judgment."[17] Tim Fuller was recalled from office on September 10;* George Boland, a lawyer who had tried three times for a council seat but had failed, took Fuller's place for the balance of his term. Penfield Tate squeaked through by 567 votes. (In the 1975 elections, however, Tate was soundly defeated in his bid for reelection.) Some say that a heavy student vote might have made a difference. The residency requirement for voters had been shortened to thirty-two days, which meant that students just back from summer vacation could not vote unless they had maintained a Boulder address all summer. However, the students' ballots might not have made a difference, for they had displayed a consistent voting apathy since 1971, when voting apparently lost its novelty.

In 1974, Clela Rorex, daughter of the county clerk in Routt County, was elected as Boulder County clerk and recorder. After two and one-half months in office, Mrs. Rorex achieved a certain unhappy fame, which served to either entertain or enrage the community.

---

*Although other council members have been threatened with recall, Fuller is the first council member to be recalled in fact.

Dave McCord and Dave Zamora, two twenty-seven-year-old homosexuals from Colorado Springs, sought a marriage license in El Paso County and were turned down, the clerk there saying, "We don't do that sort of thing here. Maybe you should go to Boulder."[18] And so they did. Mrs. Rorex requested a memorandum on the legality of same-sex marriage licenses from the district attorney's office, and deputy William Wise replied, "Same-sex marriage licenses are not specifically prohibited, or at least...There is no statutory law prohibiting the issuance of a license...."[19] Mr. Wise did not advise the county clerk further, but since she felt that "it is not for me to legislate morality,"[20] Mrs. Rorex issued the license to McCord and Zamora, saying, "Too many public officials are concerned with their public image and therefore shy away from controversial issues."[21] A few days later, two homosexual women asked for and received the second license. Two men from Wyoming, hearing of these developments, traveled down to Boulder to receive a third such license. A county clerk employee who was doing the paperwork for these licenses thought it was such a good idea that he took one out for himself and a friend. From California came two men, both born outside the United States, who hoped to legally test both the same-sex marriage license and certain immigration regulations regarding homosexuals.* They were married outside the county clerk's office.

By mid-April, Ros Howard saw some interesting possibilities in the marriage license situation and brought his neighbor's mare to town, tethering her outside the courthouse. Howard had put flowers in her mane and called her Dolly. (Actually, the horse's name was "Lightnin'," but Howard thought "Dolly" was more appropriate.) Said the sixty-six-year-old Howard, "If a boy can marry a boy, and a girl can marry a girl, why can't a lonesome old cowboy get hitched to his favorite saddle mare?"[22] Employees in the clerk's office remained calm and asked if Dolly had had her blood tests. "No," said Howard, "she hasn't but she leads a clean life."[23] When Howard had to admit that Dolly was only eight years old, the clerk's office denied the license, saying that Dolly was under age. "Oh, Dolly's sure going to be disappointed,"[24] was Howard's parting shot. Throughout these proceedings, there had been no word from the state attorney general's office, but by April 25, 1975, the attorney general decided that such licenses were illegal; Mrs. Rorex did not issue another.

By 1969, it was evident, if it had not been before, that Boulder citizens and those in city government regarded one another as adversaries. Some council members and city staff said privately that citizens could not understand the magnitude and complexity of the problems facing the community. The citizens' provincial outlook and self-interests blocked an accurate view of the needs of the total community. Citizens, on the other hand, accused council of paying lip service to their complaints, accused city managers of working for vested but not public interests, and accused planners of either incompetence or plotting against their interests, or both. Planners, in the natural course of their duties, worked closely with developers, architects, and builders, often developing a first-name relationship with them. This relationship, however innocent, caused even more hostility between citizen groups and the planners.

Some Boulderites joined forces in 1969 to try for a return to the ward system, as Mrs. Pickett had attempted fourteen years earlier. With the establishment of wards, they reasoned, council could be made more responsive to the specific needs of different sections of the city. Proceedings at council, one observer complained, were "one continuous brawl,"[25] but the ward movement died, at least for the moment. The Committee for Fair Representation, headed by realtor Walter Slack, collected enough signatures in 1973 to petition for a special elections on wards, or districting. Their plan called for three council members to be elected from each of three districts, their terms to be staggered to provide continuity. At that time, five out of nine council members lived on the Hill; both North and South Boulder wanted to be part of the decision-making process. The committee insisted on a three-year residency for candidates, even though the Colorado Supreme Court had already declared such requirements unconstitutional. The districting plan also called for lowering the age limit for candidates from twenty-five to eighteen years. With this disparate assortment of proposed amendment changes before them, voters went to the polls in September 1973; the districting plan lost by a mere twenty-nine votes. Two years later, voters were asked again if they wanted to lower the age requirement for council candidates; they said no. They also turned down a proposal that council members be paid $300 a month and reacted negatively to the request that council be allowed to meet in executive session on certain occasions.

Citizens and those in government distrusted one another. Each side spoke of the other's lack of intelligence, understanding, broad-mindedness, and grasp of civic affairs. Those in city government who tried to communicate to the public the necessity of bond issues laid the responsibility for their failure on the recalcitrant Boulder voter. When a $7,470,000 bond issue for a new civic center* failed at a June 1970

---

*In May 1980, one of these two was deported to his native Australia.

*Council planned to build a new municipal building, theatre, and auditorium on the Central Park land, moving the band shell and train to another location. The bond issue failed 7,578 to 2,837. Voters felt that the project was too costly; moreover, they did not like the idea of more civic buildings in the flood plain.

election, some supporters said philosophically that the failure was due to bad timing. But Councilman Geesaman said that the people had become "myopic."[26] City Manager Tedesco said that the community is "going to pay and pay and pay... It's paying for a lack of attention to basics over the years."[27] The *Camera* concluded mildly that Boulderites would "prefer a slower pace"[28] in funding civic improvements. When Tedesco asked for another 1 percent sales tax, E.C. Pickett replied, speaking at least for some in the community:

> City Manager Tedesco tells Council in a "study session" that the city will have to find a new financial source to tap this year. Taxpayers get three guesses who will be "tapped."
> E.C. PICKETT LOAN

In June 1972, voters defeated a sales tax increase, said no to a $1 million land purchase* for civic buildings, and said no to $950,000 for bikeways. Furthermore, some voters expressed their irritation with the city for spending tax money to advertise its position on election issues.

That September, Boulder showed its negative face again. Six counties (there had been seven, but Weld County had pulled out) participated in a funding election for the Regional Transportation District, an election that would finally take the Public Service Company off the hook. The power company would no longer manage, at a considerable loss, the city's anemic bus system. (For a time, public transportation consisted of six tired old buses.) RTD, which was established in 1969, asked for a one-half percent sales tax, or $1.5 billion, to establish a regional bus system. RTD supporters spoke to Boulder in vague terms of alternative modes of travel, including rapid transit and PRT, Personal Rapid Transit. Because no definite transportation plan had been developed for Boulder, the voters wanted specific information and rejected RTD by fifty-seven votes. Douglas County also rejected RTD. "R.T.D. really didn't offer Boulder anything at all,"[29] sympathized Tim McCarty, a new RTD board member from Longmont. Even so, Boulder did not pull out of the transportation district. Public Service got out of the bus business, and Boulder got a less sickly transportation system plus another half-cent in sales tax.

Boulder voters were not totally negative in their voting habits. In August 1970, they gave Public Service Company another twenty-five-year franchise (8,452 to 1,149) with the understanding that the company welcome a recreational use around the lake near the Valmont plant. (The lake, originally called Weisenhorn's, was the scene of many a pleasant ice-skating party years ago.) Opposition to the franchise was mild, quite a difference from the 1949 days of A. Gayle Waldrop. PLAN-Boulder, a group interested in sound planning for the community, opposed the franchise, saying that the company did not maintain high enough pollution standards at its plant. Voters did say no, however, to the question of underground power lines (6,439 to 3,027), which would have required a fifty-cent surcharge on each electric bill.

Boulder was suffering from "downtown disease" by the 1950s. The building of the Denver-Boulder turnpike had resulted in greater ease of traveling to neighboring communities; gasoline seemed limitless, and new regional shopping centers outside the county pulled some Boulder consumers away from the downtown area. Signs of decay were apparent—empty store fronts, and the moving of traditional downtown firms to the edge of town. Even so, some businessmen resisted the need for changes downtown. A group of downtown businessmen called Centroplex met to investigate ways to enhance the downtown area. They saw downtown as a cultural, governmental, and financial center but were realistic about reviving full-service shopping at the city's core. The group recommended a mall development for Pearl Street. Centroplex was followed by Boulder Tomorrow, whose goals were similar, although the group recommended a "high-rise" superblock for downtown, including a nine-block area from Ninth to Eighteenth streets. In 1966, the Downtown Businessmen's Association became active and addressed itself to the revival of the downtown area. Not until the mid-1970s, however, did the city, businessmen, and other interests work together over the violent objections of a few merchants to establish The Mall at a cost of $1,850,000. Pearl Street was closed to auto traffic in June 1976 from Eleventh to Fifteenth streets; construction of the interior walkways was completed and dedicated in August 1977. The Mall, however, was not intended as a full-service regional shopping center.

Since the 1950s, Boulder had flirted with shopping centers—downtown centers, out-of-town centers, small, large, and regional centers, centers east of Thirtieth Street, centers west of Thirtieth Street, centers without public funding, and centers with public funding. As residents and council examined specifics of each shopping complex proposal, its location was argued, its design torn apart, and its very nature questioned. A few small centers developed without too much trouble; others had troubles right from the beginning. In 1955, a modest Basemar center

---
*The city wanted to buy one land parcel just east of Central Park and another at Ninth Street and Canyon Boulevard.

Pearl Street before The Mall. *Boulder Public Library from Town and Country Review*

was established on land within the city limits. At the same time, Arapahoe Village South was built by the Murchison family of Texas on a former golf course (the land was in the county); the complex was bounded by Twenty-eighth Street and Arapahoe and Folsom streets. Development of Arapahoe Village North followed. Since liquor was sold on this "county" island, and since Boulder was still technically "dry," Arapahoe Village North interests fought against annexation to the city until 1967, when Boulder went "wet."

Crossroads Shopping Center was also built with Texas money and on land outside the city; the 400,000-square-foot development encountered no difficulty in 1963. When developer Gerri von Frellick started construction, he had to clear away a field of boulders left on the site by the flood of 1894. After Crossroads was completed, the railroad tracks along Canyon Boulevard were removed, and Boulder planners "suddenly" realized that Canyon was a natural east-west traffic carrier. But there was Crossroads—in the way. The State Highway Department, as well as county authorities, participated in considerable negotiations with private interests to connect Canyon Boulevard with Arapahoe Street; they wanted to swing to the south of Crossroads. However, negotiations broke down. Hence, Boulder has a main east-west artery that dead-ends at a shopping center in the middle of town.

Even though City Planner Trafton Bean warned council that too much land was being zoned for commercial use, it became apparent that, through the years, no one in city government was paying much attention to this view. Boulder continued its flirtation with shopping center developers. The process usually went like this: There would be an announcement in the press of an outstanding shopping proposal that would not only meet everyone's shopping needs but would be beautiful, would not impinge upon nearby residential neighborhoods, would not be endangered by flooding, would have no traffic or parking problems, and would not contribute to urban sprawl and pollution. Each proposal would employ good land-use concepts as outlined in the Boulder Comprehensive

Pearl Street is closed; the former main street is torn up. *Boulder Public Library from Town and Country Review*

The Mall is beginning to take shape. *Boulder Public Library from Town and Country Review*

The clock goes back up. *Boulder Public Library from Town and Country Review*

The Mall is finished. *Tom Moen photo*

A Mall musician plays, hoping for contributions. *Tom Moen photo*

Lunchtime on the Downtown Boulder Mall. *Tom Moen photo*

210

Plan. Such announcements were followed by extensive public hearings where the proposal would be analyzed by a variety of residents with differing viewpoints. Insults and accusations would fly, accented by letters to the *Daily Camera*, comments on local radio stations' "public access" programs, and heavy attendance at public meetings before the Planning Commission and council. Many of the shopping center plans were dismissed as "too conventional," "too massive," "a land-use disaster," "eliminate it," or "a typical suburban shopping center surrounded by a sea of cars,"[30] One Planning Commission member, after one such lengthy session, commented to a reporter, "Maybe we don't need one."[31]

For example, a "downtown superblock," the land between Ninth and Eleventh streets and Canyon Boulevard and Walnut Street, was considered by different developers at different times. In the summer of 1977, developer Orrin Ericson of Minneapolis brought his proposals and his men to Boulder to "unveil" what he considered an outstanding shopping complex for Boulder. Mr. Ericson's unusual legal and financial difficulties were given an airing in the press; hence, when his plans were scheduled for public hearing, a large number of Boulder citizens found it irresistible not to attend. The well-suited and well-groomed Ericson men met their first group of Boulder residents, not at all well-suited and somewhat disheveled and scruffy—in fact, downright sloppy in appearance. The residents presented a menacing appearance. The encounter could not be described as "pleasant." One of the Ericson men muttered, apparently to himself, "Now I know how Custer felt."[32] Ericson's team, as had many, many other out-of-town developers before him, presented what they thought was a reasonable, creative, and exciting approach to a downtown regional shopping center. As any six-month resident of Boulder could have predicted, the Minneapolis developers were greeted with suspicion, derision, and disbelief. Critics of the plan brought up traffic and parking problems, questions that had plagued Boulder's prospective shopping center developers for the last fifteen years. Solutions for these traffic and parking problems, offered by both the city and the developer, seemed vague and incomprehensible to Boulder's shopping center critics. Many of the proposed sites lay in the Boulder Creek flood plain. Certainly, Mr. Ericson's proposed "superblock" did. When resident Karl Norton asked Ericson if he had a special approach when building upon a flood plain, one of Ericson's designers answered confidently, "That is taken care of. We're planning to build a four-foot berm around the development. The building will act as a dike."[33] It was apparent that Ericson, as well as other developers, had not done their homework to address Boulder's special needs and problems.

Shopping centers were proposed for sites along Twenty-eighth Street and for various locations on Arapahoe Street as far east as Forty-seventh Street. Even the University of Colorado's land within its east campus was considered for shopping center development. Sites in Gunbarrel and Niwot, properties along the Diagonal Highway and on Valmont at Forty-seventh Street—all were announced in the press as possible spots for a regional shopping complex. The North and South Arapahoe Village sites were also slated for intensive center development. All these were studied, argued, and tentatively approved but were finally dismissed after lengthy consideration. (One proposal was defeated by council on a four to four vote.) Capture of Boulder pocketbooks must have been considered a mecca, for some developers came back again and again to the area, looking for the perfect spot for a center. Major department stores such as Sears, May D & F, and The Denver were courted by both developers and city government officials. At one point, Sears looked seriously at one of the proposed sites but drew back, saying, "Old mining claims are obscuring possible transfer of the title...We could build a building and someone could come in and start mining in our hardware department."[34] (Sears wanted the city to pass an ordinance prohibiting mining within the city limits.) A number of the shopping developments included plans for an east-west rapid transit corridor that would connect Boulder's downtown, Crossroads, and a regional shopping complex to the east. On some occasions, when developers looked over sites outside the city limits, city officials, fearful that heavy development elsewhere would contribute to urban sprawl, conducted themselves in such a way that they were accused of meddling in the affairs of neighboring communities. In January 1975, much in the same spirit as if announcing the prospects of a gold or silver mine, a *Camera* headline read, "Boulder may get a new shopping center yet."[35]

In December 1978, one developer who had previously considered several sites in Boulder returned to the area, but not to Boulder. The Jack Jacobs Company proposed to nearby Louisville that it build a Centennial Valley Mall on one million square feet of county land. The little town's government cleared the way for such development with a speed unknown in Boulder. Enmity between the two communities erupted, with strongly worded insults exchanged. Council member Paul Danish referred to Louisville's project as an "environmental pig."[36] Louisville replied that it was not the first time Boulder had interfered in other towns' business. Boulder turned quickly to what was here already—Crossroads. With a view to stopping a regional shopping center at Louisville and at other locations in the county, council approved with uncharacteristic speed in April 1979 the redevelopment of Crossroads with the understanding that the center would also be expanded to one million square feet. Despite the threat of a number of lawsuits from merchants in the Crossroads area, the voters approved the establishment of a Boulder Urban Renewal Authority, charged with the responsibility to develop a regional shopping complex for Boulder.

The affairs of BURA did not run smoothly. BURA members often conducted business in such a manner as to increase the fears of an already suspicious public. For example, bond acquisition was secured at five minutes before midnight on one occasion. The number of lawsuits against the city increased to such an extent that the selling of bonds to support the project was difficult. (Moreover, some Boulderites felt it was wrong to spend public funds on a private shopping center.) Opponents to Crossroads redevelopment called for an election to reconsider the matter; both sides spent considerable time in court. On one occasion, a petition for another election, containing the names of some 6,500 Boulder citizens, was pushed aside by council on the advice of the city attorney. However, after directed by the courts to hold a second election, council reluctantly slated a vote for April 7, 1981. BURA won handsomely (in general, North Boulder did not favor BURA, but South Boulder did) and the renovation of Crossroads continued.

Chapter Fifteen

While some Boulderites devoted themselves to the study and criticism of shopping center plans, others joined forces to help guide the shape of Boulder in other ways. PLAN-Boulder was formed in September 1959; its first project was the passage of the Blue Line, an attempt to preserve the mountain setting for the community. Ten years later, some members of PLAN-Boulder helped to write parts of the first Comprehensive Plan (approved in 1970). The group also contributed its ideas to the revised Boulder Valley Comprehensive Plan (approved in 1978). So that Boulder residents might have a chance to see the mountains, the organization worked to get on the ballot in 1971 a height limit ordinance that would prohibit new buildings over fifty-five feet. (Fifty-five feet seemed a natural cutoff because most mature trees grow to that height. Furthermore, Boulder's firefighting equipment was not designed to be effective over fifty-five feet.) The ordinance passed, but just barely. In 1976, PLAN-Boulder and other Boulder residents spoke in favor of the Danish Plan; its purpose was to limit and direct Boulder's growth by restricting the building of multiresidential units to an average of 450 units per year for a five-year period.* PLAN-Boulder did not approve of the conversion of so many apartments to condominiums, because the practice removed housing from the rental market that moderate-income families could afford. PLAN-Boulder also campaigned for the preservation of open space throughout the county and was responsible for turning away some "gigantic developers,"[1] because "If there are too many people, it will irrevocably change Boulder in a way that would be bad for everyone."[2]

The members of Historic Boulder had been active ever since Boulder's Central School had been torn down to make way for a parking lot; their interest was in the preservation of old residences and other buildings that they considered historically important to the character of the city. Another Boulder group, PURE, People United to Reclaim the Environment, was formed in 1969 to fight those developments which would further pollute the area's water and air. Many Boulderites wanted to know more about planning, but there were those who still did not trust planners. E.C. Pickett has a word or two on planners:

> This is the age of the man with the plan. Never have so many persons and organizations come forward with such a variety of schemes for reforming other people and improving the world. The reformer with his blue prints is in his hey day.
> E.C. PICKETT LOAN

> Let's NOT save the world, let's seek for the reformation of the reformer. Reform —as they understand it —consists of A & B putting their heads together and deciding what C should be forced to do for D.
> E.C. PICKETT LOAN

---

*A specific goal of 1.5 to 2 percent growth was spelled out in the Danish Plan, although it did not include restrictions on the building of single-family residences or structures that included four units on a lot already platted before the ordinance took effect.

Bulldozers at work on Central School; a parking lot is needed. *A.A. Paddock Collection*

Destruction of this kind stimulated formation of Historic Boulder in 1970. *Boulder Public Library from Town and Country Review*

Mrs. Pickett's "what C should be forced to do for D" best describes why, in the 1960s and 1970s, Boulder neighborhoods organized to fight "city hall." Neighborhood groups regarded themselves as "C," at the bottom of the city's list of priorities, forced to accommodate the needs of "D," those people yet to move to Boulder. Such groups as the University Hill League, the Mapleton Hill Neighborhood Association, and the Highland Lawn, Whittier, and Martin Acres* groups were forced to adopt a "watch-dog" attitude so that their interests could be protected. Other neighborhoods followed suit to stop what they regarded as incursions into their residential areas. Some city officials accused these neighborhood groups of selfish, provincial, and narrow-minded interests, incapable of seeing the broader picture and not sensitive to the needs of all of Boulder's citizens. On the other hand, those in the neighborhoods answered that they could see the broader picture very well, and they did not like what they saw. They lamented the growing traffic and parking problems on residential streets, the rising decibels of noise from cars, motorcycles, sirens, and rock concerts, as well as the increasing airplane noise overhead. One council member was so devoted to multiresidential living that he considered the typical single-family home, surrounded by grass and gardens, an immoral way to live. Although most neighborhood activists supported the principles of the revised Boulder Valley Comprehensive Plan and could see that population density should increase in developments that were already urban in character, they called for more imagination in the planning process.

In planning for those residents who have yet to come to Boulder, they said, do not forget the needs of those already here. Neighborhood groups warned council on a number of occasions that, in proposing greater urban densities, the city government might destroy the very qualities that made Boulder life so appealing. The 1978 Comprehensive Plan called for fewer single-family residential developments than did the 1970 Comprehensive Plan. The newer plan reserved less space for low-density development and emphasized high-density housing. The perspective of planners and that of neighborhoods was quite different; when the "core" neighborhoods were slated for what planners called "sensitive infill,"[3] the affected neighborhoods called it "overcrowding."

In some ways, the Comprehensive Plan of 1978 was weakened in its attempt to be all things to all people. Something was there for the nature-lover, the urbanite, the elderly, the young, and other groups. Greater attention was given in the new plan to the needs of single-parent families and working couples with no children, for they were moving to Boulder in greater numbers than the "conventional" family. One council member suggested that it was ridiculous to assume children needed grass and a place to roam; they could benefit by apartment life just as other children had in various parts of the country.

It was obvious that with the rising price and lessening availability of gasoline, "country" shopping centers would become obsolete. Perhaps with the turning to other sources of energy, coal mining might again become profitable in Boulder County. Perhaps oil rigs and gas towers would again dot the Boulder County landscape. The planners hoped to "rechannel" the waterways of Boulder County in order to lessen the damage of flooding to those buildings already in the floodway. In the Comprehensive Plan's discussion of the possible extension of fire, police, water, and sewer services to other parts of the Boulder Valley, a paternalistic and condescending quality was noted by Boulder's neighbors in the valley, which only served to further enrage them.

With this background of condescension and distrust, it was understandable that the prospect of a new development caused further friction between Boulder and the outlying communities. System Development Corporation, a California-based computer software concern, announced its intention in 1980 to locate along the southern boundary of the county on land that was designated as open space by the Boulder Valley Comprehensive Plan. Officials of SDC had their introduction to the ways of Boulder city officials and liked it not at all. As one columnist for the *Daily Camera* put it, "if God hadn't wanted to create the argument, he never would have made Boulder."[4] The SDC further enraged some council members by approaching Superior, Louisville, and Lafayette to ask that one of these communities annex the open-space land in question, thereby removing it from the comprehensive plan. Council decided, with help from the county commissioners, to buy the land outright so that the issue could be put "on hold" until an election might determine if Boulder residents wanted SDC or any other business to settle in Boulder County on land not reserved for business use by the Boulder Valley Comprehensive Plan. After the usual exchange of insults, SDC announced it would not locate in Boulder County, and an election was deferred.

Pow Wow, a forty-year-old Boulder institution, was not mentioned in the Boulder Valley Comprehensive Plan. During the 1940s, Rollie Leonard gave his farm lands along Twenty-eighth Street to Pow Wow for its perpetual use. In 1957, Pow Wow's finances were not as strong as they could have been, and the group was forced to give eleven and one-half acres to the city in lieu of back taxes. The city, in turn,

---

*Martin Acres is named after Billy Martin, the man to whom George Lytle cried, "Eureka. Eureka. Billy, come up here. I've found it!" Martin came down from Caribou in 1875 and bought land in Boulder, which his family eventually subdivided into Martin Acres.

gave some of the land to the YMCA for its building, encouraged the relocation of Junior Achievement on the site, and eventually developed three playing fields on the former pasture land. When the city decided that Fourteenth Street downtown should be made a through street to Canyon Boulevard, Boulder's handsome old railroad depot had to be moved. The Boulder Jaycees offered to care for the depot and moved it to another spot on the Pow Wow land.

A crowded, congested Twenty-eighth Street was no longer a suitable spot for Pow Wow's rodeo entertainment. The property was "prime for development"[5] and other activities were "systematically crowding Pow Wow out of its present location."[6] When Pow Wow asked council to rezone its remaining property to a commercial use so that the group could sell the land and move on, enough council members balked so that the request was denied. Pow Wow went to court. When Pow Wow won the right to have the property rezoned, they sold the land without a clear idea where they were going to relocate. After looking over and rejecting several site possibilities, Pow Wow turned to a parcel of land along the Diagonal Highway at Fifty-fifth Street. Board member Stan Johnson liked its "western location"[7] and hoped that a Pow Wow relocation out that way would be "less bother"[8] to Boulder's city fathers. Unfortunately for Pow Wow, the land in question had been designated open space by the Comprehensive Plan. After a number of appearances before city boards and council and county boards and the commissioners, the Fifty-fifth and Diagonal land was denied a Pow Wow rodeo use. Pow Wow, forced to cancel many of its 1980 activities, started looking again for a home. Perhaps, said Jim Bowers of the Pow Wow Board, "Pow Wow doesn't really have a place in this community."[9] Another Pow Wow Board member, Dale Marcotte, said, "Rodeo is one of the truly American traditions. It saddens me to see the city forcing the Pow Wow Association to leave Boulder."[10] After looking over properties near the Boulder Reservoir, the board considered leaving Boulder to locate near Louisville. Still suffering the stings of Boulder's superior attitude in the shopping center matter, the *Louisville Times* said with some glee that Pow Wow was Boulder's "unwanted stepchild...The western theme does not fit in with Boulder's sophisticated ideas of theatre, dance, and esoteric philosophies, hence is not worth sacrificing even one acre of open space land."[11] Louisville welcomed Pow Wow; the Boulder institution had a new home.

There must have been a number of "unsophisticated"[12] voters left in Boulder, however, for on September 9, 1980 the community again turned down a proposal to build a performing arts center. The proposal was tied to the removal of the sales tax on food, as well as a rise in the tax itself. The scheme did not appeal to Boulder voters who were unhappy, as usual, with council on a number of issues. As longtime letter writer Norbert F. Tabery said, "the carrot of the food tax repeal may appeal to rabbits, but Boulder voters are not rabbits."[13] Tabery pointed out further that many Boulderites were still unhappy about the manner in which Crossroads development had been handled.

Boulder in the late 1970s had become a far more diverse community than Boulder City of the 1860s, when modest farmers and merchants ventured into the Boulder valley looking for gold. True, some descendants of those early settlers still lived in Boulder County. They lived side by side, with the town's newcomers, with whom some had little in common. Elsewhere in the country, the suburban movement of a generation before had spawned a group of wanderers who moved from housing tract to housing tract, without apparent roots or ties to whatever municipality in which they found themselves. Some of these suburbanites came to Boulder because they were transferred here by such corporations as International Business Machines, Ball Brothers Research, or Storage Technology. Many of the hippies of the 1970s, now with gray streaks in their hair, settled down to life in the community that they once upset. When the presence of a nuclear installation at Rocky Flats became intolerable, they, as well as many other Boulder County residents, joined the periodic demonstrations against the nuclear facility south of town.

People poured in from all parts of the country. It seemed like an invasion. Northeasterners, particularly from New York and New Jersey, arrived in Boulder in the late 1970s, bringing with them Eastern ways and their unique brand of provincialism. "Westerners are constantly reminded of the hopeless backwardness of life outside"[14] New York. "Once arrived...these sun-starved Northeasterners do not dutifully buy a Stetson hat and a squash blossom string tie to remind themselves that indeed it is a privilege to live in Colorado."[15] Instead, they demanded the services in Boulder to which they were accustomed in the East.

In addition to the religious groups common to most American communities, Boulder became the home for some nine hundred American Buddhists (that is, Buddhists who were reared in Catholic, Protestant, or Jewish homes, not born to the faith). In general, this group seemed disinclined to mix with other Boulderites to take part in civic affairs; their separatism, however innocent, was viewed with suspicion in some quarters. Professors, some 20,000 students, government scientists, corporation men, gurus and their followers, tourists seeking Mork and Mindy, health food nuts, esoteric meditation groups, rolfing enthusiasts, bicycle racers, organic gardeners, joggers,

The Reverend Katsuzo Sawada leads a group of protesters against the Rocky Flats plant south of Boulder. *Boulder Public Library from Town and Country Review*

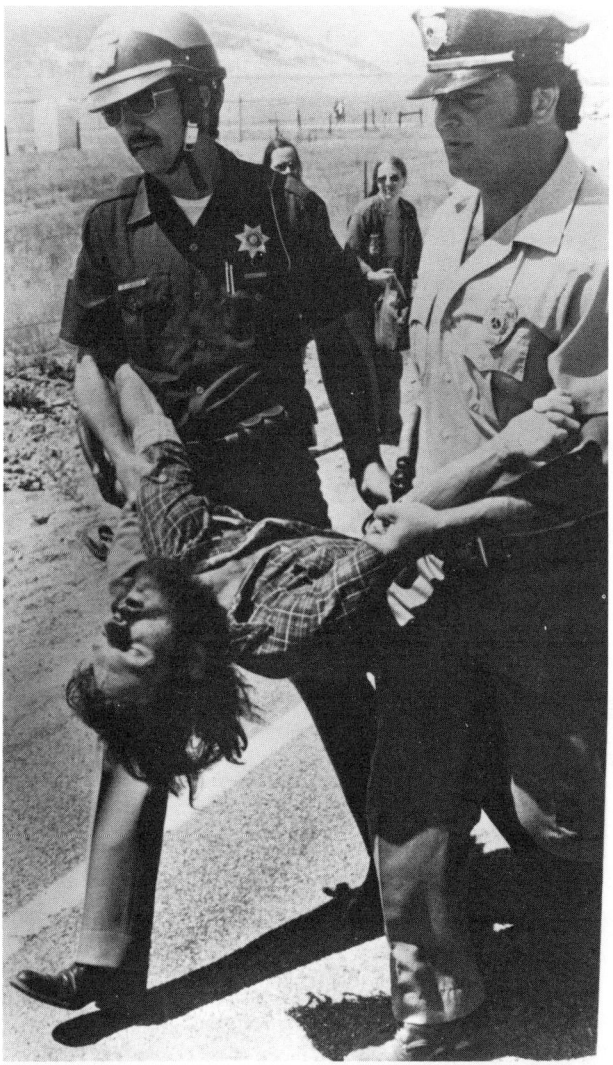

A demonstrator is carried away by police from the Rocky Flats plant. *Boulder Public Library from Town and Country Review*

nude bathers, a smattering of blue-collar workers, and a few "red necks" left over from the early 1970s completed the diverse mix.

The one group that was not fully represented in Boulder to the extent that it was in other communities was low-income families. True, poor people have always lived in Boulder, but not in such numbers as elsewhere, and not in condominiums. The Spanish-speaking residents, some of whose ancestors settled Colorado hundreds of years ago, worked in the county; few could afford to live in the city. The problems of migrant workers, who toiled on the farms of the county, seemed far away to most Boulderites. In general, Boulder's residents, no matter where they came from, were highly educated; most were prepared for jobs in one of Boulder's "clean" industries. The gulf between those from privileged backgrounds and those of modest origins seemed far greater in Boulder than in some American communities. It was not uncommon for those with limited resources to settle in nearby Longmont, Louisville, or Lafayette, or in the mountains. They could not afford the housing that Boulder had to offer in a rapidly inflated market. This situation caused some residents to wonder if Boulder would eventually become a "haven for the rich." The signs were there. Just as Boulder City Town Company's $1,000 lots discouraged settlers in 1859, so did modern Boulder's $100,000 lots.

Boulder County's farmers, working some of the best soil in the nation, on land that was passed over as the Great American Desert 160 years before, wrestled with high interest rates, growing seed and fuel bills,

Another kind of demonstration—against an abortion clinic. *Boulder Public Library from Town and Country Review*

Celebrating the kick-off for United Way Crusade. *Boulder Public Library from Town and Country Review*

Rocky Mountain Rescue unit at work in the mountains west of Boulder. *Boulder Public Library from Town and Country Review*

A Boulder bicycle classic race, Red Zinger ends near North Boulder Park. *Boulder Public Library from Town and Country Review*

Boulder novices cycling downtown during Red Zinger. *Boulder Public Library from Town and Country Review*

Dangerous but exciting. Tubing down Boulder Creek in the spring. *Boulder Public Library from Town and Country Review*

A Boulder institution: Walter Tickel sees school children across busy Ninth Street. *Boulder Public Library from Town and Country Review*

and inadequate wholesale food prices. They battled plagues of grasshoppers as did the Wellman brothers in 1859 and wondered if they should accept the latest offer from the subdivision developers. Farmer Leo Burger said, "This is beautiful land. I haven't seen any place else I like better...."[16] But, he added, "There are times I feel pretty disgusted."[17] Another problem on the Colorado plains faced the farmer: the eastern Colorado underground water table, called the Ogallala aquifer, a layer of water-bearing rock, was dropping. The availability of water had dictated the nature and location of settlement in the Southwest since the 1850s. Boulder was fortunate to have garnered enough water so that population expansion was possible.

Boulder was becoming a city, whether those who lived here when Boulder was a town liked it or not. One observer was despondent over Boulder's propsects. "Gone with Boulder's spacious housing and wide streets is the Western tradition of independence and self-reliance."[18] One angry resident summarized her views of the population invasion: "Boulder is full of rude, empty-headed, pushy fat cats and their offspring, and the nice people are being gradually pushed out or phased out."[19] Another wrote, "...I don't have to like a stratified life, and that is certainly where we're heading. We have just about fixed it so that everyone must be 23...Some old neighbors give up and move out because they don't feel welcome anymore on their own street."[20] Just as the last remnants of gold and silver camps disappeared in the mountains, so would the comfort and friendliness of small-town life. Perhaps Boulder, the city, would develop its own special character from the unusually diverse people it had attracted in the 1970s. Perhaps its characteristic feistiness and its appetite for a good civic fight would be its salvation.

Another Boulder institution: Ordinarily lit during Christmas holidays, the star remained lit during the jailing of Americans in Iran. *Boulder Public Library from Town and Country Review*

Boulder is now a city. *A.A. Paddock Collection*

End Notes

Introduction

[1] Amos Bixby, "History of Boulder County," in *History of Clear Creek and Boulder Valleys,* (Chicago: O.L. Baskin and Company, 1880), p. 381.

[2] *Boulder County Herald,* editorial by O.H. Wangelin, February 15, 1888.

[3] Bixby, op. cit., p. 382.

Chapter One

[1] W.B. Vickers, "History of Colorado," in *History of Clear Creek and Boulder Valleys,* (Chicago: O.L. Baskin and Company, 1880), p. 18.

[2] Ibid.

[3] *The Journals of Zebulon M. Pike,* vol. 2, (Norman: University of Oklahoma Press, 1966), p. 62. (Pike called Purcell by the name of Pursley.)

[4] Ibid., p. 27.

[5] Quoted in Colin B. Goodykoontz, *Colorado: Short Studies of its Past and Present,* (Boulder: University of Colorado Press, 1927).

[6] Ibid.

[7] Ibid.

[8] A.C. Patton, *Green Rocks,* (n.p., c 1904).

Chapter Two

[1] *Boulder County News,* July 14, 1876.

[2] Amos Bixby, "History of Boulder County," in *History of Clear Creek and Boulder Valleys.* (Chicago: O.L. Baskin and Company, 1880), p. 379.

[3] Ibid.

End notes 4-10 refer to letters published in LeRoy Hafen, ed., *Colorado Gold Rush, 1858-59, Contemporary Letters and Reports,* Southwest History Series, vol. 10, (Philadelphia: Porcupine Press, 1974).

[4] A.A. Brookfield to Friend Norton, January 26, 1859, p. 221.

[5] Ibid., p. 220.

[6] John Poisal, letter, January 30, 1859 (later published in the *Kansas Weekly Herald*), p. 222.

[7] O.P. Goodwin to General Eastin, February 12, 1859, pp. 229-30.

[8] A.A. Brookfield to his wife, February 27, 1859, p. 242.

[9] Ibid., p. 243.

[10] A.A. Brookfield to Friend Norton, March 5, 1859, p. 248.

[11] Peter Watts, *A Dictionary of the Old West,* (New York: Knopf, 1977), p. 125.

[12] Bixby, op. cit., p. 380.

Chapter Three

[1] LeRoy Hafen, ed., *Colorado Gold Rush, 1858-59, Contemporary Letters and Reports,* Southwest History Series, vol. 10, (Philadelphia: Porcupine Press, 1974), p. 241, letter from John Buell to the *Missouri Democrat.*

[2] Sniktau, *The Mining Review,* (Georgetown, Colorado), vol. 4, no. 2 (April 1874).

[3] Sniktau, *The Mining Review,* (Georgetown, Colorado), vol. 4, no. 1 (March 1874).

[4] Ibid.

[5] Ibid.

[6] Letter from the Reverend Jacob Adriance, Ames, Nebraska, to the Reverend John A. Davis of Boulder, April 14, 1904, Western Historical Collections, University of Colorado at Boulder.

[7] *Colorado Banner,* November 8, 1877.

[8] Sniktau, *The Mining Review,* (Georgetown, Colorado), vol. 4, no. 2 (April 1874).

[9] Amos Bixby, "History of Boulder County," in *History of Clear Creek and Boulder Valleys.* (Chicago: O.L. Baskin and Company, 1880), p. 426.

[10] Adriance, op. cit.

Chapter Four

[1] Charles Harrinton, *Summering in Colorado,* (Denver: Richards and Company, 1874).

[2] Nathan Thompson, "Ten Years as First Pastor of the Congregational Church of Boulder, Colorado, 1865-1875," First Congregational Church, Boulder, Colorado.

[3] Amos Bixby, "History of Boulder County," in *History of Clear Creek and Boulder Valleys.* (Chicago: O.L. Baskin and Company, 1880), pp. 390-91.

[4] Lynn Perrigo, *A Municipal History of Boulder, Colorado,* (Boulder: Boulder Publishing Company, 1947).

[5] Ibid.

[6] Isabella Bird, *A Lady's Life in the Rocky Mountains,* (Norman: University of Oklahoma Press, 1960), p. 197. (First published by John Murray, London, in 1879.)

[7] Ibid.

[8] *Boulder County Pioneer,* August 24, 1869.

[9] Ibid., September 14, 1869.

[10] Bixby, op. cit., pp. 392-93.

[11] Ibid.

[12] Most of the information on road building was taken from a paper written for the Boulder Historical Society by Martin Parsons, 1945.

[13] *Rocky Mountain News,* July 20, 1864.

[14] Robert L. Perkin, "Sand Creek," in *A Colorado Reader,* Carl Ubbelohde, ed. (Boulder: Pruett Publishing Company, 1960), p. 130.

[15] Ibid., p. 131.

[16] Jean Afton, "George Bent's Sand Creek," paper, 1978, Western Historical Collections, University of Colorado at Boulder.

[17] Margaret Coel explores the controversy surrounding the death of Chief Left Hand in her book *Chief Left Hand, Southern Arapaho,* (Norman: University of Oklahoma Press, 1981). The reader is also directed to three letters written by George Bent. One is found in the Western Historical Collections, University of Colorado at Boulder. The other two are in the George Bent Letters Collection, Denver Public Library, Denver, Colorado.

Chapter Five

[1] Alice Weber, "George Lytle, Colorado Pioneer, paper, 1932, Western Historical Collections, University of Colorado at Boulder.

[2] Ibid.

[3] Ibid.

[4] Ibid.

[5] J.H. Tice, *Over the Plains and on the Mountains,* (St. Louis: Industrial Age Printing, 1872), p. 110.

[6] Patrick Ourada, "Chinese in Colorado," *Colorado Magazine,* 29: 278.

[7] Muriel Sibell Wolle, *Stampede to Timberline,* (Chicago: Sage Swallow, 1949), p. 502.

[8] Amos Bixby, "History of Boulder County," in *History of Clear Creek and Boulder Valleys.* (Chicago: O.L. Baskin and Company, 1880), p. 428.

[9] Donald C. Kemp, *Silver, Gold and Black Iron,* (Denver: Sage Swallow, 1960), p. 62.

[10] *Boulder County Herald,* August 19, 1885.

[11] Duane A. Smith, *Silver Saga, the Story of Caribou, Colorado,* (Boulder: Pruett Publishing Company, 1974), p. 203.

[12] Ibid., p. 227.

[13] Ibid., p. 228.

[14] John Buchanan, "History of a Ghost Town," paper written for the Boulder Historical Society, 1944.

Chapter Six

[1] *Boulder County News,* May 20, 1871.

[2] Ibid., December 3, 1875, article by Amos Bixby.

[3] *Boulder County Herald,* August 15, 1883.

[4] *Town Minutes,* July 24, 1875.

[5] Ibid., October 5 and November 25, 1875.

[6] *Boulder County Herald,* August 15, 1883.

[7] Ibid., February 26, 1890 and July 23, 1890.

[8] Ibid., March 26, 1890.

[9] Boulder *Daily Camera,* October 20, 1891.

[10] Ibid., June 20, 1893.

[11] Ibid., February 14, 1896.

[12] *Boulder County News,* December 1, 1871.

[13] *Town Minutes,* July 6, 1880.

[14] Ibid., June 17, 1875.

[15] Ibid.

[16] *Boulder County News,* August 23, 1878.

[17] *Town Minutes,* November 1871, p. 18.

[18] Ibid., p. 38.

[19] *Boulder County Herald,* May 18, 1881.

[20] Some of this information is from Hal Nees of the Boulder Police Department, who wrote "The Boulder Police Department, A History," (n.p., Hall of Justice, Boulder, Colorado, 1976).

[21] Boulder *Daily Camera,* article by Joseph Wolff, March 28, 1908.

[22] *Boulder County News,* December 8, 1871.

[23] *Boulder News and Courier,* March 14, 1879.

[24] *Boulder County News,* February 14, 1873.

[25] *Boulder County Herald,* March 29, 1882.

[26] Ibid., October 12, 1881.

[27] Ibid., April 10, 1884.

[28] William H. Burger, "Boulder in the 80s and 90s," paper written for the Boulder Historical Society, 1945.

[29] Quoted in F.O. Repplier, *As a Town Grows,* (Boulder, Colo.: School District No. 3, 1959), p. 34.

[30] *Boulder County News,* September 18, 1874.

[31] *Town Minutes,* October 5, 1874.

[32] *Boulder County Herald,* January 12, 1884.

[33] Ibid., March 22, 1882.

[34] Ibid., September 9, 1885.

Chapter Seven

[1] William H. Burger, "Boulder in the 80s and 90s," paper written for the Boulder Historical Society, 1945.

[2] Ibid.

[3] Ibid.

[4] Ibid.

[5] Ibid.

[6] Ibid.

[7] Quoted in F.O. Repplier, *As a Town Grows,* (Boulder, Colo.: School District No. 3, 1959), p. 34.

[8] *Boulder County Herald,* September 17, 1884.

[9] Wentworth and Flexner, *Dictionary of American Slang,* (New York: Thomas Y. Crowell Company, 1975).

[10] Burger, op. cit.

[11] *Boulder County Herald,* November 19, 1890.

[12] Boulder *Daily Camera,* Souvenir Industrial Edition, December 15, 1902.

[13] *Boulder County Pioneer,* February 17, 1869.

[14] Ibid., May 19, 1869.

[15] Burger, op. cit.

[16] *Manual of the Public Schools, 1895-96,* Papers of William V. Casey, Boulder Valley School District, Boulder, Colorado.

[17] Nathan Thompson, "Ten Years as First Pastor of the Congregational Church of Boulder, Colorado, 1865-1875," First Congregational Church, Boulder, Colorado.

[18] Jane Sewall, *Jane, Dear Child,* (Boulder: University of Colorado Press, 1957), p. 41.

[19] *Boulder County News,* September 1877.

[20] Sewall, op. cit., p. 47.

[21] Ibid.

[22] Boulder *Daily Camera,* October 22, 1897.

[23] Quoted in Mary Dartt, *On the Plains and Among the Peaks, or how Mrs. Maxwell Made Her Natural History Collection,* (Philadelphia: Claxton, Remson, Haffelfinger, 1879), p. 11.

[24] Ibid., pp. 8-9.

[25] Ibid., pp. 118-19.

Chapter Eight

[1] John A. and Alan Lomax, "The Hard-Working Miners," in *American Ballads and Folk Songs,* (New York: MacMillan, 1934), p. 437.

[2] Dale Fetherling, *Mother Jones, the Miners' Angel,* (Carbondale, Ill.: Southern Illinois University Press, 1974).

[3] Boulder *Daily Camera,* March 1, 1892.

[4] Ibid., March 9, 1892.

[5] Ibid., March 2, 1892.

[6] Ibid., March 9, 1892.

[7] Ibid., March 15, 1892.

[8] Ibid., May 31 to June 4, 1894 (combined reissue).

[9] Ibid.

[10] Ibid.

[11]Ibid.

[12]Ibid.

[13]Mrs. Frank Bauer, tape prepared by the American Association for University Women, Boulder Public Library, Boulder, Colorado, 1975.

[14]Cleveland McCarty, article on the Rocky Mountain Climbers Club for the Chautauqua Association, 1976.

[15]Eben Fine, *Remembered Yesterdays.* (Boulder, Colo.: Johnson Publishing Company, 1957), p. 15.

[16]Ibid., p. 13.

Chapter Nine

[1]Helen Hunt Jackson, *Bits of Travel at Home,* (Boston: Robert Brothers, 1878), p. 302.

[2]Quoted in article by John Andrews, Boulder *Daily Camera,* January 25, 1976.

[3]Ibid.

[4]*Chautauqua Bulletin,* 1902.

[5]*Boulder County Herald,* March 16, 1881.

[6]Frederick Law Olmsted, Jr., "The Improvement of Boulder, Colorado," Report to the Boulder City Improvement Association, 1910, p. 5.

[7]Ibid., p. 13.

[8]Ibid., p. 3

[9]Ibid.

[10]Ibid.

[11]Ibid., p. 4.

[12]Ibid., p. 28.

[13]Ibid., p. 29.

[14]Ibid., p. 59.

[15]Ibid., p. 65.

[16]*Boulder County Herald,* April 29, 1871.

[17]Boulder *Daily Camera,* Souvenir Industrial Edition, article by L.C. Paddock, December 15, 1902, p. 17.

[18]Ibid.

[19]Ibid., July 28, 1891.

[20]For an historical account of Western Cutlery, read Harvey Platts, *The Knife-makers Who Went West,* (Longmont, Colo: Long's Peak Press, Inc., 1978).

Chapter Ten

[1]*Town Minutes,* November 1871, p. 30.

[2]Boulder *Daily Camera,* editorial by L.C. Paddock, April 2, 1909.

[3]Ibid.

[4]Ibid., March 3, 1909.

[5]Ibid., April 7, 1909.

[6]Ibid., November 1, 1923.

[7]Ibid., September 10, 1917.

[8]Ibid.

[9]Ibid.

[10]Ibid., February 11, 1918.

[11]Ibid., editorial by L.C. Paddock, January 2, 1918.

[12]Ibid., April 2, 1919.

[13]Ibid., August 29, 1922.

[14]*Boulder News Herald,* April 7, 1923.

[15] Boulder *Daily Camera,* April 5, 1923.

[16] *Ordinances, City of Boulder, 1882-1902,* April 15, 1901, pp. 571-72.

[17] Boulder *Daily Camera,* May 8, 1903.

[18] Ibid., January 9, 1908.

[19] *Boulder Daily Herald,* July 5, 1913.

[20] *Rocky Mountain American,* April 24, 1925.

[21] Ibid.

[22] John Rolfe Burroughs, *Steamboat in the Rockies.* (Ft. Collins, Colo.: Old Army Press, 1974), pp. 179-80.

[23] James H. Davis, "Colorado Under the Klan," *Colorado Magazine.* 42, no. 2, (spring 1965), pp. 93-108.

[24] Quoted in article by John Holliday, Jr., Boulder *Daily Camera,* January 30, 1976.

[25] Gerald Lynn Marriner, "Klan Politics in Colorado," *Journal of the West,* January 1976, p. 76.

Chapter Eleven

[1] Boulder *Daily Camera,* October 7, 1918.

[2] Ibid., October 10, 1918.

[3] Ibid., November 7, 1918.

[4] Pat Jorgensen, "Two Boulder Women," *Flatirons Magazine,* spring 1974, p. 37.

[5] Thomas L. Green, "Junius Lewis and the Golden Chest Mining Company," *Colorado Magazine,* 50: 24.

[6] Ibid.

[7] Ibid.

[8] Boulder *Daily Camera,* article by Pat Raybon, June 20, 1976.

[9] Interview with Don McInnes, June 1977.

[10] Ibid.

[11] Boulder *Daily Camera,* December 29, 1934.

[12] Ibid.

[13] Ibid., September 21, 1936.

[14] Ibid.

[15] Ibid., May 4, 1938.

[16] Ibid., January 30, 1926.

[17] Ibid., July 4, 1980, Bill Richards quoted by Karen Fisher's "Old-Timers Recall Fourth as City Celebration."

[18] Much of this information on Pow Wow came from an interview with Lyndon Switzer, early organizer, July 1976.

[19] F.O. Repplier, *As A Town Grows,* (Boulder, Colo.: School District No. 3, 1959), p. 139.

[20] Ibid., p. 140.

[21] Ibid.

[22] Interview with Faye Curtin, 1975.

Chapter Twelve

[1] Boulder *Daily Camera,* May 5, 1948.

[2] Ibid., July 5, 1951.

[3] Interview with A.A. Wickstrom, May 1977.

[4] Boulder *Daily Camera,* October 12, 1947.

[5] Ibid., October 29, 1947.

[6] Ibid.

[7] Ibid.

[8] Ibid.
[9] Ibid.
[10] Ibid., June 20, 1951.
[11] Ibid., March 3, 1948.
[12] Ibid., March 8, 1950.
[13] Ibid., April 21, 1948.
[14] Ibid., January 5, 1949.
[15] Ibid., January 19, 1949.
[16] Ibid.
[17] Ibid., January 5, 1949.
[18] *Boulder Progress,* June 1957, published by National State Bank, Hugh S. McCaffrey, ed.
[19] *Town and Country Review,* August 11, 1971.
[20] Boulder *Daily Camera,* headline, April 2, 1958.
[21] Ibid.
[22] Ibid., Mr. Lefferdink is quoted.
[23] *London Times,* July 11, 1971.
[24] *Town Minutes,* 1881.
[25] *Boulder County Herald,* September 3, 1891.
[26] Ibid., June 6, 1892.
[27] Interview with Harold Copeland, June 1977.
[28] Interview with Bly Curtis, April 1977.
[29] The ads of E.C. Pickett may be found in the Reference Department, Boulder Public Library, Boulder, Colorado.
[30] Boulder *Daily Camera,* December 7, 1955.
[31] Ibid., April 13, 1965, statement of Dr. Roy L. Cleere, State Health Director.
[32] Ibid., April 27, 1965, letter of Jo Weber.
[33] Ibid., April 25, 1965, letter of Norbert F. Tabery.
[34] Ibid., May 6, 1965.

Chapter Thirteen
[1] Boulder *Daily Camera,* December 3, 1960.
[2] Ibid., December 8, 1960.
[3] Ibid., December 5, 1960, editorial by James Corriell.
[4] Ibid.
[5] Ibid., December 8, 1960.
[6] Ibid., letter by Elloween Keane.
[7] Ibid.
[8] Ibid., December 9, 1960, letter by John Pryor.
[9] Ibid., December 13, 1960.
[10] A collection of some of E.C. Pickett's ads are on file with the Reference Department, Boulder Public Library.
[11] George Vranish, quoted by Alice Trembour, *Boulder Monthly Magazine,* June 1979.
[12] Boulder *Daily Camera,* May 12, 1965, letter by Florence Sibert.
[13] *See* End Note 10.
[14] Boulder *Daily Camera,* November 1, 1969.
[15] Ibid., letter by Donna G. Jones.
[16] *Colorado Daily,* September 28, 1967.
[17] Boulder *Daily Camera,* October 24, 1959.

[18]Ibid.

[19]Ibid.

[20]Ibid., December 23, 1968.

[21]Ibid.

[22]Ibid.

[23]Ibid., January 14, 1969.

[24]Ibid., January 21, 1969.

[25]Ibid.

[26]Ibid.

Chapter Fourteen

[1]Boulder *Daily Camera,* August 15, 1969.

[2]Ibid., August 17, 1979.

[3]Ibid.

[4]Ibid., August 14, 1969.

[5]*Colorado Daily,* October 30, 1975, article by Timothy Lange.

[6]"Summary of Boulder Jaycees Transient Investigation," Boulder Public Library, Boulder, Colorado, n.d.

[7]Boulder *Daily Camera,* May 31, 1970, article by Larry Knudsen.

[8]*Denver Post,* June 29, 1978.

[9]Boulder *Daily Camera,* August 17, 1969.

[10]*Colorado Daily,* October 31, 1975, article by Timothy Lange.

[11]*Town and Country Review,* April 3, 1974.

[12]*Colorado Daily,* October 31, 1975, article by Timothy Lange.

[13]Ibid.

[14]Boulder *Daily Camera,* April 8, 1974.

[15]Ibid.

[16]Ibid., April 18, 1974.

[17]Ibid., September 6, 1974.

[18]*Longmont Times-Call,* March 28, 1975.

[19]Boulder *Daily Camera,* March 27, 1975.

[20]Ibid.

[21]Ibid.

[22]*Denver Post,* April 16, 1975.

[23]Ibid.

[24]Ibid.

[25]Boulder *Daily Camera,* January 21, 1969, letter by Ray Alsbury.

[26]Ibid., June 24, 1970.

[27]Ibid.

[28]Ibid.

[29]Ibid., April 9, 1973.

[30]Ibid., June 20, 1975.

[31]Ibid., August 6, 1976.

[32]Statement made at a public meeting, September 28, 1978.

[33]Statement made at a public meeting, September 28, 1978.

[34]Boulder *Daily Camera,* March 26, 1970 and January 21, 1971.

[35]Ibid., January 26, 1975.

[36]Ibid., September 28, 1978.

Chapter Fifteen

[1] *Colorado Daily,* October 24, 1979, statement by Dick Harris, president of PLAN-Boulder.
[2] Ibid.
[3] *Boulder Valley Comprehensive Plan,* rev., 1978.
[4] Boulder *Daily Camera,* October 16, 1980, column by Ken Frizell.
[5] *Town and Country Review,* May 8, 1974, statement by Marvin Sparn.
[6] Ibid.
[7] *Denver Post,* November 23, 1978.
[8] Ibid.
[9] Ibid.
[10] Ibid.
[11] *Louisville Times,* August 1, 1979, editorial by Percy Conarroe.
[12] Boulder *Daily Camera,* September 29, 1980, letter by Norbert F. Tabery.
[13] Ibid.
[14] *New York Times,* February 11, 1980, article by Charles Hinds, p. 19.
[15] Ibid.
[16] Boulder *Daily Camera,* April 27, 1980.
[17] Ibid.
[18] *New York Times,* op. cit.
[19] Boulder *Daily Camera,* August 5, 1980.
[20] Ibid., July 27, 1980, "The Old and the New," by Bill Jordan.

A face from the past: As a mason carved the stone of First Methodist Church at Fourteenth and Spruce streets, northeast corner, in 1891, his small daughter died. The grieving father carved her face in the church wall where it can be seen today. *Tom Moen photo*

Bibliography

Adriance, The Reverend Jacob (Ames, Nebraska). "Letter to The Reverend John A. Davis, Boulder, Colorado, April 14, 1904." Western Historical Collections, University of Colorado at Boulder.

Afton, Jean. "George Bent's Sand Creek," Paper. 1978. Western Historical Collections, University of Colorado at Boulder.

Arps, Louise Ward, and Kingery, Elinor Eppich. *High Country Names; Rocky Mountain National Park.* Estes Park: Rocky Mountain Nature Association, 1972.

Athearn, Robert C. *High Country Empire; The High Plains and Rockies.* Lincoln: University of Nebraska Press, 1960.

———. *The Coloradans.* Albuquerque: University of New Mexico Press, 1976.

———. "Clippings on Early Colorado Education." Boulder, Colo.: *School and University Review* 7, no. 2 (Spring, 1977): pp. 3-5.

Baker, James H., and Hafen, LeRoy, eds. *History of Colorado.* 5 vols. Denver: Linderman Company, 1927.

Baker, Joseph N. "An Administration and Operational Study of the Boulder, Colorado Police Department." March 1964. Boulder Public Library, Boulder, Colorado.

Balsley, Robert. *Early Gold Hill.* n.p., c 1971.

Bancroft, Hubert Howe. *History of Nevada, Colorado and Wyoming, 1540-1888,* vol. 25. San Francisco: The History Company, 1890.

Barker, Jane Valentine. *76 Historic Homes of Boulder, Colorado.* Boulder: Pruett Publishing Company, 1976.

———. *Historic Homes of Boulder County.* Boulder: Pruett Publishing Company, 1979.

Barney, Libeus, *Letters of the Pike's Peak Gold Rush.* San Jose, Calif.: Talisman Press, 1959.

Bird, Isabella. *A Lady's Life in the Rocky Mountains.* Norman: University of Oklahoma Press, 1960. (First published in London: John Murray, 1879.)

Bixby, Amos. "History of Boulder County," *History of Clear Creek and Boulder Valleys.* Chicago: O.L. Baskin and Company, 1880.

Bluemel, Elinor. *One Hundred Years of Colorado Women.* n.p., 1973.

Boulder City Town Company, minutes and records, 1859-1861. Western Historical Collections, University of Colorado at Boulder.

Boulder Jaycees. "Summary of a Transient Investigation." December 1971. Boulder Public Library, Boulder, Colorado.

Boulder *Town Minutes.* Central Files, City of Boulder, Colorado.

Boulder Valley Comprehensive Plan, revised 1978. Boulder Public Library, Boulder, Colorado.

Brace, Mabel Maxwell. *Thanks to Abigail; a Family Chronicle.* n.p., 1948.

Bradley, Ruth. *Dellie: A Lotus in the Dust, from Bangkok to Boulder.* n.p., n.d.

Brown, Robert L. *Ghost Towns, Past and Present.* Caldwell, Idaho: The Caxton Printers, Ltd., 1972.

Buchanan, John. "History of a Ghost Town." Paper on Caribou, Colorado, for the Boulder Historical Society, 1944.

Burger, W.H. "Boulder in the 80s and 90s." Paper for the Boulder Historical Society, 1945.

____. "History of Boulder House, a Pioneer Hotel." Paper for the Boulder Historical Society, 1945.

Burroughs, John Rolfe. *Steamboat in the Rockies.* Fort Collins, Colo.: Old Army Press, 1974.

Casey, William Van Cleave. Papers, notes, and manuscripts. Boulder Valley School District, Boulder, Colorado.

A Century of the Colorado Census. Suzanne Shulze, comp. Greeley: Michener Library, University of Northern Colorado, 1976, rev. 1977.

Clint, Florence. *Boulder County Area Key* for genealogists, 1969.

Cobb, Bertha and Ernest. *Anita.* New York: G.P. Putnam's Sons, 1920.

Coel, Margaret. *Chief Left Hand, Southern Arapaho.* Norman: University of Oklahoma Press, 1981.

Conarroe, Carolyn. *The Louisville Story.* Louisville, Colo.: privately published, 1978.

Crossen, Forest. *The Switzerland Trail of America.* Boulder, Colo.: Pruett Press, 1962.

Crofutt, George A. *Crofutt's Grip-Sack Guide to Colorado.* Omaha, Neb.: The Overland Publishing Company, 1881.

Dallas, Sandra. *Gaslights and Gingerbread; Representative Victorian Houses in Colorado.* Denver: Sage Books, 1965.

Dana, Edward S. *Textbook of Mineralogy.* New York: John Wiley and Son, 1898.

Dartt, Mary. *On the Plains and Among the Peaks; or How Mrs. Maxwell Made Her Natural History Collection.* Philadelphia: Claxton, Remsen, Haffelfinger, 1879.

Davis, James H. "Colorado Under the Klan." *Colorado Magazine* 42, no. 2 (spring 1965): pp. 93-108.

Davis, William E. *Glory, Colorado, History of the University of Colorado to 1963.* Boulder, Colo.: Pruett Press, 1965.

DeMund, Mary. *Women Physicians in Colorado.* n.p., Range Press, 1976.

Eberhart, Perry. *Guide to the Colorado Ghost Towns and Mining Camps.* Denver: Sage Books, 1959, rev. 1974.

Feitz, Leland. *Colorado Trolleys, A Quick History of Colorado's Streetcar Lines.* Colorado Springs: Little London Press, 1971.

Fetherling, Dale. *Mother Jones, the Miners' Angel.* Carbondale, Ill.: Southern Illinois University Press, 1974.

Fine, Eben. *Remembered Yesterdays.* Boulder, Colo.: Johnson Publishing Company, 1957.

Fossett, Frank. *Colorado; its Gold and Silver Mines, Farms and Stock Ranges, Health and Pleasure Resorts.* New York: C.G. Crawford, 1879.

Frink, Maurice. *The Boulder Story, Historical Portrait of a Frontier Town.* Boulder: Pruett Publishing Company, 1965.

Fritz, Percy S. *Colorado, The Centennial State.* New York: Prentice Hall, 1941.

____. "Mining History of Boulder County." Paper for the Boulder Historical Society, April 1945.

____. "Constitutions and Laws of Early Mining Districts in Boulder County." Ph.D. thesis, 1933. Western Historical Collections, University of Colorado at Boulder.

Gardiner, Dorothy. *Snow Water.* New York: Doubleday, 1939.

____. Papers and letters. Western Historical Collections, University of Colorado at Boulder.

Gladden, Sanford. *Hotels of Boulder, Colorado from 1860.* Boulder, Colo.: privately published, 1970.

_____. *Tales of Boulder for Young Folks,* nos. 1 and 2. Boulder, Colo.: privately published, 1975.

_____. *Early Boulder Series.* No. 1: *Miscellany,* 1974; No. 2: *Fire Protection,* 1974; No. 3: *Education-Public Schools,* 1974; No. 4: *Miscellany* No. 2, 1975; No. 5: *Ladies of the Night,* 1979; privately published.

_____. *Index. History of Clear Creek and Boulder Valleys.* Chicago: O.L. Baskin and Company, 1880. Comp. in 1970.

Goodwin, Elizabeth F. "The Growth of a Community, Planning and Development, City of Boulder, 1859-1966." Boulder Public Library, Boulder, Colorado.

Goodykoontz, Colin B. *Colorado: Short Studies of its Past and Present.* Boulder, Colo.: University of Colorado Press, 1927.

Graf, Nelly. *No Vacancy.* Denver: University of Denver Press, 1951.

Green, Thomas L. "Junius Lewis and the Golden Chest Mining Company." *Colorado Magazine,* 50 (1973): pp. 24-40.

"A Guide to Boulder's Heritage." Planning Department, City of Boulder, 1976.

Gurney, Jann; Heaton, Barbara; and King, Jean. *Mountain Memories, a History of Jimtown, Colorado.* n.p., c 1976.

Hafen, LeRoy. *Colorado and Its People.* 4 vols. New York: Lewis Publishing Company, 1948.

_____. *Mountain Men and the Fur Trade.* 10 vols. Glendale: Arthur H. Clark Company, 1971.

_____. *Overland Routes of the Gold Fields, from Contemporary Diaries, 1859.* Glendale: Arthur H. Clark Company, 1942.

_____. *Reports from Colorado: the Wildman Letters, 1859-1865.* Glendale: Arthur H. Clark Company, 1961.

_____. *Colorado Gold Rush, Contemporary Letters and Reports, 1858-59.* Southwest History Series, vol. 10. Philadelphia: Porcupine Press, 1974 (Reprint).

Hall, Frank. *History of Colorado.* 4 vols. Chicago: Blakely Printing Company, 1889-1895.

Harper, Robert. *Colorado Mines.* Denver: Carson, Hurst and Harper, 1891.

Harrinton, Charles. *Summering in Colorado.* Denver: Richards and Company, 1874.

Hilton, Suzanne. *The Way It Was, 1876.* Philadelphia: Westminster Press, 1975.

Hollister, Ovando. *Mines of Colorado.* Springfield, Mass.: Samuel Bowles and Company, 1867.

Isern, Thomas D. "The Colorado Territory." *Journal of the West,* vol. 16, no. 2 (April 1977): pp. 57-71.

Jackson, Helen Hunt. *Bits of Travel at Home.* Boston: Robert Brothers, 1878.

Jones, Billy M. *Health Seekers of the Southwest, 1817-1900.* Norman: University of Oklahoma Press, 1967.

Kelly, William R. "Irrigation Beginnings in Colorado." Paper, Western Historical Collections, University of Colorado at Boulder.

Kemp, Donald C. *Silver, Gold and Black Iron; A Story of the Grand Island Mining District of Boulder County, Colorado.* Denver: Sage Swallow, 1960.

Lavender, David. *The Rockies.* New York: Harper and Row, 1968.

_____. *Bent's Fort.* Garden City: Doubleday and Company, Inc., 1954.

Lehrer, Margaret J., ed. *Up the Hemline; being a true account of one hundred years of classroom experience in Colorado.* Delta Kappa Gamma Society, Omega Chapter, Colorado Springs, 1976.

Lovelace, Walter. "The Pioneer Trail Through Historic Boulder." Map and commentary. 1968.

Manual of the Public Schools, 1895-96. Boulder Valley School District, Boulder, Colorado.

McCaffrey, Hugh, ed. *Boulder Progress,* quarterly publication of the National State Bank, 1950s and 1960s.

Marriner, Gerald Lynn. "Klan Politics in Colorado." *Journal of the West*. vol. 15, no. 1 (January 1976): pp. 76-101.

McCarty, Cleveland. Article on the Rocky Mountain Climbers Club, Chautauqua Association, 1976.

Meyring, Geneva. *Nederland, Then and Now*. Boulder, Colo.: n.p., 1941.

Mining in Boulder County. Boulder, Colo.: Boulder County Metal Mining Association, 1910.

Montgomery, Mabel Guise. *A Story of Gold Hill, Colorado; Seventy-odd Years in the Heart of the Rockies*. n.p., 1930.

Mumey, Nolie, ed. *Diary of Edward Dunsha Steele, Across the Plains to Boulder, Colorado, 1859*. Boulder, Colo.: Johnson Publishing Company, 1960.

Mutel, Cornelia F. *From Grassland to Glacier, an ecology of Boulder County, Colorado*. Boulder, Colo.: Land Grant Publishing Company, 1976.

Nees, Hal. "The Boulder Police Department, A History." Paper, 1976.

Oehlerts, Donald E., comp. *Guide to Colorado Newspapers, 1859-1963*. Denver: Bibliographical Center for Research, Rocky Mountain Region, Inc., 1964.

Olmsted, Frederick Law. "The Improvement of Boulder, Colorado." Report to the Boulder City Improvement Association, 1910.

Ourada, Patricia. "Chinese in Colorado." *Colorado Magazine,* 29: pp. 273-278.

Parsons, Martin B. "Toll Road History of Boulder County." Paper for the Boulder Historical Society, 1945.

Patton, A.C. *Green Rocks*. n.p., 1904.

Perrigo, Lynn T. *A Municipal History of Boulder, Colorado, 1871-1946*. Boulder, Colo.: Boulder Publishing Company, 1946.

____. "A Condensed History of Boulder, Colorado." *Colorado Magazine,* 29: pp. 37-49.

Picturesque Boulder, Gems of Boulder County. Boulder, Colo.: S.B. Macky, publishers, 1901.

Pike, Donald G. "Reconnoitering the Barrier." *The American West* 9, no. 4 (September 1972): pp. 28-60.

Pike, Zebulon M. *The Journals of Zebulon M. Pike*. vol. 2. Norman: University of Oklahoma Press, 1966.

Platts, Harvey. *The Knife-makers Who Went West*. Longmont, Colo.: Long's Peak Press, Inc., 1978.

Repplier, F.O. *As A Town Grows*. Boulder, Colo.: District No. 3, Boulder, Colorado, 1959.

Representative Men of Colorado. Denver, Colo.: Rowell Art Publishing Company, 1902.

Representative Women of Colorado. J.A. Sample, comp. Denver, Colo.: Alexander Art Publishing Company, 1911.

Rinhart, Floyd and Marion. "Martha Maxwell's Peaceable Kingdom." *The American West* 13, no. 5 (September-October, 1976): pp. 34-63.

Runnells, Donald D. *Boulder, A Sight to Behold*. Guidebook. Boulder, Colo.: First National Bank, 1976.

Sage, Rufus B. *Rocky Mountain Life*. Boston: Milton Howes and Company, 1857.

Sanford, Mrs. Bryon. *The Journals of Mollie Dorsey Sanford in Nebraska and Colorado Territory, 1857-1866*. Lincoln: University of Nebraska Press, 1959.

Schoolland, J.B. *Boulder Then and Now*. Boulder, Colo.: Pruett Press, Inc., 1967, rev. 1979.

Scott, Glenn R. "Historic Trail Map of the Greater Denver Area, Colorado." U.S. Geological Survey, 1976.

Sewall, Jane. *Jane, Dear Child*. Boulder, Colo.: University of Colorado Press, 1957.

Shaffer, Ray. *A Guide to Places on the Colorado Prairie*. Boulder, Colo.: Pruett Publishing Company, 1975.

Smith, Duane A. *Silver Saga, The Story of Caribou, Colorado.* Boulder, Colo.: Pruett Publishing Company, 1974.

Smith, Phyllis. "History of Mapleton School." Boulder, Colo.: n.p., 1975.

Smith, William S. "Caribou as it Appeared in the Year 1904." Boulder, Colo.: n.p., n.d.

Sniktau (pen name of E.H.N. Patterson). "Early Days in Boulder County." Georgetown: *The Mining Review,* March, April, May 1874.

Spitler, Laura A., and Walther, Lou. *Gem of the Mountain Valley, History of Broomfield.* Broomfield Centennial-Bicentennial Commission, 1975.

Sprague, Marshall. *Colorado, A Bicentennial History.* New York, W.W. Norton, 1976.

Spring, Agnes Wright. "Rush to the Rockies, 1859." *Colorado Magazine* 36, no. 2: pp. 83-121.

Stafford, Jean. *The Collected Short Stories of Jean Stafford.* New York: Farrar, Straus, and Giroux, 1944, second printing, 1969.

Steinel, Alvin T. *History of Agriculture in Colorado.* Ft. Collins, Colo.: State Agricultural College, 1926.

Stoehr, C. Eric. *Bonanza Victorian.* Albuquerque: University of New Mexico Press, 1975.

Stone, Wilbur Fiske. *History of Colorado.* 4 vols. Chicago: S.J. Clark Publishing Company, 1918-19.

"The Switzerland Trail of America." Commentary and map. Boulder County Historical Society, Boulder, Colorado.

Taylor, Bayard. *Colorado, A Summer Trip.* (Letters originally printed in the *New York Tribune.*) New York: Putnam, 1967.

Thompson, Nathan. "Ten Years as First Pastor of the Congregational Church of Boulder, Colorado, 1865-1875." Congregational Church, Boulder, Colorado

Tice, J.H. *Over the Plains and on the Mountains.* St. Louis: Industrial Age Printing, 1872.

Trenholm, Virginia Cole. *The Arapahoes, Our People.* Norman: University of Oklahoma Press, 1970.

Ubbelohde, Carl, ed. *A Colorado Reader.* Boulder, Colo.: Pruett Publishing Company, 1962.

Ubbelohde, Carl; Benson, Maxine; Smith, Duane A. *A Colorado History.* Boulder, Colo.: Pruett Publishing Company, 1972, rev. 1976.

Vickers, W.B. "History of Colorado." *History of Clear Creek and Boulder Valleys.* Chicago: O.L. Baskin and Company, 1881.

Villard, Henry. *The Past and Present of Pike's Peak Gold Regions.* St. Louis: 1860. (Reprinted by Princeton University Press, 1972.)

Waldrop, A. Gayle, ed. "American Town Hastening to be History." Editorials of Col. L.C. Paddock, Boulder *Camera* 1891-1921. *Colorado Magazine* 13: pp.186-195.

Weber, Alice. "George Lytle, Colorado Pioneer." Paper, Western Historical Collections, University of Colorado at Boulder.

_____. "Story of the Orphan Boy." Paper, Western Historical Collections, University of Colorado at Boulder.

Werstein, Irving. *Labor's Defiant Lady, the Story of Mother Jones.* New York: Thomas Y. Crowell Company, 1969.

Westermeier, Clifford. *Colorado's First Portrait, Scenes By Early Artists.* Albuquerque: University of New Mexico Press, 1970.

Westermeier, Therese S. *Women Too at CU.* Boulder, Colo.: University of Colorado Centennial Commission, 1976.

Wolle, Muriel Sibell. *Stampede to Timberline, the Ghost Towns and Mining Camps of Colorado.* Chicago: Sage Swallow Books, 1949, rev. 1974.

_____. *Timberline Tailings, Tales of Colorado's Ghost Towns and Mining Camps.* Chicago: Sage Swallow Books, 1977.

Newspapers Consulted:

Boulder Camera and *Boulder Daily Camera*
Boulder County Herald
Boulder County News
Boulder County News and Herald
Boulder County Pioneer
Boulder News and Courier
Colorado Banner
Colorado Daily
Denver Post
London Times
Longmont Times-Call
Louisville Times
The Mining Review, Georgetown
New York Times
Rocky Mountain American
Rocky Mountain News
Town and Country Review

Appendix 1

Members of the Nebraska City Party
Captain Thomas A. Aikins, leader
James Aikins, son of Captain Aikins
Samuel J. Aikins, nephew of Captain Aikins
Albert Atcheson
Alfred A. Brookfield
John P. Brown
Silas D. Burns
Henry Wilson Chiles
Charles M. Clouser
Lewis C. Davenport
W.H. Dickens
Daniel Gordon and brother
John R. Hall
Thaddeus R. Hamilton
Thomas Lorton, Brookfield's brother-in-law
James P. McChesney
William "Billy" C.B. Moore
John Rothrock
Theodore Squires
Wheelock brothers
Captain Abram K. Yount

Appendix 2

Signers, Articles of Organization, Boulder City Town Company
February 10, 1859*

James Able (or Abel)
Charles Aikins
Thomas A. Aikins, vice-president
Albert G. Baber
Albert Baker
Albert E. Baugh
George Bicknell, director
Daniel Blocher
George Briggs
Alfred A. Brookfield, president
John P. Brown
W.S. Buckwalter, secretary
John L. Buell, director
Isaac S. Buell
Silas D. Burns
John Cassity
William H. Cheatly
Henry Wilson Chiles (or Childs)
Charles M. Clouser
Nicholas Connelly
Charles E. Cook
Albert Corbin
David S. Corbin
M.D. Cousert (or Cowsart)
Lewis C. Davenport
Denison J. Ely
J.T. Fay
Oliver P. Goodwin, director
George Hacklemann
Thaddeus R. Hamilton, director
John R. Hall, director
Addison W. Harris

David Horsfal
S.D. Hotchkiss
William K. Hughey
W.W. Jones
A.K. Kennedy
Thomas Lorton
John Mackay
Denis McManus (or McMinus, or Manis)
James P. McChesney
Alfred Miller
William B. Moore, director
John Morin
A.B. Perrington
John Rothrock
T.S. Schofield, treasurer
William S. Scourfield
R.L. Simpson
B.A. Sinn (or Sims)
Theodore Squires
G.W. Thorp
Marquis W. Towner
Daniel Wagstaff
James Wagstaff
E.S. Warren
J.E. Williams
George R. Williamson, director
F. Winslow
David M. Wooley
J.L. Younker (or T.S.)

Some signatures are difficult to read and make the spelling of names uncertain.

Appendix 3

Members, Charter Convention
City of Boulder

H.O. Andrew, attorney
Jonas Bergheim, clothier
Ida Campbell, Women's Club
William V. Casey, superintendent of schools
Ira DeLong, professor
E.S. Evans, painter
Edward Fair, real estate salesman
Charles Fawcett, florist
Wesley Foster, beekeeper
H.P. Gamble, attorney
S.A. Greenwood, farmer and county commissioner
Dr. W.P. Harlow, physician
Louis Herman, merchant
Clair Mann, instructor
Joe McCabe, plumber
Flora Silliman McHarg, attorney
H.B. Millard, printer
F.C. Moys, hardware merchant
Charles O'Conner, attorney
W. Flint Smith, merchant
C.O. Van Note, contractor

Appendix 4

Early Dates in Boulder Education

June	1860	Pioneer School opens
October	1860	First public school building in Colorado constructed
	1863	Organization of School District No. 3
	1872	Central School opens
	1877	University of Colorado opens for college students and preparatory students
	1882	Pine Street School opens
	1884	Change to graded classrooms
	1889	Mapleton School opens for elementary and high school students
	1892	Highland School opens
		Mount St. Gertrude Academy opens
	1893	State Preparatory moves to Highland School
	1895	State Preparatory School has its own building at Seventeenth and Pearl streets
	1898	Chautauqua opens
	1899	Jefferson School opens
	1903	Washington and Lincoln schools open
		Pine Street School changes its name to Whittier School
	1905	University Hill School opens
	1916	Open-air school at Mapleton School opens
	1924	North Side Intermediate School opens
	1937	Boulder High School opens
	1938	First kindergartens for Boulder
	1944	North Side Intermediate School changes its name to Casey Junior High School
	1949	Foothills Elementary School opens
	1950	University Hill Primary opens
	1953	Base Line Junior High School opens
	1955	Park Elementary School opens
	1956	Flatirons Elementary School opens
		Columbine Elementary School opens
	1958	Crestview Elementary School opens
	1960	Centennial Junior High School opens
	1961	Establishment of Boulder Valley School District through reorganization

Appendix 5

Population Changes in Boulder County

	1860	1870	1880	1890	1900	1910	1920	1930	1940	1950	1960	1970	1980
BOULDER COUNTY	850* 1,456★	1,721	9,723	14,082	21,544	30,330	31,861	32,456	37,418	48,296	74,254	131,889	186,979
Boulder	c300	343	3,069	3,330	6,150	9,539	11,006	11,223	12,958	19,999	37,718	66,870	76,228
Caribou			549	169	44	51	47						
Eagle Rock			130	213									
Left Hand		213	425										
Longmont			773	1,543	2,201	4,256	5,848	6,029	7,406	8,099	11,489	23,209	42,902
Louisville			450	596	966	1,708	1,799	1,681	2,023	1,978	2,073	2,409	5,586
Lafayette				410	970	1,802	1,815	1,842	2,062	2,090	2,612	3,498	9,014
Magnolia			157	72	183	201	77	43	51	211✓			
Nederland			279	111	182	446	291	285	584	266	272	492	1,166
Pella				383									
Altona				255	218	170	172	163	178	175			
Valmont				487	713	778	824	918	920	743			
Canfield				398	345	330	446	699	517	433			
Marshall-Langford				233	443	813	707	415	454	465			
Ward				424	300	129	74	34	118	10	9	32	128
Jamestown				212	164	157	150	69	190	118	107	185	224
Gold Hill				425	407	192	51	56	125				
Sunshine				317	429	197	21	40					
Salina				206	462	305	173	125					
Lyons				574	547	632	570	567	654	689	706	958	1,133
Niwot				235	437	673	710	820	727	653			
Sunset				68	152	96	38						
Hygiene					527	750	737	752	706	706			
Sugar Loaf					156	226	80	81	82	211			
Allenspark				255	100	76	53	148	134	110 ☆			
Broomfield □					161	142	167	217	193	176		7,261	19,885
Noland					119	63							
Eldora					395	81	35	16	31				
Superior					252	349	233	160	205	134	173	171	212
Hessie					72								
Lakewood							68						
Rowena							47						
Albion			200										
Cardinal		200 ■											
Francis				200									
Erie													1,252
Gunbarrel area													5,170

*A district "commencing at Guy House and running to the Four-Mile House on the Gregory Road, Boulder and South Boulder Central District, Gold Hill, Gold Dirt, Gamble Gulch, Deadwood, and all districts and territory north and west of the above named.

★ Governor's report, Colorado Territory, January 4, 1867.
✓ Includes Sugar Loaf.
□ Not incorporated until the 1960s.
☆ Includes Magnolia.
■ 1872 population.

Appendix 6

The Development of Boulder's Newspapers

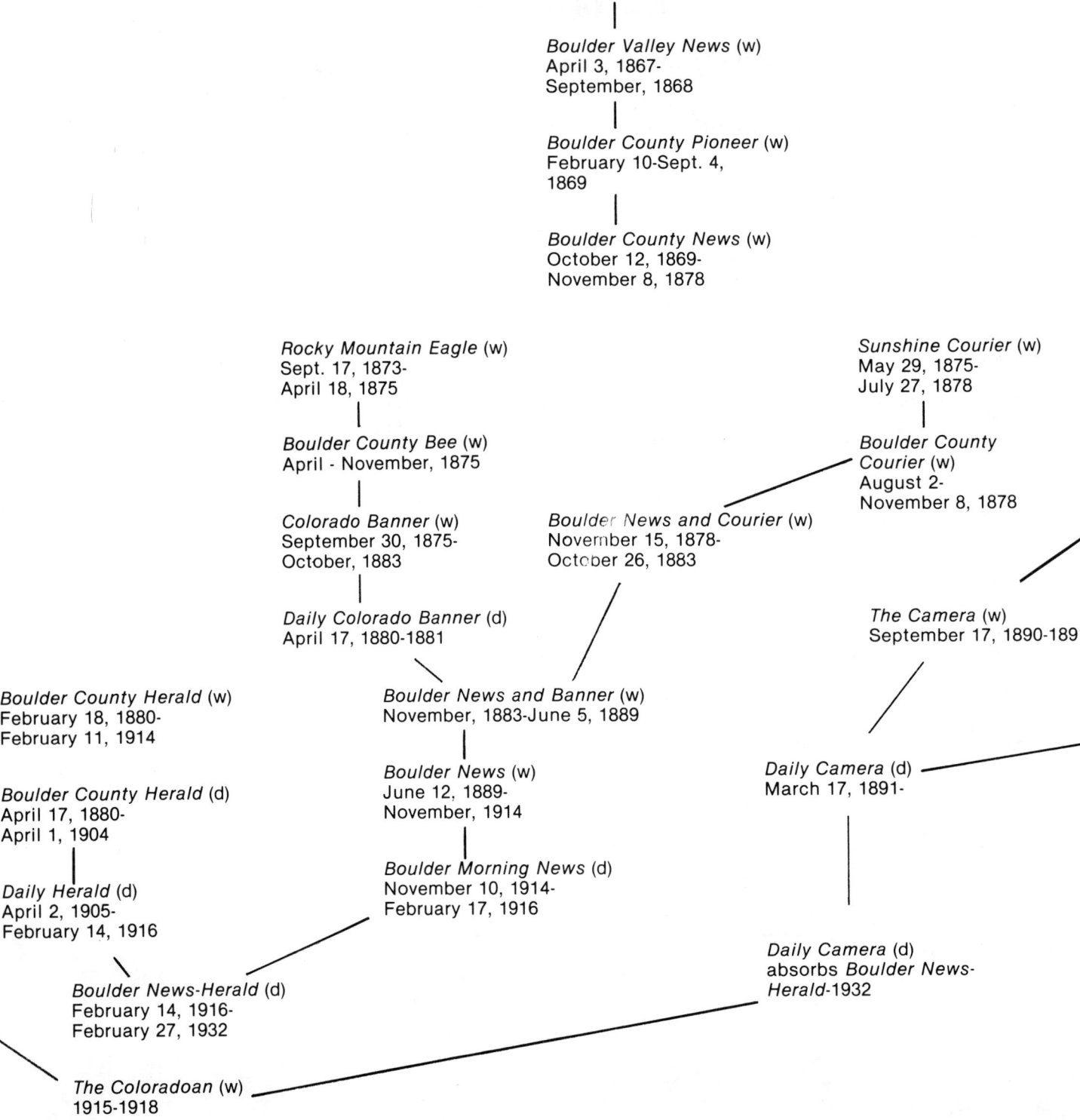

244

Boulder Sentinel (w)
July-Sept. 1871

Boulder Sentinel (w)
June, 1884-
November 29, 1890

Local Miner (w)
1888-1889

Boulder Tribune (w)
October 18, 1888-
September 21, 1921

Boulder County Miner (w)
June 1, 1905-
December 30, 1921

*Boulder County Miner
and Farmer* (w)
January 6, 1921-
May 1, 1947

Boulder County Journal (w)
September 22, 1932-
September 29, 1933

The Journal (w)
October 6, 1933-
April 20, 1944

*Boulder County
Journal* (w)
May 8, 1947-1952

Portfolio
1879

Silver and Gold
1892-1952

Colorado Daily
February 5, 1952-

Colorado Representative (w)
June 10, 1897-1899

Boulder Representative (w)
October 17, 1899-
February 12, 1903

Semi-Weekly Times (sw)
February 17, 1903-
September 29, 1903

Weekly Times (w)
October 8, 1903-
February 11, 1904

Times (w)
February 18-
December 29, 1904

Boulder County Times (w)
January 5, 1905-
February 14, 1907

Other Boulder Papers:

Friday Social and Industrial Review (w)
May 12, 1899-1900
Oil News-1901-2
Labor Leader-1900-2
Boulder Advertizer (w) 1903-4
Boulder Citizen (w) March 27-April 4, 1909 - organ of Prohibition Party
Progressive Citizen (d) March 23-April 17, 1917
Saturday Truth (w) 1903-4
Free America (w) September-October, 1904
Rocky Mountain American (w) January 31, 1925-July 31, 1925-organ of the Ku Klux Klan
Broadcaster (w) 1938-9
Boulder Mirror (w) October 7, 1942-1944
Boulder Advertiser (w) April 15, 1932-1933
Boulder Sentinel (w) April 4-18, 1946
Boulder Forum (w) June 23, 1950-October 15, 1950
Boulder Reporter (w) July 10-November 30, 1952
Town and Country Review (previously the *Downtown Shopper*) 1966-1979
Boulder Free Press (w) 1931-32
Wall Paper (w) November 1932-3
Boulder Star (w) November 24, 1932-January 19, 1934

Appendix 7

Boulder County Newspapers (other than Boulder)

Broomfield Star (w) 1955-1957
Broomfield Star-Builder (w) 1957-
Burlington Free Press (w) April 28-August, 1871

Caribou Post (w) May, 1871-August, 1872
Copper Rock Champion (w) June 4, 1892-1893

Wall Street Gold Miner (w) Delphi July, 1897-March, 1902

Eldora Miner (w) 1897-1903
Eldora Record (w) 1902-1909

Home Miner (w) Hygiene 1884-1885

Jamestown Miner (w) 1882-1883
Jamestown Whim (w) 1882-1883

Lafayette Inquirer (w) 1890-1
Boulder County Record (w) Lafayette 1892-3
Lafayette-Louisville Miner (w) 1892-1894
Birla (w) Lafayette 1894-5
Lafayette News (w) 1898-April 7, 1906
Lafayette Leader (w) February, 1905
News-Free Press (w) Lafayette April 14, 1906-November 4, 1910
Lafayette Enterprise (w) 1910-1917
Boulder Valley Lens-Shopper (w) Lafayette May 14-September 3, 1954

Longmont Sentinel (w) June-August 1871
Colorado Press (w) Longmont August 23, 1871-August 21, 1872
Longmont Press (w) August 28, 1872-1888
Inter-Ocean (w) Longmont September, 1873-April, 1879
Valley Home and Farm (w) Longmont 1877-September 1879
Home Mirror (m) 1878-1883
Longmont Post (w) 1878-1879
Longmont Ledger (w, sw) September 12, 1879-
Longmont Progress (w) 1888-1894
Longmont Times (w) 1888-March, 1931
Longmont Times (d) 1894-March, 1931

Longmont Call (w) September, 1898-March, 1931
Longmont Daily Call (d) April 1931-
Longmont Daily Tribune (d) 1912-1913
Longmont Times-Call (d) April, 1931
Boulder County Courier (w) 1939-1940
Sunrise Sentinel (w) 1962-1963

Louisville Miner (w) 1887-1888
Louisville-Lafayette Advance (w) 1892-1897
Brooks Vindicator (w) 1896-1897
Colorado Sun (w) 1896-1901
Louisville Journal (w) 1900-1902
Black Diamond World (w) October, 1901-1909
Louisville News (w) 1908-1915
Louisville Times (w) 1913-
Louisville Enterprise (w) 1914-1915

Lyons News (w) 1890-1
Long's Peak Rustler (w) Lyons 1891-1894
Lyons Topics (w) 1894-1897
St. Vrain News (w) Lyons 1898-1899
Lyons Herald (w) 1899-1900
Lyons Recorder (w) 1900-March 26, 1943
Midland Miner (m) Lyons 1901-4

Nederland Record (w) 1908-1909
Tungsten Light -Nederland 1916
Nederland Bugle -(ir) Spring, 1960-

Niwot News (w) April 19, 1912-February 28, 1913
Niwot Tribune (w) August 19, 1921-September 26, 1958

Sunshine Courier (w) May 29, 1875-July 27, 1878

Valmont Bulletin (w) January 1, 1866-March, 1867

Boulder County Miner (w) Wallstreet April 4, 1902-September 2, 1904

Free Coinage (w) Ward 1892-1893
Ward Miner (w) 1893-March, 1902
Ward Gazette (w) 1898-February, 1899

Appendix 8

Origin of Place Names
*Mining Camps, Settlements, Towns,
Geographic Landmarks in Boulder County*

Aikins Gulch: Site of county's first gold discovery near Gold Hill. Named after the Aikins party, first gold-seekers in the area, 1858. Now called *Lickskillet Gulch.*

Albion or Camp Albion: A mining camp five miles northeast of Caribou, north of Silver Lake near North Boulder Creek. Had population of 200 in 1880. Noted for its gold, silver, and asbestos. Was headquarters for Snowy Range Mining District. ("Albion" is Celtic word for "white, snowy," or "alp.")

Allenspark: A town eight miles north of Ward, settled by Alonzo Nelson Allen in 1864, platted in 1897 in hopes it would become one of the largest communities in Colorado. Also Allenspark Mining District.

Altona: A settlement eight miles northwest of Boulder at the mouth of Left Hand Canyon. Altona had a post office (1879-1916), grocery, bank, school, and tollgate. Peter Haldi ranch there. The settlement was first called *Modoc,* then *Davenport,* then *Ni Wot* in 1872, renamed *Altona* in 1879.

Ballarat or Balarat: An 1876 mining camp three and one-half miles north of Jamestown, site of Smuggler mine and Smuggler boarding house. Area noted for telluride and fluorspar. Once had a post office, school, voting precinct. Washed away in the flood of 1894. (Perhaps "ballarat" is from Australia; a mining center in Victoria is called Ballarat.)

Bald Mountain: A mining district established June 10, 1864. Bald Mountain is now called Niwot Mountain.

Batesville: An 1875 settlement on North Boulder Creek near the Upper Falls. Settled by L.M. Bates.

Bloomerville: A small mining camp and railroad stop two miles southwest of Ward.

Blue Bird: A camp three miles north of Caribou. Site of the Great Northern mine.

Boettcher: A railroad stop two miles south of Longmont, site of cement company established by Charles Boettcher in the early 1920s.

Boone's: A stage stop just south of Longmont.

Boulder City or Boulder: A town so named because of the numerous rocks in the area. Part of lower Boulder may have been called *Eleven Cabins* before the Boulder City Town Company was formed in February 1859. In 1878, Boulder City became Boulder, incorporated by the state of Colorado.

Boulder Diggings: May have been name of early camp at Gold Hill. Was destination of early Methodist-Episcopal Mission from Iowa whose diaries stated the camp was fourteen miles from Boulder. Colonel Chivington was the mission's presiding elder before he fought at Sand Creek.

Brainerd's Camp: A camp three miles below Ward. Founded by Colonel Wesley Brainerd.

Broomfield: A community ten miles from Boulder in southeastern corner of the county. Said to have been named after a field of broom corn by visiting railroad men who needed a name for a new railroad stop. Was originally called *Zang's Spur* after the Zang family of Denver who bought property here in 1885, raised Percheron horses, and managed a brewery which produced Zang's Beer.

Brownsville or *Brown's Crossing:* One of five early names for Nederland. When N.W. Brown (called "Bolly" because of his bald head) settled there in 1870, the settlement took his name. See *Nederland.*

Burlington: Name of 1862 settlement one mile from the later-formed Chicago-Colorado colony at Longmont. Absorbed by Longmont in 1871.

Canfield: A coal-mining settlement and railroad stop eleven miles east of Boulder, three and one-half miles north of Lafayette. Isaac Canfield and his brother settled there in 1874. Site of Rob Roy, Star, and Jackson coal mines. Previously called *Tabor Station.*

Capitol Hill: A railroad stop one mile southeast of Lafayette. Town plat filed in 1907 by Colorado Coal Mining Company.

Cardinal or *New Cardinal:* A town three miles southeast of Caribou, which was platted in 1870 with five streets. Two years later, 200 people lived there. In 1878-1883, 2,000 people lived there. Was railroad terminus for Caribou, as well as refuge for Caribou's evicted prostitutes. Some of Cardinal's cabins were built with wood blackened by forest fires.

Cardinal City or *Old Cardinal:* An 1870 settlement two miles northeast of Caribou.

Caribou: An 1870 silver mining settlement four miles northwest of Nederland, close to the Continental Divide. (Altitude: 10,000 feet.) George Lytle is credited with the town's name; he had just returned from Cariboo Diggings in British Columbia. (A caribou is a small arctic reindeer.)

Central: Name of a mining district established September 7, 1866, which included Jamestown, Ballarat, and Springdale. Previously called *Utilla.*

Chambers' Fort: A military fort on the Chambers' farm near Valmont, where Boulder County men trained for their military service at Sand Creek.

Chapman: A railroad stop two miles northwest of Hygiene.

Camp Chief Niwot: A small camp seven miles north of Boulder.

Clarasdorf: (Camp Rogers) A small camp on the Middle Boulder, four miles east of Lakewood.

Clarkston: A platted town just north of Broomfield. Settled in 1897 by C.A. Clark.

Clifton: A railroad stop six miles east of Boulder.

Copeland's: A camp two miles northwest of Allenspark.

Copper Rock: Some had great hopes for this mining camp, located just beyond Wallstreet. Orphan Boy gold mine opened in 1891-92. The name probably came from a green stain on a nearby cliff. Also a railroad stop, the camp disappeared with the flood of 1894.

Corona: A settlement on the Grand-Boulder county line, near the Continental Divide.

Crescent: A railroad stop and camp downstream from Pinecliffe.

Crisman or *Camp Crisman:* A mining camp seven miles north of Boulder (altitude: 6,700 feet) at Sunshine Gulch on Four Mile Creek. Noted for its telluride and silver, site of Logan mine, whose gold was so pure it was taken directly to the Denver Mint, under guard. Obed Crisman founded the camp in 1874. Area also noted for its French wine cellar stocked by the Ardourel family.

Culbertson: A railroad stop east of Boulder near Owen Lake. Site of Culbertson's Mill.

Davenport: see *Altona.*

Davidson: William Davidson established this settlement in 1874, which was six to eight miles east of Boulder and north of Coal Creek, near Louisville. Site of Davidson Coal and Iron Mining Company. Davidson also operated first general store in Boulder. Also Davidson Mesa.

Dayton: Nederland's name in 1861. See *Nederland.*

Delphi: Original name for Wallstreet. See *Wallstreet.*

Dixon: A settlement upstream from Orodell on Middle Boulder Creek, near Bummer Gulch.

Dixon's Mill: A railroad stop two miles east of Longmont, 1909-1916.

Downer: A railroad stop four miles southwest of Longmont, 1909-1916.

Eagle Rock: An 1891 mining settlement north of Magnolia on Boulder Creek. Later called *Camp Wheelman.*

Eldora: An 1890s mining camp whose first name was *Happy Valley.* Area boomed in 1896 with the name of *Eldorado Camp,* until a miners' payroll was missent to California's Eldorado Camp. Name changed to *Eldora.* Camp is three miles from Nederland and five miles east of Continental Divide.

Eldorado Camp: see *Eldora.*

Eldorado Springs: A settlement southeast of Boulder on South Boulder Creek. Noted spa after turn of century. Area settled in 1858-59. Called Moffat Lakes and perhaps Radium Springs. Post office was called Hawthorne in 1906. ("Eldorado" is Spanish for "the gilded.")

Eleven Cabins: Possibly the first name of the Boulder settlement. In 1858, John Rothrock built eleven cabins along Boulder Creek.

Elysian Park: Original name for Jamestown. See *Jamestown.*

Enterprise or *Camp Enterprise:* A mining camp four and one-half miles west of Jamestown. Settled by Swedish immigrants.

Erie: A community northeast of Boulder on the Boulder-Weld county line. Site of earlier coal mines.

Eversman: A railroad stop three miles south of Lafayette. Used in 1909.

Fairview: See *Goodview.*

Ferberite: An earlier name for Tungsten. See *Tungsten.*

Ferncliff: A settlement about one mile southeast of Allenspark.

Fisher: A railroad stop five miles south of Longmont. Used in 1892.

Flatirons: Boulder's fountain sandstone backdrop was probably called the Flatirons beginning in 1903, because someone thought the cliffs looked like New York's Flatiron Building, built the year before. Junius Henderson referred to the rocks earlier as the Towering Pinnacles. Photographer Joseph Sturtevant called them the Chautauqua Slabs.

Fourth of July: A camp and famous mine eight and one-half miles northwest of Eldora. Established by C.C. Alvord.

Foxtown: A nickname for Marshall. See *Marshall.*

Francis or *Camp Francis:* A camp three miles south of Ward. In 1895, two hundred people lived there. Site of spectacular snowslide on the railroad line in 1901.

Gato: Earlier name for Pinecliff. ("Gato" is Spanish for "cat.") See *Pinecliff.*

Glendale: An 1881 settlement two miles beyond Jamestown in Left Hand Canyon.

Gold Hill: First mining settlement in Boulder County, eleven miles west of Boulder. (Altitude: 8,400 feet.) May have been called Boulder Diggings prior to May 1859. Town boomed in 1860 but was consumed by forest fire shortly thereafter. Rebuilt and boomed again in 1870s with discovery of telluride. Site of Horsfal and Red Cloud mines. Also name of a mining district, the first in Colorado.

Gold Hill Station: A railroad stop between Gold Hill and Ward, just beyond Mount Alto. The railroad could not make the grade to Gold Hill.

Gold Lake: A town two miles northeast of Ward and three miles northwest of Gold Hill. Platted in 1861 and proposed for extensive resort, but town died. Also name of mining district established by February 26, 1861.

Gold Run: Name of the small creek below Gold Hill where the first gold in county was discovered in January 1859.

Goodview: A settlement just east of Valmont.

Gorham: A settlement and coal mine near Marshall. Post Office, 1899-1942.

Grand Island: An 1870s mining camp three miles northwest of Eldora on North Boulder Creek. Also name of mining district established March 16, 1861, which included Caribou. Was bordered by Middle and North Boulder creeks. (The name "Grand Island" is said to have referred to a nearby mountain of the same name, but it cannot be identified today.)

Gresham: A mining camp northeast of Jamestown. Also called *Camp Gresham.*

Gunbarrel: A community northeast of Boulder said to have been named by mailman Edward Viele, who noted that the road in that area was as straight as a gunbarrel. Or was it after Alonzo Allen, who plowed furrows "straight as a gunbarrel" on his nearby ranch.

Haddam: A settlement planned by Cyrus Hurd, three miles southeast from the Caribou mine.

Happy Valley: Original name for Eldora. See *Eldora.*

Hawthorne: Name of Eldorado Springs post office in 1906.

Hessie: A mining settlement two miles east of Eldora, founded by Captain J.H. Davis, who named it after his wife. Eighty people lived there at one time.

Highland: A railroad stop six miles northwest of Longmont, 1892-1959.

Hortonville: Early name for Orodelfan. See *Orodelfan.*

Hygiene: A community five miles northwest of Longmont which took its name from a local sanitarium, Hygiene Home, established in the 1880s by the Reverend Jacob S. Flory, minister of the Dunkard Church. Hygiene Home has since burned down. A nearby settlement called Pella (1861) and another called North Pella (1871) were absorbed by Hygiene.

Indian Peaks: Present name for the Snowy Range.

Irvington: A settlement directly east of Boulder on the county line. Site of Irvington Coal and Land Company, 1905.

Jackson's Camp: A mining settlement near Magnolia.

Jamestown or *Jimtown:* A community thirteen miles northwest of Boulder on James Creek (Jim Creek). (Altitude: 6,500 feet.) George Zweck came up from Gold Hill in 1860 to raise cattle there. Settlement called Elysian Park in 1865. Settlement then called Jimtown, but when residents applied for a post office, federal officials, fearing a racial slur in the name of Jimtown, called it Jamestown. Birthplace of Douglas Fairbanks, Sr.

John Jay Camp: Another name for Providence. See *Providence.*

Keysport: An 1870 settlement near Caribou, northeast of Cardinal. Developed by Alfred Tucker.

Lafayette: A community east of Boulder, named for Lafayette Miller. The Millers came to Longmont area in 1863. Mrs. Miller bought Lafayette land in 1871. Was a stage stop and site of Simpson coal mine.

Lakeside: A platted town five miles east of Boulder. Settled by Andrew Anderson in 1923.

Lakewood: A settlement two and one-half miles north of Nederland. Named after founder C.F. Lake. Site of Primos Mill.

Langdale or *Langdell:* A camp upstream from Orodell on Four Mile Creek.

Langford: For a time, Marshall was renamed Langford, after a local coal mine owner, but residents continued to call the town Marshall. See *Marshall.*

Left Hand: A farming settlement near Gold Hill, formerly called *Utilla.*

Left Hand Creek: A branch of St. Vrain Creek. The St. Vrain was formerly called Sublette's Creek after the Creole fur trader, Andrew Sublette, who was called "Left Hand" by the Indians in the area. The creek is named either for Sublette or Chief Left Hand of the Arapaho.

Lickskillet Gulch: Later name of Aikins Gulch. Origin of name "lickskillet" uncertain. Possibly refers to poor housekeeping of the miners who would rather lick their skillets than wash them. See *Aikins Gulch.*

Liggett: A settlement six miles east of Boulder.

Longmont: A community northeast of Boulder, so named because of its view of Long's Peak. Settled by members of Chicago–Colorado Colony. Incorporated by the Reverend Robert Collyer in 1873.

Long's Peak: A 14,255-foot mountain named after military explorer Stephen S. Long. (Earlier, French traders called the peak and adjoining Meeker Peak "Les Deux Oreilles," or "two ears.")

Lost Lake Camp: A resort two and one-half miles west of Eldora. Had a summer population of 200.

Louisville: A community southeast of Boulder, platted by miner Louis Nawatny, incorporated in 1878. Site of Acme coal mine.

Lyon or *Camp Lyon:* A mining camp one mile from Sunshine on Sand Gulch, one-half mile from Camp Tellurium.

Lyons: A community north of Boulder, named after the family of E.S. Lyon, who established the *Lyons News* in 1882.

Magnolia: An 1875 mining town eight miles from Boulder. Magnolia was the name of a whiskey popular with the miners, or it was named because of a southern settler's nostalgia for the flowers back home. Also name of a mining district.

Marnett: A settlement just east of Hygiene.

Marshall: A coal-mining settlement named for Joseph Marshall, who built a blast furnace on this site, which is southeast of Boulder. "Foxtown" was its nickname.

Mary City or *Marysville:* A mining camp just south of Eldora.

Maxwell's Mills: An earlier name for Orodelfan. J.P. Maxwell built a sawmill at this site. See *Orodelfan.*

Meeker Park: A settlement three miles north of Allenspark on Horse Creek.

Middle Boulder: One of Nederland's earlier names. See *Nederland.*

Mitchell: A railroad stop one mile south of Erie, used 1892-1902.

Modoc: An earlier name for Altona. See *Altona.*

Moffat Lakes: An earlier name for Eldorado Springs. See *Eldorado Springs.*

Morey: A railroad stop three miles north of Longmont, used 1909-1916.

Mount Alto or *Mount Alta:* A resort on the route of the Switzerland Trail's narrow gauge railroad near Sunset. A favorite spot for picnicking, its dance pavilion and lodge are gone.

Nederland: A community eighteen miles west of Boulder. (Altitude: 8,067 feet.) Originally called *Dayton* in 1861, then *Brownsville* or *Brown's Crossing* after Nathan "Bolly" W. Brown, who settled there in the late 1860s. By 1871, the town's post office was called *Middle Boulder.* When Dutch investors bought the Caribou mine and mill from A.D. Breed for $3 million, they renamed the town Nederland (Dutch for "low land"), as it seemed low compared to Caribou. Nederland was also called *Tungsten Town* for a short time.

New Cardinal: See *Cardinal.*

Ni Wot: An earlier name for Altona. See *Altona.*

Niwot: A community north of Valmont on Left Hand Creek. (Niwot is Arapaho for "left hand.")

Noland: A stone quarry community two miles northeast of Lyons. Established 1890.

North Pella: A settlement just south of Hygiene. See *Hygiene.*

Northrop: Platted town west of Erie. Settled by Reid N. Northrop in 1888.

Old Cardinal: See *Cardinal City.*

Orodell, Orodelfan, or *Orodelphan:* A camp and distribution point three miles west of Boulder on Four Mile Creek. (Name possibly meant "placer ground.") May have been called *Red Rock Camp* earlier, then *Maxwell's*

Mills, and then *Hortonville.* Site of Hunt's Concentration Works. Had a post office, sawmill, and general store. In the late 1890s, Chinese placer-mined there.

Peaceful Valley: A resort on St. Vrain Creek, about three miles southwest of Raymond's. Developed by John T. Roberts in 1918.

Pella: A trading post just south of the present Hygiene. A school was built there. Andrew Douty built a gristmill on site. First residents were from Pella, Iowa ("Pella" is Hebrew word meaning "city of refuge.") See *Hygiene.*

Pennsylvania Gulch: An earlier name for Sunset. The gulch itself is less than one mile from Sunset. See *Sunset.*

Phoenix: A camp southeast of Eldora on county line.

Pinecliff or *Pinecliffe:* An 1860s settlement (then called *Gato*) located on the Boulder-Gilpin county line on South Boulder Creek. (Altitude: 7,960 feet.) Dr. Craig established a resort there in 1900.

Pleasant View: Early name of post office at Sugar Loaf. See *Sugar Loaf.*

Poorman Hill: A mining camp close to Boulder, near the mouth of Four Mile Creek.

Potosi: Name of a silver mine at Caribou, also name of a rich South American mine. (Spanish for "city of silver.")

Primos: A mining camp two miles northeast of Lakewood, named after Primos, Pennsylvania.

Providence or *Camp Providence:* A mining camp established by J.J. Van Deren (sometimes called *John Jay Camp*) and site of the John Jay mine. Van Deren felt he was led there by divine guidance.

Puzzler or *Camp Puzzler:* A mining camp east of Ward which once had a school, post office, railroad stop, and telegraph station.

Quiggleyville: A settlement one mile east of Ward and sometime residence of Colonel Wesley Brainerd.

Radium Springs: Perhaps an earlier name for Eldorado Springs. See *Elorado Springs.*

Raymond's: A settlement five miles northwest of Jamestown.

Red Rocks Camp: An earlier name for Orodell, possibly a camp of the Nebraska City party in 1858. See *Orodell.*

Riverside: A camp on the Middle St. Vrain two miles northeast of Raymond's.

Rockville: An earlier name for Rowena. See *Rowena.*

Rowena: A mining community north of Gold Hill (Altitude: 7,000 feet.) Located on Left Hand Creek. Supported a school, post office, and telegraph station. Site of Prussian mine.

Ryssby: First Swedish settlement in Colorado, six miles southwest of Longmont, established in 1869 by members of the Ryssby parish, Smöland, Sweden.

St. Anton Highlands: A settlement three miles upstream from Boulder Falls and north of Boulder Creek.

St. Vrain: A fort built by Ceran St. Vrain in 1837-38 where the St. Vrain Creek flows into the South Platte. Also a town platted in 1887 by William Suydarn, which was south of the stage station. Stage station was built by Alonzo Allen, later of Allenspark. St. Vrain's Creek was first called Potera's Creek after a French adventurer. The creek was later known as Sublette's Creek after local fur trapper Andrew Sublette. Fort St. Vrain was first called Fort Lookout, then Fort George.

Salina or *Camp Salina:* An 1873-74 mining camp located at confluence of Four Mile Creek and Gold Run. Settled by former residents of Salina, Kansas. (Altitude: 6,700 feet.)

Snowy Range: Earlier name of Indian Peaks Range along the Continental Divide. Also name of mining district established June 17, 1861.

Springdale: A mineral springs community (Peabody's Hot Springs), ten miles west of Boulder near Jamestown. Destroyed by the flood of 1894, which took the town's bowling alley and sent it down Left Hand Creek to the town of Niwot on the plains.

Springville: A settlement of thirty families ten miles north of Boulder where the Reverend Jacob Adriance preached on his circuit ministry in August 1859. By September 1859, Reverend Adriance noted that the settlement was gone.

Stanley Crossing: Another name for Raymond's. See *Raymond's.*

Stevens' Camp: Eugene Stevens gave his name to this mining camp, which was later called Tungsten. See *Tungsten.*

Sugar Loaf: An 1862 mining camp ten miles west of Boulder on Four Mile Creek. Settled first in 1860, boomed with mining of telluride in 1870s. Boomed again in 1902 when farmer Niles found gold float in his potato patch. Post office called Pleasant View in 1890s. Also name of mining district and name of loaf-shaped mountain in area.

Sulphide Flats: An 1890s lakeside mining camp one mile south of Eldora.

Summerville: A mining camp nine miles west of Salina and nine miles from Gold Hill, on Gold Run. Center of the tellurium belt.

Sunnyside or *Sunnyside Camp: (Camp Virginia)* A mining settlement three miles upstream from Sunset and southwest of Ward.

Sunset: A mining settlement thirteen miles from Boulder on Four Mile Creek. Earlier called Pennsylvania Gulch, but renamed Sunset in 1883. Site of school, post office, telegraph station, and Columbine Hotel. The Switzerland Trail narrow gauge railroad branched here, with one line running to Eldora and the other to Ward. A boom town in the 1890s.

Sunshine: A mining community eight miles west of Boulder in the middle of the telluride belt. Named after the first baby born there, Susan Sunshine, daughter of the Peter Turners, settlers in 1874. Population was 1,500 in 1876. Site of the American mine.

Superior: A coal-mining community between Langford and Louisville. Its first residents were from Superior, Wisconsin.

Switchville: A settlement and railroad stop six miles south of Ward. See *Williamsburg.*

Switzerland Park: A mining-resort community two and one-half mile upstream from Boulder Falls on North Boulder Creek.

Tabor Station: Earlier name for Canfield. See *Canfield.*

Talcott, Tolcott, or *Camp Tolcott:* A camp southeast of Ward established by Colonel Wesley Brainerd.

Camp Tellurium: An 1890s mining settlement one mile from Sunshine on Sand Gulch and one-half mile from Camp Lyon.

Tower Junction: A settlement and railroad stop one mile southeast of Lyons.

Tungsten: A mining camp just east of Nederland on the Middle Boulder. Originally called *Stevens' Camp,* then *Ferberite.* Area was lively just before World War I. ("Tungsten" is Swedish for "heavy stone.")

Tungsten Town: Another name for Nederland. See *Nederland.*

Utilla: Another name for settlement called Left Hand. See *Left Hand.* Also name for mining district (*Central*) which was established by September 7, 1861.

Valmont: A community just east of Boulder. In 1860s, was larger than Boulder. Supported two drugstores, five general stores, a newspaper, a school, three saloons, and, later, a cheese factory. "Valmont" possibly refers to nearby buttes. The town's nickname was "Bugtown."

Camp Virginia: See *Sunnyside.*

Wallstreet: A settlement on Four Mile Creek two miles southwest of Salina. (Altitude: 7,000 feet.) Named after the New Yorkers who invested there. Called *Delphi* until 1893. Site of the Nancy Gold Mine and Tunnel Company.

Ward: A railroad stop four miles south of Longmont in 1892.

Ward: A mining community nineteen miles northwest of Boulder, located on Left Hand Creek by Indiana Gulch. Settled in 1860 by Calvin W. Ward. (Altitude: 9,450 feet.) Was stop on the Switzerland Trail narrow gauge railroad, called the "whip-lash" route. Also name of mining district established September 12, 1860.

Wheelman or *Camp Wheelman:* Another name for Eagle Rock. See *Eagle Rock.*

White Rock or *White Rock Mill:* A settlement near white rock cliffs seven miles east of Boulder. Site of early flour mill.

Williamsburg: A settlement six miles south of Ward named after early settler George Williams. Platted in early 1870s with the hope that it would become another "Caribou." Later, was switching station for railroad and was called *Switchville.*

Wolf Tongue: A mining company in Nederland whose name combines the terms "wolframite" and "tungsten."

Wondervu: A community three miles east of Pinecliff on the Gilpin-Boulder county line.

Zang's Spur: Original name for Broomfield. See *Broomfield.*

Index

abortion, 72, *218*
Acme mine, 107
Adams, Alva B., 124
Addams, Jane, 124
Adriance, Jacob, 20, 23
African Methodist Church, 175
agriculture
    early farming ventures, 14, 20, 25-27
    grasshoppers, 5, 20, 25, 27, 221
    fruit production, 27
    first fair, 27
    winterkill, 27
    irrigation, 2, 20, 25, 68
    modern farming, 217-221
    Ogallala aquifer, 221
Aikins, James, 11, 12
Aikins, Lafayette, 70
Aikins, Samuel, 11
Aikins, Thomas A., 11, *11*, 12, 14, 17, 18, 24
Aikins Gulch, 22, 54
aircraft industry, 176, 189
Akins, C.E., 149
Albion, 4, *65*, 125n
Alcantar, Antonio, 204
aldermen, 68. See also ward system of government
Allen, Oscar, 67, 70, 74
Allen Enterprises, 189
Allen Enterprises Loans, 189
Allison, W.H., 68, 156
Altona, 4, 33
Altona School, 31
Ambrook, Charles, 149
American Civil Liberties Union, 193
American House, 38
American Legion, 193
American mine, 54-55
American Park, 150
Anderson, Erik, 79
Andrew, H.O., *160*, 175
Andrews, D.M., 125n
antelope hunt, 13
Anti-Saloon League, 155
Antlers Hotel, 133, *135, 136*

Apache Indians, 5
Arapaho Glacier, 2, *5*, 20n, *169, 170, 196, 197*, 198
    discovery of, 125
    purchase by Boulder of, 151
Arapaho Indians, 5, 6, 7, *7*, 9, *9*, 10, 13, *13*, 14, 17, 30, 41, 48, 183
    words for, 5n
    spellings of, 20n
Arapaho Pass, 33
Arapaho Peak, *130*
Arapahoe Chemicals, Inc., 189
Arapahoe Street, 20, 111n, 198, 207, 211
Arapahoe Village Shopping Centers, 20n, 207, 211
arastra, 22, *22*
Arbor Day, 1, 94
Ardourel, Alphonse, 176
Ardourel, François Pierre, 66
aridity, 3
Arkansas River, 7, 13
Armistice Day parade, *157*
Armstrong, W.L., 156, 159, 160
Arnett, Anthony, 23, 36, 67, 81, 86
Arnett, R.E., *30*
Arnett Hotel, *71*, 176, 176n, *182*
Arnold, William, 141
Athearn, Robert G., 168n
Atlantic Monthly, 97
Atomic Energy Commission, 189
Auraria, 10, 12, 13, 22
Automation Industries, Inc., 189

Bailey mine, 56
Baird, William J. family, 150
Baker, Jennie Hilton, 171
Bald Mountain, 18
Baldwin, Ivy, *145*, 146
Ball Brothers Research Corporation, 189, 216
Ballarat, 4, 66, 66n, 111
Baptist, 44, 175
Baraboo, Wisconsin, 103
Barber, Caroline, 142
Barker, Hannah, 150

Barker, Dam, 150, 198
Barnard, J.W., 125n
Barney, Bill, 20-21, 149
Bartlett, J. Perry, 161n
baseball, 44, *55*
Base Line Elementary School, 194
Baseline Road, 1, 124, 202
Basemar Shopping Center, 206
Bass, Lawrence P., 111, *158, 162*, 165, *165*, 165n
Baumberger, Robert E., 185-186
Baunn, Fredericka, 72
Beach, William, 150
Beach Park, 150, 180, 203
Bean, Trafton, 207
Bear Canyon, 33, 36
Bear Canyon and Black Hawk Road Company, 33
Bear Canyon and French Gulch Wagon Road Company, 36
Bear Head, 13
Beard, E.M., 49
Beasley Ditch, *20*, 27, 116
Beaver Creek, 40
Beech Aircraft Corporation, 189
Bellairs, Ethel, 158
Bennett, Alexander Campbell, 49n
Bennett, Horace, 146
Bent, Charles, 7
Bent, George, 40, 41
Bent, William, 7
Bent's Fort, 7, 13
Bergheim, Joe, *160*
Berkley, Cloudless Morning, 27n
Berkley, Granville, 27, *27*
Berlin's Hall, 83
Betasso treatment plant, 198
Better Boulder Party, 68, 156, 171
bicycles, 85, 186, *219*
Big Thompson River, 2, 19, 195, 196, 198
Bijou water, 198
bikeways, 206
Bird, Isabella, 29, 173
Birge, Em "Bugtown", *109*, 116
Bixby, Amos, 1, 4, 14, 15, *20*, 32,

253

52, 68, 70
Black and Veatch, 195, 198
Black, T.C. Jr., *163*
Black Cloud mine, 56
Black Diamond mine, 28, 105
Black Hawk, 13, 33, 48, 49
Black Hawk Road, 49
Black Kettle, 40, *40*
Black Swan mine, 56
blacks, 84, 174-176
    Junius Lewis, 175
    Ruth Flowers, 174, *175*, 175
Blake, Gustave B., *100*
Blanchard's, 180
"bloodless third." See Third Colorado Regiment.
Blore, William, 18
blossom rock, 48n, 49
Blue Bird Cottage, 160, 172
Blue Line, 196, 213
Blue Vein Society, 175
Blum, Sheriff, 158, 159
Board of Trade Saloon, 156
Boland, George, 204
bombings. See explosions.
Bonfils, Frederick, 146
bootlegging, 158, 159, 163
Bosse, *40*
Boulder Acceptance Corporation, 189
Boulder Anti-Clique Party, 32
Boulder Brass Band, 83
Boulder Canyon, 1, 12, *19*, 33, 36, *42*, 50, 68, *87*, *126*, 150, 188, 190, 201
Boulder City
  real estate company at, 17-18
  city planners in, 18
  early descriptions of, 14, 19, 20, *25*, 25, 29, 30, 41, *43*, 44
  additions to, 45
  incorporation of, 67
  "city" dropped, 68
Boulder City Brewing Company, 78, 152, 156
Boulder City Council, 185-186, 187, 190, 191, 192, 192n, 199, 204, 205, 207, 216
  formation of first, 161, *161*
  use of "emergency clause" by, 186
  closed meetings of, 185-186
Boulder City Improvement Association (Society), 149, 150, 151
  See also Olmsted, Frederick Law, Jr.
Boulder City Town Company, *11*, 17-18, 17n, 20, 32, 149, 217, 240
Boulder Community Hospital, 150, 160, 186
Boulder Committee for Individual Freedom, 204

Boulder Comprehensive Plan, 207, 213
Boulder Council of Churches, 193
Boulder County Clerk and Recorder, 204
Boulder County Herald, 4, 54, 68, 69, 73, 74, 78, 79, 81, 83, 85, 149, 152, 190
Boulder County Metal Mining Association, 180
Boulder County News, 30, 45, 56, 73, 76
Boulder County News-Courier, 56, 73, 171-172
Boulder County Pioneer, 30, 32, 45, 85
Boulder Creamery Company, 172
Boulder Creek, 2, 12, 13, 17, 30, 38, 68, 69, 72, 73, 79, *79*, 83, 84, 103, 111, 116, *132*, 150, 180, 187, 190, 192, 211, *220*
  pollution of, 69
Boulder *Daily Camera*, 69, *90*, 98, 109, 110, 111, 141, 152, 156, 169, 173, 179, 188, 190, 192, 193, 194, 196, 198, 201, 203, 205, 211, 215
Boulder-Denver Turnpike, 188-189, *188*, 206
Boulder Electric Light and Power Company, 79, 165n, 187n
Boulder Falls, 150
Boulder Fire Station No. 1, 78, 79
Boulder Foundry and Machine Shops, 152
Boulder Hall of Justice, 202
Boulder High School, 161n, 183-184, *183*
Boulder Historical Society, 81, 86
Boulder Hook and Ladder Company, 76
Boulder Hose Company, No. 1, 72, 76, 78, 79, 164
Boulder House, 81
Boulder Humane Society, 172
Boulder Industrial Park, 152, 189
Boulder Jaycees, 216
Boulder Junior Police Band, 165, *166*
Boulder Lions Club, 180
Boulder Memorial Hospital, 102, 164, 195
Boulder Milling and Elevator Company, 152
Boulder Oil and Refining Company, 142
Boulder Oil Company, 139
Boulder Public Library, 173, 183, 193. See also libraries.
Boulder Reservoir, 196, 216
Boulder Tomorrow, 206

Boulder Union to Register People (BURP), 202
Boulder Urban Renewal Authority (BURA), 212
Boulder valley, 7, 28
Boulder Valley and Central City Wagon Road Company, 36
Boulder Valley Comprehensive Plan, 213, 215, 216
Boulder Valley News, 30
Boulder Valley Railroad, 29
Boulder Valley School District, 194
Boulder Wheel Club, 85
Bounds, B.F., 68
Bowers, Jim, 216
Boyd, Frank, *100*
Breath, Samuel M., 19, 38, 42
Breed, Abel D., 49, 53
Brighton, 165
Brookfield, Alfred A., 11, *11*, 13, 14, 18, 21, 23, 40, 44, 68
Brookfield, Emma, 11, 14, 21, 44, *148*, 149
Broomfield, 188, 189
Brown, Abner Roe, 29-30, 86, 183
Brown, Nathan W., 133
Brown, Suzie, 73
Brown, Tim, 73
Brown's Crossing, 133
Brownsville, 133
Bryan, William Jennings, 124
Buchanan, James, 33
Buckingham, Charles G., 97, 150
Buckingham, Nell, 199
Buckingham Hook and Ladder Company, 78
Buckskin Charley, 149
Buckwalter, W.S., 18
Buddhists, 216
Buffalo Springs, 40
Buffalo well, 142
building code, 187
Bull, I.S., 12
Bull Bear, *40*
Bunch, Wiley, 23
Burbank, Natt, 193
Burger, Leo, 221
Burger, W.H., 81
Burgess Drug Store, 175
Burlington, 94
Burr, Aaron, 6
buses, 165, *167*. See also Regional Transportation District.
business development, 20, 41-42, 152-153, 176, 189-190
  in Caribou, 49
Byers, William, 40

Callahan, Henry White, 91
Calvert's Stage Station, *37*
Ida Campbell, *4*, 160, *160*, 161, *161*

Campbell, Jacob, *39*
Canfield, Isaac, 29, 139, 141, *141*, 142
Canfield, 29, 85, 105, 139
Canon City, 72, 78, 139, 141
Cardinal, 52
Caribou, 4, 33, 36, 38, *46*, 47-54, *47*, *51*, *52*, *53*, 81, 133, 139n, 215n
Caribou Company, 49, 53
Caribou Hill, 48, 49
Caribou mill, 134, *135*
Caribou mine, 23, 49, 51, 53, 54, 133
Caribou Post, 48, 50
Caribou School, *60*
Caribou Silver Cornet Band, 47, 52, *61*
Carmack, Johnny, 149
Carnegie, Andrew, 173
Carnegie Library, 44, 173, 191, 199. See also libraries.
Casey, Lee, 168n
Casey, Robert, 110
Casey, William V., *89*, *90*, *160*, *186*
Casey Junior High School, 172
Cash mine, 56
Castle Rock, 143, *145*, 146
Catholics, 45, 167, 169
   first Sacred Heart of Jesus Church, *93*
"Centennial Separator," 152
Centennial Valley Mall, 211
Central mining district, 18
Central City, 33, 49, 50, 53, 175
Central mining district, 18
Central Park, 150, 180, 186, 201, 205n
Central School, 86, 88, *89*, *172*, 191, 213, *214*
Centroplex, 206
Chaffee, Jerome B., 53
Chamber of Commerce, *178*, 180, 189
Chambers, George, 40
Chambers canal, 27
Chapman Drive, 180
Charley Johnson's Saloon, 156
Charter, 156, 188, 200
   unsuccessful tries for home rule, 159-160
   convention, *4*, 160, *160*
   passage of, 160, 241
   fight of 1923, 162
   fight of 1925, 162-163
Chase, Fred, *98*, *100*
Chase, George, 69
Chautauqua, 86, 88, 117-125, *117*, *118*, *119*, *120*, *121*, *122*, *123*, *130*, *154*
   meaning of, 117n
   city purchase of land for, 117, 149, 150, 151
   early programs at, 124-125
Chautauqua Climbers Club, 125
Chautauqua Reservoir, 198
Chedsey, Nat, *100*
Cheney, Lewis, 149
Cherry Creek, 10, 11, 12, 20
Cheyenne Indians, 5, 6, 7, *7*, 72
Chicago Creek, 13
Chicago-Colorado Colony, 27
Chiles, Henry, 12
Chinese miners, *22*
   in Caribou area, 51
Chivington, John, 24, 40, *40*
chlorination of water, 156, 162, 198
Christian Church, 169
Christmas, 21
Christmas-in-the-schools controversy, 193-194
Christmas star, *221*
Church, Hattie, 171
Church, Jay, *88*
churches. See denomination by name.
Citizens Party, 68
Citizens Reform League, 68
Citizens United to Restore Boulder (CURB), 202
City Taxi and Sightseeing Company, 176
Civic Association for a Better Boulder, 192
Civilian Conservation Corps (CCC), 180
Clarasdorf, *56*, *57*
Clark, E.D., 98
Clark, T.L., *87*
Classics Club, 171
Clifton Plan, 198
climate, 3
Climax, 180, 189
clothing, 85, 86
Clouser, Charles, 12, 14, 23
Coal Creek, 2, 27, 28
coal mining, 28-29, 105-109, *106*, *107*, *108*
Cobb, Elmer, 158, *158*, 163, 165n
Cockerell, J.D.A., 152
Cockerell, Williamette Porter, 152, 172
Coffin, Onsville C., 33
Collier and Hall, 50
Collyer, Robert, 27
colonies
   Chicago-Colorado, 27
   Dearfield, 176
   Ryssby, 44
Colorado and Northern Railroad, *131*, *133*
Colorado and Northwestern Railroad, 127
Colorado and Southern Railroad, 143, 150, 187, 195
Colorado Banner, 73
Colorado Bookstore, 202
"Colorado brown stain," 198
Colorado Building, 189
Colorado Central Railroad, 28, 85
Colorado Chautauqua Association, 124
Colorado Credit Life Insurance Company, 189
Colorado Daily, 198
Colorado General Assembly, 188
Colorado Historical Society, 168n
Colorado House, *41*, 68
Colorado Mountain Club, 180
Colorado School of Mines, 133
Colorado Springs, 42, 139, 167, 168, 198
Colorado State Mill, 152
Colorado Supreme Court, 160n, 179, 192, 204, 205
Colorado Telephone Company, 85
Colorado Territorial Legislature, 24
Colorado Territory, 1, 9, 30, 32, 94
Columbia cemetery, *83*, *102*
Columbian mine, 38
Columbine mine, 108
Comanche Indians, 5
Committee for Fair Representation, 205
Committee for Individual Freedom, 204
composting, 191
Concerned Citizens, 204
Concerned Citizens for Human Rights, 204
Conger, Samuel P., 48, 49, 54, 133, 134
Conger mine, 49
Congregationalists, *26*, 44, *80*, *92*, 173
Conner, Mary, 204
Continental Divide, 1, 3, *23*, 47, 198
Coon Creek, 50
Copper Rock, 4, 38, 109-110, *110*, 111
"corduroy" road, *32*, 33
Cornish miners, 51, 54
Correll, Ruth, 204
Coulehan, J.C., 68, 74, 79
Coulehan, Robert, 110
courthouse, square, *41*, 44, 84, 149
   first, 32, 84, 149, *150*, *177*
   fire at, *179*, 180
   second, 127n, 171, 180
courts, early, 70
Cousin Jacks and Jennies, 51
Cowie, James, 116
Cowie, Marie, 172
Cracker Jack mine, 105
Crag's, 146, *146*

255

Crazy Bull, 9
"crazy stairs," 142-143, *145*
Creede, 110
Cripple Creek, 110, 174, 175
Crisman, Obed, 56
Crisman, 56-66, *57, 58*, 111
Crofutt's *Grip-Sack Guide to Colorado*, 98
cross burning, 169
   on Natt Burbank's lawn.
     See Christmas-in-the-schools.
   on Flagstaff Mountain.
     See Ku Klux Klan.
Crossroads, 207, 211, 212, 216
Crystal Springs Brewing and Ice Company, 152, 156
Culver, Gary, 23
Culver, Robert, 23, 32, 84
Culver, Mrs. Robert, 171
Culver's Flats, 84, 116
Current Events Club, 171
Curtin, Faye, 184
Curtis, Bly Ewalt, 190, 191, 198

Dabney, Charles, 23, 36, 149
Dakota Ridge Medical Building, 164
dancing, 86
Danish, Paul, 211
Danish Plan, 213, 213n
Dartt, Amy, 102
Dartt, Elizabeth (Sayre), 102n
Dartt, Josiah, 103
Dartt, Mary (Thompson), 102n, 104n
Davidson, William A., 19, 38, 42
Davidson canal, 27
Davidson mesa, 20
Davis, Bob, *77*
Davis, James H., 168n, 169
Dayton, 133
Deadwood Gulch, 13
Deardorf, Cyrus, 38
Dearfield colony, 176
Deavenport Poultry Company, 152
DeBoers, S.B., 179
DeBord, William, 74
Deep River Plantation Singers, 124
DeLong, Ira M., *160*
Democratic Party, 32, 68, 169
demonstrations, at Rocky Flats, 216, *217*
   antiwar, 202
   closing of Highway 36, 202
Dempsey, Jack, 146
Denver, 42, 54, 84, 108, 110, 139, 141, 142, 143, 158, 165, 167, 168, 174, 175, 188, 190, 202
Denver and Boulder Valley Line, 85
Denver and Interurban, 143, *145, 148*
Denver, Boulder and Northwestern Railroad, 127, *131*

Denver County Medical Society, 167
Denver Doers Club, 167
Denver Dry Goods Company, 211
Denver mint, 56
Denver Post, 146, 203
Denver *Republican*, 111
depot, *75, 112*, 176, 176n
   relocation of, 216
Develine, Edward, 152
Develine, James, 152
Diagonal highway, 198, 211, 216
Diamond, Lottie, 73-74
Dickens, W.H., 12
ditches, 2, 20, 25-27, 44, 187, 190, 192
   ditch, to Gold Run, 14
   to Pearl Street, 68
   on Pearl Street, 69
   Farmers Ditch, 1, 27, 42
   Beasley Ditch, *20*, 27
   danger to children, 176, 187
dog control, 67, 70, 187, 200
Dolly, 205
Domestic Science Club, 171
Donati's comet, 13
Donnelly, Ed, 20, 29, 33
Dougherty, Francisco, 204
Douglas County, 206
Douty, Andrew, 1, 20, 25, 42, 68, 142, 142n
Douty, Sylvester, 42
Dow, Justin, 97
Dowding, Charles H. Jr., 201
Downing, Roderick L., 188
Downtown Businessmen's Association (DBA), 206
downtown "disease," 206
dumps, garbage, 190-191
Dun, R.G., 53, 134
Dun and Bradstreet, 53
Durham, Jeanette B., 116

Eagle Rock, 36, 116
Earl, Issac T., 156
East Boulder Hose Company, 78
Eaves, Gertrude W., 172
Eben Fine Park, *79*, 103
education, 86, 88-102, 141-142, *172, 174*, 183-184, 186
   first schools, 29-30, *30, 40*
   mountain schools, 30
   School District No. 3, 30
   curriculum, 90, 94
   salaries, 91
   holidays, 94
   flag salute controversy, 193-194
   Boulder Valley School District (reorganization), 194
   "Minnie and Jake" controversy, 183-184, *183*
   chart, 242

   See also individual schools by name.
Eisenhower, Dwight, 102, 146
Eisenhower, Mamie, 146
Eldora, *65, 66*, 127, 133, 150
Eldora Springs, 3, 5, *29*, 142-146, *143, 144, 145, 146*
Eldorado Springs Canyon, *145*, 146
electric power, 83, 85, 165
Eleven Cabins, 12
Elitch's, 146
Elks Club, 186
Ellison, Jacob, 68
Elysian Park, 66
Enchanted Mesa, 199
Enterprise, Camp, 66, 133
Enterprise Road, 36
epidemics, 52, 54, 173
Episcopalians, 173
Erickson, Orrin, 211
Erie, 29, 83, 85, 108
Esquire Magazine (Esquire Coronet), 189. See Neodata.
Estes Park toll road, 111
Euler, Edward "Jack," 176
Eureka House, *37*
Evans, E.S., *160*
Evans, John, 40, *40*
explosion, 83
   at Caribou, 53
   at freight depot, 127, *128*
   at Flatirons School, 203, *203*
   at Board of Education, 203
   los seis de Boulder, 203-204

Fair, Ed, *160*
Fair, Fred, 188
Fairbanks, Sr., Douglas, 146
Farmers Ditch, 1, 27, 42, 69, 83, *92*
Faus, Jacob, *113*, 116
Fawcett, Charles, *160*
Federal Gas Company, 142
Feeney's Hall, 83, 116
Fine, Eben, 125, 151, 156, 191n
fire
   at Gold Hill, 23
   at Ward, *39*
   at Caribou, 50, 51, 53-54
   in downtown Boulder, 78
   at courthouse, *179*, 180
   on Flagstaff Mountain, 180n
   in underground coal chambers, 108-109, *108*
fire-fighting, 70, 74-79, *77*, 163-165, *163, 164*, 200
   See also fires.
fire stations, 78, 164, *164*
first camp of gold seekers, 12
First National Bank, *157*, 180
Firth Steel Company, 134

First Congregational Church, 90, 102n
Fitzpatrick, T.H., 179
Fitz-Randolph, Jane, 198
flag salute controversy, 98-102
Flagstaff Mountain, 149, 150, *170*, 180n, 193
  Sunrise Amphitheatre at, 180
Flagstaff Road, construction of, 36, *178*
  CCC rebuilds, 180
Flatirons, 12, 150, 186
  geology of, 2
  "painting" of, 186-187
Flatirons Country Club, 180
Flatirons Elementary School, 203, *203*
"float," 14, 14n, 54
flood control, 151-152, 211
flood of 1894, 110-116, *111*, *112*, *113*, *114*, 127
flooding, 2, 146, 176
  of wagon roads, 33, 36
  of Switzerland Trail, 127
  at Jamestown, *115*
Florence oil field, 139, 141
flour mills, 20, 42, 152
Flowers, Ruth, 174, 175, *175*
fluoridation controversy, 192, 198
Fonda, George, *44*, *77*, 83, 163-164
Fonda's Drug Store, 1, *44*
Fonda's Drug Store, Caribou, 49
Forget-Me-Not, 171
Forsythe, Lige, 81
Fort Chambers, 40
Fort Collins, 72
Fort George. *See* Fort St. Vrain.
Fort Jackson, 7, 9
Fort Kearney, 12
Fort Lancaster. *See* Fort Lupton.
Fort Laramie, 13
Fort Lookout. *See* Fort St. Vrain.
Fort Lupton, 7, 9
Fort Lyon, 13
Fort St. Vrain, 9, *9*, 12, 20
Fort Vasquez, 7, *7*, 9
Fortieth parallel, 1
Fortnightly, 45, 161, 171
Foster, Henry, 40
Foster, Wesley, *160*
Four Mile Canyon, 1, 12, 109, 127
Four Mile Creek, 33, 36, *57*, 111, 149
Fourth of July, 23, 94, 124
Fowler, Frank, 142, *145*, 146n
Fowler, Gene, 146n
Fowler, Jack, 146
Fox mine, 28, 105, *106*
"Foxtown," 28, 105n, *106*
Fraeb, Henry, 7
Francis, William, 169

Fred Burger's Saloon, 156
Frederick, 108, 192
freight depot, 127
freight depot explosion, *127*, *128*
freight lines, *33*, 36, *36*, 38
Frémont, John Charles, 9, *9*
French and Indian War, 5
French claims to Louisiana, 5
Friday, *9*
Fritz, Percy, 17
fruit production. *See* agriculture.
Fullen, Hiram, 54, 66
Fuller, Tim, 204, 204n
fur trade, 7, 9

galena, 66
Gamble, H.P., *160*
gambling, 70, 73
garbage, 186, 190-191
Garbarino's Saloon, 156
Garner, W.A., 142
gas production, 141, 142
Gates, Jessie, *90*
Geesaman, Richard, 206
geography, 1
geology, 1-2, 28, 142
Georgetown, 19n, 78
Georgetown Mining Review, 19n
Gilbert, Clark, 73
Gilbert, Jarvis, 67
Gilbert, Oscar, *182*
Gilbert's Drug Store, *75*
Gilman's Brass Band, 96
Gilpin, William, 9
glacier. *See* Arapaho Glacier.
Glacier Lake, 251
Gladden, Sanford, 18n
Glendale, 66, 111
Glorieta Pass, 40
"go-backers," 14
gold
  first discoveries of, 6, 9, 10, 11, 12, 13, 14
  "float," 14, 14n
  the rocker, 14
  the arastra, 22
  lodes, 22
  stamp mills, 22-23
  low-grade ore production, 54
  at Copper Rock, 109-110.
  See also tellurium.
Gold Hill, 4, 18, 19, 21-24, *23*, 32, 38, 54, *55*, 72, 83, 84, 133
Gold Hill Mountain District No. 1, 18
Gold Lake, 4, 18, 38
Gold Nugget, The, 110
Gold Run, 12, 13, 14, 18, 20, 54, 56
Golden, 19, 24, 85, 105, 190
Golden Age Mining and Milling Company, 152

Golden Chest mine, 175
Golden Chest Mining, Milling and Tunnel Company, 175
Good Templars, 155
Goodwin, Oliver P., 14, 18
Gordon, Daniel, 11
Gordon, Molly, 73
Gordon Gulch, 33
Gordon-McHenry Road, 33, 50
government, establishment of
  in Gold Hill, 18
  in Boulder County, 24, 32
  in Boulder
    board of trustees, 67-68
    aldermen, 68, 159
    city manager-council, 159-163
    employees, 159, *162*, 191n
  See also Boulder City and Boulder and Boulder City Council.
Graham, Thomas J., 22, 24
Graham mine, 105
Granado, Florencio, 204
Grand Island, 18, 133
Grand Junction, 167
Grant, Ulysses S., 53
Granville Phillips, 189
grasshoppers, 5, 20, 25, 221.
  See also agriculture.
Great American Desert, 6, *6*, 12, 217
Great Depression, 176, 180, 183
Great Oil Basin, *140*
Greeley, 27, 78, 176
Green Lake, 151
Green Mountain, *177*, 180
Green Rocks, 9-10
Greenback Party, 68
greenbelt acquisition, 199, 200
Greenman, Ernest, 125, 180
Greenwood, S.A., *160*
Gregory, John, 13, 33
Gregory Canyon, 33, 36, 150, *177*, 180
Gregory mines, 22
Gresham, 66
Grieder, Florence, 193
growth, problems with, 213
Gunbarrel, 29, 139, 211
Gyp, story of, 9-10

Hafen, LeRoy, 7n
Hale Science Building, *99*
Hall, Felicia Grace, 172
Hamilton, O.P., 56
Hanging Rock, 68
Harbeck, Kate, 172
Hare system of voting, 161, 162, 163, 185, 186
Harkins, Edna, 174, *174*
Harlow, W.P., *160*
Harmon, G.D., 33
Harmon Falls, 142

257

Harper's Magazine, 104
Harrinton, Charles, 25
Hartley, Joe, *39*
Hartley, John, *39*
Hauck, Robert, 14n
Hayden, Ferdinand V., 139, 141
Haystack Field, 142
Haystack Mountain, 142
Head, Claud F., 158
health department, establishment of, 197, 198
health problems
  in Caribou, 52, 54
  and the flu epidemic, 52, 54, 173
  with transients, 201
  See also tuberculosis.
Heap of Buffalo, *40*
Hecla mine, 105, 108
height ordinance, 189, 213
Heinrich, O.E., *160*, 162, *162*
Henderson, Junius, 150
Hennig, Lillie E., 176, 179
Hennig, Louis F., 176-179
Henry, O.E., 78
Henry's Saloon, 156
Herman, Louis, *160*
Hessie, 133
Hetzer Hotel, *135*
High Altitude Laboratory, 189
High License Party, 68, 155, 156
high school, 88, 90-91.
  See also State Preparatory School, Boulder High School.
Highland Hose Company, 78
Highland Lawn neighborhood group, 215
Highland School, 90, *93*, *95*
Hill, Nathaniel, 49, 54
hippies, 201-203, 216
Historic Boulder, 88, 213, *214*
Hitchcock, Hiram, 56
Hogue, A.J. "Toots," 176
holidays, 21, 23, 78, 94, *95*
Holk, Christian, 54
Holley, Charles F., 24, 32
Holstein, Ben, *100*
home rule. See charter.
homosexual rights controversy, 204
homosexuals, 204-205
Hoosier Ledge mine, 56
Horse Creek Treaty, 13
Horsfal, David, 18
Horsfal mine, 19, 22
hose companies. See fire-fighting or by individual name.
hose company competitions, *77*, 78, *78*
Hotel Boulderado, *149*, 172
House of Happiness, 174, *174*
Housel, Peter, 17, 17n, 23, 33
housing problems, 187, 213

Howard, Roswell, 205
Huey, William, 12
Huggins Park, 149
Hughes, Charles Evans, 124
Hungerford, Adrianna, 156
Hutchens, Charlie Bowman, 124
Hygiene, 25, 29
Hypatia, 171

ice skating, 83
Idaho Springs, 13
immigration society, 45
incorporation of Boulder City, 67, 68
Independent Champions of the Red Cross, 155
Independent Taxi Company, 176
Indian Peaks, 1, 2, 153
Indians. See under tribal name.
Industrial mine, 107
Industrial Workers of the World (IWW) 108n
influenza epidemic, 173
Ingram, J.E., *160*
International Business Machines (IBM) 189, 216
Ione, 7
irrigation, 2, 20, 25, 68.
  See also ditches and water acquisition.

Jaakola, Una, 204
Jack Jacobs Company, 211
Jackson, George, 13, 54
Jackson, Helen Hunt, 102, 134, *134*
Jackson, O.T., 176
"Jackson County," 24
jails, 70-72, *72*.
  See also law enforcement.
James (Jim) Creek, 111
Jamestown, 3, 23, *62*, *63*, 66, 111, *115*, 146, 153, 180
Jaramillo, Joe, 107
Jasper, Peter, 85
Jay, Dr., 116
Jefferson, Thomas, 6
Jefferson School, 90
Jefferson Territory, 24, 70
Jews, 167, 169
Jim Conway Saloon, 156
John Jay Camp, 66
Johnson, Andrew, 28
Johnson, Bert, 196
Johnson, Chester, *181*
Johnson, Ed, 183
Johnson, Emil A., *162*, 164-165
Johnson, Stan, 216
Jones, Billy M., 174n
Jones, Donna G., 198
Jones, Mother, 108, 108n
Jones, W.W., 12

Jones Drug Store, 202
Juhl, Earl, 191
Julesburg, 12
Junior Achievement, 216

Kansas City Symphony, 124
Kansas-Nebraska Act, 17
Kansas Territory, 1
Kerouac, Jack, 201
Kerr, David, 105
Keystone mine, 66
Kikionga mine, *138*
kindergarten, 184
Kingsley, Marietta, 73, 116
Kiowa Indians, 5, 6
Kitchen, William, 28
Kitchen's Bank, 28
"kite route," 143
Klingler, F.J., *93*, 160, 162
klondike, 38
Kneale, Helen family, 142, 146
Knecht, Robert, 198, 200
Knight, John H., 133, 134
Kohler Reservoir, 196, 198
Kossler's Lake, 36
Krupp, Hugo, 134
Ku Klux Klan, 158, 162, 165-169, *168*

Lady Franklin mine, 66
Lafayette, 29, 85, 105, 107, 164, 169, 215, 217
Lake, C.F., 134
Lakewood, 134, 198
Langford, Augustine, 28
Langford, Nathaniel P., 28n
Langford, 28
Langford Hose Team, *78*
Langley, B.F., 13
Langridge, B.A., 139, 141
LaSalle, 5
Lashley, Theodore, 150
law enforcement, 69-74, *158*, *162*, *165*, 165, *166*, 200
  early courts, 70
  jails, 70-72, *72*
  lynching, 72
  abortion, 72-73
  Junior Police, 165
  acquisition of equipment, 165
Leadville, 38, 54, 143, 180
League of Women Voters, 200
Lee, Linda M., 165
Lee, Mylo, 28
Lee, William, 28
Lefferdink, Allen J., 189-190, 201
Left Hand, Chief, 7n, 13, 40, 41
Left Hand, 72
Left Hand Canyon, 1, *2*, 23, *31*, 33, 150
Left Hand Creek, 2, 7n, 14, 111, 116

legislature. *See* Colorado General Assembly.
Leonard, Rollie, 215
Les Deux Oreilles, 6n
letters from the gold fields, 14
Lewis, Junius, 175
libraries
   early reading rooms, 45, 172
   and liquor, 45
   Clara H. Savory, 172, 173
   Carnegie Library, 44, 173, 191, 199
   Library Commission, 161
   bond elections, 199
   George Reynolds Library, 199
   Boulder Public Library, 173, 183, 193
Lincoln School, 142
liquor, licenses to sell, 67, 68, 155-156, 187
   by-the-drink controversies, 159, 186, 199
   "islands" and "peninsulas," 186, 192, 199, 206
   See also prohibition and temperance.
Little Bear, 41
Little Maud mine, 66
Little Miami mine, 54
Little Raven, *13*
Lizard Head Pass, 187
Loach, William, 134
Locke, John Galen, 167, 168, 169
Lockwood, Fred, 111, 116
Logan, John A., 56
Logan mine, 56
London Times, 190
Long, J.D., 152
Long, Stephen H., 6-7, *6*, 12, 27
Longmont, 14n, 27-28, 85, 94, 139, 165, 168, 173, 180, 188, 194, 206, 217
Longmont High School, 194
Long's Gardens, 152
Long's Peak, 1, 6n, 125
Lorton, Thomas, 11
los seis de Boulder, 204
Louisiana, 5, 6, *6*
Louisville, 29, 76, 85, 105, 107, 108, 158, 169, 186, 211, 215, 216, 217
Louisville Times, 216
Lovelace, Susan Mary, 91, 172
Loveland, 142
Lovers Hill. *See* Sunset Hill.
Ludlow massacre, 108, 108n
Lumina, Sister Mary, 91
Lupton, Lancaster P., 7
lynching, 3, 72
Lyon, Camp, 56
Lyons, 2, 14, 165
Lyons formation, 2

Lytle, George, 48, 49, 215n

Macky, A.J., *21*, 32, 76, *77*, 96, *101*, 102
Macky Auditorium, 171
Macky Hose Company No. 2, 76, *77*, 78, 79
Macleay, Mabel, 172, 173, *173*, 176
Madera, "Shep," 156
Magnolia, *59, 60*, 66
Magnolia Hill, 36
Mahoney, John, 23
mail service, 20, 85
Mall, Boulder Downtown, 1, 206, *208, 209, 210*
Mall, Centennial Valley, 211
Mallinckrodt, Mr., 116
Mann, Clair V., *160*
Many Whips, 13
Mapleton Avenue, 84, 179
Mapleton Hill, 32, 83, 162, 164, 179, 187
Mapleton Hill Neighborhood Association, 215
Mapleton School, 1, *10*, 90, *91, 92*, 98, 172, 174, *174*, 184, *184*
Marcotte, Dale, 216
Marine Street, 20
Marinus Express, 20
Marmots, 146
Maro the Magician, 124
Marshall, Helen, 172
Marshall, Joseph W., 28
Marshall, 28, *28, 29*, 105, 105n, *106*, 107, *107*, 108, *108*, 191
Martin, Marvin, 183
Martin, William, 48, 49, 53, 215n
Martin Acres, 215
Martin Park, 180
Martinez, Reyes, 204
Mary City, 133
Mary Rippon Outdoor Theatre, 180
Masters, A.F., 179
Maxwell, James A., *79*, 103
Maxwell, James P., 36, 37, 67, *67*, 84, 102n, 151
Maxwell, Mabel, 103
Maxwell, Martha, *79*, 102, 102n, 103-104, *103*, 172
Maxwell Reservoir, 196, 198
Maxwell Street, 124
May, Robert, 163
May D-F, 211
May Day, 94, *95*
McAllister, Dan, 116
McAllister, W.W. 164
McCammon, Hugh, 48, 49
McCarty, Tim, 206
McCaslin, Mamie, 23
McCaslin, Matthrew, 18
McClintock, H.C., 176

McCook, Edward, 73
McCord, Dave, 205
McDonald, Bob, *33*
McDonald, Frankie, 73
McFarland, Robert, 41
McHarg, Flora S., *4*, 160-161, 160n, *160*
McInnes, Don, 176, 179, 180
McKenna, William G., 134
McKenzie, Neil, 139, 139n, *140, 141*, 141, 142
McKeown, James, 201-202
McMasters, Raymond, 165
McMenamin, Delia, 175
McVey, John W., 175
Means, W. Rice, 169
Meeker Peak, 6n
Melvina mine, 56
Merryman, John family, 116
Mesa Ski Slope, 186
Mesa Vista Sanitarium, 174
Metcalf, Eli, 33
Methodist Episcopal Church, 24, *43*, 44
Methodists, 20, 24, 30, 44, 52, 54, *232*
Middle Boulder, 23, 133
Middle Boulder Creek, 2, *56*
Midget Mill, 134
Miles, Dr., 173
Millard, H.B., *160*
Miller, Glenn, 146
mineral springs, 3, 66, 142-146
mining, 211. *See also* gold, silver, telluride, tungsten, galena, coal, uranium. *See also* mining camps by name.
mining districts, establishment of, 18
   law and order in, 18, 69-70
   chart of, 18
   in Jamestown, 66
Ministerial Association, 163
"Minnie and Jake," *183*, 183-184
Minute Men of America, 169
Miser's Dream, 38
Mishler, Samuel, 48, 49
Missouri Republican, 11
Missouri River, 5, 11, 70
Mitchell, Fred, 152
Mitchell mine, 105
Moaning Dove, 48
Moffat, David, 53
Moffat Lakes Resort Company, 142
Moffat Road, 143, 146
Molloy, Florence, 172, 173, *173*, 176, 180
Molloy, Mary, 180
Monarch No. 2, 107
Monarch Haulers, 192
Monroe, Joe, 116

259

Moore, William "Billy,", 12
Moorhead, Frank, *94*, 161, 186
Morency, H.L., 186
Morley, Clarence, 168, 169, 176
Mormons, 33n
Mother Jones, 108, 108n
Mount Alto, 127, *129, 132*
Mount St. Gertrude Academy, 83, *83, 88,* 91, 116, 174
Mount St. Gertrude Fire Station, *164*
Mount Sanitas, 2
Mountain Bell, 188
Mountain House, *60,* 133
Mountain Lion mine, 66
mountain men, 5, 7, *7,* 9
Moys, F.C., *160,* 161, *161,* 162
municipal buildings, *72, 159,* 191n

Nafe, Bob, *160*
Nancy mill, *4*
Napolean, 5
narrow gauge railroad, *126,* 127, 127n
Narrows, The, 38
National Bureau of Standards, 189
National Center for Atmospheric Research, 189, 196-198
National Guard, 108n, 168
National Science Foundation, 189
Navajo Indian children, 174
Nawatny, Louis, 105
Nebraska City, 11, 12, 14, 21
Nebraska City party, 11-15, *11,* 239
Nebraska Territory, 1, 17, 18
Nederland, 23, 36, 38, 47, 50, 51, 53, 54, 84, 133-134, *134, 135, 136, 137,* 150, 151, 173, 180, 201
Nederland House, 133
Nederland School, 180
Negroes. See blacks.
neighborhood groups, 215
Neilsen, A.C., 189
Neodata, Inc., 189
Neva, *40*
New Eldorado Hotel, 142, 146
New Spain, 5
New York Independent, 102
Newlon, Paul, 168
newspapers, 30-31, 50, 56, 244-245, chart of, 246
Nichols, David, 23, 29, 40, *40,* 41, 73, 94
Ninth Street, *111, 112,* 187, 199
Ni Wot Mining Company, 19, 38
Niwot, Chief. See Left Hand.
Niwot, 139, *141,* 211
Nixon, Richard, 202
No-Man's Land, 5
Non-Partisan Party, 68
Norlin, George, 169

Norlin Library, 199
North Boulder Creek, 2, 33, 198
North Boulder Park, 151, 180
North Boulder Recreation Center, 199
North Side Intermediate School, *91,* 172
Northern Coal Field, 29, 105, 108
Northern Colorado Conservancy District, 196
Northern Colorado Power Company 165, 187n
Norton, C.D., 36
Norton, Henry Clay, 20, 33
Norton, Karl, 211
Norton, Vic, *98,* 100
Notanee, *40*

Ogallala, 12
Ogallala aquifer, 221
oil, 29, 139-142, *139, 140,* 215
Oil News, 141
Old Main, 88, 94, 96, *97,* 98
Old Whiterock, 139
Olmsted, Frederick Law, Jr., 151-152 159, 187
100-day volunteers, 40
open-air school, 174, *174*
Orodell, 33, 36
Orphan Boy mine, 109, 110
Ourada, Patrick K., 51

Packer, Alfred, 116
Paddock, Lucius C., 69, 83, 152, 156
Paget, Karen, 204
Panic of 1857, 12
Papa's Shoeshine Parlor, 175
Parallel Dome, 142
Parce, W.W., 150
Paris Dry Cleaning Parlor, 168
Paris Universal Exposition (1900), 133-134
Park Allen Hotel, 190
Parker, Judge, 70
Parkhurst, Suzie, 172
parking, 187
Parkman, Francis, 9
parks and recreation, 44, 149-150, 151-152, 199.
  See also parks by name.
Partridge shingle mill, 30
Patterson, D.C., 54
Patterson, E.H.N. (Sniktau), 19, 19n
Pay Dirt Pow Wow. See Pow Wow.
Peabody's Hot Springs, 66
Pearl Street, 1, 44, 69, 70, *70,* 72, 73, 74, 84, 85, 167, 175, 187, *207, 208*
Pease, Clarence, *98*
Peerless mine, 105, 108-109

Pei, I.M., 189
Pell, William, 20, 23, 27
People United to Reclaim the Environment (PURE), 213
People's Clinic, 201
performing arts center bond issues, 205, 205n, 206, 216
Peterman, Clara, 171
Peterson mine, 105
Peyton, Thomas J., 188
Philadelphia Exposition (1876), 53, 56, 104
Phoenix Hook and Ladder Company 76, 79
Pickel, John, 23, 49, 133
Pickett, E.C., 192, 194-195, 198, 199, 201, 202, 205, 206, 213, 215
Pickford, Mary, 146
Pike, Zebulon, 6, *6*
Pine Street School, *10,* 88, *89.*
  See also Whittier School.
Pioneer School, 29, *29, 40*
Place, Richard G., 152
placer mining. See gold.
PLAN-Boulder, 196, 206, 213
planning, city, 18, 151-152, 205, 213, 215
  See also Olmsted, Frederick Law, Jr.
Planning and Parks Commission, 162, 187, 187n
Planning Commission, 211
Platteville, 7
Platts, H.N., 152
police. See law enforcement.
political parties. See individual party names.
pollution, 191, 213
  of Boulder Creek, 192, 201
Poorman mine, 49
population, 41, 68, 176
  chart showing, 243
Populist Party, 68, 139n
Pound, Daniel, 36
Pound, Ephraim, 68
Pow Wow, 125, 180-183, *181, 182,* 215-216
  relocation in Louisville, 216
power development, 83, 85, 165
  See also power companies by name.
Prather, Rolla C., 179
pre-emption, 17, 18, 149
Pre-emption Law of 1841, 7
Presbyterians, 44, *44,* 161
Primos, 134
Primos Chemical Company, 134
prize fight, 73
prohibition, 152, 155-159
  See also temperance and liquor.
Prohibition Alliance, 155

260

Prohibition Party, 68, 155
prostitution, 52, 70, 73-74, *73*, 155
Providence, Camp, 66
public health, 69, 173-174, 186, 190, 198
Public Service Company, 165, 187n
   absorbs local power companies, 187n
   franchise fight of 1949, 187-188
   franchise election of 1970, 206
   and buses, 165, 206
   uses water, 195
Pudlik, John, 192
Pueblo, 158, 167
Purcell, James, 5, 6

railroads, 28, 29, 85, *126,* 127, *127, 128, 129, 130, 132*
   See also individual names of railroads.
Ralston, 30
Randall, R.M., 116
Rattlesnake Gulch, 146
Read, Margaret, 172
reading rooms. See libraries.
recall election, 204
recall election threats, 162, 163, 192, 204
Recht, Christian, 161n
Recluse Club, 171
recreation. See parks and recreation.
Red Ash mine, 105
Red Cloud mine, 54
Red Rocks, 1, 2, 12, 42, *42,* 150
Red Rocks Mill, 42, 152
red sunflower, 152
Red Zinger, *219*
Reeves, Alice Cleora, 175
Reeves, George, 175
Regent Hall, 202
Regional Transportation District (RTD), 165, 206
religion, 44
   circuit ministries, 20, 44
   flag salute controversy, 98-102
   Christmas-in-the-schools controversy, 193-194
   See individual religious groups by name.
Republican Party, 32, 67, 68, 167-168, 169
reservoirs, 2, 68, 69, 150, 151, 196, 198
   See reservoir by name.
residency requirements for voting, 204, 205
Rex No. 1 mine, 105
Reynolds, George, 199
Reynolds Library, 199
Rhodes, Joseph, 27
Rich-land Corporation, 191

Ricketts, Crockett, 68, 117, 124
Ricketts, Elizabeth, 111n
Riethmayer, Leo C., 190
Rink Auditorium, 83, *84*
riot, 202
Rippon, Mary, 45, 97, *98,* 171, 172
Rischar orchestra, *120*
Ritchie Gulch, 33
road building, 32-38, 50
Rob Roy mine, 29, 139
Roberts, Janet, 189, 204
Roberts, Walter Orr, 189, 198
Roche, John, 108
Roche, Josephine, 108
rock-drilling contests, 125, 180-183
rocker, 14
Rockville, *58, 59*
Rocky Flats, plant at, 189
   demonstrations at, 216, *217*
Rocky Mountain American, 167, 169
Rocky Mountain Climbers Club, 125, 180
Rocky Mountain Fuel Company, 108
"Rocky Mountain Joe." See Joseph B. Sturtevant.
Rocky Mountain Museum, 102
Rocky Mountain National Park, 1, 151
Rocky Mountain News, 18, 40, 168n
Rocky Mountain Rescue team, *219*
rodeo. See Pow Wow.
roller skating, 51, 83, *84*
Romero, Neva, 204
Roose, Arthur, *94*
Roosevelt, Elliott, 190
Rorex, Clela, 205-206
Rothrock, John, 11, 12, *12,* 23
Rowena, *58, 59*
Rowland, Ebenezer, *21*
Rowland, Mrs. Ebenezer, *7*
Rowland, Georgiana, *10, 122*
Rowland, Judson, *98*
Royal Arch, *123,* 125
Rudd property, 198
"The Ruins," 190, 201
Runyan, Damon, 146
Russell, Martha M., 172
Russell, William Green, 10, 11
Ryssby, 44

Sage, Rufus B., 7n
St. John's Episcopal Church, 201
St. Vrain, Ceran, 7, 9
St. Vrain, Marcellin, 9, *9*
St. Vrain, Altona, Gold Hill, and Gregory Road Company, 33
St. Vrain Canyon, 1, 33
St. Vrain Creek, 2, 13, 25, 111
St. Vrain School District, 194
sales tax, 187, 199-200, 206, 216
Salina, 56, 111, 127

Salomon, Edwin, 188
saloons, 45, 70, 155, 156
Salter, W.D., 165
"salting," 18n
Salvation Army, 169
same sex marriages licenses, 204-205
Sand Creek, 13, 14, 24, 40-41, *40*
Sanitarium, 102, *103,* 124
Savory, Clara H., 172, 173
Sawada, Katsuzo, *217*
sawmills, 29
Sayre, Hal, 102n
Schirmer, J.F.L., 54
Schmoll, Hazel, 172
Scholfield, T.S., 18
Schoolland, John, 187
Schools. See education.
   See also individual school names.
Scott, J.D., 18
Scott Carpenter Park, 150, 190, 190n, 199
Scrooby Mining Company, 134
Sears, Frank, 49
Sears, Roebuck Company, 211
Seltzer House, *64,* 66
semi-centennial celebration, 148, *148*
Settlemire, Claude, 173
Seventh-Day Adventists, build Sanitarium, 102, 173
   and the flag salute controversy, 98-102
Sewall, Jane, 96-97
Sewall, Joseph A., 96, 97
Sewall Hall, 190
sewers, first, 69
   bond issues for, 190-191, 192, 192n, 198
   pollution of Boulder Creek, 192
   fees, 195
sexual preference amendment, 204
Shaw's Botanical Gardens, 103
Shedd, William G., 56
Shep, 188-189, *188*
Sherman House, *46,* 49, 54
Sherwood, Jean Wirt, 172
shopping center controversies, 206-212
   See also shopping center by name.
Sibert, Florence, 198
Sides, Vernon and Revilo, 165
sidewalks, 42-44, 84
sign ordinance, 179
silver, 36
   See also Caribou.
Silver Lake, 125, 151, 198
Silver Lake Dam, 196
Silver Wing Aircraft Corporation, 176
Simons, William, 187
Simpson, John, 105
Simpson mine, 107

261

Sink (Sunken Gardens), 187
Sioux Indians, 5, 6
Sisters of Charity, 116, 174
ski tow, 186
Skinner, Hilma, 204
Slack, Walter, 205
sledding, 83
Smith, Duane A., 57
Smith, Edgar, 66
Smith, J. Alden, 54, 56
Smith, J.C., 33n, 49n, 53
Smith, J. Corder, 193
Smith, Mack, *30*
Smith, Marinus G., 20, 27, 29, 40, 67, 70, 94, 94n
Smith, Nelson K., 36
Smith, W. Flint, *160*
smoking ban, 186
Smoky Hill route, 40
Smuggler mine, 66
Sniktau. See E.H.N. Patterson.
Snodgrass, John, 9-10
Snodgrass, Josephine, 9-10
Snowy Range, 1, 5, *7*, 18, 21, 47
Sobrino, Madame and Signor, 116
Socialist Party, 68
Solander, Daniel, 73
Solander, Mary, 72-73
Sorby, Peter A., 7
Sousa, John Phillip, 124
South Arapaho Peak, 124
South Boulder Canyon, 1, 32
South Boulder Creek, 2, 13, 20, 25, 36, 42, 142, 146, 149
South Boulder Recreation Center, 199
South Platte River, 2, 5, 6, 7, *7*, 9, 12, 20, 33, 192
Southern Arapaho Indians. See Arapaho Indians.
Southern Cheyenne Indians. See Cheyenne Indians.
Spanish claims to Louisiana, 5
Spanish interest in Colorado region, 5-6
Spokes of the Wheel, 198
Spoontz, M.A., 124
Spring Gulch, 159
Springdale, 3, 4, 64, 66, *115*
Springdale, 20, 23
Spruce Park, 199
Squires, Frederick, 32, 36, 40, 41, 67, 68, 73, 84, 90
Squires, Miranda, *41,* 42
Squires, Theodore, 11
Squires-Tourtellot House, *26, 41,* 172
stamp mills, 22-23
State Preparatory School, 90-91, *94, 171, 172,* 175, *175,* 183
Steppler, Joseph, 54

Sternberg, DeKalb, 152
Sternberg, Jay, 152
Sternberg flour mill, 79, 116
Stevens, Annie, 83
Stevens, Eugene, 134n
Stevens Camp, 134n
Stillman Hotel, 176
stock market, *141*
Stockton, L.C., 142
Storage Technology Corporation, 216
Streamer's Drug Store, *42*
street lighting, 85
street signs, 85, 187
streetcars, horsedrawn, 85
    electric line to Chautauqua, *122,* 124
    expansion, 124, *147,* 165
streets, 69, 162, 179
Streich, Art, *94*
strike, railroad, 127
strikes in coal fields, 108
Sturtevant, Joseph B., 98, 111, *121,* 124, 143
Sublette, Andrew, 7, 7n, *7*
Sublette's Creek, 7n
subsidence, 107-108
suffrage, women, 68
sugar beets, 28
Sugar Loaf, 18, 33, 111, *138*
Sugar Loaf Hill, 33
"sugar moon," 158
Sulphide Flats, 133
Summerville, 56
Sunday, Billy, 124, 156
Sundquist, Charles O., *160*
Sunnyside, 38
Sunset, 38, *60, 61,* 109, 111, 127, 175
Sunset Hill, 116, 180
Sunset Rock, 12
Sunshine, 44, 54, *55,* 56
Sunshine Canyon, 10, 12, 33, 69, 150
Sunshine Courier, 56
Sunshine Creek, 12, 149
Sunshine Hill, 33
Sunshine Reservoir, 150, 198
Sunshine School, *31*
"superblock," 211
Superior, 29, 107, 215
Superior Metals Building, 176
Surguine, Ray, 189
Swedish immigration, 44, 66
Switchville, 54
Switzer, Lyndon, *182*
Switzerland Trail, *38, 61,* 127, *129, 130, 132,* 180
Syntex Corporation, 189
Systems Development Corporation (SDC), 215

Tabery, Norbert F., 216
Table Mesa Drive, 36
Table Mountain, 198
Tabor, H.A.W., 38
Tabor Station, 29, 139
tally-ho, 38, *87,* 124
Tally-ho Stable, 152
Tanner, Nina, *138*
Tanner, W.L., 138
Tarbox, Horace, 20, 29, 70
Tate, Penfield, 204
taxes, 187, 199-200, 206
    See also sales tax.
taxi-cab wars, 176-179
taxi service, 172
taxidermy, 102-104
Taylor, George, 142
Tedesco, Ted, 200, 201, 202, 206
telephone service, 85
Telephone Stable, 152
Teller House, 53
Telluride, 187
tellurium, 23, 54-66, 54n
Tellurium, Camp, 56
temperance, 27, 78, 155-159.
    See also prohibition and liquor.
Teran, Heriberto, 204
Texas-Colorado organization, 124
Texado Park. See Chautauqua.
Third Colorado Regiment, 14, 40, *40,* 41
Thompson, Harris, 186, 189
Thompson, Nathan, 25, 44, 94n, 102n
Thompson Engineering Company, 189
Thornton, Dan, 190
Tice, T.H., 49
Tickel, Walter, *220*
Todd, William, 54
toll roads, 32-38
    Boulder-Denver Turnpike, 188-189
toll stations, 36, *44,* 188-189
Tourtellot, George, 76
Tourtellot, Jonathan, 27, 36, 41
Tourtellot, Maria, 41-42, *41*
town square, *41,* 44, 149
Towner, Marcus W., 18
traffic problems, 187
transients, 201-203
transportation
    wagon roads map, 34-35
    road building, 32-38, 50
    toll roads, 32-38, 188-189
    railroads, 28, 29, 85
    streetcars, 85, 124, 165
    buses, 165, *167*
    Regional Transportation District, 165, 206
trash burning controversies, 69, 186, 191-192

treaties with Indians, 13, 40
tree planting, 67, 84
Trojan Ranch, 172, *173*
Trucksess, Frances, 193
trustees, board of, 67-68, 155
tuberculosis, 7, 12, 84, 125, 173-174, 175
Tulagi, 187
Tull, William, 72
Tunnel, Milkman, 116
tungsten, 133-134, 133n
Tungsten, 134n
Tungsten Light, 134
Tungsten Town, 134, 134n
Tunnell mine, 56
Turner, E. Robert, 198
Turner, Peter, 56
Turner, Susan Sunshine, 56
Tyler, Clinton M., 36, 83
Tyler, young, *100*

"Ugly Ones." See Arapaho Indians.
Union Pacific Railroad, 127, 142
United Mine Workers, 108, 108n
U.S. Bank mine, 56
U.S. Congress, 17
United Way Crusade, *218*
University Hill, *88, 102,* 150, 179, 187, 202
University Hill League, 215
University Hospital, 171, 172
University of Colorado, *10,* 20, 32, 40, 88, 90, 94-98, *97, 99, 101,* 146, 160, 164, 169, 171, 175, 176, 180, 183, 187, 189, 190, 194, 195, 202, 211
uranium, 152-153
Ute Indians, 5, 9, 13, 21, 149
Ute Trail, 33
Utilla, 18
Valmont, 13, 23, 30, 40, 44, *44,* 83
Valmont Bulletin, 30
Valmont buttes, 2
Valverdan Park, 150, 190n
van Deren, J.J., 66
Vasquez, Louis, 7
Victoria mine, 56
Vietnam war referendum, 202
Volstead Act, 155, 158
von Frellick, Gerri, 207
voting controversies, 161, 162, 163, 185, 186, 192, 205

wagon roads map, 34-35
  See also road building.
  See also wagon roads by name.
Waldrop, A. Gayle, 185, 186, 187, 188, 206
Wallstreet, *4,* 109, 127, *137*
Wangelin, O.H., 4
Wannemaker, W.H., 14, 133, 134

War Memorial Park, 150, 187
Ward, Calvin W., 38
Ward, 1, 18, 19, 23, 36, 38, *38, 39,* 127, *131,* 159
ward system of government, 68, 192, 192n, 205
Wardenburg Student Health Center, 171
Washington lode, 28
Washington Park, 150
Washington School, 141
washouts. See flooding.
water, acquisition of, 2, 68-69, 151, 176, 195-196, 198, 221
  See also ditches and irrigation.
Water Street, 73, 85, 116
waterways, 2.
  See also ditches.
  See streams by name.
Watterson, Henry, 124
Webb, E.D., 81, 156
Weber, Alice, 49
Webster, Mary, 52
Weisenhorn, Frank, 152, 156
Weisenhorn's Lake, 83, 206
Welch, C.C., 105
Welch mine, 105
Weld, Camp, *40*
Weld County, 29, 108, 176, 206
Wellman brothers, 20, 25, 36, 221
Wells Fargo, 36, 38
Werley, Pete J., *47,* 49
Westdyke, Robert, 200
Western Cutlery and Manufacturing Company, 152, 176, 189
Western Light and Power Company, 187n
Westlake, William, 70
Weston, Joseph, 17
Weston, Sarah Emery, 17
Wheeler, Alfred, *87*
Wheeler, H.M., *87,* 125n
Wheeler, S.R., *87*
Wheelock brothers, 11
White Antelope, *40*
White, Perry, 25
White Rock Mill, 79
Whiteley, Emma Tyler, *99*
Whiteley, Richard H., *101,* 124
Whiteman, Paul, 146
Whitney, George, 116
Whittier, John Greenleaf, 88
Whittier neighborhood, 215
Whittier School, 88, 180, *186*
  See also Pine Street School.
Wickstrom, A.A., 186, 196
Wilkinson, James, 6
Williams, John, 125n
William's Fort
  See Bent's Fort.
Williamsburg, 54

Williamson, George, 33
Winchell, Walter, 146
winds, 3, 200
Wisconsin Gold Mining Company, 14n
Wise, William, 205
Wittemyer, Bea, *182*
Wittemyer, Leonard, *182*
Wolcott, Ed, *98*
Wolf Tongue Company, 134
Wolff, Joseph, 27, *27*
wolframite, 134
Wolle, Muriel Sibell, 52
women, 14
  in politics, 68, 171
  form groups, 171-172
Women's Christian Temperance Union (WCTU), 2, *154,* 156
Women's Club of Boulder, 84, 150, 171
Women's League, 171
Wood Mountain Gulch, *22*
Wooley, David, 12
Works Progress Administration (WPA), 180
World War I, 150
World War II, 187
Worthing, John, 179
Wright, Alpheus, 67, 73, 156, 172
Wynkoop, W.C., 67
Wyoming, 68, 155, 158, 205

Yellow Pine mine, 56
Young American Party, 67
Young Men's Christian Association (YMCA), 216
Yount, Abram K., 12, 152
Yount, Ella, 152, 171
Yount mill, *42, 79*
youth hostel, 201-202

Zamora, Dave, 205
Zang's beer, 156
zoning, 79, 187, 189, 216
Zubrow, Reuben, 199
Zweck, George, 23